Abraham Lincoln
THE PRAIRIE YEARS
IN TWO VOLUMES

✦

Volume

1

Jackknife signature of Abe Lincoln on his ax handle, New Salem, Illinois, 1834.

Original in Oliver R. Barrett Collection, Chicago

Abraham Lincoln
THE PRAIRIE YEARS

✦

BY

CARL SANDBURG

✦

WITH 105 ILLUSTRATIONS FROM
PHOTOGRAPHS, AND MANY CARTOONS,
SKETCHES, MAPS, AND LETTERS

VOLUME ONE

NEW YORK
HARCOURT, BRACE & COMPANY

To
AUGUST AND CLARA SANDBURG
WORKERS ON THE ILLINOIS PRAIRIE

Preface

For thirty years and more I have planned to make a certain portrait of Abraham Lincoln. It would sketch the country lawyer and prairie politician who was intimate with the settlers of the Knox County neighborhood where I grew up as a boy, and where I heard the talk of men and women who had eaten with Lincoln, given him a bed overnight, heard his jokes and lingo, remembered his silences and his mobile face.

The Mayor of Galesburg in 1858, Henry Sanderson, is the only individual of casual record who carried warm cistern water to a bathtub for Lincoln and saw Lincoln taking a bath. There in Galesburg Clark E. Carr, author of "The Illini," repeated Bill Green's remark about Lincoln, "He can make a cat laugh." And there Lincoln when bantered about his backwardness with women, answered, "A woman is the only thing I am afraid of that I know will not hurt me."

The folk-lore Lincoln, the maker of stories, the stalking and elusive Lincoln is a challenge for any artist. He has enough outline and lights and shadows and changing tints to call out portraits of him in his Illinois backgrounds and settings—even had he never been elected President.

Perhaps poetry, art, human behavior in this country, which has need to build on its own traditions, would be served by a life of Lincoln stressing the fifty-two years previous to his Presidency. Such a book would imply that if he was what he was during those first fifty-two years of his life it was nearly inevitable that he would be what he proved to be in the last four.

Then, too, the vortex in which he stood during the last four years of his life was forming in the years he was growing. The embryo of modern industrial society was taking shape. The history of transportation, of world colonization and world markets based on power-driven machinery, of international trade, finance, and standardization, weave through the destiny of Lincoln. He wore home-made moccasins as a boy, rawhide boots from a factory as a young man, and dressed calfskin shoes in still later years. A vast play of economic action, in whatever impressionistic manner, must move in the record of Lincoln.

And then Lincoln from a child on was intensely companionable, keenly sensitive to the words and ways of people around him. Therefore those people, their homes, occupations, songs, proverbs, schools, churches, politics, should be set forth with the incessant suggestion of change that went always with western pioneer life. They are the backgrounds on which the Lincoln life moved, had its rise and flow, and was moulder and moulded.

Of all the sources from which men are to gather impressions of the personality of Lincoln, the foremost singly important one is the collection of his letters and papers, the speeches and writings of the man himself. This is the high document, always, to be lived with and brooded over, to be scrutinized and forgotten and gone back to and searched again with all gifts of imagination, intuition, experience, prayer, silence, sacrifice, and the laughter next door to tears.

The first widely read biography of Lincoln, excluding campaign sketches, was by Josiah Gilbert Holland of New York, who characterized Lincoln as "a Christian gentleman." Ward Hill Lamon's book, in 1872, attacked the claims of Holland. Sixteen years later came the notable biography wherein William H. Herndon, the law partner of Lincoln, set forth a mass of documents, recollections, impressions. With the same period goes the ten-volume "History of Abraham Lincoln" by John G. Nicolay and John Hay, and Henry C. Whitney's "Life on the Circuit with Lincoln." The evidence seemed about complete when Ida Tarbell made her investigations that put fresh color into the early life of Lincoln, theretofore pictured as drab and miserable beyond the fact.

Death and time have obliterated people and houses that Miss

Tarbell visited nearly thirty years ago with note book, camera, and portfolio; her services as a recorder and writer, her sketches, interviews, photographs, surveys, of that period of so many now vanished vestiges, are an achievement and a leading contribution.

Since then further essential testimony has come from Henry B. Rankin, a law student under Lincoln, and Jesse W. Weik, who had so loyally and ably collaborated with Herndon. Also there have come the researches of Dr. William E. Barton; his painstaking, extended investigations are of material value.

Rankin and Barton have softened the tinting that has clung through report and gossip to Mary Todd Lincoln and have so placed the Ann Rutledge legend that it may stand as a tragic lyric rather than as a lurid melodrama.

Meantime the University of Illinois directed the production of a solid, crowded statement of the Lincoln-Douglas debates, followed by a monumental five-volume centennial history of the State of Illinois. Meantime also, the collection and classification of materials by the Illinois State Historical Society and the Chicago Historical Society has proceeded, while the Huntington, McLellan and Morgan collections and others such as those of Oliver R. Barrett, Joseph B. Oakleaf, Frederick H. Meserve, Clark Bissett, Emanuel Hertz, besides many more, have increased beyond all proportions at first considered probable.

Several thousand books, pamphlets, brochures, have been written and printed about Lincoln. The bibliography of Daniel Fish, published in 1906, listed 1,080 books. J. B. Oakleaf of Moline, Illinois, bringing the Fish enumeration to the year 1925, adds 1,600 items.

In a single private collection are biographies of Lincoln in French (five in number), German (four), Italian, Portuguese, Russian, Yiddish, Greek, Turkish, Japanese (three), Chinese (two), and Hawaiian.

At intervals and often with curious surprise, come new glints of illumination on Lincoln. Thus reminiscences gathered by Allen Thorndike Rice, Dorothy Lamon, A. K. McClure, Horace White; Eleanor Atkinson's haunting sketch of Dennis

Hanks; the Old Salem league publications; the transcript by Henry C. Whitney of the "Lost Speech" of 1856; the reprint in 1921 by the Woman's Club of Elizabethtown, Kentucky, of the history of that community as written by Samuel Haycraft and published in a local newspaper in 1869.

Besides these materials I have used the reminiscences of Thomas G. Lowry, whose published volume was limited to 200 copies, and notes taken in extended conversations with Joseph W. Fifer, former Governor of Illinois and during many years an intimate of Leonard Swett and Richard Oglesby.

In the McLellan manuscripts of the John Hay library of Brown University, in the collections of the Chicago and Illinois Historical societies and in private collections, I have met sixty-five unpublished letters and papers in Lincoln's handwriting. I visited the Shenandoah Valley farm site of Lincoln's grandfather, the Lincoln birthplace and the Kentucky and Indiana regions, traveled down the Mississippi River, walked the docks of New Orleans, spent weeks in Springfield, Petersburg, New Salem, Bloomington, and towns in Illinois where Lincoln lived.

Lincoln's last speech in Illinois, at Tolono, I first met in a file of the *New York Herald*. Old newspaper files in the Chicago Public Library, and various source materials in the Newberry Library, were of service. The forty large volumes of newspaper clippings about Lincoln, gathered by the Chicago Historical Society during the centennial year of 1909, yielded letters, sketches, interviews, and memoirs of worthy authenticity. Local newspaper files such as *The Galesburg Republican-Register*, *The Galesburg Evening Mail*, *The Bloomington Pantagraph*, *The Alton Telegraph,* supplied quaint original material. Oliver R. Barrett loaned me an almost complete file of the *New York Herald* covering a critical period when that newspaper had at Springfield a correspondent with fine understanding of Lincoln; also Mr. Barrett supplied many rare copies of newspapers published in Illinois during the forty years previous to 1860.

Such items as letters and papers of Alexander Stephens characterizing Lincoln; the Lincoln & Herndon office as seen through

the letters of Herndon to Theodore Parker in Joseph Fort Newton's book; the monographs of William H. Townsend on Lincoln
as defendant and litigant; the diary of Orville H. Browning; the
researches of Cole and Pease in Illinois history; the Tracy "Un-
collected Letters"; the studies of William E. Dodd in wheat,
railroads, finance, from 1840 to 1860 and his remarkable paper,
"The Fight for the Northwest"—these are but a few instances
of documents and material, brought forth in the past eight years,
that go to form the Lincoln impression.

We might list also the *Atlantic Monthly* publication of "The
Bear Hunt" doggerel from the manuscript owned by J. Pierpont
Morgan; the Black Hawk War history and the biography of
Stephen A. Douglas written by Frank Stevens of Sycamore,
Illinois; the Louis A. Warren brochure "From White House to
Log Cabin"; biographies of James A. Buchanan and Lyman
Trumbull; the Herndon broadsides and a letter of Mrs. Lincoln
reprinted by H. E. Barker of Springfield, Illinois, besides that
copy of the *Cleveland* (Ohio) *Plaindealer* which publishes for
the first time the text of a letter written by Mrs. Lincoln to her
husband; the Addison G. Procter recollections of the 1860 Chicago Republican convention; and the writings of Lincoln edited
by Arthur Lapsley, with an introduction by Theodore Roosevelt.
In so out of the way a volume as the autobiography of John
James Ingalls of Kansas one comes across the first statement of
an exact figure as to how much money Lincoln's campaign
managers in Illinois spent to nominate him for president in 1860.

No letter written by Lincoln to his wife has ever come to light
publicly during all the years in which the streams of biography
have run on endlessly. Such a letter, and a long quaint one,
constituting a rarely fine document on the relationship between
Lincoln and his wife, is loaned for use in this book through the
courtesy of Alexander W. Hannah of Chicago. In the same year
of 1925 we have seen the publication by Oliver R. Barrett of the
1858 address showing Lincoln with head bent in defeat just before
the fall elections, hinting, with no cheap regrets, at the treachery

of supposed friends and mentioning how he and his associates
had been "bespattered with every imaginable odious epithet."

The Barrett collection began more than thirty-five years ago
when Oliver R. Barrett as a boy of fifteen started to gather
letters, manuscripts, photographs, of Lincoln and reminiscences
from men and women who had met Lincoln in life. There in
Pittsfield, county seat of Pike County, Illinois, the old settlers
had heard Lincoln deliver speeches, had sat at turkey dinners
with him, and had passed the **Gilmer** house, where Lincoln, going
to a conference in the house, had lifted Lizzie **Gilmer** off the front
gate, kissed her and put her back on the gate; they remembered
the little red-headed boy, John G. Nicolay, who was a printer's
devil at the office of the Pike County *Free Press*, and the boy
John Hay who went to school and wrote "contributions" for the
Free Press. There Barrett grew up; later he was a Peoria lawyer,
familiar with the "orgmathorial" humor and savor of the old
Eighth Circuit Bar and the stump politics of central Illinois;
then he moved to Chicago. Keen in the scrutiny of evidence and
shrewd in his analysis of documents; a man droll, inventive,
quizzical and lovable in the company of children; a long distance
walker, a fisherman, story-teller, bookman; a man who takes a
ten or fifteen mile hike at midnight or dawn when the impulse
moves him; a man who enjoys being ungrammatical when with
ungrammatical people; with the restless urge of the pony express
rider modulated by the peaceful preoccupations of the antiquarian
—Oliver R. Barrett requires further portraiture. As a collab-
orator and commentator he has given honest values to some of
these pages.

Frederick H. Meserve gave full access to his collection of
200,000 photographs and was ready with seasoned counsel on
Lincoln photographs; he loaned the bronze life mask for the two
photographs by Edward Steichen; they deliver the enigmatic
Lincoln whose range of laughter and tears was far and deep.

Going farther month by month in stacks and bundles of fact
and legend, I found invisible companionships that surprised me.
Perhaps a few of those presences lurk and murmur in this book.

NOTE

WHEN I TRIED TO MAKE A COMPLETE LIST OF THE PERSONS WHO GAVE VALUABLE TIME AND HELP TOWARD THE MAKING OF THIS BOOK, THE SERIES OF NAMES GREW SO LONG THAT IT WOULD OVER-BALANCE THE PLAN OF THE BOOK TO INCLUDE THEM IN PROPER STYLE WITH JUST AND MEASURED ACKNOWLEDGMENTS. I CAN ONLY SAY THAT I AM GRATEFUL BEYOND WORDS TO THE MANY WHO ASSOCIATED THEIR EFFORTS, OFFERED FREE COMMENT, WORTHY COUNSEL, AND PERFORMED ERRANDS.

List of Photographs, Cartoons, Sketches, Maps, and Letters

Abraham Lincoln
THE PRAIRIE YEARS

Abraham Lincoln
THE PRAIRIE YEARS

Chapter 1

IN the year 1776, when the thirteen American colonies of England gave to the world that famous piece of paper known as the Declaration of Independence, there was a captain of Virginia militia living in Rockingham County, named Abraham Lincoln.

He was a farmer with a 210-acre farm deeded to him by his father, John Lincoln, one of the many English, Scotch, Irish, German, Dutch settlers who were taking the green hills and slopes of the Shenandoah Valley and putting their plows to ground never touched with farming tools by the red men, the Indians, who had held it for thousands of years.

The work of driving out the red men so that the white men could farm in peace was not yet finished. In the summer of that same year of 1776, Captain Abraham Lincoln's company took a hand in marches and fights against the Cherokee tribes.

It was a time of much fighting. To the south and west were the red men. To the north and east were white men, the regiments of British soldiers, and Virginia was sending young men and corn and pork to the colonial soldiers under General George Washington. Amos Lincoln, a kinsman of Abraham, up in Massachusetts, was one of the white men who, the story ran, rigged out as Indians, went on board a British ship and dumped a cargo of tea overboard to show their disobedience, contempt, and defiance of British laws and government; later Amos was a captain of artillery in the colonial army.

3

There was a Hananiah Lincoln who fought at Brandywine under Washington and became a captain in the Twelfth Pennsylvania regiment; and Hananiah was a first cousin of Abraham. Jacob Lincoln, a brother of Abraham, was at Yorktown, a captain under Washington at the finish of the Revolutionary War. These Lincolns in Virginia came from Berks County in Pennsylvania.

Though they were fighting men, there was a strain of Quaker blood running in them; they came in part from people who wore black clothes only, used the word "thee" instead of "you," kept silence or spoke "as the spirit of the heart moved," and held war to be a curse from hell; they were a serene, peaceable, obstinate people.

Now Abraham Lincoln had taken for a wife a woman named Bathsheba Herring. And she bore him three sons there amid the green hills and slopes of the Shenandoah Valley, and they were named Mordecai, Josiah, and Thomas. And she bore two daughters, named Mary and Nancy.

This family of a wife and five children Abraham Lincoln took on horses in the year 1782 and moved to Kentucky. For years his friend, Daniel Boone, had been coming back from trips to Kentucky, sometimes robbed of all his deerskins and bearskins and furs of fox and mink, sometimes alone and without the lusty young bucks who had started with him for Kentucky. And listening to Boone's telling of how the valleys were rich with long slopes of black land and blue grass, how there were game and fish, and tall timber and clear running waters— and seeing the road near his farm so often filled with parties of men and families headed for the wilderness beyond the mountains—he began thinking about taking up land for himself over there. It was his for forty cents an acre. He wanted to be where he could look from his cabin to the horizons on all sides—and the land all his own—was that it? He didn't know. It called to him, that country Boone was talking about.

Boone and his friends had worn a trail following an old buffalo path down the Shenandoah Valley to Lexington and around to Cumberland Gap in Tennessee, then northwest into Kentucky. It had become more than a trail, and was called the Wilderness Road. It was the safest way to Kentucky because the British and the Indians still had a hold on the Ohio River water route, the only other way to reach Kentucky.

Moving to Kentucky had been in Abraham Lincoln's thoughts for some time, but he didn't finally decide to go until the state of Virginia started a land office and made new laws to help straighten out tangled land-titles in Kentucky.

While Bathsheba was still carrying in her arms the baby, Thomas, it happened that Abraham Lincoln sold his farm, and in accordance with the laws of Virginia she signed papers giving up her rights to her husband's land, declaring in writing on 'the 24th day of September, 1781, that "she freely and voluntarily relinquished the same without the Force threats or compulsion of her husband." Then they packed their belongings, especially the rifle, the ax, and the plow, and joined a party which headed down the Wilderness Road through Cumberland Gap and up north and west into Kentucky.

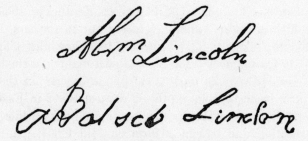

Abraham and Bathsheba (or Batsab) Lincoln sign their names to a deed in the courthouse of Rockingham County, Virginia.

Tall mountains loomed about them with long blue shadows at sunup and sundown as they traveled, camped, broke camp, and traveled again. And as they watched the mountains they slanted their keenest eyes on any moving patch of shrub or tree —the red men who ambushed enemies might be there.

There had been papers signed, and the land by law belonged to the white men, but the red men couldn't understand or didn't wish to understand how the land was gone from them to the white men. Besides, the red men had been fighting among themselves for favorite hunting grounds and fishing waters; there had been hundreds of years of fighting; now they were fighting white men by the same weapons, ways, and ambushes as they fought red men. And so, though the scenery was good to look at, the white men traveling the Wilderness Road kept a keen eye on the underbrush and had scouts ahead at the turn of the road and scouts behind.

Some towns and villages then were paying a dollar to two dollars apiece for Indian scalps.

Coming through safe to Kentucky, Abraham Lincoln located on the Green River, where he filed claims for more than 2,000 acres. He had been there three or four years when, one day as he was working in a field, the rifle shot of an Indian killed him. His children and his children's children scattered across Kentucky, Tennessee, Indiana, and Illinois.

Tom Lincoln, the child of Abraham and Bathsheba, while growing up, lived in different places in Kentucky, sometimes with his kith and kin, sometimes hiring out to farmers, mostly in Washington County, and somehow betweenwhiles managing to learn the carpenter's trade and cabinet-making. He bought a horse—and paid taxes on it. He put in a year on the farm of his uncle, Isaac Lincoln, on the Wautauga River in East Tennessee. He moved to Hardin County in Kentucky while still a young bachelor, and bought a farm on Mill Creek, paid taxes on the farm, kept out of debt, and once bought a pair of silk suspenders for a dollar and a half at a time when most men were using homemade hickory-bark galluses.

As Tom Lincoln came to his full growth he was about five feet, nine inches tall, weighing about 185 pounds, his muscles and ribs close-knit, so that one time a boy joking with him tried to find the places between his ribs but couldn't put a finger in between any place where a rib ended and the muscle began. His dark hazel eyes looked out from a round face, from under coarse black hair. He was a slow, careless man with quiet manners, would rather have people come and ask him to work on a job than to hunt the job himself. He liked to sit around and have his own thoughts.

He wasn't exactly lazy; he was sort of independent, and liked to be where he wasn't interfered with. A little slab of bacon with hoecake or a little corn-bread and milk every day, and he was satisfied. He drank whisky but not often. The sober Baptists saw more of him than those who were steady at licking up liquor. He was a wild buck at fighting, when men didn't let him alone. A man talked about a woman once in a way Tom Lincoln didn't like. And in the fight that came, Tom bit a piece of the man's nose off. His neighbors knew him as a good man to let alone. And his neighbors knew him for a good workman, a handy man with the ax, the saw, the drawknife, and the hammer. Though he was short-spoken, he knew yarns, could crack jokes, and had a reputation as a story-teller when he got started. He never had much time for the alphabet, could read some, and could sign his name.

Church meetings interested him. He had been to cabins on Sunday mornings; the worshipers sat where it was half dark. Windows hadn't been cut in the walls; light came in through the door; words of the sermon came from a preacher in half-shadows. And he had gone to service in the evening when the cabin was lighted by the burning logs of the fireplace. Sometimes he felt stirred inside when a young woman kneeling on the floor would turn a passionate, longing face to the roof of the cabin and call, "Jesus, I give everything to thee. I give thee all. I give thee all. I am wholly thine!"

He had heard different preachers; some he liked better than others; some he was suspicious of; others he could listen to by the hour. There was a Reverend Jesse Head he had heard preach over at Springfield in Washington County, and he had a particular liking for Jesse Head, who was a good chair-maker, a good cabinet-maker, and an active exhorter in the branch of the

Methodist church that stood against negro slavery and on that account had separated from the regular church. When Tom joined the Baptists it was in that branch of the church which was taking a stand against slavery.

Chapter 2

DURING those years when Tom Lincoln was getting into his twenties, the country in Hardin County and around Elizabethtown was still wilderness, with only a few farms and settlements. Kentucky had been admitted to the Union of states; there were places in the state where civilization had dented the wilderness; but it was still a country of uncut timber, land unknown to the plow, a region where wolves and bear, wild animals and the Indians still claimed their rights and titles, with tooth and fang, claw and club and knife.

They talked in Elizabethtown about Miles Hart, who lived near by, and how he was killed by the Indians after he had used up his powder, how his wife Elizabeth and her two children were taken by the Indians, and how, on an outdoor march with the Indians, she was sent away, as Indian squaws were, by herself, to build a fire in the snow and give birth to her child. The child lived six months, but its mother was several years in the hands of the Indians before a Frenchman bought her near Detroit and sent her back to her relatives in Kentucky, where she again married and was raising a family. It was nearly twenty years since Elder John Gerrard, the Baptist preacher, had come to Hardin County. He preached nine months, and then one day, when a hunting party was surprised by Indians, all got away except Elder Gerrard, who was lame, and whether the Indians killed him, burned him at the stake, or took him along as a slave, nobody ever heard. There were many things to talk about around Elizabethtown. There was a negro living there called General Braddock, a free man; he had been given his freedom because, when his master's cabin was attacked by Indians, he had killed nine of the red men and saved the lives of his owner's family.

There was the time when Henry Helm and Dan Vertrees were killed by the Indians; a red man wrestled a gun away from a white man and had his war-ax raised to bring down and split the head of the white man; it was then Nicholas Miller, quick as a cat, made a jump, snatched the white man away and killed the Indian. One man who saw it, John Glenn, said, "Miller snatched the white man from the Indian as he would a chicken from a hawk." There was talk about how, even though the wilderness life was full of danger, men kept coming on, the Wilderness Road and the Ohio River bringing more and more settlers year by year, some speaking in one form or another the language of Daniel Boone, calling himself "an instrument ordained by God to settle the wilderness." Also there were those who knew that Dragging Canoe, chief of the Chickamauga tribe of Indians, after a powwow when white men and red signed papers at Wautauga, had pointed his finger northwest toward Kentucky, saying words translated as "Bloody ground! . . . And dark and difficult to settle." It seemed that the ground, the soil, and the lay of the land in Kentucky had an old name among the Indians as a land for war.

As the crossroads grew into settlements in Hardin County, there was hard feeling between the crowd around Elizabethtown and the settlers in the valley over near Hodgen's mill, about where the county seat should be located and the courthouse built. On election days, when the members of the county board were chosen, the voters clashed. The hard feeling lasted nearly ten years. At least fifty combats of fist and skull took place, though it was generally understood that the only time the fighting was not strictly fair and square rough-and-tumble combat was when a young man named Bruce tried to gash his enemies by kicking them with shoes pointed with sharp iron pieces shaped like the "gaffs" which are fastened to the feet of fighting cocks Bruce himself being a rooster-fight sport.

The first jail in Elizabethtown cost the county $42.60. The

sheriff was discouraged with it, and in 1797 a new jail was built, costing $700.00, with stocks and whipping-post. Many of the prisoners were in for debt and both white and black men were lashed on their naked backs at the public whipping-post. The stocks were built so that each prisoner had to kneel with his hands and head clamped between two grooved planks. If the prisoner was dead drunk he was laid on his back with his feet in the stocks and kept there till he was sober.

The same year the jail was built, it happened that a man in for debt set fire to it when the jailer was away; the prisoner was nearly roasted to death but was saved, though the jail burned down; after which he was indicted for arson, and acquitted because he was a first-rate bricklayer and the town needed his work.

The time of the grand "raisin'" of the courthouse in 1795 in the middle of August was remembered; on that day forty strong men raised the frames and big logs into place while many women and children looked on, and at noon the men all crowded into the Haycraft double log-house to eat hearty from loaves of bread baked in a clay oven, roast shotes, chickens, ducks, potatoes, roast beef with cabbage and beans, old-fashioned baked custard and pudding, pies, pickles, and "fixin's."

Grand juries held their sessions in the woods alongside the courthouse. In 1798 their entire report was, "We present Samuel Forrester for profane swearing"; on several occasions they mention Isaac Hynes, the sheriff, for "profane swearing." The sheriff was a distiller and his stillhouse was in one year recommended for use as the county jail.

When people spoke of "the time Jacob was hung," they meant the year 1796 and the negro slave, Jacob, who was "reproved for sloth" and killed his owner with an ax; a jury fixed the value of the slave at 80 pounds, or $400; he broke jail, was taken again, and on hanging day the sheriff hired another black man "to tie the noose and drive the cart from under," leaving the murderer hanging in mid-air from the scaffold. A large crowd came in Sunday clothes, with lunch baskets, to see the law take its course

If in that country they wished to speak of lighter things, they could talk about pancakes; it was a saying that a smart woman, a cook who was clever, could toss a pancake off the skillet up through the top of the chimney and run outdoors and catch it coming down. Eggs were five cents a dozen. And one year a defendant in a case at law got a new trial on showing that in his case the jury, after retiring and before agreeing on a verdict, "did eat, drink, fiddle, and dance." Such were some of the community human cross-weaves in the neighborhood where Tom Lincoln spent the years just before he married.

Chapter 3

TOM LINCOLN was looking for a woman to travel through life with, for better or worse. He visited at the place of Christopher Bush, a hard-working farmer who came from German parents and had raised a family of sons with muscle. "There was no back-out in them; they never shunned a fight when they considered it necessary; and nobody ever heard one of them cry 'Enough.' "

Also there were two daughters with muscle and with shining faces and steady eyes. Tom Lincoln passed by Hannah and gave his best jokes to Sarah Bush. But it happened that Sarah Bush wanted Daniel Johnson for a husband and he wanted her.

Another young woman Tom's eyes fell on was a brunette sometimes called Nancy Hanks because she was a daughter of Lucy Hanks, and sometimes called Nancy Sparrow because she was an adopted daughter of Thomas and Elizabeth Sparrow and lived with the Sparrow family.

Lucy Hanks had welcomed her child Nancy into life in Virginia in 1784 and had traveled the Wilderness Road carrying what was to her a precious bundle through Cumberland Gap and on into Kentucky.

The mother of Nancy was nineteen years old when she made

this trip, leaving Nancy's father, who had not married her, back
in Virginia. She could croon in the moist evening twilight to
the shining face in the sweet bundle, "Hush thee, hush thee,
thy father's a gentleman." She could toss the bundle into the
air against a far, hazy line of blue mountains, catch it in her
two hands as it came down, let it snuggle to her breast and feed,
while she asked, "Here we come—where from?"

And after they had both sunken in the depths of forgetful
sleep, in the early dark and past midnight, the tug of a mouth
at her nipples in the gray dawn matched in its freshness the first
warblings of birds and the morning stars leaving the earth to
the sun and the dew.

And while Nancy was still learning to walk and talk, her
mother Lucy was talked about in and around Harrodsburg, Kentucky, as too free and easy in her behavior, too wild in her
ways. A grand jury had taken up the case of Lucy Hanks at
one session in Harrodsburg and named her to be investigated
for immoral tendencies.

And whether some man on the jury or some officer of the
law had a spiteful heart against Lucy or whether it was a roister-
ing, jesting grand jury like the one that before agreeing on a
verdict "did eat, drink, fiddle and dance," was not clear.

What was clear in the years that had passed was that Lucy
Hanks was strong and strange, loved love and loved babies, had
married a man she wanted, Henry Sparrow, and nine children
had come and they were all learning to read and write under her
teaching. Since she had married the talk about her running
wild had let down.

After she married Henry Sparrow her daughter Nancy went
under the roof of Thomas Sparrow, a brother of Henry, and
Elizabeth Hanks Sparrow, a sister of Lucy. Under the same
roof was an adopted boy named Dennis Hanks, a son of a
Nancy Hanks who was one of three sisters of Lucy. There were
still other Nancy Hankses in Hardin County and those who
spoke of any Nancy Hanks often had to mention which one
they meant.

Tom Lincoln had seen this particular Nancy Hanks living with the Sparrows and noticed she was shrewd and dark and lonesome. He had heard her tremulous voice and seen her shaken with sacred desires in church camp-meetings; he had seen her at preachings in cabins when her face stood out as a sort of picture in black against the firelights of the burning logs. He knew she could read the Bible, and had read in other books. She had seen a few newspapers and picked out pieces of news and read her way through.

Her dark skin, dark brown hair, keen little gray eyes, out-standing forehead, somewhat accented chin and cheek-bones, body of slender build, weighing about 130 pounds—these formed the outward shape of a woman carrying something strange and cherished along her ways of life. She was sad with sorrows like dark stars in blue mist. The hope was burned deep in her that beyond the harsh clay paths, the everyday scrubbing, washing, patching, fixing, the babble and the gabble of today, there are pastures and purple valleys of song.

She had seen tall hills there in Kentucky. She had seen the stark backbone of Muldraugh's Hill become folded in thin. evening blankets with a lavender mist sprayed by sunset lights, and for her there were the tongues of promises over it all.

She believed in God, in the Bible, in mankind, in the past and future, in babies, people, animals, flowers, fishes, in foundations and roofs, in time and the eternities outside of time; she was a believer, keeping in silence behind her gray eyes more beliefs than she spoke. She knew . . . so much of what she believed was yonder—always yonder. Every day came scrubbing, wash-ing, patching, fixing. There was so little time to think or sing about the glory she believed in. It was always yonder. . . .

The day came when Thomas Lincoln signed a bond with his friend, Richard Berry, in the courthouse at Springfield in Wash-ington County, over near where his brother, Mordecai, was farm-ing, and the bond gave notice: "There is a marriage shortly intended between Thomas Lincoln and Nancy Hanks." It was June 10, 1806. Two days later, at Richard Berry's place,

Beechland, a man twenty-eight years old and a woman twenty-three years old came before the Reverend Jesse Head, who later gave the county clerk the names of Thomas Lincoln and Nancy Hanks as having been "joined together in the Holy Estate of Matrimony agreeable to the rules of the Methodist Episcopal Church."

After the wedding came "the infare," the Kentucky style wedding celebration. One who was there said, "We had bear-meat, venison, wild turkey and ducks, eggs wild and tame, maple sugar lumps tied on a string to bite off for coffee or whisky, syrup in big gourds, peach-and-honey; a sheep that two families barbecued whole over coals of wood burned in a pit, and covered with green boughs to keep the juices in; and a race for the whisky bottle."

The new husband put his June bride on his horse and they rode away on the red clay road along the timber trails to Elizabethtown. Their new home was in a cabin close to the courthouse. Tom worked at the carpenter's trade, made cabinets, door-frames, window sash, and coffins. A daughter was born and they named her Sarah. Tom's reputation as a solid, reliable man, whose word could be depended on, was improved after his quarrels with Denton Geoheagan.

He took a contract to cut timbers and help put up a new sawmill for Geoheagan; and when Geoheagan wouldn't pay he went to law and won the suit for his pay. Geoheagan then started two suits against Lincoln, claiming the sawmill timbers were not cut square and true. Lincoln beat him in both suits, and noticed that afterward people looked to him as a reliable man whose word could be depended on.

It was about this time the building of the third Hardin County jail was finished in Elizabethtown, with an old-time dungeon underground. The first jailer was Reverend Benjamin Ogden, who was a Methodist preacher, also a chair-maker and worker in wood.

In May and the blossom-time of the year 1808, Tom and Nancy with little Sarah moved out from Elizabethtown to the farm of George Brownfield, where Tom did carpenter work and helped farm.

The Lincolns had a cabin of their own to live in. It stood among wild crab-apple trees.

And the smell of wild crab-apple blossoms, and the low crying of all wild things, came keen that summer to the nostrils of Nancy Hanks.

The summer stars that year shook out pain and warning, strange laughters, for Nancy Hanks.

Chapter 4

THE same year saw the Lincolns moved to a place on the Big South Fork of Nolin's Creek, about two and a half miles from Hodgenville. They were trying to farm a little piece of ground and make a home. The house they lived in was a cabin of logs cut from the timber near by.

The floor was packed-down dirt. One door, swung on leather hinges, let them in and out. One small window gave a lookout on the weather, the rain or snow, sun and trees, and the play of the rolling prairie and low hills. A stick-clay chimney carried the fire smoke up and away.

One morning in February of this year, 1809, Tom Lincoln came out of his cabin to the road, stopped a neighbor and asked him to tell "the granny woman," Aunt Peggy Walters, that Nancy would need help soon.

On the morning of February 12, a Sunday, the granny woman was there at the cabin. And she and Tom Lincoln and the moaning Nancy Hanks welcomed into a world of battle and blood, of whispering dreams and wistful dust, a new child, a boy.

A little later that morning Tom Lincoln threw some extra wood on the fire, and an extra bearskin over the mother, went out of the cabin, and walked two miles up the road to where the Sparrows, Tom and Betsy, lived. Dennis Hanks, the nine-year-old boy adopted by the Sparrows, met Tom at the door.

In his slow way of talking—he was a slow and a quiet man—Tom Lincoln told them, "Nancy's got a boy baby." * *   A half-sheepish look was in his eyes, as though maybe more babies were not wanted in Kentucky just then.

The boy, Dennis Hanks, took to his feet, down the road to the Lincoln cabin.   There he saw Nancy Hanks on a bed of poles cleated to a corner of the cabin, under warm bearskins.

She turned her dark head from looking at the baby to look at Dennis and threw him a tired, white smile from her mouth and gray eyes.   He stood by the bed, his eyes wide open, watching the even, quiet breaths, of this fresh, soft red baby.

"What you goin' to name him, Nancy?" the boy asked.

"Abraham," was the answer, "after his grandfather."

Soon came Betsy Sparrow.   She washed the baby, put a yellow petticoat and a linsey shirt on him, cooked dried berries with wild honey for Nancy, put the one-room cabin in better order, kissed Nancy and comforted her, and went home.

Little Dennis rolled up in a bearskin and slept by the fireplace that night.   He listened for the crying of the newborn child once in the night and the feet of the father moving on the dirt floor to help the mother and the little one.   In the morning he took a long look at the baby and said to himself, "Its skin looks just like red cherry pulp squeezed dry, in wrinkles."

He asked if he could hold the baby.   Nancy, as she passed the little one into Dennis's arms, said, "Be keerful, Dennis, fur you air the fust boy he's ever seen."

And Dennis swung the baby back and forth, keeping up a chatter about how tickled he was to have a new cousin to play with.   The baby screwed up the muscles of its face and began crying with no let-up.

Dennis turned to Betsy Sparrow, handed her the baby and said to her, "Aunt, take him!   He'll never come to much."

So came the birth of Abraham Lincoln that 12th of February

* * *These words are from the Eleanor Atkinson interview with Dennis Hanks.   Throughout this work conversational utterances are based word for word on sources deemed authentic.—The Author.*

in the year 1809—in silence and pain from a wilderness mother on a bed of corn-husks and bearskins—with an early laughing child prophecy he would never come to much.

And though he was born in a house with only one door and one window, it was written he would come to know many doors, many windows; he would read many riddles and doors and windows.

The Lincoln family lived three crop years on the farm where baby Abraham was born. It was a discouraging piece of land with yellow and red clay, stony soils, thick underbrush, land known as "barrens." It was called the Rock Spring farm because at the foot of one of its sloping hills the rocks curved in like the beginning of a cave; coats of moss spotted the rocks and rambled with quiet streaks of green over the gray; a ledge of rock formed a beckoning roof with room for people to stand under; and at the heart of it, for its centre, was a never-ending flow of clear, cool water.

With the baby she called Abe in her arms, Nancy Hanks came to this Rock Spring more than once, sitting with her child and her thoughts, looking at running water and green moss. The secrets of the mingled drone and hush of the place gave her reminders of Bible language, "Be ye comforted," or "Peace, be still."

Cooking, washing, sewing, spinning, weaving, helping keep a home for a man and two babies, besides herself, in a one-room cabin, took a good deal of her time. If there were flies creeping over the face of the baby Abe, she had to drop her work and shoo the flies away. There were few hours in the year she was free to sit with her child and her thoughts, listening to the changing drone and hush of Rock Spring saying, "Be ye comforted," or "Peace, be still."

The baby grew, learning to sit up, to crawl over the dirt floor of the cabin; the gristle became bone; the father joked about the long legs getting longer; the mother joked about how quick he grew out of one shirt into another.

Sparrows and Hankses who came visiting said, "He's solemn

as a papoose." An easy and a light bundle he was to carry when the family moved to a farm on Knob Creek, eight miles from Hodgenville, on the main highway from Louisville to Nashville.

Chapter 5

ON the Knob Creek farm the child Abraham Lincoln learned to talk, to form words with the tongue and the roof of the mouth and the force of the breath from lungs and throat. "Pappy" and "Mammy," the words of his people meaning father and mother, were among the first syllables. He learned what the word "name" meant; his name was Abraham, the same as Abraham in the Bible, the same as his grandfather Abraham. It was "Abe" for short; if his mother called in the dark, "Is that you, Abe?" he answered, "Yes, Mammy, it's me." The name of the family he belonged to was "Lincoln" or "Linkun," though most people called it "Linkern" and it was sometimes spelled "Linkhorn."

The family lived there on Knob Creek farm, from the time Abe was three or so till he was past seven years of age. Here he was told "Kaintucky" meant the state he was living in; Knob Creek farm, the Rock Spring farm where he was born, Hodgenville, Elizabethtown, Muldraugh's Hill, these places he knew, the land he walked on, was all part of Kentucky.

Yet it was also part of something bigger. Men had been fighting, bleeding, and dying in war, for a country, "our country"; a man couldn't have more than one country any more than he could have more than one mother; the name of the mother country was the "United States"; and there was a piece of cloth with red and white stripes having a blue square in its corner filled with white stars; and this piece of cloth they called "a flag." The flag meant the "United States." One summer morning his father started the day by stepping out of the front door and shooting a long rifle into the sky; and his father explained it was the day to make a big noise because it was the "Fourth of

July," the day the United States first called itself a "free and independent" nation.

His folks talked like other folks in the neighborhood. They called themselves "pore" people. A man learned in books was "eddicated." What was certain was "sartin." The syllables came through the nose; joints were "j'ints"; fruit "spiled" instead of spoiling; in corn-planting time they "drapped" the seeds. They went on errands and "brung" things back. Their dogs "follered" the coons. Flannel was "flannen," a bandanna a "bandanner," a chimney a "chimbly," a shadow a "shadder," and mosquitoes plain "skeeters." They "gethered" crops. A creek was a "crick," a cover a "kiver."

A man silent was a "say-nothin'." They asked, "Have ye et?" There were dialogues, "Kin ye?" "No, I cain't." And if a woman had an idea of doing something she said, "I had a idy to." They made their own words. Those who spoke otherwise didn't belong, were "puttin' on." This was their wilderness lingo; it had gnarled bones and gaunt hours of their lives in it.

Words like "independent" bothered the boy. He was hungry to understand the meanings of words. He would ask what "independent" meant and when he was told the meaning he lay awake nights thinking about the meaning of the meaning of "independent." Other words bothered him, such as "predestination." He asked the meaning of that and lay awake hours at night thinking about the meaning of the meaning.

Chapter 6

SEVEN-YEAR-OLD Abe walked four miles a day going to the Knob Creek school to learn to read and write. Zachariah Riney and Caleb Hazel were the teachers who brought him along from A B C to where he could write the name "A-b-r-a-h-a-m L-i-n-c-o-l-n" and count numbers beginning with one, two, three, and so on. He heard twice two is four.

The schoolhouse was built of logs, with a dirt floor, no window, one door. The scholars learned their lessons by saying them to themselves out loud till it was time to recite; alphabets, multiplication tables, and the letters of spelled words were all in the air at once. It was a "blab school"; so they called it.

The Louisville and Nashville pike running past the Lincoln cabin had many different travelers. Covered wagons came with settlers moving south and west, or north to Ohio and Indiana; there were peddlers with knickknacks to spread out and tell the prices of; congressmen, members of the legislature meeting at Lexington, men who had visited Henry Clay at Ashland.

Coming back from a fishing trip, with one fish, Abe met a soldier who came from fighting in the Battle of New Orleans with General Jackson, and Abe, remembering his father and mother had told him to be good to soldiers, handed the soldier the one fish.

The Lincolns got well acquainted with Christopher Columbus Graham, a doctor, a scientist, who was beginning to study and write books about the rocks, flowers, plants, trees, and wild animals of Kentucky; Graham slept in the bed while the Lincolns slept on the floor of the cabin, more than once; he told in the evening talk about days camping with Daniel Boone, and running backward with Boone so as to make foot-tracks pointing forward to mislead the Indians; he talked about stones, leaves, bones, snake-skins he was carrying in a sack back to Louisville; he mentioned a young storekeeper at Elizabethtown, named John James Audubon, who had marvelous ways with birds and might some day write a great book about birds. The boy Abe heard traveling preachers and his father talk about the times when they held church meetings in cabins, and every man had his rifle by his side, and there were other men with rifles outside the cabin door, ready for Indians who might try to interrupt their Sabbath worship. And the boy never liked it when the talkers slung around words like "independent" and "predestination," because he lay awake thinking about those long words.

Abe was the chore-boy of the Knob Creek farm as soon as he grew big enough to run errands, to hold a pine-knot at night lighting his father at a job, or to carry water, fill the woodbox, clean ashes from the fireplace, hoe weeds, pick berries, grapes, persimmons for beer-making. He hunted the timbers and came back with walnuts, hickory and hazel nuts. His hands knew the stinging blisters from using a hoe-handle back and forth a summer afternoon, and in autumn the mash of walnut-stain that wouldn't wash off, with all the rinsing and scrubbing of Nancy Hanks's homemade soap. He went swimming with Austin Gollaher; they got their backs sunburnt so the skin peeled off.

Wearing only a shirt—no hat nor pants—Abe rode a horse hitched to a "bull-tongue" plow of wood shod with iron. He helped his father with seed corn, beans, onions, potatoes. He ducked out of the way of the heels of the stallion and brood mares his father kept and paid taxes on.

The father would ride away to auctions, once coming home with dishes, plates, spoons, and a wash basin, another time with a heifer, and again with a wagon that had been knocked down to the highest bidder for 8½ cents.

Abe and his sister picked pails of currants and blueberries for mother Nancy to spread in the sun to dry and put away for winter eating. There were wild grapes and pawpaws; there were bee trees with wild honey; there were wild crabapples and red haws. If it was a good corn year, the children helped shell the corn by hand and put it between two big flat stones, grinding it into cornmeal. The creeks gave them fish to fry. Tom Lincoln took his gun and brought back prairie turkey, partridge, rabbit, sometimes a coon, a bear, or a deer; and the skins of these big animals were tanned, cut and sewed into shirts, trousers, moccasins; the coonskins made caps.

There were lean times and fat, all depending on the weather, the rains or floods, how Tom Lincoln worked and what luck he had fishing and hunting. There were times when they lived on the fat of the land and said God was good; other times when they just scraped along and said they hoped the next world would be better than this one.

It was wilderness. Life dripped with fat and ease. Or it

took hold with hunger and cold. All the older settlers remembered winter in the year 1795, when "cold Friday" came; Kentucky was "cold as Canada," and cows froze to death in the open fields. The wilderness is careless.

Between the roadway over the top of Muldraugh's Hill and the swimming-hole where Abe Lincoln and Austin Gollaher ducked each other, there are tall hills more correctly called limestone bluffs. They crowd around Knob Creek and shape the valley's form. Their foundations are rocks, their measurements seem to be those of low mountains rather than hills. They seem to be aware of proportions and to suggest a quiet importance and secrets of fire, erosion, water, time, and many repeated processes that have stood them against the sky so that human settlers in the valley feel that around them are speakers of reserves and immensities.

The valley through which Knob Creek wanders there near Muldraugh's Hill, shooting its deep rushes of water when the hill rains flush the bottoms, has many keepers of the darker reticences of the crust of the earth and the changers that hold on to their lives there. That basic stream has a journal of its movement among pools inconceivably quiet in their mirrorings during days when the weather is fair and the elements of the sky at ease, and again of movement among those same pools when the rampages between the limestone banks send the water boiling and swirling. The naming of Muldraugh's Hill was a rich act in connotation, for it has whisperings of namelessly shrewd and beautiful wishes that the older and darker landscapes of Ireland breathe.

Trees crowd up its slopes with passionate footholds as though called by homes in the rocky soil; their climbings have covered sides and crests till they murmur, "You shall see no tall hills here unless you look at us." Caverns and ledges thrust their surprises of witchery and wizardry, of gnomes and passwords, or again of old-time intimations and analogues, memories of reckless rains leaving wave-prints to hint or say Muldraugh's Hill and the Knob Creek valley are old-timers in the making of the world, old-timers alongside of the two-footed little mover known as man. In the bottom lands the honeysuckle ranges with a strength nothing less than fierce; so deep are its roots that, unless torn away by the machines of man, the bees count on every year a boomer harvest of its honey-stuff; black and brown butterflies, spotted and streaked with scrolls and alphabets of unknown tongues from the world of wings—these come back every year to the honeysuckle.

Redbud, wild rose, and white daisies that look like scatterings of snow on green levels rise up with their faces yearly. Birds have made the valley a home; oncoming civilization has not shut off their hopes; homes for all are here; the martins learned a thousand years before the white man came that ten martins that fight with despair can kill and pick the eyes out of the head of a hawk that comes to slaughter and eat martins. And horses have so loved the valley, and it has so loved them in return, that some of the fastest saddle and riding nags remembered of men got their flying starts here.

Such was the exterior of the place and neighborhood where Abe Lincoln grew up from three to seven years of age, where he heard travelers talk, where he learned to write and sign his name, where, in fact, he first learned the meanings of names and how to answer, "Yes, it's me," if his mother called in the dark, "Is that you, Abe?"

Chapter 7

In the year 1816 Tom Lincoln was appointed road surveyor. The paper naming him for that office said he was named in place of George Redman to repair the road "leading from Nolen to Pendleton, which lies between the Bigg Hill and the Rolling Fork." It further commanded "that all hands that assisted said Redman do assist Lincoln in keeping said road in repair." It was a pasty red clay road. That the county was beginning to think about good roads showed that civilization was breaking through on the wilderness. And that Tom Lincoln was named as road surveyor showed they were holding some respect for him as a citizen and taxpayer of that community. At the county courthouse the recorder of deeds noticed that Thomas Lincoln signed his name, while his wife, Nancy, made her mark.

Thomas Lincoln
Nancy X Lincoln
her mark

Knob Creek settlers taking their corn to Hodgens Mill or riding to Elizabethtown to pay their taxes at the court or collect bounties on wolfskins at the county courthouse, talked a good deal about land-titles, landowners, landlords, land-laws, land-lawyers, land-sharks. Tom Lincoln about that time was chopping down trees and cutting brush on the Knob Creek land so as to clear more ground, raise corn on it and make a farm out of it. And he wasn't satisfied; he was suspicious that even if he did get his thirty acres cleared and paid for, the land might be taken away from him. This was happening to other settlers; they had the wrong kind of papers. Pioneers and settlers who for years had been fighting Indians, wolves, foxes, mosquitoes, and malaria had seen their land taken away; they had the wrong kind of papers. Daniel Boone, the first man to break a path from civilization through and into the Kentucky wilderness, found himself one day with all his rich, bluegrass Kentucky lands gone, not an acre of his big farms left; he had the wrong kind of papers; that was why he moved from Kentucky to Missouri.

Though Tom Lincoln was paying taxes on his thirty-acre farm, he was sued as a "tresspasser." He had to prove he wasn't a squatter—which he did. He went to court and won his suit. His little thirty-acre piece was only one of many pieces of a 10,000-acre tract surveyed in 1784 and patented to one man, Thomas Middleton, in 1786.

One-room, one-window, dirt-floor log cabin near Hodgenville, Kentucky, where Lincoln was born.

Along Knob Creek where the boy, Abe Lincoln, grew up till he was seven years old. Here his feet knew clear streams and clean gravel. The bottom photograph shows the Old Swimming Hole.

Poor white men were having a harder time to get along.
Hardin County had been filling up with negroes, slave black
men, bought and sold among the rich and well-to-do. The
Hodgens, La Rues, and other first families usually had one or
two, or six or a dozen, negroes. More than half the population
of Hardin County were colored. And it seemed that as more
slave black men were brought in, a poor white man didn't count
for so much; he had a harder time to get along; he was free
with the freedom of him who cannot be sold nor bought, while
the black slave was free with the security of the useful horse,
mule, cow, goat, or dog whose life and health is worth money
to the owner.

Already, in parts of Kentucky and farther south, the poor
white men, their women and children, were using the name of
"nigger" for the slaves, while there were black slaves in families
of quality who used the name of "po' w'ite" for the white people
who owned only their clothes, furniture, a rifle, an ax, perhaps
a horse and plow, and no land, no slaves, no stables, and no
property to speak of.

While these changes were coming in Kentucky, the territory
of Indiana came into the Union as a state whose law declared
"all men are born equally free and independent" and "the holding any part of the human creation in slavery, or involuntary
servitude, can only originate in usurpation and tyranny." In
crossing the Ohio River's two shores, a traveler touched two
soils, one where the buying and selling of black slaves went on,
the other where the negro was held to be "part of human creation" and was not property for buying and selling. But both
soils were part of the Union of states.

Letters and reports reaching Hardin County about this time
told of rich, black lands in Indiana, with more bushels of corn
to the acre than down in Kentucky, Government land with clear
title, the right kind of papers, for two dollars an acre. This
helped Tom Lincoln to decide in the year 1816 to move to Indiana. He told the family he would build a flatboat, load the
household goods on it, float by creeks to the Ohio River, leave

the household goods somewhere along the river while he went afoot up into Indiana, located his land, and registered it. Then he would come back, and the family, afoot and on horseback, would move to the new farm and home.

Chapter 8

THE boy, Abe, had his thoughts, some running ahead wondering how Indiana would look, some going back to his seven little years in Kentucky. Here he had curled around his mother's apron, watched her face and listened to her reading the Bible at the cabin log-fire, her fingers rambling through his hair, the hands patting him on the cheek and under the chin. God was real to his mother; he tried to make pictures in his head of the face of God far off and away in the sky, watching Kentucky, Hodgenville, Knob Creek, and all the rest of the world He had made. His thoughts could go back to the first time on a winter night around the fire when he lay flat on his stomach listening to his father as he told about his brothers, Mordecai and Josiah, and their father, Abraham Lincoln, who had staked out claims for more than 2,000 acres of land on the Green River. One day Abraham Lincoln and his three boys were working in a field; all of a sudden the father doubled up with a groan of pain and crumpled to the ground, just after the boys had heard a rifle-shot and the whining of a bullet. "Indians," the boys yelled to each other.

And Mordecai ran to a cabin, Josiah started across the fields and woods to a fort to bring help, while Tom Lincoln—little knee-high Tom—stooped over his father's bleeding body and wondered what he could do. He looked up to see an Indian standing over him, and a shining bangle hanging down over the Indian's shoulder close to the heart.

The Indian clutched upward with his hands, doubled with a groan and crumpled to the ground; Mordecai with a rifle at a peephole in the cabin had aimed his rifle at the shining bangle hanging down close to the Indian's heart, and Tom was so near he heard the bullet plug its hole into the red man.

And for years after that Mordecai Lincoln hated Indians with a deadly hate; if he heard that Indians were loose anywhere in a half-day's riding, he took his best rifles, pistols, and knives, and went Indian-killing.

There was Dr. Christopher Columbus Graham from Louisville, telling how the Indians were chasing Daniel Boone, and Boone saw a grapevine climbing high up a big oak; and he cut the grapevine near the root, took a run and a swing and made a jump of forty feet, so the Indians had to lose time finding sight and smell of his foot-tracks again.

And there were caves, worth remembering about in that part of Kentucky, and especially the biggest one of all, Mammoth Cave, fifty miles south; they said a thousand wagons could drive in and there would be room for another thousand.

And there was the foxy Austin Gollaher, his playmate. Up a tree he climbed one time, Abe dropped a pawpaw down into a coonskin cap; he guessed it was Austin's cap he was putting a smear of pawpaw mash in, but Austin had seen the trick coming and changed caps. So he had to wipe the smear out of his own cap.

Once he was walking on a log across Knob Creek when the rains had raised the creek. Just under the log, and under his feet, was the rush of the yellow muddy water. The log was slippery, his feet slippery. His feet went up in the air, he tumbled to the bottom of the creek; he came up, slipped again, came up with his nose and eyes full of water, and then saw Austin Gollaher on the bank holding out a long pole. He took hold of the pole and Austin pulled him to the bank.

Maybe he would grow up; his feet would be farther away from his head and his chin if he grew up; he could pick apples without climbing a tree or throwing clubs—if he grew up. Maybe then, after growing up, he would know more about those words he heard men saying, "in-de-pend-ent," "pre-des-ti-na-tion." Daniel Boone—yes, he could understand about Daniel

Boone—wearing moccasins and a buckskin shirt. But George Washington and Thomas Jefferson, and the President in Washington, James Madison—they were far off; they were sort of like God; it was hard to make pictures of their faces.

How many times he had gone to the family Bible, opened the big front cover, and peeped in at the page which tells what the book is! There were the words: "The Holy Bible, containing the Old and New Testaments, with Arguments prefixed to the Different Books and Moral and Theological Observations illustrating each Chapter, composed by the Reverend Mr. Osterwald, Professor of Divinity." And then pages and pages filled with words spelled out like the words in the spelling-book he had in school. So many words: heavy words—mysterious words!

About wolf heads, he could understand. He saw a man in Elizabethtown one time carrying two big wolf heads. The man had shot the wolves and was going to the courthouse, where they paid money for wolf heads. Yes, this he could understand. Wolves kill sheep and cattle in the fields; they come to the barns for pigs and chickens; he had heard them howling and sniffing on winter nights around the Knob Creek cabin and up the hills and gorges.

And there was his mother, his "mammy," the woman other people called Nancy or Nancy Hanks. . . . It was so dark and strange about her. There was such sweetness. Yet there used to be more sweetness and a fresher sweetness. There had been one baby they buried. Then there was Sally—and him, little Abe. Did the children cost her something? Did they pull her down? . . . The baby that came and was laid away so soon, only three days after it came, in so little a grave: that hurt his mother; she was sick and tired more often after that. . . . There were such lights and shadows back in her eyes. She wanted— what did she want? There were more and more days he had to take care of her, when he loved to bring cool drinking water to her—or anything she asked for.

Well—a boy seven years old isn't supposed to know much; he goes along and tries to do what the big people tell him to do. . . . They have been young and seen trouble: maybe they know. . . . He would get up in the morning when they called him; he would run to the spring for water. . . . He was only seven years old—and there were lots of frisky tricks he wanted to know more about

He was a "shirt-tail boy." . . . Three boys teased him one day when he took corn to Hodgen's Mill; they wouldn't be satisfied till he had punched their noses. . . . A clerk in the store at Elizabethtown gave him maple sugar to sit on a syrup keg and suck while his mother bought salt and flour. And the clerk was the only man he knew who was wearing store clothes, Sunday clothes, every day in the week. . . . The two pear trees his father planted on the Rock Spring farm . . . the faces of two goats a man kept down in Hodgenville . . . Dennis Hanks saying, "Abe, your face is solemn as a papoose."

It wouldn't be easy to forget that Saturday afternoon in corn-planting time when other boys dropped the seed-corn into all the rows in the big seven-acre field—and Abe dropped the pumpkin seed. He dropped two seeds at every other hill and every other row. The next Sunday morning there came a big rain in the hills; it didn't rain a drop in the valley, but the water came down the gorges and slides, and washed ground, corn, pumpkin seeds, and all clear off the field.

A dark blur of thoughts, pictures, memories and hopes moved through the head of little seven-year-old Abe. The family was going to move again. There was hope of better luck up north in Indiana. Tom's older brother, Josiah, was farming along the Big Blue River. Rich black corn-land was over there in "Indianny," more bushels to the acre than anywhere in Kentucky.

Chapter 9

IN the fall of the year 1816, Abe watched his father cut down trees, cut out logs, and fasten those logs into a flatboat on Knob

Creek. Abe ran after tools his father called for, sometimes held a hammer, a saw and a knife in his hands ready to give his father the next one called for. If his father said, "Fetch me a drink of water," the boy fetched; his legs belonged to his father. He helped carry chairs, tables, household goods, and carpenter's tools, loading them onto the flatboat. These, with four hundred gallons of whisky, "ten bar'ls," Tom had loaded onto the boat, made quite a cargo. Tom Lincoln, who was not much of a drinking man, had traded his farm for whisky, which was a kind of money in that day, and $20.00 cash.

Nancy Hanks and Sarah and Abe stayed on the farm while the husband and father floated down Knob Creek to Salt River and into the Ohio River. Tom was out of luck when the flatboat turned over so that the tool chest, household goods and four barrels of whisky slid out of the boat. Most of the whisky and some of the other goods he managed to fish up from the river bottom. Then he crossed the Ohio River, landed on the Indiana side at Thompson's Ferry and left his whisky and household goods at the house of a man called Posey.

He started off on foot into the big timbers of what was then Perry County, later divided into Spencer County. He decided to live and to farm on a quarter-section of land on Little Pigeon Creek; he notched the trees with his ax, cleared away brush and piled it, as the Government land-laws required. This was his "claim," later filed at the Land Office in Vincennes, Indiana, as the Southwest Quarter of Section Thirty-two, Town Four South, Range Five West, to be paid for at $2.00 an acre. His Indiana homestead was now ready for a cabin and a family; he walked back to the Knob Creek home in Kentucky and told the family he reckoned they'd all put in the winter up in "Indianny."

They had fifty miles to go, in a straight line "as the crow flies," but about one hundred miles with all the zigzags and curves around hills, timbers, creeks, and rivers.

Pots, pans, kettles, blankets, the family Bible, and other things were put into bags and loaded on two horses. Nancy and Sarah climbed on one horse, Tom and Abe on the other. When it was hard going for the horses, the father and mother walked. Part of the way on that hundred-mile ride made little Abe's eyes open. They were going deeper into the wilderness. In Kentucky there were ten people to the square mile and in Indiana only three. As Abe sat on the horse plodding along, he saw miles and miles of beeches, oaks, elms, hard and soft maples, hung and run over with the scarlet streamers and the shifting gray hazes of autumn.

Then they came to the Ohio River. The Frenchmen years before named it "La Belle Rivière," meaning it was a sheen of water as good to look at as a beautiful woman. There she lay —the biggest stretch of shining water his eyes had ever seen. And Abe thought how different it was from Knob Creek, which he could walk across on a log—if he didn't let his feet slip from under. They crossed the river, and at the house of the man called Posey they got a wagon, loaded the barrels of whisky and the household goods, and drove sixteen miles to their "claim." The trail was so narrow that a few times Tom Lincoln got off the wagon with an ax and cut brush and trees so the wagon could pass through. It was a hired wagon and horses they came with, and the wagon and horse-team were taken back to Posey.

Tom Lincoln, his wife, boy, and girl, had arrived on a claim at Little Pigeon Creek, without a horse or a cow, without a house, with a little piece of land under their feet and the wintry sky high over. Naked they had come into the world; almost naked they came to Little Pigeon Creek, Indiana.

The whole family pitched in and built a pole-shed or "half-faced camp." On a slope of ground stood two trees about fourteen feet apart, east and west. These formed the two strong corner-posts of a sort of cabin with three sides, the fourth side open, facing south. The sides and the roof were covered with poles, branches, brush, dried grass, mud; chinks were stuffed where the wind or the rain was trying to come through. At the open side a log-fire was kept burning night and day. In the two far corners inside the camp were beds of dry leaves on the ground.   To these beds the sleepers brought their blankets and bearskins.

Here they lived a year.   In the summer time and fair weather, the pole-shed was snug enough.   When the rain storms or wind and snow broke through and drenched the place, or when the south or southwest wind blew the fire-smoke into the camp so those inside had to clear out, it was a rough life.

The mother sang.   Nancy Hanks knew songs her mother, Lucy, had heard in Virginia.   The ballad of Fair Ellender told of the hero coming home with the Brown Girl who had lands and gold.   Fair Ellender taunted: "Is this your bride?   She seemeth me plagued brown."   And for that, the Brown Girl leaped over a table corner and put a slim little knife through Fair Ellender's heart.   Then out came the hero's sword and he cut off the Brown Girl's head and "slung it agin the wall." Then he put the sword through his own heart.

And there was the ballad of Wicked Polly, who danced and ran wild and told the old folks, "I'll turn to God when I get old, and He will then receive my soul."   But when death struck her down while she was young and running wild, she called for her mother, and with rolling eyeballs, cried, "When I am dead, remember well, your wicked Polly screams in hell."

Tom chopped logs for a cabin forty yards away while Abe did the best he could helping Nancy and Sarah trim the branches off the logs, cut brush, clear ground for planting, hoe weeds, tend the log-fire.   The heaviest regular chore of the children was walking a mile away to a spring and carrying a bucket of water back home.   Their food was mostly game shot in the woods near by; they went barefoot most of the year; in the winter their shoes were homemade moccasins; they were up with the sun and the early birds in the morning; their lighting at night was fire-logs and pine-knots.   In summer and early fall the flies and mosquitoes swarmed.

In the new cabin Tom Lincoln was building, and on this little Pigeon Creek farm, the Lincoln family was going to live fourteen years.

Chapter 10

As Abe Lincoln, seven years old, going on eight, went to sleep on his bed of dry leaves in a corner of the pole-shed there on Little Pigeon Creek, in Indiana, in the winter of 1816, he had his thoughts, his feelings, his impressions. He shut his eyes, and looking-glasses began to work inside his head; he could see Kentucky and the Knob Creek farm again; he could see the Ohio River shining so far across that he couldn't begin to throw a stone from one side to the other.

And while his eyes were shut he could see the inside of the pole-shed, the floor of earth and grass, the frying-pan, the cooking-pot, the water-pail he and his sister carried full of water from the spring a mile away, and the log-fire always kept burning. And sometimes his imagination, his shut eyes and their quick-changing looking-glasses would bring the whole outdoor sky and land indoors, into the pole-shed, into the big shifting looking-glasses inside of his head. The mystery of imagination, of the faculty of reconstruction and piecing together today the things his eyes had seen yesterday, this took hold of him and he brooded over it.

One night he tried to sleep while his head was working on the meaning of the heavy and mysterious words standing dark on the pages of the family Bible; the stories his mother told him from those pages; all the people in the world drowned, the world covered with water, even Indiana and Kentucky, all people drowned except Noah and his family; the man Jonah swallowed by a whale and after days coming out of the belly of the whale; the Last Day to come, the stars dropping out of the sky, the world swallowed up in fire.

And one night this boy felt the southwest wind blowing the log-fire smoke into his nostrils. And there was a hoot-owl crying, and a shaking of branches in the beeches and walnuts outside, so that he went to the south opening of the shed and looked

out on a winter sky with a high quarter-moon and a white shine
of thin frost on the long open spaces of the sky.

And an old wonder took a deeper hold on him, a wonder about
the loneliness of life down there in the Indiana wilderness, and
a wonder about what was happening in other places over the
world, places he had heard people mention, cities, rivers, flags,
wars, Jerusalem, Washington, Baltimore.

He might have asked the moon, "What do you see?" And
the moon might have told him many things.

That year of 1816 the moon had seen sixteen thousand wagons
come along one turnpike in Pennsylvania, heading west, with
people hungry for new land, a new home, just like Tom Lincoln.
Up the Mississippi River that year had come the first steamboat to curve into the Ohio River and land passengers at Louisville. The moon had seen the first steamboat leave Pittsburgh
and tie up at New Orleans. New wheels, wagons, were coming,
an iron horse snorting fire and smoke. Rolling-mills, ingots,
iron, steel, were the talk of Pennsylvania; a sheet copper mill
was starting in Massachusetts.

The moon could see eight million people in the United States,
white men who had pushed the Indians over the eastern mountains, fighting to clear the Great Plains and the southern valleys
of the red men. At Fallen Timbers and at Tippecanoe in
Indiana, and down at the Great Bend of the Tallapoosa, the
pale faces and copper faces had yelled and grappled and
Weatherford had said, "I have done the white people all the
harm I could; if I had an army I would fight to the last; my
warriors can no longer hear my voice; their bones are at Tal-
ladega, Tallushatches, Emuckfaw, and Tohopeka; I can do no
more than weep." The red men had been warned by Jefferson
to settle down and be farmers, to double their numbers every
twenty years as the white people did, the whites in "new
swarms continually advancing upon the country like flocks of
pigeons."

The moon had seen two men, sunburned, wind-bitten and

scarred, arrive at the White House just four years before Abe Lincoln was born. The two men had been on a three-year trip, leaving Washington in 1802, riding and walking across the Great Plains, the Rockies and Sierras, to the Pacific Coast country, and then back to Washington. What those two, Lewis and Clark, had to tell, opened the eyes of white people to what a rich, big country they lived in. Out along that trail Jefferson could see "new swarms advancing like flocks of pigeons."

And how had these eight million people come to America, for the moon to look down on and watch their westward swarming? Many were children of men who had quarreled in the old countries of Europe, and fought wars about the words and ways of worshiping God and obeying His commandments. They were Puritans from England, French Huguenots, German Pietists, Hanoverians, Moravians, Saxons, Austrians, Swiss, Quakers, all carrying their Bibles. Also there were Ulster Presbyterians from North Ireland, and Scotch Presbyterians. They came by their own wish. Others who came not by their own wish were fifty thousand thieves and murderers sent from British prisons and courts. Dr. Samuel Johnson, the same man who said, "Patriotism is the last refuge of a scoundrel," had called Americans "a race of convicts." Convicted men in England, offered the choice of hanging or being shipped to America, had given the answer, "Hang me."

The moon had seen boys and girls by thousands kidnaped off the streets of English cities and smuggled across to America. And each year for fifty years there had come a thousand to fifteen hundred "indentured servants," men and women who had signed papers to work for a certain master, the law holding them to work till their time was up.

The moon had seen sailing-ships start from ports in Europe and take from six weeks to six months crossing the Atlantic. Aboard those ships often were "stench, fumes, vomiting, many kinds of sicknesses, fever, dysentery, scurvy, the mouth-rot, and the like, all of which come from old and sharply salted food and meat, also from bad and foul water."

Such were a few of the things known to the fathers and grandfathers of part of the eight million people in America that the
moon was looking down on in the winter nights of 1816. And
in the years to come the moon would see more and more people
coming from Europe.

Seldom had the moon in its thousands of years of looking
down on the earth and the human family seen such a man as
the Napoleon Bonaparte whose bayonets had been going in
Europe for fifteen years, shoving kings off thrones, changing
laws, maps, books, raising armies, using them up, and raising new
armies, until people in some regions were saying, "The red roses
of this year grow from the blood-wet ground of the wars we
fought last year." And at last the terrible Napolcon was caged,
jailed, on the lonely island of St. Helena. Crying for the "liberty
and equality" of France to be spread over the world, he had led
armies to believe and dream of beating down all other armies
in Europe that tried to stand against him. Then he was a lean
shadow; he had become fat; the paunch stuck out farther than is
allowed to conquerors. He had hugged armfuls of battle-flags
to his breast while telling an army of soldiers, "I cannot embrace
you all, but I do so in the person of your general." It hurt his
ears when, captured and being driven in an open carriage, he
heard sarcastic people along the streets mock at him with the
call, "Long live the Emperor!" He would die far from home,
with regrets, the first man to be Napoleonic.

When Napoleon sold to Jefferson the Great Plains between
the Mississippi River and the Rocky Mountains, the moon saw
only a few Indians, buffalo hunters and drifters, living there.
The price for the land was fifteen million dollars; Jefferson had
to argue with people who said the price was too high. Such
things the moon had seen. Also, out of war-taxed and war-
crippled Europe the moon could see steady lines of ships taking
people from that part of the Round World across the water to
America. Also, lines of ships sailing to Africa with whisky,
calico, and silk, and coming back loaded with negroes.

And as the wagons, by thousands a year, were slipping through the passes of the Allegheny Mountains, heading west for the two-dollar-an-acre Government land, many steered clear of the South; they couldn't buy slaves; and they were suspicious of slavery; it was safer to go farming where white men did all the work. At first the stream of wagons and settlers moving west had kept close to the Ohio River. Then it began spreading in a fan-shape up north and west.

The moon could see along the pikes, roads, and trails heading west, broken wagon-wheels with prairie grass growing up over the spokes and hubs. And near by, sometimes, a rusty skillet, empty moccasins, and the bones of horses and men.

In the hot dog-days, in the long rains, in the casual blizzards, they had stuck it out—and lost. There came a saying, a pithy, perhaps brutal folk proverb, "The cowards never started and the weak ones died by the way."

Such were a few of the many, many things the moon might have told little Abe Lincoln, nearly eight years old, on a winter night in 1816 on Little Pigeon Creek, in the Buckhorn Valley, in southern Indiana—a high quarter-moon with a white shine of thin frost on the long open spaces of the sky.

He was of the blood and breath of many of these things, and would know them better in the years to come.

Chapter 11

DURING the year 1817, little Abe Lincoln, eight years old, going on nine, had an ax put in his hands and helped his father cut down trees and notch logs for the corners of their new cabin, forty yards from the pole-shed where the family was cooking, eating, and sleeping.

Wild turkey, ruffed grouse, partridge, coon, rabbit, were to be had for the shooting of them. Before each shot Tom Lincoln took a rifle-ball out of a bag and held the ball in his left hand; then with his right hand holding the gunpowder horn he pulled the stopper with his teeth, slipped the powder into the barrel, followed with the ball; then he rammed the charge down the barrel with a hickory ramrod held in both hands, looked to his trigger, flint, and feather in the touch-hole—and he was ready to shoot —to kill for the home skillet.

Having loaded his rifle just that way several thousand times in his life, he could do it in the dark or with his eyes shut. Once Abe took the gun as a flock of wild turkeys came toward the new log cabin, and, standing inside, shot through a crack and killed one of the big birds; and after that, somehow, he never felt like pulling the trigger on game-birds. A mile from the cabin was a salt lick where deer came; there the boy could have easily shot the animals, as they stood rubbing their tongues along the salty slabs or tasting of a saltish ooze. His father did the shooting; the deer killed gave them meat for Nancy's skillet; and the skins were tanned, cut, and stitched into shirts, trousers, mitts, moccasins. They wore buckskin; their valley was called the Buckhorn Valley.

After months the cabin stood up, four walls fitted together with a roof, a one-room house eighteen feet square, for a family to live in. A stick chimney plastered with clay ran up outside. The floor was packed and smoothed dirt. A log-fire lighted the inside; no windows were cut in the walls. For a door there was a hole cut to stoop through. Bedsteads were cleated to the corners of the cabin; pegs stuck in the side of a wall made a ladder for young Abe to climb up in a loft to sleep on a hump of dry leaves; rain and snow came through chinks of the roof onto his bearskin cover. A table and three-legged stools had the top sides smoothed with an ax, and the bark-side under, in the style called "puncheon."

A few days of this year in which the cabin was building, Nancy told Abe to wash his face and hands extra clean; she combed his hair, held his face between her two hands, smacked him a kiss on the mouth, and sent him to school—nine miles and back—Abe and Sally hand in hand hiking eighteen miles a day. Tom Lincoln used to say Abe was going to have "a real eddication," explaining, "You air a-goin' to larn readin', writin', and cipherin'."

He learned to spell words he didn't know the meaning of, spelling the words before he used them in sentences. In a list of "words of eight syllables accented upon the sixth," was the word "incomprehensibility." He learned that first, and then such sentences as "Is he to go in?" and "Ann can spin flax."

Some neighbors said, "It's a pore make-out of a school," and Tom complained it was a waste of time to send the children nine miles just to sit with a lot of other children and read out loud all day in a "blab" school. But Nancy, as she cleaned Abe's ears in corners where he forgot to clean them, and as she combed out the tangles in his coarse, sandy black hair, used to say, "Abe, you go to school now, and larn all you kin." And he kissed her and said, "Yes, Mammy," and started with his sister on the nine-mile walk through timberland where bear, deer, coon, and wildcats ran wild.

Fall time came with its early frost and they were moved into the new cabin, when horses and a wagon came breaking into the clearing one day. It was Tom and Betsy Sparrow and their seventeen-year-old boy, Dennis Hanks, who had come from Hodgenville, Kentucky, to cook and sleep in the pole-shed of the Lincoln family till they could locate land and settle. Hardly a year had passed, however, when both Tom and Betsy Sparrow were taken down with the "milk sick," beginning with a whitish coat on the tongue. Both died and were buried in October on a little hill in a clearing in the timbers near by.

Soon after, there came to Nancy Hanks Lincoln that white coating of the tongue; her vitals burned; the tongue turned brownish; her feet and hands grew cold and colder, her pulse slow and slower. She knew she was dying, called for her children, and spoke to them her last choking words. Sarah and Abe leaned over the bed. A bony hand of the struggling mother went out, putting its fingers into the boy's sandy black hair; her fluttering guttural words seemed to say he must grow up and be good to his sister and father.

So, on a bed of poles cleated to the corner of the cabin, the body of Nancy Hanks Lincoln lay, looking tired . . . tired . . . with a peace settling in the pinched corners of the sweet, weary mouth, silence slowly etching away the lines of pain and hunger drawn around the gray eyes where now the eyelids closed down in the fine pathos of unbroken rest, a sleep without interruption settling about the form of the stooped and wasted shoulder-bones, looking to the children who tiptoed in, stood still, cried their tears of want and longing, whispered "Mammy, Mammy," and heard only their own whispers answering, looking to these little ones of her brood as though new secrets had come to her in place of the old secrets given up with the breath of life.

And Tom Lincoln took a log left over from the building of the cabin, and he and Dennis Hanks whipsawed the log into planks, planed the planks smooth, and made them of a measure for a box to bury the dead wife and mother in. Little Abe, with a jackknife, whittled pine-wood pegs. And then, while Dennis and Abe held the planks, Tom bored holes and stuck the whittled pegs through the bored holes. This was the coffin, and they carried it the next day to the same little timber clearing near by, where a few weeks before they had buried Tom and Betsy Sparrow. It was in the way of the deer-run leading to the saltish water; light feet and shy hoofs ran over those early winter graves.

So the woman, Nancy Hanks, died, thirty-six years old, a pioneer sacrifice, with memories of monotonous, endless everyday chores, of mystic Bible verses read over and over for their promises, and with memories of blue wistful hills and a summer when the crab-apple blossoms flamed white and she carried a boy-child into the world.

She had looked out on fields of blue-blossoming flax and hummed "Hey, Betty Martin, tiptoe, tiptoe"; she had sung of bright kingdoms by and by and seen the early frost leaf its crystals on the stalks of buttonweed and redbud; she had sung:

> You may bury me in the east,
> You may bury me in the west,
> And we'll all rise together in that morning.

To Exercise Multiplication

There were 40 men concerned in payment, a sum of money and each man paid 12.71£ how much was paid in all ——

12.71
40
40)50840
1241

If 1 foot contain 12 inches I demand how many there are in 126 feet ——

126
12
252
126
12)1512
126

of Compound Division.

Q What is compound Division

A When several numbers of Divers Denomination is given to be divided by 1 common divisor this called Compound Division —

£   S   D
2)48 – 12 – 6¾
24 – 6 – 3½
2
48 – 12 – 6½

lb   oz   dr
5)16 – 12 – 10
9 – 5 – 13
5
46 – 12 – 10

Abraham Lincoln His Book

Young Abe's homemade arithmetic.

Original in Barrett Collection

THE

KENTUCKY PRECEPTOR,

CONTAINING

A NUMBER OF USEFUL LESSONS

FOR READING AND SPEAKING.

COMPILED FOR THE USE OF SCHOOLS.

BY A TEACHER.

Delightful task ! to rear the tender thought,
To teach the young idea how to shoot,
To pour the fresh instruction o'er the mind,
To breathe the enlivening spirit, and to fix
The generous purpose in the glowing breast.
                                    THOMPSON.

THIRD EDITION, REVISED, WITH CONSIDERABLE ADDITIONS.

COPY-RIGHT SECURED ACCORDING TO LAW.

LEXINGTON, (KY.)

PUBLISHED BY MACCOUN, TILFORD & CO.

1812.

Ox yoke carved by Lincoln; young steers yoked in this helped haul the Lincoln family across the Wabash to the new prairie home in Illinois in 1831.

Original yoke in University of Illinois Library

Title page of Abe Lincoln's school reader in Indiana; he borrowed it from Josiah Crawford.

Reduced size from original in Barrett Collection

Chapter 12

SOME weeks later, when David Elkin, elder of the Methodist church, was in that neighborhood, he was called on to speak over the grave of Nancy Hanks. He had been acquainted with her in Kentucky, and to the Lincoln family and a few neighbors he spoke of good things she had done, sweet ways she had of living her life in this Vale of Tears, and her faith in another life yonder past the River Jordan.

The "milk sick" took more people in that neighborhood the same year, and Tom Lincoln whipsawed planks for more coffins. One settler lost four milch cows and eleven calves. The nearest doctor for people or cattle was thirty-five miles away. The wilderness is careless.

Lonesome and dark months came for Abe and Sarah. Worst of all were the weeks after their father went away, promising to come back.

Elizabethtown, Kentucky, was the place Tom Lincoln headed for. As he footed it through the woods and across the Ohio River, he was saying over to himself a speech—the words he would say to Sarah Bush Johnston, down in Elizabethtown. Her husband had died a few years before, and she was now in Tom's thoughts.

He went straight to the house where she was living in Elizabethtown, and, speaking to her as "Miss Johnston," he argued: "I have no wife and you no husband. I came a-purpose to marry you. I knowed you from a gal and you knowed me from a boy. I've no time to lose; and if you're willin' let it be done straight off."

Her answer was, "I got debts." She gave him a list of the debts; he paid them; a license was issued; and they were married on December 2, 1819.

He could write his name; she couldn't write hers. Trying to explain why the two of them took up with each other so quickly,

Dennis Hanks at a later time said, "Tom had a kind o' way with women, an' maybe it was somethin' she took comfort in to have a man that didn't drink an' cuss none."

Little Abe and Sarah, living in the lonesome cabin on Little Pigeon Creek, Indiana, got a nice surprise one morning when four horses and a wagon came into their clearing, and their father jumped off, then Sarah Bush Lincoln, the new wife and mother, then John, Sarah, and Matilda Johnston, Sarah Bush's three children by her first husband. Next off the wagon came a feather mattress, feather pillows, a black walnut bureau, a large clothes-chest, a table, chairs, pots and skillets, knives, forks, spoons.

Abe ran his fingers over the slick wood of the bureau, pushed his fist into the feather pillows, sat in the new chairs, and wondered to himself, because this was the first time he had touched such fine things, such soft slick things.

"Here's your new mammy," his father told Abe as the boy looked up at a strong, large-boned, rosy woman, with a kindly face and eyes, with a steady voice, steady ways. The cheek-bones of her face stood out and she had a strong jaw-bone; she was warm and friendly for Abe's little hands to touch, right from the beginning. As one of her big hands held his head against her skirt he felt like a cold chick warming under the soft feathers of a big wing. She took the corn-husks Abe had been sleeping on, piled them in the yard and said they would be good for a pig-pen later on; and Abe sunk his head and bones that night in a feather pillow and a feather mattress.

Ten years pass with that cabin on Little Pigeon Creek for a home, and that farm and neighborhood the soil for growth. There the boy Abe grows to be the young man, Abraham Lincoln.

Ten years pass and the roots of a tree spread out finding water to carry up to branches and leaves that are in the sun; the trunk thickens, the forked limbs shine wider in the sun, they pray with their leaves in the rain and the whining wind; the tree arrives, the mystery of its coming, spreading, growing, a secret not even known to the tree itself; it stands with its arms

stretched to the corners the four winds come from, with its murmured testimony, "We are here, we arrived, our roots are in
the earth of these years," and beyond that short declaration, it
speaks nothing of the decrees, fates, accidents, destinies, that
made it an apparition of its particular moment.

Abe Lincoln grows up. His father talks about the waste of
time in "eddication"; it is enough "to larn readin', writin',
cipherin' "; but the stanch, yearning stepmother, Sarah Bush
Lincoln, comes between the boy and the father. And the father
listens to the stepmother and lets her have her way.

Chapter 13

WHEN he was eleven years old, Abe Lincoln's young body began
to change. The juices and glands began to make a long, tall
boy out of him. As the months and years went by, he noticed
his lean wrists getting longer, his legs too, and he was now looking
over the heads of other boys. Men said, "Land o' Goshen, that
boy air a-growin'!"

As he took on more length, they said he was shooting up into
the air like green corn in the summer of a good corn-year. So
he grew. When he reached seventeen years of age, and they
measured him, he was six feet, nearly four inches, high, from the
bottoms of his moccasins to the top of his skull.

These were years he was handling the ax. Except in spring
plowing-time and the fall fodder-pulling, he was handling the ax
nearly all the time. The insides of his hands took on callus
thick as leather. He cleared openings in the timber, cut logs
and puncheons, split firewood, built pig-pens.

He learned how to measure with his eye the half-circle swing
of the ax so as to nick out the deepest possible chip from off a
tree-trunk. The trick of swaying his body easily on the hips so
as to throw the heaviest possible weight into the blow of the ax
—he learned that.

On winter mornings he wiped the frost from the ax-handle,

sniffed sparkles of air into his lungs, and beat a steady cleaving of blows into a big tree—till it fell—and he sat on the main log and ate his noon dinner of corn bread and fried salt pork—and joked with the gray squirrels that frisked and peeped at him from high forks of near-by walnut trees.

He learned how to make his ax flash and bite into a sugar-maple or a sycamore. The outside and the inside look of black walnut and black oak, hickory and jack oak, elm and white oak, sassafras, dogwood, grapevines, sumac—he came on their secrets. He could guess close to the time of the year, to the week of the month, by the way the leaves and branches of trees looked. He sniffed the seasons.

Often he worked alone in the timbers, all day long with only the sound of his own ax, or his own voice speaking to himself, or the crackling and swaying of branches in the wind, and the cries and whirs of animals, of brown and silver-gray squirrels, of partridges, hawks, crows, turkeys, sparrows, and the occasional wildcats.

The tricks and whimsies of the sky, how to read clear skies and cloudy weather, the creeping vines of ivy and wild grape, the recurrence of dogwood blossoms in spring, the ways of snow, rain, drizzle, sleet, the visitors of sky and weather coming and going hour by hour—he tried to read their secrets, he tried to be friendly with their mystery.

So he grew, to become hard, tough, wiry. The muscle on his bones and the cords, tendons, cross-weaves of fiber, and nerve centres, these became instruments to obey his wishes. He found with other men he could lift his own end of a log—and more too. One of the neighbors said he was strong as three men. Another said, "He can sink an ax deeper into wood than any man I ever saw." And another, "If you heard him fellin' trees in a clearin', you would say there was three men at work by the way the trees fell."

He was more than a tough, long, rawboned boy. He amazed men with his man's lifting power. He put his shoulders under a new-built corncrib one day and walked away with it to where the farmer wanted it. Four men, ready with poles to put under it and carry it, didn't need their poles. He played the same trick with a chicken house; at the new, growing town of Gentryville near by, they said the chicken house weighed six hundred pounds, and only a big boy with a hard backbone could get under it and walk away with it.

A blacksmith shop, a grocery, and a store had started up on the crossroads of the Gentry farm. And one night after Abe had been helping thresh wheat on Dave Turnham's place, he went with Dennis Hanks, John Johnston, and some other boys to Gentryville where the farm-hands sat around with John Baldwin, the blacksmith, and Jones, the storekeeper, passed the whisky jug, told stories, and talked politics and religion and gossip. Going home late that night, they saw something in a mud puddle alongside the road. They stepped over to see whether it was a man or a hog. It was a man—drunk—snoring—sleeping off his drunk—on a frosty night outdoors in a cold wind.

They shook him by the shoulders, doubled his knees to his stomach, but he went on sleeping, snoring. The cold wind was getting colder. The other boys said they were going home, and they went away leaving Abe alone with the snoring sleeper in the mud puddle. Abe stepped into the mud, reached arms around the man, slung him over his shoulders, carried him to Dennis Hanks's cabin, built a fire, rubbed him warm and left him sleeping off the whisky.

And the man afterward said Abe saved his life. He told John Hanks, "It was mighty clever of Abe to tote me to a warm fire that night."

So he grew, living in that Pigeon Creek cabin for a home, sleeping in the loft, climbing up at night to a bed just under the roof, where sometimes the snow and the rain drove through the cracks, eating sometimes at a table where the family had only one thing to eat—potatoes. Once at the table, when there were only potatoes, his father spoke a blessing to the Lord for potatoes; the boy murmured, "Those are mighty poor blessings." And Abe made jokes once when company came and Sally Bush

Lincoln brought out raw potatoes, gave the visitors a knife apiece, and they all peeled raw potatoes, and talked about the crops, politics, religion, gossip.

Days when they had only potatoes to eat didn't come often. Other days in the year they had "yaller-legged chicken" with gravy, and corn dodgers with shortening, and berries and honey. They tasted of bear meat, deer, coon, quail, grouse, prairie turkey, catfish, bass, perch.

Abe knew the sleep that comes after long hours of work outdoors, the feeling of simple food changing into blood and muscle as he worked in those young years clearing timberland for pasture and corn crops, cutting loose the brush, piling it and burning it, splitting rails, pulling the crosscut saw and the whipsaw, driving the shovel-plow, harrowing, planting, hoeing, pulling fodder, milking cows, churning butter, helping neighbors at house-raisings, log-rollings, corn-huskings.

He found he was fast, strong, and keen when he went against other boys in sports. On farms where he worked, he held his own at scuffling, knocking off hats, wrestling. The time came when around Gentryville and Spencer County he was known as the best "rassler" of all, the champion. In jumping, foot-racing, throwing the maul, pitching the crowbar, he carried away the decisions against the lads of his own age always, and usually won against those older than himself.

He earned his board, clothes, and lodgings, sometimes working for a neighbor farmer. He watched his father, while helping make cabinets, coffins, cupboards, window frames, doors. Hammers, saws, pegs, cleats, he understood first-hand, also the scythe and the cradle for cutting hay and grain, the corn-cutter's knife, the leather piece to protect the hand while shucking corn, and the horse, the dog, the cow, the ox, the hog. He could skin and cure the hides of coon and deer. He lifted the slippery two-hundred-pound hog carcass, head down, holding the hind hocks up for others of the gang to hook, and swung the animal clear of the ground. He learned where to stick a hog in the under side of the neck so as to bleed it to death, how to split it in two, and carve out the chops, the parts for sausage grinding, for hams, for "cracklings."

Farmers called him to butcher for them at thirty-one cents a day, this when he was sixteen and seventeen years old. He could "knock a beef in the head," swing a maul and hit a cow between the eyes, skin the hide, halve and quarter it, carve out the tallow, the steaks, kidneys, liver.

And the hiding-places of fresh spring water under the earth crust had to be in his thoughts; he helped at well-digging; the wells Tom Lincoln dug went dry one year after another; neighbors said Tom was always digging a well and had his land "honey-combed"; and the boy, Abe, ran the errands and held the tools for the well-digging.

When he was eighteen years old, he could take an ax at the end of the handle and hold it out in a straight horizontal line, easy and steady—he had strong shoulder muscles and steady wrists early in life. He walked thirty-four miles in one day, just on an errand, to please himself, to hear a lawyer make a speech. He could tell his body to do almost impossible things, and the body obeyed.

Growing from boy to man, he was alone a good deal of the time. Days came often when he was by himself all the time except at breakfast and supper hours in the cabin home. In some years more of his time was spent in loneliness than in the company of other people. It happened, too, that this loneliness he knew was not like that of people in cities who can look from a window on streets where faces pass and repass. It was the wilderness loneliness he became acquainted with, solved, filtered through body, eye, and brain, held communion with in his ears, in the temples of his forehead, in the works of his beating heart.

He lived with trees, with the bush wet with shining raindrops, with the burning bush of autumn, with the lone wild duck riding a north wind and crying down on a line north to south, the faces of open sky and weather, the ax which is an individual one-man instrument, these he had for companions, books, friends, talkers, chums of his endless changing soliloquies.

His moccasin feet in the winter-time knew the white spaces of snowdrifts piled in whimsical shapes against timber slopes or blown in levels across the fields of last year's cut corn stalks; in the summer-time his bare feet toughened in the gravel of green streams while he laughed back to the chatter of bluejays in the red-haw trees or while he kept his eyes ready in the slough quack-grass for the cow-snake, the rattler, the copperhead.

He rested between spells of work in the springtime when the upward push of the coming out of the new grass can be heard, and in autumn weeks when the rustle of a single falling leaf lets go a whisper that a listening ear can catch.

He found his life thrown in ways where there was a certain chance for a certain growth. And so he grew. Silence found him; he met silence. In the making of him as he was, the element of silence was immense.

Chapter 14

It was a little country of families living in one-room cabins. Dennis Hanks said at a later time, "We lived the same as the Indians, 'ceptin' we took an interest in politics and religion."

Cash was scarce; venison hams, bacon slabs, and barrels of whisky served as money; there were seasons when storekeepers asked customers, "What kind of money have you today?" because so many sorts of wildcat dollar bills were passing around. In sections of timberland, wild hogs were nosing out a fat living on hickory nuts, walnuts, acorns; it was said the country would be full of wild hogs if the wolves didn't find the litters of young pigs a few weeks old and kill them.

Farmers lost thirty and forty sheep in a single wolf raid. Toward the end of June came "fly time," when cows lost weight and gave less milk because they had to fight flies. For two or three months at the end of summer, horses weakened, unless covered with blankets, under the attacks of horse-flies; where one lighted on a horse, a drop of blood oozed; horses were hitched to branches of trees that gave loose rein to the animals, room to move and fight flies.

Men and women went barefoot except in the colder weather; women carried their shoes in their hands and put them on just before arrival at church meetings or at social parties.

Rains came, loosening the top soil of the land where it was not held by grass roots; it was a yellow clay that softened to slush; in this yellow slush many a time Abe Lincoln walked ankle-deep; his bare feet were intimate with the clay dust of the hot dog-days, with the clay mud of spring and fall rains; he was at home in clay. In the timbers with his ax, on the way to chop, his toes, heels, soles, the balls of his feet, climbed and slid in banks and sluices of clay. In the corn-fields, plowing, hoeing, cutting, and shucking, again his bare feet spoke with the clay of the earth; it was in his toenails and stuck on the skin of his toe-knuckles. The color of clay was one of his own colors.

In the short and simple annals of the poor, it seems there are people who breathe with the earth and take into their lungs and blood some of the hard and dark strength of its mystery. During six and seven months each year in the twelve fiercest formative years of his life, Abraham Lincoln had the pads of his foot-soles bare against clay of the earth. It may be the earth told him in her own tough gypsy slang one or two knacks of living worth keeping. To be organic with running wildfire and quiet rain, both of the same moment, is to be the carrier of wave-lines the earth gives up only on hard usage.

Chapter 15

HE took shape in a tall, long-armed cornhusker. When rain came in at the chinks of the cabin loft where he slept, soaking through the book Josiah Crawford loaned him, he pulled fodder two days to pay for the book, made a clean sweep, till there wasn't a blade left on a cornstalk in the field of Josiah Crawford.

His father was saying the big boy looked as if he had been

roughhewn with an ax and needed smoothing with a jack-plane. "He was the ganglin'est, awkwardest feller that ever stepped over a ten-rail snake fence; he had t' duck to git through a door; he 'peared to be all j'ints."

His stepmother told him she didn't mind his bringing dirt into the house on his feet; she could scour the floor; but she asked him to keep his head washed or he'd be rubbing the dirt on her nice whitewashed rafters. He put barefoot boys to wading in a mud-puddle near the horse-trough, picked them up one by one, carried them to the house upside down, and walked their muddy feet across the ceiling. The mother came in, laughed an hour at the foot-tracks, told Abe he ought to be spanked—and he cleaned the ceiling so it looked new.

The mother said, "Abe never spoke a cross word to me in his life since we lived together." And she said Abe was truthful; when Tilda Johnston leaped onto Abe's back to give him a scare on a lonely timber path, she brought the big axman to the ground by pulling her hands against his shoulders and pressing her knee into his backbone. The ax-blade cut her ankle, and strips from Abe's shirt and Tilda's dress had to be used to stop the blood. By then she was sobbing over what to tell her mother. On Abe's advice she told her mother the whole truth.

As time went by, the stepmother of Abe became one of the rich, silent forces in his life. Besides keeping the floors, pots, pans, kettles, and milk-crocks spick and span, weaving, sewing, mending, and managing with sagacity and gumption, she had a massive, bony, human strength backed with an elemental faith that the foundations of the world were mortised by God with unspeakable goodness of heart toward the human family. Hard as life was, she was thankful to be alive.

Once she told Abe how her brother Isaac, back in Hardin County, had hot words with a cowardly young man who shot Isaac without warning. The doctors asked Isaac if they could tie him down while they cut his flesh and took out the bullet. He told them he didn't need to be tied down; he put two lead musket-balls in between his teeth and ground his teeth on them while the doctors cut a slash nine inches long and one inch deep till they found the bullet and brought it out. Isaac never let out a moan or a whimper; he set his teeth into the musket-balls, ground them into flat sheets, and spat them from his mouth when he thanked the doctors.

Sally Bush, the stepmother, was all of a good mother to Abe. If he broke out laughing when others saw nothing to laugh at, she let it pass as a sign of his thoughts working their own way. So far as she was concerned he had a right to do unaccountable things; since he never lied to her, why not? So she justified him. When Abe's sister, Sarah, married Aaron Grigsby and a year after died with her newborn child, it was Sally Bush who spoke comfort to the eighteen-year-old boy of Nancy Hanks burying his sister and the wraith of a child.

A neighbor woman sized him up by saying, "He could work when he wanted to, but he was no hand to pitch in like killing snakes." John Romine made the remarks: "Abe Lincoln worked for me, but was always reading and thinking. I used to get mad at him for it. I say he was awful lazy. He would laugh and talk—crack his jokes and tell stories all the time; didn't love work half as much as his pay. He said to me one day that his father taught him to work, but he never taught him to love it."

A misunderstanding came up one time between Abe Lincoln and William Grigsby. It ended with Grigsby so mad he challenged Abe to a fight. Abe looked down at Grigsby, smiled, and said the fight ought to be with John Johnston, Abe's stepbrother. The day was set for the fight; each man was there with his seconds; the mauling began, with the two fighters stripped to the waist, beating and bruising each other with bare knuckles.

A crowd stood around, forming a ring, cheering, yelling, hissing, till after a while they saw Johnston getting the worst of it. Then the ring of people forming the crowd was broken as Abe Lincoln shouldered his way through, stepped out, took hold of Grigsby and threw that fighter out of the center of the fight-ring.

Then Abe Lincoln called out, "I'm the big buck of this lick." And looking around so his eyes swept the circle of the crowd he let loose the challenge, "If any of you want to try it, come on and whet your horns." A riot of wild fist-fighting came then between the two gangs and for months around the Jones grocery store there was talk about which gang whipped the other.

After a fox-chase with horses, Uncle Jimmy Larkin was telling how his horse won the race, was the best horse in the world, and never drew a long breath; Abe didn't listen; Uncle Jimmy told it again, and Abe said, "Why don't you tell us how many short breaths he drew?" It raised a laugh on Jimmy, who jumped around threatening to fight, till Abe said quietly, "Now, Larkin, if you don't shut up I'll throw you in that water."

Asked by Farmer James Taylor if he could kill a hog, he answered, "If you will risk the hog I'll risk myself."

He had the pride of youth that resents the slur, the snub, besides the riotous blood that has always led youth in reckless exploits. When he was cutting up didoes one day at the Crawford farm-house, Mrs. Crawford asked, "What's going to become of you, Abe?" And with mockery of swagger, he answered, "Me? I'm going to be president of the United States." His father's yellow cur, which always yelped and gave warning when Abe and John Johnston tried to get off for a coon-hunt or a trip to Jones's store, was picked up and taken along one night on a coon-hunt. The skin of the coon they killed that night was sewed onto the "yaller cur," which ran for home, was caught by bigger dogs and torn to pieces. Sore at some action of Josiah Crawford, who had purple veins on a large nose, Abe nicknamed him "Blue Nose" so that the nickname stuck.

He drew a red ear at a husking bee, kissed Green Taylor's girl, and in a fight the next day hit Green Taylor with an ear of corn, making a gash and a scar for life. For the day of the marriage of his sister Sarah to Aaron Grigsby, he wrote "Adam and Eve's Wedding Song," telling in doggerel how the Lord made woman from a rib taken from Adam's side. The three final verses read:

The woman was not taken
From Adam's feet, we see,
So he must not abuse her,
The meaning seems to be.

The woman was not taken
From Adam's head, we know,
To show she must not rule him—
Tis evidently so.

The woman she was taken
From under Adam's arm,
So she must be protected
From injuries and harm.

A farcical poem from Abe's pen was recited, with the climactic verse:

But Betsy she said, "You cursed baldhead,
My suitor you never can be.
Beside, your ill shape proclaims you an ape,
And that never can answer for me."

A favorite that Abe asked Dennis Hanks to sing began with the lines, "The turbaned Turk that scorns the world, and struts about with his whiskers curled," while Dennis had still another beginning, "Hail Columbia, happy land! If you ain't drunk then I'll be damned." But when Abe tried singing, "Poor Old Ned," Dennis would say he had the tune wrong and couldn't sing anyhow. Visitors to the Lincoln house were shown in a copy-book the scribbling:

Abraham Lincoln
his hand and pen.
he will be good but
god knows When.

In the hanging ballad of "John Anderson's Lamentations," Abe made his own verses, of which these are two:

Much intoxication my ruin has been,
And my dear companion hath barbarously slain:
In yonder cold graveyard the body doth lie;
Whilst I am condemned, and shortly must die.

Remember John Anderson's death, and reform
Before death overtakes you, and vengeance come on.
My grief's overwhelming; in God I must trust:
I am justly condemned; my sentence is just.

Driving a horse at the mill, he was sending the whiplash over the nag and calling, "Git up, you old hussy; git up, you old hussy." The horse let fly a hind foot that knocked down the big boy just as he yelled, "Git up." He lay bleeding, was taken home, washed, put to bed, and lay all night unconscious. As his eye winkers opened the next day and he came to, his tongue struggled and blurted, "You old hussy," thus finishing what he started to say before the knockdown.

He grew as hickory grows, the torso lengthening and toughening. The sap mounted, the branches spread, leaves came with wind clamor in them. A scorn sprang up betwixt him and the Grigsbys, who forgot to invite him to the double wedding of Reuben and Charles Grigsby on the same day marrying Betsy Ray and Matilda Hawkins. Shotes were roasted with fancy fixings, dancers tripped singing "Weevily Wheat," the brides and grooms were put to bed, but the young buck, Abe Lincoln, was not there. It was then he put into circulation a piece of writing titled, "The Chronicles of Reuben." It read:

Now there was a man whose name was Reuben, and the same was very great in substance; in horses and cattle and swine, and a very great household. It came to pass when the sons of Reuben grew up that they were desirous of taking to themselves wives, and being too well known as to honor in their own country they took a journey into a far country and there procured for themselves wives. It came to pass also that when they were about to make the return home they sent a messenger before them to bear the tidings to their parents. These, enquiring of the messengers what times their sons and wives would come, made a great feast and called all their kinsmen and neighbors in and made great preparations. When the time drew nigh they sent out two men to meet the grooms and their brides with a trumpet to welcome them and to accompany them. When they came near unto the house of Reuben, the father, the messenger came on before them and gave a shout, and the whole multitude ran out with shouts of joy and music, playing on all kinds of instruments. Some were playing on harps, some on viols, and some blowing on ram's horns. Some also were casting dust and ashes towards heaven, and chief among them all was Josiah, blowing his bugle and making sound so great the neighboring hills and valleys echoed with the resounding acclamation. When they had played and their harps had sounded till the grooms and brides approached the gates, Reuben, the father, met them and welcomed them to his house. The wedding feast being now ready they were all invited to sit down and eat, placing their bridegrooms and their wives at each end of the table. Waiters were then appointed to serve and wait on the guests. When all had eaten and were full and merry they went out again and played and sung till night, and when they had made an end of feasting and rejoicing the multitude dispersed, each going to his own home. The family then took seats with their waiters to converse while preparations were being made in an upper chamber for the brides and grooms to be conveyed to their beds. This being done the waiters took the two brides upstairs, placing one in a bed at the right hand of the stairs and the other on the left. The waiters came down, and Nancy the mother then gave directions to the waiters of the bridegrooms, and they took them upstairs but placed them in the wrong beds. The waiters then all came downstairs. But the mother being fearful of a mistake, made enquiry of the waiters, and learning the true facts took the light and sprang upstairs. It came to pass she ran to one of the beds and exclaimed, "O Lord, Reuben, you are in bed with the wrong wife." The young men, both alarmed at this, sprang up out of bed and ran with such violence against each other they came near knocking each other down. The tumult gave evidence to those below that the mistake was certain. At last they all came down and had a long conversation about who made the mistake, but it could not be decided. So endeth the chapter.

One of the Grigsbys put the copy of "The Chronicles" in Abe Lincoln's handwriting up under the roof rafters of a house, where it was to stay hidden till carpenters came to put on a new roof. It was a lampoon, boisterous with the laughter of a strong young man, and yet keen with an accuracy of intentions that could deliver the thrust, "Being too well known as to honor in their own country they took a journey into a far country and there procured for themselves wives," and the fling at "Blue Nose" Josiah Crawford in "Chief among them all was Josiah, blowing his bugle."

Further back of its immediate surface of drollery, it had a finger of derision pointed at pretensions of grandeur; a whirl of little javelins at the assumption that Ivanhoe on a high horse or Babylonians in golden slippers might come and be at ease among the barefoot farmers and the fleabitten mares working on the land of Spencer County, Indiana.

Betsy Ray said years afterward: "Yes, they did have a joke on us. They said my man got into the wrong room, and Charles got into my room. But it wasn't so. Lincoln wrote that for mischief. Abe and my man often laughed about it."

Chapter 16

WHILE young Abe was growing up, he heard his father and John and Dennis Hanks tell neighbors this and that about their families, what kind of men and women they had for relatives, kinfolk, blood connections. And young Abe learned there were things the Lincolns and Hankses didn't care to tell the neighbors concerning Abe's mother Nancy and his grandmother Lucy.

About 1825 Lucy Hanks, the grandmother of Abe, had died, near to sixty years of age, the mother of eight children, James, Thomas, Henry, George, Elizabeth, Lucy, Peggy, and Polly. James and Henry had become ministers of the gospel. The children were all well brought up, and spoken of as honest, industrious, law-abiding and God-fearing citizens. Their father, Henry Sparrow, had married Lucy Hanks in 1791. She could read and write though her father and brothers couldn't.

Such things the Lincolns and Hankses were free to talk about with any of their neighbors, either in corn-shucking time or in the winter around the stove in Jones's store. They were proud of Lucy Hanks and her husband and the eight children respectably brought up.

They were less free to say that Nancy Hanks, the mother of Abe, was born in Virginia in 1784 when Lucy Hanks was nineteen years old, and seven years before Lucy married. And

Joseph Hanks, the father of Lucy, had taken his family to Kentucky that same year.

In November, 1789, a grand jury of Mercer County had named Lucy Hanks as a loose woman; the clerk of the court was ordered to issue a summons for her arrest by the sheriff. Then five months had gone by, and Lucy Hanks came to the courthouse in Harrodsburg, Kentucky, and signed a certificate that she would marry Henry Sparrow on that day or as she wrote it, "enny other day." And she had waited a year, to show him perhaps what kind of life she could lead for the sake of a man she wanted to marry. And at the end of that year came the wedding of Lucy Hanks and Henry Sparrow. "And it turned out to be a love match."

Then two years passed and Joseph Hanks, the father of Lucy, died and left a will. To his son William (father of the same John Hanks who worked in the cornfields with young Abe Lincoln) was bequeathed "one gray horse called Gilbert." And he left his son Thomas "one sorrel horse called Major," while the son Joseph fell heir to "one sorrel horse called Bald" besides 150 acres of land. To his daughter Elizabeth he gave "one heifer yearling called Gentle," to his daughter Polly "one heifer yearling called Lady," and to his daughter Nancy "one heifer yearling called Peidy." The residue then went to his wife Nanny.

Thus the dead man had remembered in his will and given a piece of his property to four sons, three daughters and his wife. He had named and mentioned all of his family—except Lucy. She was the disobedient child, the daughter who had erringly darkened his door sills, and he died with a heart hardened against her, unforgiving to the last.

Yet it seemed that his punishment of Lucy made little difference with his daughter, Nancy, who lived to make a mistake like that of Lucy. For in 1799 Nancy's son, Dennis Hanks (who later helped Abe Lincoln build corncribs around Gentryville) was born several years before his mother married Levi Hall and moved to Indiana to die in the same plague that took away her husband and her niece Nancy Hanks, the mother of Abe Lincoln.

Thus life came and went and there were men and women who seemed to have been candles lighted and to be seen till a sudden gust of wind had come and their lights no longer met the eyes; they had been; they no longer were.

One of the sisters of Lucy Hanks worth talking about was Betsy, the one given the heifer called Gentle. She had married Thomas Sparrow; they wanted children of their own but the wanted children didn't come; so they took into their house the children of others. When Lucy Hanks married Henry Sparrow, then Betsy and Tom Sparrow took in Nancy Hanks and raised Nancy Hanks till she married Tom Lincoln; to outsiders Nancy Hanks was sometimes known as Nancy Sparrow. They took in Dennis Hanks when Levi Hall married Nancy Hanks, the mother of Dennis. Yes, one of the sisters worth talking about was the big-hearted, ready-handed Betsy Sparrow with her door open and welcome to the children not so welcome in the homes of her sisters. She it was who had gone two miles down the road the morning little Abe Lincoln was born, to help wash the new baby and put a yellow petticoat on him.

Such were tissues of fact twisted through and around the births and the deaths of the men and the women of the Lincoln and Hanks clan, talked about sometimes in hushed and sober moments, sometimes perhaps late at night when monotonous, multitudinous rain came on the roof in late winter and early spring, when a chill was still on the air and the frost not yet out of the ground, and the logs of the home fire threw shadows that lengthened, lessened, and lengthened again along the puncheon floor and among the rafters where seed corn hung.

Back in the shadows of the years had lived the dark, strange woman, Lucy Hanks, with flame streaks in her. And the years had beaten on her head, and circumstance had squeezed at her heart and tried to smother her hopes. And she had lived to pick a man she wanted to marry and borne him eight children and brought them up to read and write in a time when few could read and still fewer could write so much as their own names.

Young Abe Lincoln was free to have his thoughts about this mother of his mother. He could ask himself about what is called "good" and what is called "bad" and how they are criss-crossed in the human mesh. He could ask whether sinners are always as crooked as painted; whether people who call themselves good are half the time as straight as the way they tell it.

Maybe he ought to go slow in any deep or fixed judgments about people. Did the ghost of his lovable mother or the phantom of his lovely grandmother seem to whisper something like that?

Chapter 17

A MILE across the fields from the Lincoln home was the Pigeon church, a log-built meeting-house put up in 1822 after many discussions among members about where to locate. On June 7, 1823, William Barker, who kept the minutes and records, wrote that the church "received Brother Thomas Lincoln by letter." He was elected the next year with two neighbors to serve as a committee of visitors to the Gilead church, and served three years as church trustee. Strict watch was kept on the conduct of members and Tom served on committees to look into reported misconduct between husbands and wives, brothers and sisters, of neighbor against neighbor.

William Barker once entered the subscriptions for the support of the church as follows: "We the undersined do asign our names to pay the sevrial somes annexed to our names in produce this fall to be delivered betwixt the first and 20th of December the produce is as follows corn wheat whiskey pork Linnen wool or any other article or material to do the work with. the produce will be Dilevered at the meting hoas in good marchanable produce." Among the subscribers was recorded, "undersined"— "Thomas Lincoln in corn manufactured pounds 24."

Along with the earliest settlers in Indiana had come Catholic priests, and Baptist and Presbyterian preachers, and Methodist circuit riders. Churches had been organized, and the members, with prayer and songs, hewed the logs and raised the frames of their meeting-houses for worship. Time had been when the circuit-rider traveled with Bible in one hand and rifle in the other, preaching to members, sinners, and "scorners" in settlers' cabins or in timber groves. To the members, the Bible, and the lands, names, stories, texts, and teachings of the Bible, were overshadowing realities, to be read, thought over, interpreted, and used in daily life. To "grow in grace" and to arrive at "grace abounding," to be "strong in sperrit," to "cast out delusion," were matters connected definitely with the daily life of arising, building a fire, breaking the ice sheets on water, and starting a kettle to boil, and then going forth to the chores of the barn and the horse-trough, the corncrib, the pigpen. Such biblical words as "malice," "mercy," and "charity" were topics of long explanations.

Most of the church people could read only the shortest words in the Bible, or none at all. They sat in the log meeting-house on the split-log benches their own axes had shaped, listening to the preacher reading from the Bible by the light of fire-logs. The pronunciation of the words Egypt, Mesopotamia, Babylon, Damascus, set minds to work imagining places less real to them than Rockport, Boonville, Vincennes, Cincinnati. Epithets and texts enunciated often by preachers became tissues of their spiritual lives; the words meant something beyond the actual words in "weeping and wailing and gnashing of teeth," "an eye for an eye, and a tooth for a tooth," "by the waters of Babylon." They could see the direct inference to be drawn from, "The fathers have eaten sour grapes and the children's teeth are set on edge," or the suggestions in "Let not your heart be troubled," or "Let him who is without sin cast the first stone," or "As ye would that others should do unto you, do ye even so unto them."

Their own morning-glories, honeysuckle, and blooming perennials came to leafage out of the rhythmic text, "Consider the lilies of the field, how they grow; they toil not, neither do they spin; and yet I say unto you, that even Solomon in all his glory was not arrayed like one of these." They felt enough portents in the two words, "Jesus wept," for the arrangement of that as a verse by itself.

At the Pigeon church one of the favorite hymns was "How Tedious and Tasteless the Hours," and another, "Oh, to Grace How Great a Debtor!" and another began with the lines:

> When I can read my title clear
> To mansions in the skies.

To confess, to work hard, to be saving, to be decent, were the actions most praised and pleaded for in the sermons of the preachers. Next to denying Christ, the worst sins were drinking, gambling, fighting, loafing, among the men, and gossiping, back-biting, sloth, and slack habits, among the women. A place named Hell where men, women, and children burned everlastingly in fires was the place where sinners would go.

In a timber grove one summer Sunday afternoon, a preacher yelled, shrieked, wrung his hands in sobs of hysterics, until a row of women were laid out to rest and recover in the shade of an oak-tree, after they had moaned, shaken, danced up and down, worn themselves out with "the jerks" and fainted. And young Abe Lincoln, looking on, with sober face and quiet heart, was thoughtful about what he saw before his eyes.

The Sabbath was not only a day for religious meetings. After the sermon, the members, who rode horses many miles to the meeting-house, talked about crops, weather, births and deaths, the growing settlements, letters just come, politics, Indians, and land-titles.

Families had prayers in the morning on arising, grace at breakfast, noon prayers and grace at dinner, grace at supper, and evening prayers at bedtime. In those households, the manger at Bethlehem was a white miracle, the Black Friday at Golgotha and the rocks rolled away for the Resurrection were near-by realities of terror and comfort, dark power and sustenance. The Sabbath day, Christmas, Easter, were days for sober thoughts and sober faces, resignation, contemplation, rest, silence. Verses in the Gospel of St. John had rhythm and portent. "I am the way, the truth, and the life. . . . He that believeth in me shall not perish but shall have everlasting life."

Besides a wisdom of short syllables covering all the wants of life in the Lord's Prayer, they found a melodious movement of musical intention in the arrangement of its simple words. It was like a walk from a green valley to a great mountain to pronounce with thoughtful cadence: "Give us this day our daily bread. And forgive us our trespasses as we forgive those who trespass against us. And lead us not into temptation but deliver us from evil."

The glisten of dewdrops on wheat straws, in the gray chill of daybreak on harvest fields, shone in the solemn assurance of, "Yea, though I walk through the valley of the shadow of death, I will fear no evil: . . . thy rod and thy staff they comfort me."

There was occupation of the imaginative gift, a challenge even to the sleeping or crying senses of color and form, hidden in the picture of Jacob's ladder stretching from the man in earth-slumber up beyond the limits of sky; in the drama of Jonah entering the belly of the whale and later issuing forth from that darkness; in the swift stride of the four horsemen of the apocalypse; in the coat of many colors worn by Joseph and the dream of seven years of famine to come upon Egypt; in the flawless and clear-eyed sheep-boy David, walking with sling and stone to win battle against the stiff-necked giant Goliath by reason of one fierce stone pounded home to the forehead of the swaggerer; in the massive prefigurements of preparation for calamity or destruction of mortal pride to be found in the episodes of Noah's ark and the upthrust and come-down of the Tower of Babel.

After a day of plowing corn, watching crop pests, whittling bean-poles, capturing strayed cattle and fixing up a hole in a snake-rail fence, while the housewife made a kettle of soap, hoed the radishes and cabbages, milked the cows, and washed the baby, there was a consolation leading to easy slumber in the beatitudes: "Blessed are the meek: for they shall inherit the earth. . . . Blessed are the pure in heart, for they shall see God. Blessed are the peacemakers: for they shall be called the children of God." It was not their business to be sure of the arguments and the invincible logic that might underlie the Bible promises of heaven and threats of hell; it was for this the preacher was hired and paid by the corn, wheat, whisky, pork, linen, wool, and other produce brought by the members of the church.

The exquisite foretokening, "In my Father's house are many mansions: if it were not so I would have told you," was but a carrying farther of the implications of that cry from the ramparts of the unconquerable, "O death, where is thy sting? O grave, where is thy victory?"

Beyond Indiana was something else; beyond the timber and underbrush, the malaria, milk-sick, blood, sweat, tears, hands hard and crooked as the roots of walnut trees, there must be something else.

Young Abraham Lincoln saw certain of these Christians with a clean burning fire, with inner reckonings that prompted them to silence or action or speech, and they could justify themselves with a simple and final explanation that all things should be done decently and in order. Their door-strings were out to sinners deep in mire, to scorners seemingly past all redemption; the Jesus who lived with lawbreakers, thieves, lepers crying "Unclean!" was an instrument and a light vivifying into everyday use the abstractions behind the words "malice," "mercy," "charity."

They met understanding from the solemn young Lincoln who had refused to join his schoolmates in torturing a live mud-turtle, and had written a paper arguing against cruelty to animals; who when eleven years old took his father's rifle and shot a prairie turkey and had never since shot any game at all; who could butcher a beef or hog for food but didn't like to see rabbit blood; who wanted to be a river steamboat pilot but gave up in simple obedience when his father told him he was needed at home; who as a nine-year-old boy helped get a traveling preacher to speak some sort of final ceremonial words over the winter grave of Nancy Hanks Lincoln; who would bother to lug on his shoulders and save from freezing the body of a man overloaded with whisky; who had seen one of his companions go insane and who used to get up before daylight and cross the fields to listen to the crooning, falsetto cackling, and disconnected babbling of one whose brain had suddenly lost control of things done decently and in order.

The footsteps of death, silent as the moving sundial of a tall sycamore, were a presence. Time and death, the partners who operate leaving no more track than mist, had to be reckoned in the scheme of life. A day is a shooting-star. The young Lincoln tried to rhyme this sentiment:

> Time! what an empty vapor 'tis!
> And days how swift they are:
> Swift as an Indian arrow—
> Fly on like a shooting star,
> The present moment just is here,
> Then slides away in haste,
> That we can never say they're ours,
> But only say they're past.

His mother Nancy Hanks and her baby that didn't live, his sister Sarah and her baby that didn't live—time and the empty vapor had taken them; the rain and the snow beat on their graves. The young man who was in his right mind and then began babbling week in and week out the droolings of a disordered brain—time had done it without warning. On both man and the animals, time and death had their way. In a single week, the milk-sick had taken four milch-cows and eleven calves of Dennis Hanks, while Dennis too had nearly gone under with a hard week of it.

At the Pigeon Creek settlement, while the structure of his bones, the build and hang of his torso and limbs, took shape, other elements, invisible, yet permanent, traced their lines in the tissues of his head and heart.

Chapter 18

PIONEERS are half gypsy. The lookout is on horizons from which at any time another and stranger wandersong may come calling and take the heart, to love or to kill, with gold or with ashes, with bluebirds burbling in ripe cornfields or with rheumatism or hog cholera or mortgages, rust and bugs eating crops and farms into ruin.

They are luck-hunters. And luck—is it *yonder?* Over the horizon, over yonder—is there a calling and a calling? The pioneers, so often, are believers in luck . . . out yonder.

And always the worker on land, who puts in crops and bets on the weather and gambles in seed corn and hazards his toil against so many whimsical, fateful conditions, has a pull on his heart to believe he can read luck signs, and tell good luck or bad luck to come, in dreams of his sleep at night, in changes of the moon, in the manners of chickens and dogs, in little seeming accidents that reveal the intentions and operations of forces beyond sight and smell.

They have noticed certain coincidences operating to produce certain results in the past. And when again those coincidences arise they say frankly, "I'm superstitious—what happened before is liable to happen again." The simple saying among simple people, "If a bird lights in a window there will be a death in that house," goes back to the fact that there have been deaths, and many of them, in houses to which a bird came and sat on a window-sill and picked his wings and put on dark assumptions.

Down in Indiana, as Abe Lincoln grew up, he cherished his sweet dreams, and let the bitter ones haunt him, and tried to search out from the muddled hugger-mugger of still other dreams whether the meaning was to be sweet or bitter. His father had had portentous dreams; his father told how in a night's sleep once he saw a wayside path to a strange house; he saw the inside walls, the chairs, the table, the fireplace in that house;

at the fireside a woman was sitting, and her face, eyes, and lips
came clear; she was paring an apple; she was the woman to be
his wife. This was the dream, and in his night's sleep it came
again and again; he could not shake it off. It haunted him till
he went to the path, followed the path to the house, went inside
and there saw the woman, sitting at the fireside paring an apple;
her face, eyes, and lips were those he had seen so often in his
night sleep; and the rest of his dream came to pass. Tom Lincoln had told this to his son, Abe, and the boy searched his
dreams for meanings. He learned to say of certain coincidences,
"I'm superstitious," feeling that what had happened before
under certain combinations of events would probably happen
again.

Even the water underground, the streams and springs, were
whimsical, unreliable, ran by luck, it seemed, in southern Indiana. Not far from the Lincolns was a region where rivers
dipped down into limestone and faded out of sight. "Lost
rivers," they were called. In Wyandotte Cave a walker could
go fifteen miles around the inside. In some counties there was
no telling when a good well would give out and say, "No more
water here."

Abe's father hired a man to come with a witch-hazel and tell
by the way the magic stick pointed where to dig a well that
wouldn't go dry. The well was dug where the witch-hazel said
it should be dug. And that well went dry just as others before
had on the Lincoln farm.

Besides superstitions there were sayings, to be spoken and
guessed about, old pieces of whim and wisdom out of bygone
generations of Kentuckians, of English, Scotch, and Irish souls.
Potatoes, growing underground, must be planted in the dark of
the moon, while beans, growing above-ground, must be planted
in the light of the moon. The posts of a rail fence would sink
in the ground if not set in the dark of the moon. Trees for
rails must be cut in the early part of the day and in the light
of the moon. If in planting corn you skipped a row there would
be a death in the family. If you killed the first snake you saw

in the spring, you would win against all your enemies that year.
If rheumatism came, skunk-grease or red worm-oil rubbed where
the ache was would cure it.

Steal a dishrag, people said, and hide it in a tree-stump and
your wart will go away. If you have many warts, tie as many
knots in a string as there are warts, and bury the string under
a stone. A dog crossing a hunter's path means bad luck unless
he hooks his two little fingers together and pulls till the dog is
out of sight. Feed gunpowder to dogs and it will make them
fierce. To start on a journey and see a white mule is bad luck.
If a horse breathes on a child, the child will have the whooping-
cough. Buckeyes carried in the pocket keep off the rheumatism.

When a man is putting up a crop of hay or shucking a field
of corn or driving a load of wood, the weather has a particular
interest for him. Out of the lives of farmers, timber-workers,
ox-drivers, in Kentucky and Indiana, have come sayings:

If the sun shines while it is raining, it will rain again the next
day; birds and hens singing during the rain indicate fair weather;
if roosters crow when they go to roost it is a sign of rain; the first
thunder in the spring wakes up the snakes from their winter
sleep; when chickens get on a fence during a rain and pick themselves, it is a sign of clear weather; when the rain gets thick and
heavy, almost like mist, it will turn cold; if a bobwhite says bob
only once there will be rain; rain from the east rains three days
at least; if it rains before seven it will clear before eleven; if
there is lightning in the north it will rain in twenty-four hours;
lightning in the south means dry weather.

"If a man can't skin he must hold a leg while some one else
does," was a saying among the butcher gangs Abe Lincoln worked
with. Men in those gangs would indicate a short distance by
saying it was "far as you can throw a bull by the tail." A
strong whisky "would make a rabbit spit in a dog's face." There
were admonitions: "Spit against the wind and you spit in your
own face," or "Don't see all you see, and don't hear all you hear."

Then, too, there were sayings spoken among the men only,
out of barn-life and handling cattle and hogs; the daily chores

required understanding of the necessary habits of men and animals.

And naturally in field and kitchen, among young and old, there were the phrases and epithets, "as plain as the nose on your face; as easy as licking a dish; as welcome as the flowers in May; as bare as the back of my hand; before the cat can lick her ear; as red as a spanked baby."

And there were eloquent Irish with blessings, maledictions, and proverbs. "Better be red-headed than be without a head." "No man can live longer at peace than his neighbors like." "I think his face is made of a fiddle; every one that looks on him loves him." "She's as dirty as a slut that's too lazy to lick herself." "A liar must have a good memory." "It's an ill fight where he that wins has the worst of it." "Hills look green that are far away." "It will be all the same after you're dead a hundred years."

Among the young people were whimsies often spoken and seldom believed. Fancy was on a loose leash in some of these. "If you can make your first and little finger meet over the back of your hand, you will marry." "If you spit on a chunk of firewood and speak your sweetheart's name, he will come before it burns out." "The new moon must never be seen through the trees when making a wish." "If a butterfly comes into the house a lady will call wearing a dress the color of the butterfly." "If you sing before breakfast you will cry before night." "If the fire roars there will be a quarrel in the family."

"If two hens fight in the barnyard there will be two ladies calling." "If your ears burn somebody is gossiping about you." "If your hand itches you will get a present or shake hands with a stranger; if your right foot itches you are going on a journey; if the left foot itches you are going where you are not wanted; if your nose itches away from home you are wanted at home, but if your nose itches at home some one is coming to see you; if your right eye itches you will cry and if it is the left eye you will laugh." "If you break a looking-glass you will have seven years of bad luck." "If you let a baby under a year old look in the mirror it will die." "It is bad luck to step over a broom."

Among the games played at parties by the young people in Indiana was the farm classic "Skip-to-My-Lou" which tells of a little red wagon painted blue, a mule in the cellar kicking up through, chickens in the haystack shoo shoo shoo, flies in the cream jar shoo shoo shoo, rabbits in the bean patch two by two.

> Hurry up slow poke, do oh do,
> Hurry up slow poke, do oh do,
> Hurry up slow poke, do oh do,
> Skip to my Lou, my darling.
>
> I'll get her back in spite of you,
> I'll get her back in spite of you,
> I'll get her back in spite of you,
> Skip to my Lou, my darling.
>
> Gone again, what shall I do?
> Gone again, what shall I do?
> Gone again, what shall I do?
> Skip to my Lou, my darling.
>
> I'll get another one sweeter than you,
> I'll get another one sweeter than you,
> I'll get another one sweeter than you,
> Skip to my Lou, my darling.

And there were other classics such as "Way Down in the Pawpaw Patch," "All Chaw Hay on the Corner," "Pig in the Parlor," "Old Bald Eagle, Sail Around," and "Pop Goes the Weasel." The game of "Old Sister Phœbe," with a quaint British strain, had song couplets:

> Old Sister Phoebe, how merry were we,
> The night we sat under the juniper tree,
> The juniper tree, high-o, high-o,
> The juniper tree, high-o.
>
> Take this hat on your head, keep your head warm,
> And take a sweet kiss, it will do you no harm.
>
> It will do you no harm, but a great deal of good,
> And so take another while kissing goes good.

In "Thus the Farmer Sows His Seed," an ancient human dialogue is rehearsed:

> Come, my love, and go with me,
> And I will take good care of thee.
>
> I am too young, I am not fit.
> I cannot leave my mamma yet.
>
> You're old enough, you are just right,
> I asked your mamma last Saturday night.

Among a people who spun their own wool and wove their own
cloth, as their forefathers had done, there was the inheritance
of the game of "Weevily Wheat," danced somewhat like the
Virginia Reel, with singing passages:

> O Charley, he's a fine young man,
> O Charley, he's a dandy,
> He loves to hug and kiss the girls,
> And feed 'em on good candy.
>
> The higher up the cherry tree,
> The riper grow the cherries,
> The more you hug and kiss the girls,
> The sooner they will marry.
>
> My pretty little pink, I suppose you think
> I care but little about you.
> But I'll let you know before you go,
> I cannot do without you.
>
> It's left hand round your weevily wheat.
> It's both hands round your weevily wheat.
> Come down this way with your weevily wheat.
> It's swing, oh, swing, your weevily wheat.

Among the best-remembered favorites in the neighborhood
around the Lincoln farm in Indiana were "Skip to My Lou,"
"Old Sister Phœbe," "Thus the Farmer Sows His Seed," and
"Weevily Wheat."

They had patriotic songs for the Fourth of July, chief of which was "Hail Columbia," printed as follows:

> Hail! Columbia, happy land!
> Hail! ye heroes, heav'n-born band,
> Who faught and bled in freedom's cause,
> Who faught, &c.
>
> And when the storm of war is gone,
> Enjoy the peace your valor won;
> Let independence be your boast,
> Ever mindful what it cost,
> Ever grateful for the prize,
> May its altar reach the skies.

Chapter 19

THE farm boys in their evenings at Jones's store in Gentryville talked about how Abe Lincoln was always reading, digging into books, stretching out flat on his stomach in front of the fire-place, studying till midnight and past midnight, picking a piece of charcoal to write on the fire shovel, shaving off what he wrote, and then writing more—till midnight and past midnight. The next thing Abe would be reading books between the plow handles, it seemed to them. And once trying to speak a last word, Dennis Hanks said, "There's suthin' peculiarsome about Abe."

He wanted to learn, to know, to live, to reach out; he wanted to satisfy hungers and thirsts he couldn't tell about, this big boy of the backwoods. And some of what he wanted so much, so deep down, seemed to be in the books. Maybe in books he would find the answers to dark questions pushing around in the pools of his thoughts and the drifts of his mind. He told Dennis and other people, "The things I want to know are in books; my best friend is the man who'll git me a book I ain't read." And sometimes friends answered, "Well, books ain't as plenty as wildcats in these parts o' Indianny."

This was one thing meant by Dennis when he said there was "suthin' peculiarsome" about Abe. It seemed that Abe made the books tell him more than they told other people. All the other farm boys had gone to school and read "The Kentucky Preceptor," but Abe picked out questions from it, such as "Who has the most right to complain, the Indian or the negro?" and Abe would talk about it, up one way and down the other, while they were in the cornfield pulling fodder for the winter. When Abe got hold of a storybook and read about a boat that came near a magnetic rock, and how the magnets in the rock pulled all the nails out of the boat so it went to pieces and the people in the boat found themselves floundering in water, Abe thought it was funny and told it to other people. After Abe read poetry, especially Bobby Burns's poems, Abe began writing rhymes himself. When Abe sat with a girl, with their bare feet in the creek water, and she spoke of the moon rising, he explained to her it was the earth moving and not the moon—the moon only seemed to rise.

John Hanks, who worked in the fields barefooted with Abe, grubbing stumps, plowing, mowing, said: "When Abe and I came back to the house from work, he used to go to the cupboard, snatch a piece of corn bread, sit down, take a book, cock his legs up high as his head, and read. Whenever Abe had a chance in the field while at work, or at the house, he would stop and read." He liked to explain to other people what he was getting from books; explaining an idea to some one else made it clearer to him. The habit was growing on him of reading out loud; words came more real if picked from the silent page of the book and pronounced on the tongue; new balances and values of words stood out if spoken aloud. When writing letters for his father or the neighbors, he read the words out loud as they got written. Before writing a letter he asked questions such as: "What do you want to say in the letter? How do you want to say it? Are you sure that's the best way to say it? Or do you think we can fix up a better way to say it?"

As he studied his books his lower lip stuck out; Josiah Crawford noticed it was a habit and joked Abe about the "stuck-out lip." This habit too stayed with him.

He wrote in his Sum Book or arithmetic that Compound Division was "When several numbers of Divers Denominations are given to be divided by 1 common divisor," and worked on the exercise in multiplication; "If 1 foot contain 12 inches I demand how many there are in 126 feet." Thus the schoolboy.

What he got in the schools didn't satisfy him. He went to three different schools in Indiana, besides two in Kentucky—altogether about four months of school. He learned his A B C, how to spell, read, write. And he had been with the other barefoot boys in butternut jeans learning "manners" under the school teacher, Andrew Crawford, who had them open a door, walk in, and say, "Howdy do?" Yet what he tasted of books in school was only a beginning, only made him hungry and thirsty, shook him with a wanting and a wanting of more and more of what was hidden between the covers of books.

He kept on saying, "The things I want to know are in books; my best friend is the man who'll git me a book I ain't read." He said that to Pitcher, the lawyer over at Rockport, nearly twenty miles away, one fall afternoon, when he walked from Pigeon Creek to Rockport and borrowed a book from Pitcher. Then when fodder-pulling time came a few days later, he shucked corn from early daylight till sundown along with his father and Dennis Hanks and John Hanks, but after supper he read the book till midnight, and at noon he hardly knew the taste of his cornbread because he had the book in front of him. It was a hundred little things like these which made Dennis Hanks say there was "suthin' peculiarsome" about Abe.

Besides reading the family Bible and figuring his way all through the old arithmetic they had at home, he got hold of "Æsop's Fables," "Pilgrim's Progress," "Robinson Crusoe," and Weems's "The Life of Francis Marion." The book of fables, written or collected thousands of years ago by the Greek slave, known as Æsop, sank deep in his mind. As he read through the book a second and third time, he had a feeling there were fables all around him, that everything he touched and handled, everything he saw and learned had a fable wrapped in it somewhere. One fable was about a bundle of sticks and a farmer whose sons were quarreling and fighting.

There was a fable in two sentences which read, "A coachman, hearing one of the wheels of his coach make a great noise, and perceiving that it was the worst one of the four, asked how it came to take such a liberty. The wheel answered that from the beginning of time, creaking had always been the privilege of the weak." And there were shrewd, brief incidents of foolery such as this: "A waggish, idle fellow in a country town, being desirous of playing a trick on the simplicity of his neighbors and at the same time putting a little money in his pocket at their cost, advertised that he would on a certain day show a wheel carriage that should be so contrived as to go without horses. By silly curiosity the rustics were taken in, and each succeeding group who came out from the show were ashamed to confess to their neighbors that they had seen nothing but a wheelbarrow."

The style of the Bible, of Æsop's fables, the hearts and minds back of those books, were much in his thoughts. His favorite pages in them he read over and over. Behind such proverbs as, "Muzzle not the ox that treadeth out the corn," and "He that ruleth his own spirit is greater than he that taketh a city," there was a music of simple wisdom and a mystery of common everyday life that touched deep spots in him, while out of the fables of the ancient Greek slave he came to see that cats, rats, dogs, horses, plows, hammers, fingers, toes, people, all had fables connected with their lives, characters, places. There was, perhaps, an outside for each thing as it stood alone, while inside of it was its fable.

One book came, titled, "The Life of George Washington, with Curious Anecdotes, Equally Honorable to Himself and Exemplary to His Young Countrymen. Embellished with Six Steel Engravings, by M. L. Weems, formerly Rector of Mt. Vernon Parish." It pictured men of passion and proud ignorance in the government of England driving their country into war on the American colonies. It quoted the far-visioned warning of Chatham to the British parliament, "For God's sake, then, my lords, let the way be instantly opened for reconciliation. I say instantly; or it will be too late forever."

The book told of war, as at Saratoga. "Hoarse as a mastiff of true British breed, Lord Balcarras was heard from rank to rank, loud-animating his troops; while on the other hand, fierce as a hungry Bengal tiger, the impetuous Arnold precipitated heroes on the stubborn foe. Shrill and terrible, from rank to rank, resounds the clash of bayonets—frequent and sad the groans of the dying. Pairs on pairs, Britons and Americans, with each his bayonet at his brother's breast, fall forward together faint-shrieking in death, and mingle their smoking blood." Washington, the man, stood out, as when he wrote, "These things so harassed my heart with grief, that I solemnly declared to God, if I know myself, I would gladly offer myself a sacrifice to the butchering enemy, if I could thereby insure the safety of these my poor distressed countrymen."

The Weems book reached some deep spots in the boy. He asked himself what it meant that men should march, fight, bleed, go cold and hungry for the sake of what they called "freedom."

"Few great men are great in everything," said the book. And there was a cool sap in the passage: "His delight was in that of the manliest sort, which, by stringing the limbs and swelling the muscles, promotes the kindliest flow of blood and spirits. At jumping with a long pole, or heaving heavy weights, for his years he hardly had an equal."

Such book talk was a comfort against the same thing over again, day after day, so many mornings the same kind of water from the same spring, the same fried pork and corn-meal to eat, the same drizzles of rain, spring plowing, summer weeds, fall fodder-pulling, each coming every year, with the same tired feeling at the end of the day, so many days alone in the woods or the fields or else the same people to talk with, people from whom he had learned all they could teach him. Yet there ran through his head the stories and sayings of other people, the stories and sayings of books, the learning his eyes had caught from books; they were a comfort; they were good to have because they were good by themselves; and they were still better to have because they broke the chill of the lonesome feeling.

He was thankful to the writer of Æsop's fables because that writer stood by him and walked with him, an invisible companion, when he pulled fodder or chopped wood. Books lighted lamps in the dark rooms of his gloomy hours. . . . Well—he would live on; maybe the time would come when he would be free from work for a few weeks, or a few months, with books, and then he would read. . . . God, then he would read. . . . Then he would go and get at the proud secrets of his books.

His father—would he be like his father when he grew up? He hoped not. Why should his father knock him off a fence rail when he was asking a neighbor, passing by, a question? Even if it was a smart question, too pert and too quick, it was no way to handle a boy in front of a neighbor. No, he was going to be a man different from his father. The books—his father hated the books. His father talked about "too much eddication"; after readin', writin', 'rithmetic, that was enough, his father said. He, Abe Lincoln, the boy, wanted to know more than the father, Tom Lincoln, wanted to know. Already Abe knew more than his father; he was writing letters for the neighbors; they hunted out the Lincoln farm to get young Abe to find his bottle of ink with blackberry brier root and copperas in it, and his pen made from a turkey buzzard feather, and write letters. Abe had a suspicion sometimes his father was a little proud to have a boy that could write letters, and tell about things in books, and outrun and outwrestle and rough-and-tumble any boy or man in Spencer County. Yes, he would be different from his father; he was already so; it couldn't be helped.

In growing up from boyhood to young manhood, he had survived against lonesome, gnawing monotony and against floods, forest and prairie fires, snake-bites, horse-kicks, ague, chills, fever, malaria, "milk-sick."

A comic outline against the sky he was, hiking along the roads of Spencer and other counties in southern Indiana in those years when he read all the books within a fifty-mile circuit of his home. Stretching up on the long legs that ran from his moccasins to the body frame with its long, gangling arms, covered with linsey-woolsey, then the lean neck that carried the head with its surmounting coonskin cap or straw hat—it was, again, a comic outline—yet with a portent in its shadow. His laughing "Howdy," his yarns and drollery, opened the doors of men's hearts.

Starting along in his eleventh year came spells of abstraction. When he was spoken to, no answer came from him. "He might be a thousand miles away." The roaming, fathoming, searching, questioning operations of the minds and hearts of poets, inventors, beginners who take facts stark, these were at work in him. This was one sort of abstraction he knew; there was another: the blues took him; coils of multiplied melancholies wrapped their blue frustrations inside him, all that Hamlet, Koheleth, Schopenhauer have uttered, in a mesh of foiled hopes. "There was absolutely nothing to excite ambition for education," he wrote later of that Indiana region. Against these "blues," he found the best warfare was to find people and trade with them his yarns and drolleries. John Baldwin, the blacksmith, with many stories and odd talk and eye-slants, was a help and a light.

Days came when he sank deep in the stream of human life and felt himself kin of all that swam in it, whether the waters were crystal or mud.

He learned how suddenly life can spring a surprise. One day in the woods, as he was sharpening a wedge on a log, the ax glanced, nearly took his thumb off, and left a white scar after healing.

"You never cuss a good ax," was a saying in those timbers.

Chapter 20

Sixteen-year-old Abe had worked on the farm of James Taylor, at the mouth of Anderson Creek, on that great highway of traffic, the Ohio River. Besides plowing and doing barn and field work, he ran the ferryboat across the Ohio. Two travelers wanted to get on a steamboat one day, and after Abe sculled them to it and lifted their trunks on board they threw him a half-dollar apiece; it gave him a new feeling; the most he had ever earned before that was at butchering for thirty-one cents a day. And when one of the half-dollars slipped from him and sank in the river, that too gave him a new feeling.

At Anderson Creek ferry, he saw and talked with settlers, land buyers and sellers, traders, hunters, peddlers, preachers, gamblers, politicians, teachers, and men shut-mouthed about their business. Occasionally came a customer who looked as if he might be one of the "half horse, half alligator men" haunting the Ohio watercourse those years. There was river talk about Mike Fink, known on the Ohio as the "Snapping Turtle" and on the Mississippi as "The Snag," the toughest of the "half horse, half alligator" crowd; he was a famous marksman and aiming his rifle from his keel-boat floating the Ohio had shot off the tails of pigs running loose in the bottom lands; once Mike ordered his wife off his barge, covered her with autumn leaves while he threatened to shoot her, set fire to the leaves, so that Mrs. Fink ran with clothes and hair on fire and jumped into the river, to hear her husband saying, "Ye will make eyes at the men on other boats, will ye?"

Along the water-front of Louisville, Mike Fink had backed up his claim, "I can outrun, outhop, outjump, throw down, drag out, and lick any man in the country; I'm a Salt River roarer; I love the wimming and I'm chockfull of fight." They tried him for crimes in Louisville and acquitted him for lack of sufficient evidence; he waved a red bandanna for a good-by and told them he would come back to face their other indictments.

One of Mike's nicknames was "The Valley King." In a dispute with a man who claimed to have royal blood of France in his veins, Mike closed the argument by kicking the representative of royalty from the inside of a tavern to the middle of a street, with the words, "What if you are a king? Ain't we all kings over here?" His keel-boat was named "The Lightfoot." Mike's rival among the "half horse, half alligator" men was Little Billy, whose challenge ran, "I'm Little Billy, all the way from North Fork of Muddy Run and I can whip any man in this section of the country. Maybe you never heard of the time the horse kicked me an' put both his hips out o' j'int—if it ain't true, cut me up for catfish bait. I'm one o' the toughest —live forever and then turn to a white-oak post. I can outrun, outjump, outswim, chaw more tobacco and spit less, drink more whisky and keep soberer, than any man in these parts."

Among the bad men of the river, rough-and-tumble fighting included gouging of eyes, thumb-chewing, knee-lifting, head-butting, the biting off of noses and ears, and the tearing loose of underlips with the teeth. "Fights was fights in them days." Travelers had a proverb that a tavern was hardly safe if the proprietor had a nose or an ear off. It was a sign the landlord couldn't take care of himself.

Many travelers carried jugs of whisky, with corncob stoppers. Their common names for the raw article were such as "Red Eye," "Fire Water," "Cider Royal," "Blue Ruin," "Fool Water," "Bug Juice," though there were special brands indicative of lore and lingo with their names, "Clay and Huysen," "Race Horse," "Ching Ching," "Tog," "Rappee," "Fiscal Agent," "T. O. U.," "Tippena Pecco," "Moral Suasion," "Vox Populi," "Ne Plus Ultra," "Shambro," "Pig and Whistle," "Silver Top," "Poor Man's Punco," "Split Ticket," "Deacon," "Exchange," "Stone Wall," "Virginia Fence," "Floater," and "Shifter."

In Louisville, men played billiards all night, and there were no closing hours for the saloons and poker-rooms; a legend ran of one gambler dealing the cards when alarm was sounded that a steamboat at the river landing was on fire, and he went on asking the players, "How many?" as though steamboats caught fire every day. The Hope Distillery Company, capitalized at $100,000, was operating with grain from the near-by Kentucky and Scioto River valleys, while one Dr. McMurtrie called the Hope concern "a gigantic reservoir of damning drink; they manufacture poison for the human race; of what avail are the reasonings of philanthropists?"

So risky was travel that the Indiana legislature specifically permitted travelers to carry concealed weapons of any kind. There were traders from Cincinnati to New Orleans who were familiar with a regular dialogue, which they rehearsed to each other when they had the same room or bed in a tavern. "Stranger," one would say, "it's been a mighty long time since you and me slep' together." "Yep," came the regulation answer. "Got the same old smell you used to have?" "You *bet*." "Air you as lousy as ever?" "That's me." "Put 'er thar!" Then with a handshake and a swig from the jug they went to their sleep. There were tales of mosquitoes of a certain breed along the Ohio River; two could kill a dog, ten a man.

Men who had made trips up and down the river more than once had a song with a chorus:

> Hard upon the beach oar!
> She moves too slow.
> All the way to Shawneetown,
> Long time ago.

A song, "The Hunters of Kentucky," written by Samuel Woodworth, the author of "The Old Oaken Bucket," was heard occasionally amid the Ohio River traffic. It was about the Kentuckians at the Battle of New Orleans; a force of 2,250 of them had marched overland, arriving half-naked; women of New Orleans cut and sewed 1,127 "pairs of pantaloons" for them from wool blankets, in less than five days. Part of the song ran:

And if a daring foe annoys,
    No matter what his force is,
We'll show him that Kentucky boys
    Are alligator-horses.

After telling about the breastworks erected for the battle, the song had this to say:

Behind it stood our little force,
    None wished it to be greater,
For every man was half a horse
    And half an alligator.

Lawyers with books in their saddlebags took the ferryboat across the Ohio; law and order was coming to that wild young country, they believed; they could remember only ten years back how the law of the Territory of Indiana provided that a horse-thief should have two hundred lashes with a whip on his bare back and stay in jail till the horse was paid for, and the second time he was caught horse-stealing he was shot or hanged; for stealing cattle or hogs the thief had his shirt taken off and was given thirty-nine lashes.

Hunters crossed Anderson Creek ferry who could tell how George Doty in 1821 up in Johnson County killed 300 deer. They said Noah Major, one of the first settlers in Morgan County, estimated there were 20,000 deer in that county when he came in 1820, six years before. Circuit riders could tell about Peter Cartwright, who twenty years before was riding the Salt River district in Kentucky, occasionally getting over into Indiana; once Cartwright labored with a community of Shakers till eighty-seven of that sect were "rescued from the delusion." Those circuit riders could tell about Samuel Thornton Scott, the Presbyterian wilderness preacher, who swam the White River, losing his hat and one boot, arriving at Vincennes, as one friend said, "neither naked nor clad, barefoot nor shod."

Old-timers came along who could tell how the Indians in 1809 were stealing horses, burning barns and fences, killing settlers, running off with cattle and chickens, and how General

Hopkins with 1,200 soldiers burned the Indian villages along the Wabash, their log cabins, gardens, orchards, stationed rangers to hunt down every Indian they found, till the time came when there was not a red man on the Wabash or south of that river in the state of Indiana.

Others could tell of Daniel Ketcham, who was taken by Indians, kept over winter near Madison, loaded like a mule and marched to one of the Miami rivers, where his skin was blacked and he was handed a looking-glass and told to have a last look at himself before burning at the stake. A daughter of the chief, wearing five hundred silver brooches, made a thirty-minute speech, words flying fast and with defiance. Then she let Ketcham loose, two Indian women washed the black off him "and the white blood out"; he was taken to the tent of their mother, who offered him her hand but, being drunk, fell off her seat before he could take the hand. He carried wood, pounded corn, escaped and returned home to his wife, who had pledged neighbors that Ketcham, who was a famous wheat-stacker, would be home in time for stacking that year.

The ferry boy at Anderson Creek watched and listened to this human drift across the Ohio River, the bushwhackers and bad men who called themselves bad, and the others who called themselves good. Civilization went by, boats and tools breaking ways. Steamboats came past in a slow and proud pageantry making their fourteen- to twenty-day passage from New Orleans to Pittsburgh; geography became fact to the boy looking on; the flags on the steamboats were a sign of that long stretch of country the steamboats were crossing. Strings of flatboats passed, loaded with produce, pork, turkeys, chicken, cornmeal, flour, whisky, venison hams, hazel-nuts, skins, furs, ginseng; this was farm produce for trading at river ports to merchants or to plantation owners for feeding slaves. Other trading boats carried furniture, groceries, clothes, kitchenware, plows, wagons, harness; this was from manufacturing centres, consignments to storekeepers and traders. Houseboats, arks, sleds, flatboats with small cabins in which families lived and kept house, floated

toward their new homesteads; on these the women were washing, the children playing. The life-flow of a main artery of
American civilization, at a vivid line of growth, was a piece of
pageantry there at Anderson Creek.

Chapter 21

YOUNG Abe was out with ax, saw, and draw-knife building himself a light flat-boat at Bates's Landing, a mile and a half down
the river from Anderson's Creek. He was eighteen years old,
a designer, builder, navigator; he cut down trees, hewed out
planks, pegged and cleated together the bottoms and sides of
his own boat, wood from end to end.

Pieces of money jingled in his pockets. Passengers paid him
for sculling them from Bates's Landing out to steamboats in
the middle of the Ohio River.

He studied words and figurations on pieces of money. Thirteen stars stood for the first Thirteen States of the Union. The
silver print of an eagle spreading its wings and lifting a fighting
head was on the half-dollar. As though the eagle were crying
high, important words, above its beak was inscribed "E Pluribus
Unum"; this meant the many states should be One, young Abe
learned.

Circled with the thirteen stars were the head and bust of a
motherly-looking woman. On her forehead was the word
"Liberty." Just what did *She* mean?

Waiting for passengers and looking out on the wide Ohio to
the drooping trees that dipped their leaves in the water on the
farther shore, he could think about money and women and
eagles.

A signal came from the opposite shore one day and Lincoln
rowed across the river. As he stepped out of his boat two men
jumped out of the brush. They took hold of him and said they
were going to "duck" him in the river. They were John and
Lin Dill, brothers who operated a ferry and claimed Abe had

been transporting passengers for hire contrary to the law of
Kentucky.

As they sized up Abe's lean husky arms they decided not to
throw him in the river. He might be too tough a customer.
Then all three went to Squire Samuel Pate, justice of the peace,
near Lewisport.

A warrant for the arrest of Abraham Lincoln was sworn out
by John T. Dill. And the trial began of the case of "The Commonwealth of Kentucky versus Abraham Lincoln," charged with
violation of "An Act Respecting the Establishment of Ferries."

Lincoln testified he had carried passengers from the Indiana
shore out to the middle of the river, never taking them to the
Kentucky shore. And the Dill brothers, though sore and claiming the defendant Lincoln had wronged them, did not go so far
as to testify he had "for reward set any person over a river,"
in the words of the Kentucky statute.

Squire Pate dismissed the warrant against Lincoln. The disappointed Dills put on their hats and left. Lincoln sat with
Squire Pate for a long talk. If a man knows the law about a
business he is in, it is a help to him, the Squire told young Abe.

They shook hands and parted friends. Afterwards on days
when no passengers were in sight and it was "law day" at Squire
Pate's down the river, Abe would scull over and watch the witnesses, the constables, the Squire, the machinery of law, government, justice.

The State of Indiana, he learned, was one thing, and the State
of Kentucky, something else. A water line in the middle of a
big river ran between them. He could ask: "Who makes state
lines? What *are* state lines?"

Chapter 22

IN the year 1825, ox teams and pack horses came through Gentryville carrying people on their way to a place on the Wabash
River they called New Harmony. A rich English business man

named Robert Owen had paid $132,000.00 for land and $50,000.00 for live stock, tools, and merchandise, and had made a speech before the Congress at Washington telling how he and his companions were going to try to find a new way for people to live their lives together, without fighting, cheating, or exploiting each other, where work would be honorable yet there would be time for play and learning; they would share and share alike, each for all and all for each. In January, 1826, Owen himself, with a party of 30 people came down the Ohio River in what was called the "boatload of knowledge."

More ox wagons and pack horses kept coming past the Gentryville crossroads; about a thousand people were joined in Owen's scheme at New Harmony on the Wabash. The scheme lighted up Abe Lincoln's heart. His eyes were big and hungry as a hoot-owl's as he told Dennis Hanks, "There's a school and thousands of books there and fellers that know everything in creation." The schooling would have cost him about $100 a year and he could have worked for his board. But Tom Lincoln had other plans for his son Abe.

Across the next three years the boy grew longer of leg and arm, tougher of bone and sinew, with harder knuckles and joints. James Gentry, with the largest farms in the Pigeon Creek clearings, and a landing on the Ohio River, was looking the big boy over. He believed Abe could take his pork, flour, meal, bacon, potatoes, and produce to trade down the Mississippi River, for cotton, tobacco, and sugar. Young Abe was set to work on a flatboat; he cut the oaks for a double bottom of stout planks, and a deck shelter, two pairs of long oars at bow and stern, a check-post, and a setting pole for steering.

As the snow and ice began to melt, a little before the first frogs started shrilling, in that year of 1828, they loaded the boat and pushed off.

In charge of the boat Mr. Gentry had placed his son Allen, and in charge of Allen he had placed Abe Lincoln, to hold his own against any half horse, half alligator bush-whackers who might try to take the boat or loot it, and leave the bones of those they took it from, at Cave-in-Rock on the Illinois shore, or other spots where the skeletons of flatboatmen had been found years after the looters sold the cargo down the river. The honesty of Abe, of course, had been the first point Mr. Gentry considered; and the next point had been whether he could handle the boat in the snags and sand-bars. The two young men pushed off on their trip of a thousand miles to New Orleans, on a wide, winding waterway, where the flatboats were tied up at night to the river-bank, and floated and poled by day amid changing currents, strings of other flatboats, and in the paths of the proud white steamboats.

Whitecaps rose and broke with their foam feathers, a mile, two miles, beyond the limit of eyesight, as fresh winds blew along the Ohio River. Cave-in-Rock was passed on the Illinois shore, with its sign, "Wilson's Liquor Vault and House of Entertainment," with a doorway 25 feet high, 80 feet wide, and back of that entrance a cavern 200 feet deep, a 14-foot chimney leading to an upper room, where one time later were found 60 human skeletons, most of them rivermen lured and trapped by the Wilson gang that camped at Hurricane Island near by.

Timber-covered river bluffs stood up overlooking the river like plowmen resting big shoulders between the plow-handles; twisted dumps and runs of clay banks were like squatters who had lost hope and found rheumatism and malaria; lone pine trees had silhouetted their dry arms of branches on reefs where they dissolved and reappeared in river-mist lights as if they struggled to tell some secret of water and sky before going under.

The nineteen-year-old husky from Indiana found the Mississippi River as tricky with comic twists as Æsop's fables, as mystical, boding, and promising as the family Bible. Sand-bars, shoals, and islands were scattered along with the look of arithmetic numbers. Sudden rains, shifting winds, meant new handling of oars. A rising roar and rumble of noise might be rough water ahead or some whimsical current tearing through fallen tree-branches at the river side. A black form seems to be floating up-river through a gray drizzle; the coming out of the sun shows it is an island point, standing still; the light and air play tricks with it.

The bends of the river ahead must be watched with ready oars and sweeps or the flatboat naturally heads in to shore. Strong winds crook the course of the boat, sometimes blowing it ashore; one of the crew must hustle off in a rowboat, tie a hawser to a tree or stump, while another man on the big boat has a rope at the check-post; and they slow her down. Warning signals must be given at night, by waving lantern or firewood, to other craft.

So the flatboat, "the broadhorn," went down the Father of Waters, four to six miles an hour, the crew frying their own pork and corn-meal cakes, washing their own shirts, sewing on their own buttons.

Below Baton Rouge, among the sugar plantations known as the "Sugar Coast," they tied up at the plantation of Madame Duquesne one evening, put their boat in order, spoke their good nights to any sweet stars in the sky, and dropped off to sleep. They woke to find seven negroes on board trying to steal the cargo and kill the crew; the long-armed Indiana husky swung a crab-tree club, knocked them galley-west, chased them into the woods, and came back to the boat and laid a bandanna on a gash over the right eye that left a scar for life as it healed. Then they cut loose the boat and moved down the river.

At New Orleans they traded, sold the rest of their cargo of potatoes, bacon, hams, flour, apples, jeans, in exchange for cotton, tobacco, and sugar, and sold the flatboat for what it would bring as lumber. And they lingered and loitered a few days, seeing New Orleans, before taking steamer north.

On the streets and by-streets of that town, which had floated the flags of French, British, and American dominion, young Abraham Lincoln felt the pulses of a living humanity with far heartbeats in wide, alien circles over the earth: English sailors who sang "Ranzo" and "Boney," "Hangin' Johnny," and "O Fare-you-well, My Bonny Young Girls"; Dutchmen and French in jabber and exclamative; Swedes, Norwegians, and Russians with blond and reddish mustaches and whiskers;

Spaniards and Italians with knives and red silk handkerchiefs; New York, Philadelphia, Boston, Rome, Amsterdam, become human facts; it was London those men came from, ejaculating, " 'Ow can ye blime me?"

Women in summer weather wearing slippers and boots; creoles with dusks of eyes; quadroons and octoroons with elusive soft voices; streets lined with saloons where men drank with men or chose from the women sipping their French wine or Jamaica rum at tables, sending quiet signals with their eyes or openly slanging the sailors, teamsters, roustabouts, rivermen, timber cruisers, crap-shooters, poker sharps, squatters, horse thieves, poor whites; bets were laid on steamboat races; talk ran fast about the construction, then going on, of the New Orleans & Pontchartrain Railroad, to be one of the first steam railroads in America and the world; slaves passed handcuffed into gangs headed for cotton fields of one, two, six thousand acres in size; and everywhere was talk about niggers, good and bad niggers, how to rawhide the bad ones with mule whips or bring 'em to N' Orleans and sell 'em; and how you could trust your own children with a good nigger.

As young Abe Lincoln and Allen Gentry made their way back home to the clearings of Pigeon Creek, Indiana, the tall boy had his thoughts. He had crossed half the United States, it seemed, and was back home after three months' vacation with eight dollars a month pay in his pocket and a scar over the right eye.

That year Indiana University was to print its first catalogue, but Abe Lincoln didn't show up among the students who registered. He was between the plow handles or pulling fodder or sinking the ax in trees and brush, and reading between times "Pilgrim's Progress," a history of the United States, the life of Francis Marion, the life of Ben Franklin, and the book he borrowed from Dave Turnham, the constable. The title-page of the book said it contained, "The Revised Laws of Indiana, adopted and enacted by the general assembly at their eighth session. To which are prefixed the Declaration of Independence, the Constitution of the United States, the Constitution of the State of Indiana, and sundry other documents connected with the Political History of the Territory and State of Indiana. Arranged and published by the authority of the General Assembly."

The science of government, theories of law, and schemes of administration spread themselves before the young man's mind as he crept along from page to page, wrestling with those statutes of Indiana and other documents. It was tough plowing through that book, with the satisfaction, however, that he could keep what he earned. Crimes and punishments were listed there, in black and white, fine distinctions between murder and manslaughter, between burglary, robbery, larceny, forgery, trespass, nuisance, fraud; varied circumstances of assault and battery, affray, unlawful assembly, rout and riot; such offenses as rape, arson, kidnaping, mayhem, counterfeiting, adultery, perjury, profane swearing, selling playing cards or obscene books.

Lives of masses of people spread out before him in a panorama as he read the statutes. He read that there are crimes which shall be deemed "infamous," and these are "murder, rape, treason, man stealing, and willful and corrupt perjury"; and any man found guilty of an infamous crime "shall thereafter be rendered incapable of holding any office of honour, trust, or profit, of voting at any election, of serving as a juror, of giving testimony within this state." He read in Section 60 on page 48, "Every person of the age of fourteen years or upwards, who shall profanely curse or damn, or shall profanely swear by the name of God, Jesus Christ, or the Holy Ghost, shall be fined not less than one, nor more than three dollars, for each offence." Sharp lines were drawn between murder and manslaughter; a murderer shall be a person "of sound memory and discretion, who shall unlawfully kill any reasonable creature in being and under the peace of this state, with malice aforethought"; a manslaughterer shall be a person "who without malice, either express or implied, shall unlawfully kill another person, either voluntarily upon a sudden heat, or involuntarily, but in the commission of some unlawful act." It seemed, too, there was a stream of people born or gone wrong, for the state to take care of, the criminals in jails and prisons, the paupers in poorhouses, the insane and feeble-minded in asylums, wives with runaway husbands, and children born out of wedlock.

Chapter 23

READING the *Louisville Gazette* which came weekly to Gentryville, working out as chore-boy, field-hand and ferryman, walking a fifty-mile circuit around the home cabin, flatboating down the Ohio and Mississippi, the young man Abraham Lincoln took in many things with his eyes that saw and his ears that heard and remembered. A Virginia planter named Edward Coles had quit Virginia and come down the Ohio River with his slaves, ending his journey in Illinois, where he had deeded a farm to each of his slaves with papers of freedom. The Erie Canal in New York, a big ditch for big boats to run on, was finished; it cost seven and a half million dollars but it connected the Great Lakes and the Atlantic Ocean and it meant that the north ends of Indiana and Illinois, besides other prairie stretches, were going to fill up faster with settlers. The first railroad in the United States, a stub line three miles long, was running iron-wheeled wagons on iron rails at Quincy, Massachusetts. A settlement called Indianapolis had been cleared away. Glass and nails were arriving in southern Indiana now; there used to be none at all ten years back. The famous Frenchman, General LaFayette, came up the Mississippi from New Orleans and visited Kaskaskia, where a reception was held in a mansion with the windows kept open for the benefit of people outside who wanted to have a look in. Sam Patch, who slid down Niagara Falls once, and lived, had slid down the Genesee Falls at Rochester, New York, and was killed.

It was interesting that Henry Clay, the famous congressman and orator from Kentucky, was nicknamed "The Mill Boy of

the Slashes," and came from a family of poor farmers and used
to ride to mill with a sack of corn. It was interesting to hear
a story that Henry Clay's wife was asked by a Boston woman
in Washington, "Doesn't it distress you to have Mr. Clay gambling with cards?" and that she answered, "Oh, dear, no! He
most always wins."

Fragments of talk and newspaper items came about Daniel
Webster, and his Bunker Hill speech at the cornerstone of the
Bunker Hill monument, or John Marshall, Chief Justice of the
Supreme Court, and a decision in law, but they were far off.
There was a sharp-tongued senator from Virginia, John Ran-
dolph of Roanoke, who was bitter against John Calhoun, vice
president of the United States; and John Randolph one day
pointed his finger at Calhoun and said: "Mr. Speaker! I mean
Mr. President of the Senate and would-be President of the
United States, which God in His infinite mercy avert." And
Randolph during a hot speech would call to a doorkeeper, "Tims,
more porter," taking every ten or fifteen minutes a foaming
tumbler of malt liquor, drinking two or three quarts during a
long speech.

And neither Calhoun nor anybody else interfered with John
Randolph when, on the floor of the Senate, he called John
Quincy Adams, the President of the United States, "a traitor,"
or Daniel Webster "a vile slanderer," or Edward Livingston
"the most contemptible and degraded of beings, whom no man
ought to touch, unless with a pair of tongs." In some stories
about famous men there seemed to be a touch of the comic;
John Randolph on the Senate floor called Henry Clay a
"blackleg"; they fought a duel with pistols; Clay shot Randolph twice in the pantaloons; Randolph shot off his pistol once
"accidentally" and once in the air; both sides came through
alive and satisfied.

Southern and western congressmen kept dueling pistols in
their Washington outfits; some had special pistols inlaid with
gold. A Philadelphia gunsmith named Derringer was winning
popularity with a short pistol to be carried in the hip pocket

and used in street fights. At the "exclusive" assembly balls in Washington, the women's skirts came down to slightly above the ankles; their silk stockings were embroidered with figures called "clocks" and their thin slippers had silk rosettes and tiny silver buckles. The fashionable men of "exclusive" society affairs wore frock coats of blue, green, or claret cloth, with gilt buttons; shirts were of ruffled linen; they had baggy "Cossack" pantaloons tucked into "Hessian" boots with gold top tassels.

Everybody in the capital knew that the justices of the Supreme Court took snuff from their snuffboxes while hearing causes argued; that Henry Clay was moderate about drinking whisky, while Daniel Webster went too far; that Andrew Jackson smoked a corn-cob pipe, and his enemies were free to say Mrs. Jackson too enjoyed her daily pipe. Protests were made to the Government against the transportation of the mails on Sunday; in Philadelphia church people stretched chains fastened with padlocks across the streets to stop the passage of mail-coaches.

The stories drifted west about white men in New York City who held political processions in which they marched dressed like Indians; they had organized the Tammany Society back in 1789; the members died but Tammany lived on. The big excitement of New York politics had been the struggle of De Witt Clinton, the governor, to put through the digging of the Erie Canal, against Tammany opposition.

> Oh, a ditch he would dig from the lakes to the sea.
> The Eighth of the world's matchless Wonders to be.
> Good land! How absurd! But why should you grin?
> It will do to bury its mad author in.

So Tammany sang at the start. But De Witt Clinton stuck with the tenacity of his forefathers who had fought against the Indians and against the British king. When he won out, the rhymes ran:

> Witt Clinton is dead, St. Tammany said,
> And all the papooses with laughter were weeping;
> But Clinton arose and confounded his foes—
> The cunning old fox had only been sleeping.

There had been the four years John Quincy Adams was President. He had been elected in a three-cornered fight that ended on election day with Andrew Jackson having the most votes cast for him but not a majority. This had put the contest into Congress, where Henry Clay had thrown his forces to Adams; and Adams's first move was to appoint Clay Secretary of State. The Jackson men said it was a crooked deal. Jackson had handed in his resignation as Senator from Tennessee and started work on his political fences for 1828, while his New York Tammany friend, Martin Van Buren, was booming him up North. All the four years Adams was President, the moves in Congress were aimed at bagging the Presidency in 1828. Investigating committees worked overtime; each side dug for the other's scandals: Adams's past personal record; Jackson's handling of six deserters at Mobile in 1815, when 1,500 soldiers were drawn up at parade rest to watch thirty-six riflemen fire at six blindfolded men, each man kneeling on his own coffin; Adams's bills for wall paper and paint in renovating the White House; Jackson's alleged marriage to his wife before she was properly divorced.

In the background of all the bitter personal feelings, the slander and the slack talk of politics, a deep, significant drift and shift was going on. Part of it was the feeling of the West and Southwest, the raw and new country, against the East and New England, the settled and established country. Added to this was a feeling that Jackson stood for the rough, plain people who work, as against the people who don't. That was the issue, as the Jackson crowd presented it, so that even Abe Lincoln in Spencer County, Indiana, was caught in the drive of its enthusiasm, and wrote:

> Let auld acquaintance be forgot
> And never brought to mind;
> May Jackson be our President,
> And Adams left behind.

Jackson rode to election on a tumultuous landslide of ballots. His wife, Rachel, said, "Well, for Mr. Jackson's sake, I am glad, but for my own part I never wished it." And the home women of Nashville secretly got ready dresses of satin and silk for her to wear in Washington as the first lady of the land; then death took her suddenly; her husband for hours refused to believe she had breathed her last; he had killed one man and silenced others who had spoken against her. One woman wrote, "General Jackson was never quite the same man afterward; her death subdued his spirit and corrected his speech."

Then the new President-elect sailed down the Cumberland River to the Ohio, stopped at Cincinnati and Pittsburgh, and went on to Washington for an inauguration before a crowd of ten thousand people, whose wild cheering of their hero showed they believed something new and different had arrived in the government of the American republic. Daniel Webster, writing a letter to a friend, hit off the event by saying: "I never saw such a crowd. People have come five hundred miles to see General Jackson, and they really seem to think the country is rescued from some dreadful danger." The buckskin shirts of Kentucky settlers and the moccasins of Indian fighters from Tennessee were seen in the crowd, and along with politicians, preachers, merchants, gamblers, and lookers-on, swarmed in to the White House reception, took their turns at barrels of whisky, broke punch-bowls of glass and chinaware, emptied pails of punch, stood on the satin-covered chairs and had their look at "Andy Jackson, Our President," who was shoved into a corner where a line of friends formed a barrier to protect the sixty-two-year-old man from his young buck henchmen.

Thus began an eight-year period in which Andrew Jackson was President of the United States. He came to the White House with the mud of all America's great rivers and swamps on his boots, with records of victories in battles against savage Indian tribes and trained Continental European generals who had fought Napoleon, with shattered ribs and the bullets of Tennessee duelists and gun-fighters of the Southwest in his body; he knew little grammar and many scars, few classics and many fast horses.

Jackson came taking the place of John Quincy Adams, who was asking large funds for a national university and a colossal astronomical observatory, "a lighthouse of the skies," a lovable, decent man who knew all the capes, peninsulas, and inlets of New England, who had been across the Atlantic and stood by the Thames and the Seine rivers, and had never laid eyes on the Mississippi nor the Wabash River. Harvard went under as against the Smoky Mountains and Horseshoe Bend. Jackson came in with 178 electoral votes as against 83 for Adams, after national circulation by his enemies of a thick pamphlet entitled, "Reminiscences; or an Extract from the Catalogue of General Jackson's Youthful Indiscretions, between the Age of Twenty-Three and Sixty," reciting fourteen fights, duels, brawls, shooting and cutting affairs, in which it was alleged he had killed, slashed, and clawed various American citizens. It was told of him that he asked a friend the day after the inaugural what the people were saying of his first message. "They say it is first-rate, but nobody believes you wrote it," was the answer. To which Jackson rejoined, "Well, don't I deserve just as much credit for picking out the man who could write it?"

One nickname for him was "Old Hickory"; he had lived on acorns and slept in the rain; now he sat in a second-story room of the White House smoking a cob pipe, running the United States Government as he had run his armies, his political campaigns, his Tennessee plantation, his stable of racing horses, with a warm heart, a cool head, a sharp tongue, recklessly, cunningly; he was simple as an ax-handle, shrewd as an Indian ambush, mingling in his breast the paradoxes of the good and evil proverbs of the people.

Jackson was the son of a north-of-Irelander who came to America with only a pair of hands. "No man will ever be quite able to comprehend Andrew Jackson who has not personally known a Scotch-Irishman." His breed broke with their bare hands into the wilderness beyond the Allegheny Mountains, and more than any other one stock of blood is credited with putting the western and southwestern stretches of territory under the dominion of the central federal government at Washington. The mellowed and practiced philosopher, Thomas Jefferson, once wrote a letter with the passage, "When I was president of the Senate, he (Jackson) was a senator, and he could never speak on account of the rashness of his feelings. I have seen him attempt it repeatedly and as often choke with rage." And yet, unless the Jackson breed of men, even their extreme type, "the half horse, half alligator men," had pushed with their covered wagons, their axes and rifles, out into the territory of the Louisiana Purchase, Jefferson would have had no basis nor data for his negotiations in that mammoth land deal. Though in the presence of the ruffled linen of the Senate Jackson did "choke with rage," he faced Creek Indians, or seasoned troops from Napoleonic campaigns, or mutineers of his own army, with a cool and controlled behavior that was beyond the range of comprehension of models of etiquette in Washington.

With Jackson in the White House came a new politics, better and worse. The ax of dismissal fell on two thousand post-masters, department heads and clerks. An Administration daily newspaper, the *Washington Globe,* began publication; all office-holders earning more than one thousand dollars a year had to subscribe or lose their jobs. The editor was asked to soften an attack on an Administration enemy, and replied, "No, let it tear his heart out." Wives of Cabinet members refused to mix socially with Peggy O'Neill; talk ran that she was "fast" and of too shady a past even though now married to the Secretary of War. As the scandal dragged on, Jackson wrote hundreds of letters in her defense, sometimes using the phrase that she was "chaste as snow"; the husbands of the offended Cabinet members' wives resigned from the Cabinet; Jackson knocked the ashes from his cob pipe, appointed fresh and willing Cabinet members, and life went on as before.

When his postmaster-general, a tried and loyal friend, rebelled at making the wholesale dismissals required by the politicians, Jackson pushed him to a seat on the Supreme Court bench, and appointed a more willing post-office chief. One friend said he was an actor, that after storming at a caller, and closing the door, he would chuckle over his pipe and say, "He thought I was mad." A mail-coach robber, condemned to be hanged, reminded the President that once at a horse-race near Nashville he had told General Jackson to change his bets from a horse whose jockey had been "fixed" to lose the race; the death sentence was commuted to ten years in prison. "Ask nothing but what is right, submit to nothing wrong," was his advice on policies with European countries. He was well thought of by millions who believed there was truth lurking behind his sentiment, "True virtue cannot exist where pomp and parade are the governing passions; it can only dwell with the people—the great laboring and producing classes that form the bone and sinew of our confederacy." He was alluded to as "the Tennessee Barbarian" or "King Andrew the First" in certain circles, yet the doormats of the White House got acquainted with the shoes, boots, and moccasins of a wider range of humanity as he ran the Federal Government during those first years of the eight in which he was to be President.

Chapter 24

ALL the way down the Mississippi to the Gulf and back, Abe Lincoln had heard about Andrew Jackson in that year of 1828 when Jackson swept that country with a big landslide. In the newspapers that came to the post office at Gentryville, in the talk around Jones's store, in the fields harvesting, and at meetings, Andrew Jackson was the man talked about. With Andrew Jackson for President, the plainest kind of people could go into the White House and feel at home; with that kind of man, who smoked a cob pipe, talked horse sense, and rode reckless horses, and who had whipped the British at New Orleans, the Government would be more like what was meant in the Declaration of Independence and the Fourth of July speeches. Thus the talk ran.

Young Abe Lincoln heard it. The personality and the ways of Andrew Jackson filled his thoughts. He asked himself many questions and puzzled his head about the magic of this one strong, stormy man filling the history of that year, commanding a wild love from many people, and calling out curses and disgust from others, but those others were very few in Indiana. The riddles that attach to a towering and magnetic personality staged before a great public, with no very definite issues or policies in question, but with some important theory of government and art of life apparently involved behind the personality —these met young Abe's eyes and ears.

It was the year he wrote in the front cover of "The Columbian Class Book" the inscription, "Abe Lincoln 1828." The preface of the book said it contained "pieces calculated to interest the attention of the scholar and impress the mind with a knowledge of useful facts." And he borrowed from Josiah Crawford "The Kentucky Preceptor," the preface of that book saying, "Tales of love, or romantic fiction, or anything which might tend to instil false notions into the minds of children have not gained admission." There were essays on Magnanimity, Remorse of Conscience, Columbus, Demosthenes, On the Scriptures as a Rule of Life, the speech of Robert Emmet on why the English government should not hang an Irish patriot, stories of Indians, and the inaugural address of President Jefferson twenty-four years previous to that year. Jefferson spoke of "the agonizing spasms of infuriated man, seeking through blood and slaughter his long-lost liberty" in the French Revolution. Let America remember that free speech, and respect for the opinions of others, are measures of safety, was the advice of Jefferson.

Then Abe Lincoln read the passage from the pen of Jefferson: "If there be any among us who would wish to dissolve this Union, or to change its republican form, let them stand as monuments of the safety with which error of opinion may be tolerated where reason is left free to combat it. I know, indeed, that some honest men fear a republican government cannot be strong, that this government is not strong enough. . . . I believe this, on the contrary, the strongest government on earth."

Young nineteen-year-old Abe Lincoln had plenty to think about in that year of 1828, what with his long trip to New Orleans and back, what with the strong, stormy Andrew Jackson sweeping into control of the Government at Washington, and the gentle, teasing, thoughtful words of Thomas Jefferson: "Sometimes it is said that man cannot be trusted with the government of himself. Can he then be trusted with the government of others?"

Chapter 25

FOR more than twenty years Johnny Appleseed had been making his name one to laugh at and love in the log cabins between the Ohio River and the northern lakes. In 1806, he loaded two canoes with apple seeds at cider mills in western Pennsylvania and floated down the Ohio River to the Muskingum, along which he curved to White Woman Creek, the Mohican, the Black Fork, making a long stay on the borders of Licking Creek and in Licking County, where many farmers were already thanking him for their orchards. As he ran out of seeds he rode a bony horse or walked back to western Pennsylvania to fill two leather bags with apple seeds at cider-mills; then in the Ohio territory where he tramped, he would pick out loamy land, plant the seeds, pile brush around, and tell the farmers to help themselves from the young shoots. He went barefoot till winter came, and was often seen in late November walking in mud and snow. Neither snakes, Indians nor foreign enemies had harmed him. Children had seen him stick pins and needles into his tough flesh; when he sat at a table with a farmer family he wouldn't eat till he was sure there was plenty for the children. Asked if he wasn't afraid of snakes as he walked barefoot in the brush, he pulled a New Testament from his pocket and said, "This book is protection against all danger here and hereafter."

When taken in overnight by a farmer, he would ask if they wanted to hear "some news right fresh from heaven," and then stretch out on the floor and read, "Blessed are the meek, for they shall inherit the earth" and other Beatitudes. A woman said of his voice that it was "loud as the roar of wind and waves, then soft and soothing as the balmy airs that quivered the morning-glory leaves about his gray beard."

Once the camp-fire of Johnny Appleseed drew many mosquitoes which were burning; he quenched the fire, explaining to friends, "God forbid that I should build a fire for my comfort which should be the means of destroying any of His creatures!" During most of the year he wore no clothes except for a coffee sack with armholes cut in it; and a stump preacher once near the village of Mansfield was crying, "Where now is there a man who, like the primitive Christians, is traveling to Heaven barefooted and clad in coarse raiment?" when Johnny Appleseed came forward to put a bare foot on the pulpit stump and declare, "Here's your primitive Christian." A hornet stung him and he plucked out the hornet from a wrinkle of the coffee sack and let it go free. He claimed that his religion brought him into conversations with angels; two of the angels with whom he talked were to be his wives in heaven provided he never married on earth. What little money he needed came from farmers willing to pay for young apple trees. As settlements and villages came thicker, he moved west with the frontier, planting apple seeds, leaving trails of orchards in his paths over a territory of a hundred thousand square miles in Ohio and Indiana.

These were the years John James Audubon, who had kept a store in Elizabethtown, Kentucky, was traveling the Ohio and Mississippi River regions, with knapsack, dog, and gun, hunting birds, to paint them in oil on canvas "with their own lively animated ways when seeking their natural food and pleasure." He was among pioneers who moved from Kentucky and settled at Princeton, Indiana, a walker who walked on thousand-mile trips, leaving his wife to stay with friends while he lived with wild birds and shot them and sketched their forms.

Audubon's notebook told of canoeing in flood-swollen Mississippi river-bottom lands. "All is silent and melancholy, unless when the mournful bleating of the hemmed-in deer reaches your ear, or the dismal scream of an eagle or a heron is heard, or the foul bird rises, disturbed by your approach, from the carcass on which it was allaying its craving appetite. Bears, cougars, lynxes, and all other quadrupeds that can ascend the trees, are observed crouched among their top branches; hungry in the midst of abundance, although they see floating around them the animals on which they usually prey. They dare not venture to swim to them. Fatigued by the exertions which they have made in reaching dry land, they will there stand near the hunter's fire, as if to die by a ball were better than to perish amid the waste of waters. On occasions like this, all these animals are shot by hundreds."

Audubon went East to Philadelphia in 1824, gave an exhibition of his paintings, sold less than enough to pay for the show, and was told not to publish his work. In 1827 he began his issues of a work titled "The Birds of America," which when finished was in eighty-seven parts. That same year he reached London, where a barber cut off the ringlets of hair falling to his shoulders, and he wrote, under date of March 19, 1827, "This day my hair was sacrificed, and the will of God usurped by the wishes of Man. My heart sank low." He became an international authority, and sat up till half-past three one morning writing a paper to be read the next day before the Natural History Society of London on the habits of the wild pigeon. "So absorbed was my whole soul and spirit in the work, that I felt as if I were in the woods of America among the pigeons, and my ears filled with the sound of their rustling wings."

After reading his paper before the society, Audubon wrote the commentary: "Captain Hall expressed some doubts as to my views respecting the affection and love of pigeons, as if I made it human, and raised the possessors quite above the brutes. I presume the love of the (pigeon) mothers for their young is much the same as the love of woman for her offspring. There is but one kind of love: God is love, and all his creatures derive theirs from his; only it is modified by the different degrees of intelligence in different beings and creatures."

Thus Audubon, who had sold Sunday clothes to his customers in Elizabethtown, Kentucky. He and Abe Lincoln had footed the same red clay highways of Hardin County, floated the same Ohio and Mississippi rivers, fought in the night against other forms of life that came to kill. Both loved birds and people. Each was a child of hope.

Chapter 26

IN the fall of 1829, Abraham Lincoln was putting his ax to big trees and whipsawing logs into planks for lumber to build a house on his father's farm. But his father made new plans; the lumber was sold to Josiah Crawford; and the obedient young axman was put to work cutting and sawing trees big enough around to make wagon-wheels, and hickories tough enough for axles and poles on an ox-wagon.

The new plans were that the Lincoln family and the families of Dennis Hanks and Levi Hall, married to Abe's step-sisters, thirteen people in all, were going to move to Macon County over in Illinois, into a country with a river the Indians named Sangamo, meaning "the land of plenty to eat." The Lincoln farm wasn't paying well; after buying eighty acres for $2.00 an acre and improving it for fourteen years, Tom Lincoln sold it to Charles Grigsby for $125.00 cash before signing the papers.

The milk-sick was taking farm animals; since Dennis Hanks lost four milk-cows and eleven calves in one week, besides having a spell of the sickness himself, Dennis was saying, "I'm goin' t' git out o' here and hunt a country where the milk-sick is not; it's like to ruined me."

In September Tom Lincoln and his wife had made a trip down to Elizabethtown, Kentucky, where they sold for $123.00 the lot which Mrs. Lincoln had fallen heir to when her first husband died; the clerk, Samuel Haycraft, filled out the deed of sale, declaring that she "was examined by me privately and apart from her said husband" and did "freely and willingly subscribe to the sale." And Tom, with the cash from this sale and the money from the sale of his own farm, was buying oxen, or young steers, and trading and selling off household goods.

Moving was natural to his blood; he came from a long line of movers; he could tell about the family that had moved so often that their chickens knew the signs of another moving; and the chickens would walk up to the mover, stretch flat on the ground, and put up their feet to be tied for the next wagon trip.

The men-folks that winter, using their broadaxes and draw-knives on solid blocks of wood, shaping wagon wheels, had a church scandal to talk about. Tom Lincoln and his wife had been granted by the Pigeon church a "letter of Dismission," to show they had kept up their obligations and were regular members. Sister Nancy Grigsby had then come in with a "protest" that she was "not satisfied with Brother and Sister Lincoln." The trustees took back the letter, investigated, gave the letter again to Brother and Sister Lincoln, and to show how they felt about it, they appointed Brother Lincoln on a committee to straighten out a squabble between Sister Nancy Grigsby and Sister Betsy Crawford. And it was jotted down in the Pigeon church records and approved by the trustees.

The ox wagon they made that winter was wood all through, pegs, cleats, hickory withes, and knots of bark, holding it together, except the wheel rims, which were iron. Bundles of bed-clothes, skillets, ovens, and a few pieces of furniture were loaded, stuck, filled and tied onto the wagon; early one morning the last of the packing was done. It was February 15, 1830; Abraham Lincoln had been four days a full-grown man, a citizen who "had reached his majority"; he could vote at elections from now on; he was lawfully free from his father's commands; he could come and go now; he was footloose.

At Jones' store he had laid in a little stock of pins, needles, buttons, tinware, suspenders, and knickknacks, to peddle on the way to Illinois.

And he had gone for a final look at the winter dry grass, the ruins of last year's wild vine and dogwood over the grave of Nancy Hanks. He and his father were leaving their Indiana home that day; almost naked they had come, stayed fourteen years, toiled, buried their dead, built a church, toiled on; and now they were leaving, almost naked. Now, with the women and children lifted on top of the wagon-load, the men walked alongside, curling and cracking their whip-lashes over the horns or into the hides of the half-broken young steers.

And so the seven-yoke team of young steers, each with his head in a massive collar of hardwood, lashed and bawled at with "Gee," "Haw," "G' lang" and "Hi thar, you! Git up!" hauled the lumbering pioneer load from the yellow and red clay of Spencer County, in Southern Indiana, to the black loam of the prairie lands in Macon County, Illinois.

They had crossed the Wabash River, the state line of Illinois, and the Sangamo River, on a two-week trip with the ground freezing at night and thawing during the day, the steers slipping and tugging, the wagon axles groaning, the pegs and cleats squeaking. A dog was left behind one morning as the wagon crossed a stream; it whined, ran back and forth, but wouldn't jump in and swim across; young Lincoln took off boots and socks, waded into the icy water, gathered the hound in his arms and carried it over.

Near the Indiana-Illinois state line, Lincoln took his pack of needles and notions and walked up to a small farmhouse that seemed to him to be "full of nothing but children." They were of assorted sizes, seventeen months to seventeen years in age, and all in tears. The mother, red-headed and red-faced, clutched a whip in her fingers. The father, meek, mild, tow-headed, stood in the front doorway as if waiting for his turn to feel the thongs. Lincoln thought there wouldn't be much use in asking the woman if she wanted any needles and notions; she was busy, with a keen eye on the children and an occasional glance at her man in the doorway.

She saw Lincoln come up the path, stepped toward the door, pushed her husband out of the way, and asked Lincoln what was his business. "Nothing, madam," he answered gently, "I merely dropped in as I came along to see how things were going." He waited a moment.

"Well, you needn't wait," the woman snapped out. "There's trouble here, and lots of it, too, but I kin manage my own affairs without the help of outsiders. This is jest a family row, but I'll teach these brats their places ef I have to lick the hide off every one of 'em. I don't do much talkin' but I run this house, so I don't want no one sneakin' round tryin' to find out how I do it, either."

Around them as they crossed the first stretch of the Grand Prairie was a land and soil different from Indiana or Kentucky. There were long levels, running without slopes up or hollows down, straight to the horizon; arches and domes of sky covered it; the sky counted for more, seemed to have another language and way of talk, farther silences, too, than east and south where the new settlers had come from. Grass stood up six and eight feet; men and horses and cattle were lost to sight in it; so tough were the grass-roots that timber could not get rootholds in it; the grass seemed to be saying to the trees, "You shall not cross"; turf and sky had a new way of saying, "We are here—who are you?" to the ox-wagon gang hunting a new home.

Buffalo paths, deer tracks, were seen; coon, possum, and wolf signs were seen or heard. And they met settlers telling how the sod was so tough it had broken many a plow; but after the first year of sod-corn, the yield would run 50 bushels to the acre; wheat would average 25 to 30 bushels, rye the same, oats 40 to 60 bushels; Irish potatoes, timothy hay, and all the garden vegetables tried so far would grow. Horses and cattle, lean from short fodder through the winter, would fatten and shine with a gloss on their hair when turned loose in the wild grass in spring. Beds of wild strawberries came ripe in June and stained horses

and cattle crimson to the knees. Wild horses and wild hogs were
still to be found.

The outfit from Indiana raised a laugh as they drove their
steers and wagon into the main street of Decatur, a county-seat
settlement where court would hold its first session the coming
May. To the question, "Kin ye tell us where John Hanks' place
is?" the Decatur citizens told them how to drive four miles,
where they found John, talked over old Indiana and Kentucky
times, but more about Illinois. After the night stay, John took
the Lincoln family six miles down the Sangamo River, where he
had cut the logs for their cabin. There young Lincoln helped
raise the cabin, put in the crops, split rails for fences. He hired
out to Major Warnick near by, read the few books in the house,
and passed such pleasant talk and smiles with the major's
daughter, Mary, and with another girl, Jemima Hill, that at a
later time neighbors said he carried on courtships, even though
both girls married inside of a year after young Lincoln kept
company in those parts. He was asking himself when he would
get married, if ever.

He wrote back to Jones at Gentryville that he doubled his
money on the peddler's stock he sold; he earned a pair of brown
jean trousers by splitting four hundred rails for each yard of
the cloth. With new outlooks came new thoughts; at Vincennes,
on the way to Illinois, he had seen a printing-press for the first
time, and a juggler who did sleight-of-hand tricks. John Hanks
put him on a box to answer the speech of a man who was
against improvements of the Sangamo River; and John told
neighbors, "Abe beat him to death." More and more he was
delivering speeches, to trees, stumps, potato rows, just practicing,
by himself.

Fall came, with miasma rising from the prairie, and chills,
fever, ague, for Tom Lincoln and Sally Bush, and many doses
of "Barks," a Peruvian bark and whisky tonic mixture, bought
at Renshaw's general store in Decatur. Then came Indian
summer, and soft weather, till Christmas week. And then a
snowstorm.

For forty-eight hours, with no let-up, the battalions of a blizzard filled the sky, and piled a cover two and a half feet deep on the ground. No sooner was this packed down and frozen than another drive of snow came till there was a four-foot depth of it on the level. It was easy picking for the light-footed wolves who could run on the top crust and take their way with cattle. Wheat crops went to ruin; cows, hogs, horses died in the fields. Connections between houses, settlements, grain mills, broke down; for days families were cut off, living on parched corn; some died of cold, lacking wood to burn; some died of hunger lacking corn.

Those who came through alive, in the years after, called themselves "Snowbirds." The Lincoln family had hard days. It was hard on new settlers with no reserve stocks of meat, corn, and wood; young Lincoln made a try at wading through to the Warnick house four miles off, nearly froze his feet, and was laid up at home.

As the winter eased off, the Lincoln family moved southeast a hundred miles to Goose Nest Prairie, in the southern part of Coles County.

Chapter 27

EIGHT miles from the new farm was the town of Charleston. Young Lincoln drove there with an ox team and sold loads of cordwood split with his own ax. One afternoon he was late in selling his wood and decided with dark coming on he wouldn't try to drive his ox team to the farm. Tarlton Miles, the horse doctor, living just outside of Charleston, took him in overnight, and they sat up till midnight talking.

In the morning, Lincoln goaded his steers on out to the farm, drove wedges with a maul, split more cordwood. In the evening, as he lay on a board reading, a stranger came to the house and asked to stay overnight. Tom Lincoln said there were only two beds, one belonged to his son, and it depended on whether his son wanted to sleep with a stranger. The two shared the bed that night. . . . It was a country where the veterinary surgeon took in the ox-driver and the ox-driver took in the stranger.

Over in Cumberland County, which joined Coles, the champion wrestler was Dan Needham. It came to his ears several times that the new tall boy over at Goose Nest could throw him. "I can fling him three best out of four any day," was Needham's answer. At a house-raising at Wabash Point the two faced each other, each one standing six feet, four inches, each a prairie panther. "Abe, rassle 'im," said Tom Lincoln.

Abe held off; the crowd egged both of them on. They grappled four times and each time Needham went under. Then Needham lost his head, threatened a fist fight, calmed down with hearing Lincoln's drawling banter, and at last put out his hand with a grin and said, "Well, I'll be damned." And they shook hands.

In February, 1831, there came to the neighborhood of John Hanks, when Abe Lincoln was lingering there, a man named Denton Offut, a hard drinker, a hustler, and a talker shrewd with his tongue, easy with promises, a believer in pots of gold at the rainbow end. He would have a flatboat and cargo to go to New Orleans, all ready for Abe Lincoln, John Hanks, and John Johnston, "as soon as the snow should go off," if they would meet him on a Sangamo River branch near the village of Springfield. They were there at the time set but Denton Offut wasn't; they walked to Springfield, asked for Offut, found him drunk at the Buckhorn Tavern, and helped sober him.

Offut hired them at twelve dollars a month, gave them permission to go onto Government timber-land and get out gunwales for the flatboat, while the rest of the needed lumber could come from Kirkpatrick's sawmill, charged to Offut. They slung together a camp outfit and started building, with Lincoln calling himself "chief cook and bottle-washer." A sleight-of-hand performer came along and giving his show asked for an empty hat to take eggs out of. Lincoln offered his hat in a hesitating way, saying he hesitated not so much out of respect for the hat as for the eggs.

Two men, whose canoe turned over and got away from them were shivering in a tree on a raw April day with the freshet-flooded Sangamo River under them. Lincoln got out across the rampaging waters to the tree, on a log with a rope tied to it; the men in the tree straddled the log and were pulled on shore. People began talking about Lincoln's cool wit.

Thirty days saw the flatboat finished, loaded, and on her way, with Lincoln on deck in blue homespun jeans, jacket, vest, raw-hide boots with pantaloons stuffed in, and a felt hat once black but now, as the owner said, "sunburned till it was a combine of colors." On April 19, rounding the curve of the Sangamo at the village of New Salem, the boat stuck on the Cameron mill-dam, and hung with one third of her slanted downward over the edge of the dam and filling slowly with water, while the cargo of pork-barrels were sliding slowly so as to overweight one end.

She hung there a day while all the people of New Salem came down to look at the river disaster, which Lincoln fixed by un-loading the pork barrels into another boat, boring a hole in the end of the flatboat as it hung over the dam, letting the water out, dropping the boat over the dam and reloading. As she headed toward the Mississippi watercourse, New Salem talked about the cool head and ready wit of the long-shanked young man with his pantaloons stuffed in his rawhide boots.

Again Lincoln floated down the Mississippi River, four to six miles an hour, meeting strings of other flatboats, keel-boats, arks, sleds, proud white steamboats flying flags. Stepping off their flatboat at New Orleans, Lincoln and Hanks went nearly a mile, walking on flatboats, to reach shore. Stacks of pork and flour from the West, and piles of cotton bales from the South, stood on the wharves. Some shippers, about one in six, were cursing their luck; on the long haul from north of the Ohio River their pork and flour had spoiled; all they got for their trip was the view of the Mississippi River scenery. In New Orleans, Lincoln saw advertisements of traders offering to "pay the highest prices in cash for good and likely Negroes" or to "attend to the sale and purchase of Negroes on commission." A firm advertised:

"We have now on hand, and intend to keep throughout the entire year, a large and well-selected stock of Negroes, consisting of field hands, house servants, mechanics, cooks, seamstresses, washers, ironers, etc., which we can sell and will sell as low or lower than any other house here or in New Orleans; persons wishing to purchase would do well to call on us before making purchases elsewhere, as our fresh and regular arrivals will keep us supplied with a good and general assortment; our terms are liberal; give us a call."

One trader gave notice: "I will at all times pay the highest cash prices for Negroes of every description, and will also attend to the sale of Negroes on commission, having a jail and yard fitted up expressly for boarding them." Another announced: "The undersigned would respectfully state to the public that he has forty-five Negroes now on hand, having this day received a lot of twenty-five direct from Virginia, two or three good cooks, a carriage driver, a good house boy, a fiddler, a fine seamstress, and a likely lot of field men and women; all of whom he will sell at a small profit; he wishes to close out and go on to Virginia after a lot for the fall trade." There were sellers advertising, "For sale—several likely girls from 10 to 18 years old, a woman 24, a very valuable woman 25, with three very likely children," while buyers indicated wants after the manner of one advertising, "Wanted—I want to purchase twenty-five likely Negroes, between the ages of 18 and 25 years, male and female, for which I will pay the highest prices in cash."

An Alabama planter advertised, "Runaway—Alfred, a bright mulatto boy, working on plantation; about 18 years old, pretty well grown, has blue eyes, light flaxen hair, skin disposed to freckle; he will try to pass as free-born." Another Alabama planter gave notice: "One hundred dollars reward for return of a bright mulatto man slave, named Sam; light sandy hair, blue eyes, ruddy complexion, is so white as very easily to pass for a free white man."

Lincoln saw one auction in New Orleans where an octoroon girl was sold, after being pinched, trotted up and down, and handled so the buyer could be satisfied she was sound of wind and limb. After a month's stay he worked his passage, firing a steamboat furnace, up the Mississippi River, stayed a few weeks on his father's farm in Coles County, Illinois, and then spoke the long good-by to home and the family roof.

Saying good-by to his father was easy, but it was not so easy to hug the mother, Sally Bush, and put his long arms around her, and lay his cheeks next to hers and say he was going out into the big world to make a place for himself.

The father laughed his good-by, and not so long after told a visitor: "I s'pose Abe is still fooling hisself with eddication. I tried to stop it, but he has got that fool idea in his head, and it can't be got out. Now I hain't got no eddication, but I get along far better'n ef I had. Take bookkeepin'—why, I'm the best bookkeeper in the world! Look up at that rafter thar. Thar's three straight lines made with a firebrand: ef I sell a peck of meal I draw a black line across, and when they pay, I take a dishcloth and jest rub it out; and that thar's a heap better'n yer eddication." And the visitor who heard this told friends that Thomas Lincoln was "one of the shrewdest ignorant men" he had ever seen.

With his few belongings wrapped in a handkerchief bundle tied to a stick over his shoulder, Abraham was on his way to New Salem.

Chapter 28

ABRAHAM LINCOLN, in the spring of the year 1831, is spending a night at the cabin of John Hanks, planning his canoe trip down the Sangamo River to New Salem, where he is going to work on his new job in the store of Denton Offut.

Spring breezes move in the oaks and poplars. The branches of the trees register their forks and angles in flat black shadows over the white flat spread of moon-silver on the ground.

For a moment there flits through his head the memory of the

face of an auburn-haired girl, a head with corn-silk hair; he had seen her at New Salem; he would see her again there.

And as Abraham Lincoln stepped out of the cabin door of the Hanks home that night in 1831, he might have looked up and asked the moon to tell him about the comings and goings of men and machines, guns and tools, events and enterprises, the drift of human struggle and history, over and around the earth.

And the moon might have told him many things that spring night in the year 1831.

The ships and guns of the white men of western Europe were beginning to travel world routes. A vast interwoven fabric of international selling, buying, manufacturing, merchandising, with its circles of operation around the earth, was starting to develop. Coal and iron, steam and steel, and new ways to use them, had been found. In Lancashire and West Riding, England, and in Lyons, France, were new cities with miles of smokestacks sending their scrolls of soot against the sky; under them were roaring power-driven looms, the rattling and clicking spindles and bobbins of machines weaving cloth from American cotton, from Australian wool. The machines had knuckles and fingers weaving faster than any man or woman ever had woven by hand; a boy or a woman watching a machine did the work ten men or twenty used to do. And the ships and guns of England, France, the Netherlands, had gone out over the earth and found millions of new customers for the cloths, fabrics, prints, from these factories, where "the iron man" did the heavy work, the iron man who neither ate nor drank nor slept nor revolted nor took strong drink and came late to work.

The human swarms of India, Asia Minor, Egypt, of Tripoli, Tunis, and Algeria, were on the routes of British, French, and Dutch ships that unloaded the factory goods and took on food products and raw materials to bring to their home countries. The British dominions in America, Australia, New Zealand, were on the regular pathways of the British merchant ships. The bayonets of France in Algiers had established dependable busi-

Log cabin the twenty-year-old Abe Lincoln helped his father build on Goose Nest Prairie in Coles County, Illinois.

From original photograph in the Barrett Collection

Grub hoe used by Abe Lincoln at New Salem (left). Doorstep of
Goose Nest Prairie cabin with Lincoln bureau and clock (right).

Bureau made by Thomas Lincoln in Indiana (left). "Movers'"
wagon (right).

ness relations.   At the straits of the Dardanelles, Mohammedan and Christian soldiers had been fighting till the waters of the Black Sea and the straits of Constantinople and the Dardanelles were opened for the international navigation of all merchant ships.   Governments were learning to speak of protectorates, suzerainties, spheres of influence, zones of understanding.

A new form of world civilization was shaping, founded on the production of merchandise by power-driven machinery and the selling and trading of that merchandise in markets as far off as cargoes could be carried by sailing vessels—and by the new incoming steamboats.   Merchants, manufacturers, and bankers could now operate with the earth as their region of action.   This was the large fact of history before which it seemed all other facts bent and crumpled.   Old sleeping, mysterious dynasties of Asia gave way before it and let open their arabesque portals, at the request or bidding of diplomats, salesmen, or the demands of fleets and squadrons.

Yet it was happening that the millions of new customers for the factory-made goods of Europe were not able to buy all that the new power-driven looms and spindles could turn out.   Factories shut their doors and turned workmen out.   And one day in Lancashire an army of men out of work broke into the factories and smashed a thousand looms.   In Paris a tailor had invented a chain-stitch sewing-machine worked with a treadle, and workmen who hated labor-saving machines had wrecked a new factory with eighty of these sewing-machines in it.   At Lyons, France, workmen out of jobs rioted with banners inscribed, "Live working or die fighting."   In Germany the rulers were in fear of university students who had organized societies and were taking the word "Liberty" for a password.   When a student killed a royal spy named Kotzebue, he was put to death, and in Prussia there were 203 students arrested and 94 condemned to death.   In middle and eastern Europe was agitation for the serfs to be set free.   One French king was told of as the last to die decently in bed as a sovereign; he pointed at the bed and said the next king of France would not die in that bed.

Neither dying nor living was a safe and comfortable thing for the kings of Europe amid the rapid zigzag of events.

Thomas Babington Macaulay of the House of Commons in England delivered a warning that the king and the nobles of France had not come back to stay; they were only "playing at despotism." He urged: "The old laws are forgotten. The old titles have become laughing-stocks. To those gay and elegant nobles who studied military science as a fashionable accomplishment, and expected military rank as a part of their birthright, have succeeded men born in lofts and cellars; educated in the half-naked ranks of the revolutionary armies, and raised by ferocious valor and self-taught skill, to dignities with which the coarseness of their manners and language forms a grotesque contrast. The Bastille is fallen, and can never more rise from its ruins. Is this a romance? Has the warning been given in vain? Have they forgotten how the tender and delicate woman —the woman who would not set her foot on the earth for tenderness and delicateness, the idol of gilded drawing-rooms, the pole-star of crowded theatres, the standard of beauty, the arbitress of fashion, the patroness of genius—was compelled to exchange her luxurious and dignified ease for labor and dependence; perhaps even to draw an infamous and miserable subsistence from those charms which had been the glory of royal circles—to sell for a morsel of bread her reluctant caresses and her haggard smiles—to be turned over from a garret to a hospital and from a hospital to a parish vault? Have they forgotten all this?"

Since 1815, Macaulay declared, the history of England had been "almost entirely made up of the struggles of the lower orders against the government, and of the efforts of the government to keep them down." In bitterness of sarcasm and irony, he mocked: "The people are distressed and tumultuous. They must be kept down by force. The army must be increased; and the taxes must be increased. Then the distress and tumult are increased; and then the army must be increased again! The country will be governed as a child is governed by an ill-tempered nurse—first beaten *till* it cries, and then beaten *because* it cries!"

And with a sincere analysis that contained no hint of irony nor sarcasm, Sir Robert Peel told Parliament: "The United States has been rapidly undergoing a change from a republic to a mere democracy. The influence of the executive—the influence of the government—has been daily becoming less, and more power has consequently been vested in the hands of the people. And yet, in that country, there is land uncultivated to an extent almost incalculable—there is no established church, no privileged orders —property exists on a very different tenure from that on which it is held in this country; therefore let not the people of England be deceived, let them not imagine from the example of the United States, that because democracy has succeeded and triumphed there, it will also succeed and triumph here."

Such were a few of the drifts of thought and action at work in Europe in the year 1831 and years just before. Thus ran the ferment and stew of human conditions that made sections of the people of Europe so restless that they looked to see where else over the earth they could go. There was an appeal to them in "land uncultivated to an extent almost incalculable," land at $1.25 an acre, in "no established church, no privileged orders," and in "property on a different tenure." That appeal would hold across several decades, sending millions in the long suffocating voyage across the ocean to make their gamble in the new country. In the history of America across coming decades, that never-ending stream of newcomers to its soil would be a factor in the ever westward moving of frontiers, in the structure of railroads, cities, armies.

As the ships from Europe came into American ports the ten years following the year 1831, they would deliver 600,000 emigrants, four times as many as in the preceding ten years. Factory and farm jobs, railroad and canal construction jobs called them, work in lumber woods, brickyards, dockyards; the first words they learned were "job," "work," "boss," "dollars," "cents," "eat," "sleep." Railroads were to be built; wooden rails covered with iron strips, then iron ways. Thousands of Irishmen hired out with pick, shovel and wheelbarrow. R. W.

Emerson wrote in his journal, "The poor Irishman, the wheel-barrow is his country." On the Erie Canal and the Great Lakes route to the north, on the wagon roads to Pittsburgh and the Ohio River route to the south, the human traffic was thicker and heavier, as well as on the newer Cumberland road between the two older routes. There were now about 10,000,000 white people in the United States, and about 2,300,000 colored slaves.

The people lived in three sections or regions, each section with a character of its own in products, land, and people. There was the North with a long belt of factories, shops, and mills running from southern Maine to Chesapeake Bay. There was the South with its cotton, tobacco, rice, and slaves. There was the West with its corn, wheat, pork, furs. In some respects these sections or regions were three separate countries, with different ways of looking at life; their soil, climate, slang, and subtleties of personal communication were different.

And behind that tissue of time called the Future, events were operating, shaping lines of destiny for these three sections or regions of America. First of these events was the coming of the railway. An American-made, horizontal-boiler engine was running on the first stub line called the Baltimore & Ohio Railway. Processes for smelting iron with anthracite coal by use of a hot-air blast were almost ready. The transportation revolution was breaking. Blunt facts stood up: iron production jumped from 54,000 tons in 1810 to 165,000 tons in 1830 and would go to 347,000 tons in 1840. Beyond the little narrow Atlantic states, where the dinky B. & O. engines puffed along fifteen miles an hour and slipped on the uphill drag, there were the Great Plains, where miles were measured by thousands, vast level stretches of territory where the building and running of railroads would be easier and faster than anywhere else in the world.

McCormick, Hussey, and other men were fixing their wits on the making of harvesting machines, so that one farmer alone on a mower would cut as much grain as a gang of field hands with scythe and cradle. Morse was nearly ready to connect the Mississippi Valley with the Atlantic seaboard by instantaneous wire communication. Electricity was to be moved from the laboratory to the workshop and have its horsepower measured and harnessed. These were events sleeping behind that tissue of time called the Future, almost ready to step out into the drama called History.

The South, in the early thirties, was an empire of cotton blossoms, and cotton bales, held in the loose leashes of cotton planters who lived on horseback accustomed to command. The old-time tobacco and rice planters had closed their silver snuff-boxes, spoken muffled farewells to the power they once held, and acknowledged some new and terrible chapter was in the writing for the South. In some counties in Virginia, half the population had been swept out and away downward into the Cotton Belt; John Randolph said publicly his plantation was going bankrupt; at an auction sale in 1829, the stately white home of Thomas Jefferson was bidden in for $2,500; the speech, the tone of voice, and the human slant of the Declaration of Independence were fading out from approved conversation. As a region the South covered 880,000 square miles; less than one-fourth held in its grip the controlling economic and political element; on a peculiar strip of land, where cotton crops laughed with snow-white harvests, there lived in 1830 about a million and a half people, one in three a negro. The dominant interest each year was the cotton crop; Massachusetts, Connecticut, New York, Great Britain, France sent more and more ships every year for this cotton crop; its bales in 1830 were worth $29,000,000. On a crisscross neck of land running from lower North Carolina to the Red River counties of Louisiana and Arkansas was rising the cotton civilization. A phenomenon with a star of destiny, the talk of the world, was the South. Pot-luck hunters and rainbow-chasers came from states north, from Britain, Ireland, and continental Europe, hoping a small gamble would bring quick rich returns. Land wore out as the soil was mined and exploited without care or manure; so the worked-out land was left empty or rented to poorer whites, while the big planters turned west and farther west to fresh and virgin soils. Virginia cotton production slumped from 25,000,000 pounds in 1826 to 10,000,000 pounds in 1834; in the same time the cotton crops of Mississippi, far below the Allegheny Mountains, leaped from 20,000,000 to 85,000,000 pounds. The exploitation was decisive, blind, relentless. Superb timber on a million and more acres of land was cut down and burned or the trees girdled, the sap choked and the trunks deadened, to make room for more cotton crops. The covenants of the Federal Government with the Red Indian tribes were torn to scraps of paper while the Cherokee, Choctaw, Creek, and Chickasaw Indian tribes were charged with "an attempt to establish an independent government," and driven off their rich and wide tracts of land, to make room for cotton crops and the cotton civilization of the white man.

Sections of the South outside the Cotton Belt became economic tributaries of it; in parts of Virginia the breeding of negroes for the slave-labor markets farther south had become a recognized live-stock business, selling 6,000 negroes south every year; Alexandria was a loading point for brigs hauling cargoes of black freight to New Orleans; Delaware and Maryland were pouring fresh supplies into the famous barracoons or slave barracks selling and shipping regularly from Washington, D. C.; along the Wilderness Road and through Cumberland Gap moved kaffles or chain gangs headed away from the worn-out cotton lands of Virginia into strips of virgin soil south and west. The ships of smugglers on the high seas and the wagons of legitimate traders and breeders on the inland highways were carrying the fresh labor supplies called for by the big planters as imperative requisites toward larger cotton crops. Mississippi had doubled her negro labor supply in ten years; Alabama had tripled hers. Tax assessors had counted more than two million slaves, taxable at more than a billion dollars. This negro labor-supply was the backbone of wealth production, connecting directly with the economic supremacy of the South as shown in its exports of cotton, tobacco, and rice between 1821 and 1830, which were valued at $33,000,-

000.00 as against a total of only $20,000,000.00 for all other states.

"Slave labor is more productive than free labor," was the argument of Thomas R. Dew, president of a Virginia college, replying before a legislative committee to other Virginians who were asking for a gradual emancipation of slaves. He pointed to the 470,000 slaves of Virginia as worth $94,000,000.00 and nearly equal in value to one-half the assessed value of all the houses and lands of the state, or $206,000,000.00. He respectfully challenged Jefferson's statement, "The whole commerce between master and slave is a perpetual exercise of the most boisterous passions," and countered, "Look to the slaveholding population and you everywhere find them characterized by noble and elevated sentiments; the most cruel masters are those who have been unaccustomed to slavery; it is well known that northern gentlemen who marry southern heiresses are much severer masters than southern gentlemen. The slaves of a good master are his warmest, most constant, and most devoted friends; we have often heard slave-holders affirm that they would sooner rely upon their slaves' fidelity and attachment in the hour of danger, than on any other equal number of individuals." He referred to the population of Virginia as "consisting of three castes, free white, free colored, and slave colored."

In 200 years there had been only three slave insurrections, with less than 100 lives lost, declared Dew, in discussing the Nat Turner insurrection in which negro slaves one summer night killed 60 white persons in Southampton County. It was an action to be traced chiefly to a fanatical leader who heard voices in the air telling him he was sent from Heaven to save the slaves; an eclipse of the moon followed by a green sun were signs the work of emancipation should begin.

Slave labor is superior to free labor in southern climates, it was urged. "The slave districts in China, according to travelers, are determined by latitude and agricultural products; the wheat-growing districts have no slaves, but the rice-, cotton-, and sugar-growing districts situated in warm climates have all of them slaves." The sweeping postulates were stated: "The exclusive owners of property ever have been, ever will and perhaps ever ought to be, the virtual rulers of mankind. It is the order of nature and of God that the being of superior faculties and knowledge, and therefore of superior power, should control and dispose of those who are inferior. It is as much in the order of nature that men should enslave each other as that other animals should prey upon each other."

Circumstances beyond control of the southern states had brought slavery; it was a long age in developing and would take a long age to go; it was rooted so deep that no rash or sudden act could cut it loose. "The original sin of introduction rests not on our heads," declared Dew. "With regard to the assertion that slavery is against the spirit of Christianity, we are ready to admit the general assertion, but deny, most positively, that there is anything in the Old or New Testament to show the master commits any offense in holding slaves. No one can read the New Testament without seeing and admiring that the meek and humble Savior of the world in no instance meddled with the established institutions of mankind; he came to save a fallen world, and not to excite the black passions of men, and array them in deadly hostility against each other; He nowhere encourages insurrection; he nowhere fosters discontent, but exhorts always to implicit obedience and fidelity."

A church association in Georgia had formally decided that when slave husbands and wives were separated by sale, either could marry again as though the other had died; "such separation, among persons situated as our slaves are, is civilly a separation by death, and in the sight of God, it would be so viewed." In North Carolina, to sell or to give a slave any book, the Bible not excepted, was punishable with 39 lashes for a free negro or a $200.00 fine for a white man. The statute urged that "teaching slaves to read and write tends to excite dissatisfaction in their minds, and to produce insurrection and rebellion." Twenty lashes "well laid on" was the penalty for slaves meeting for "religious worship" before sunrise or after sunset in South Carolina; in one year, thirty-five slaves were executed at Charleston, after trial and conviction on a charge of intended insurrection. Any meeting of slaves at any school, day or night, for instruction in reading or writing, was held by the laws of Virginia to be an act of unlawful assembly, punishable with twenty lashes on the back of any slave found in such school. In Louisiana, the penalty for teaching slaves to read and write was one year's imprisonment; in Georgia $500.00 fine and imprisonment.

In South Carolina and Georgia, any person finding more than seven slaves together in the highway without a white person could give each one twenty lashes. In Maryland, for "rambling, riding, or going abroad in the night, or riding horses in the daytime, without leave," a slave could be whipped, have his ears cropped, be branded on the cheek with the letter R, or punished by any method which would not render the slave "unfit for labor."

Prices of slaves fluctuated with the market price of cotton. The coasts of Florida and the bayous of Louisiana were favorite places for the landing of wild Africans, to be later mixed with squads of American-born blacks and sold off singly or in couples. The captain of *La Fortuna,* a 90-ton schooner, brought 217 slaves from the African Gold Coast to Havana, Cuba, sold them for $77,469, itemized a net profit of $41,438.54 to the shipowners for an investment during six months of $3,700.00 in the schooner, and a capital all told amounting to less than $21,000.00 That is, they doubled their money in six months. The *Napoleon,* a Baltimore clipper, earned a profit of $100,000.00 in one trip; she brought to the Cuban market 250 full-grown men and 100 picked boys and girls; cost per head was $16.00; they sold for an average of $360.00 per head. A first-class ship for carrying from 300 to 400 slaves cost less than $30,000.00 and earned from $35,000.00 to $100,000.00 each voyage. Three to four voyages soaked the timbers of the vessel with such filth that no crew could sail it; seamen said the odor of a slave ship could be sniffed definitely in the ocean air more than "five miles down wind "

The slaves were packed "spoon-fashion" in a space three feet, ten inches high, between decks, the men ironed together, two and two by the ankles, the women and children left unironed.

Cargoes were usually loaded on the west African coast where there were stations or depots to which negro African tribal chiefs brought slaves, captives from defeated tribes, for sale; that is, negroes sold negroes to white men; most often the payment was in rum. In the later days of the trade there were larger lots of children in the cargo; they were easier to handle. Sometimes the negro men and women refused to eat; they were flogged under commands to eat—and to sing and dance. Some tricked the captains into heavy blows, till they knew death was coming; then they smiled quiet mockery at the captains, saying, "Soon we shall be free." Home ports of many of the ships were in New England; at one time Newport alone had 150 ships hauling these oversea cargoes of perishable freight.

For more than 200 years, ships had sailed to the west African coast, shackled their loads of live stock, and hauled them to American harbors. John Rolfe, the white man who married the Indian princess Pocahontas, recorded in his diary one day in 1619 the arrival of a ship in the harbor of Jamestown, "a dutch man of warre that sold us twenty Negars." And since 1619, two centuries past, their increase through importation and birth had gone on till the census takers reckoned two million and more negro slaves in the South.

Most of this negro labor supply was on the large plantations, where the approved unit was a hundred slaves to a thousand acres. On a single plantation might be found coal-black Africans with slant skulls and low foreheads, direct from the jungles, speaking a guttural mumble; men and women of brown or bronze faces, with regular features; some who came evidently from Arabia or northern Africa, with flashes of intelligence and genius from old civilizations; and persons thirty-one thirty-seconds white blood and one thirty-second negro blood, white in color, having manners, skill, and accomplishments, held as slaves.

The bulk of slaves were on the large one- or two-thousand-acre cotton plantations. Yet a slave-owner might be a small farmer raising crops with the help of one or two slaves who worked side by side with him in the fields. Or, the owner of a copper-faced slave might be a copper-faced Indian, as happened in a few instances. Or again the owner might be a free negro; there were mulattoes and quadroons in New Orleans who owned negro house-slaves. There were nearly 200,000 free negroes in the South; most of them had been given papers of freedom by their masters. Every child of a negro slave-mother was lawfully born as a slave and the property of her owner; there were slaves who knew their owners were their fathers. There were slim and appealing mulatto girls who sold for prices upward of $3,000.00 each. There were free negroes who had earned their freedom, had been arrested and convicted of violations of law, and sold at auction back into slavery. There were free negroes, who had come back asking to live as slaves again, which happened in cases of negroes given freedom on the plantation of John Randolph. There were house negroes who considered themselves superior to field negroes; there were field negroes who had contempt for struggling white farmers, called "po' w'ite trash."

There were negroes who had been jailed and charged with crimes in New York, shackled, put on ships and unloaded at Gulf-coast states; one ship from New York came to New Orleans with 70 such negroes from New York prisons; the brig *Mary Ann* in 1818 took 36 negroes from Perth Amboy, New Jersey, to New Orleans, where a newspaper remarked: "It is probable the greater part of these unfortunate creatures were stolen; negro trading seems to be actively carried on through certain great villains holding their headquarters in New Jersey."

Great Britain, France, and Sweden had an agreement to handle slave-traders as "pirates, felons, and robbers"; they had agreed to search each other's ships. The United States held off from this agreement—and the favorite flag of the slave ships along the coast of Africa was the Stars and Stripes. The American flag was protection against search from any vessels except American cruisers, operating under orders from the Secretary of the Navy at Washington, who was responsible to a President who was a slaveholder.

Thus in the early thirties was weaving the fabric of an empire, a pastoral and agricultural nation, with its foundations resting on three chief conditions: (1) the special fertility of a certain strip of land for cotton crops; (2) the raising of the cotton crop by negro slave labor; (3) the sale of that crop to northern American and to English cotton-mills that sold their finished products in a constantly widening world market. The planters who had control of its destiny, in so far as there was control rather than blind luck and brute hazard, were men of pride, valor, and cunning; they lived on horseback, accustomed to command.

The North was a section of country fumbling and groping toward control of water power, iron, steel, canals, railways, ocean-going boats. Her controlling men sat in office chairs, accustomed to add and subtract, measure and multiply, with maps, statistics, diagrams and designs before their eyes. By one route and another, the money of American regions was streaming toward banks in New York, Philadelphia, and Boston. Brickyards were running night and day in order that new factories and mills might rise on the banks of swift-running rivers whose water power would operate woolen and cotton mills. The ten years before 1830 had seen the mills of New England and the Middle States triple their output twice over. The shipping, mercantile, fisheries, and farming interests of New England slipped back from their places of importance to make room for the manufacturing interests, which, with their allied banks, were taking the chief control.

Cotton mills were the industrial phenomenon; each year they called for increasing tens of millions of pounds of cotton from the South; they produced cotton goods worth $2,500,000 in 1820, and their value kept mounting till in 1831 the total was $15,500,-000; in the same period the woolen-mill output increased from less than $1,000,000 to more than $11,000,000. It was a process that shook up culture, religion, and politics in New England and so mixed the currents of its destinies that Daniel Webster wrote, "We are disgraced beyond help or hope; there is a Federal interest, a Democratic interest, a bankrupt interest, an orthodox interest, and a middling interest; but I see no national interest, nor any national feeling in the whole matter." The spinning-wheels and distaffs of millions of homes had become old-fashioned; their place was the garret and attic; spinning was to be done in cotton and woolen mills and clothes were to be cheap.

From thousands of farms the people moved into the industrial cities to go to work, men, women, and children, in the mills. Other thousands of New England farmers were selling out and moving via the Erie Canal over into the Mohawk Valley and western New York, or out still farther west into Ohio, Indiana, Michigan, and Illinois. Some could tell of the New England farmer who called a minister to pray for better crops from the soil; and the minister, after looking over the stony and stingy soil, had said, "This farm doesn't need prayer—what this farm needs is manure!"

Farmers' daughters filled the cotton mills in Lowell, Massachusetts; they started work at five o'clock in the morning and worked till seven o'clock in the evening, with a half-hour off for breakfast, and forty-five minutes off at noon for dinner; they spent fourteen hours a day at the factory and had ten hours a day left in which to sleep and to refresh themselves and to improve their minds and bodies. One girl, operating a single spinning-machine, carrying 3,000 spindles, spun as much cotton cloth as 3,000 girls working by hand a single thread at a time on the old-fashioned spinning-wheel. In fifteen years the price of ordinary cloths for sheeting had dropped from forty cents a yard to eight and one-half cents a yard.

Bells rang at "break of day" in some factory towns; the workers tumbled out of sleep, crept into their clothes and reported at the factory gates in fifteen minutes, when the gates closed. An hour or two later, twenty-five minutes was allowed for breakfast, and at noon twenty-five minutes was again allowed for dinner. The gates were opened at eight o'clock at night to let the workers go back to supper, play, amusements, recreation, education, strong drink, sleep, or whatever they chose till the ringing of the bell again the next morning at "break of day." The Hope factory in Rhode Island ran on this plan. In the Eagle Mill at Griswold, Connecticut, the work-day lasted fifteen hours and ten minutes. At Paterson, New Jersey, women and children began the day's work at half-past four o'clock in the morning. Overseers in some textile mills cracked a cowhide whip over women and children. "The only opportunities allowed to children generally, employed in manufactories, to obtain an education, are on the Sabbath and after half-past eight o'clock of the evening of other days," declared the report of a committee of the newly organized New England Association of Farmers, Mechanics, and Other Workingmen.

In language dark as the early winter dawns in which boys and girls went to work rubbing sleep from their eyes, the association declared its purpose to be "the organization of the whole laboring class," with the express hope "to imbue our offspring with abhorrence for the usurpations of aristocracy, so that they shall dedicate their lives to a completion of the work which their ancestors commenced in their struggle for *national,* and their sires have continued in their contest for *personal,* independence." The first labor paper on the American continent, *The Workingman's Advocate,* had been started in New York by two English workingmen. It was followed by *The Mechanics' Free Press.*

A jury in New York City heard the evidence against striking workingmen charged with "conspiring to raise wages" and awarded a fine of one dollar. The growing wage-earning class was organizing trade associations, and in Philadelphia had formed its first central body of such associations. Strikes were called to raise wages, to bar from work the nonunion men known later as "rats" and "scabs." But most of all the strikes were aimed to get the ten-hour work-day. In politics this labor movement stood against jailing for debt, against banking monopoly, for easier access to public lands, for schools open to all, for the

United States mails to run on the Sabbath, for limitation of ownership of land to 160 acres per person, and for "abolition of chattel slavery and of wages slavery."

Thread, yarn, twine, sheeting, shirting, ticking, print cloth, gingham, and bags were leaving North Atlantic states for all parts of the world. They went west on the Erie Canal and the Great Lakes; they were on Ohio River flatboats going west and south; they were loaded on pack horses and mules moving in four parallel columns from Independence, Missouri, for the seventy-day trip to Santa Fe, where they were traded for gold dust, buffalo skins, rugs, Mexican blankets. The South was buying back in finished cloth part of the cotton it raised. Ships leaving North Atlantic ports carried cargoes for South America. The United States had become in 1830 second only to England in the amount of cotton it bought for its humming spindles. In 1831, were reported 795 mills, 1,246,500 spindles and 70,000 mill workers. The industrial and commercial fact of cotton had moved into world history as a reckonable factor. The seeds of a "tree wool," gathered in India by Englishmen and planted in Bermuda and from there transplanted to South Carolina and Georgia, had spread and grown till they were part of the lives and work of millions of people.

Yet the development was merely in its beginnings. In New York and Pennsylvania, companies were organizing to mine the iron and coal fields. In the coming ten years the railroads and steamboats would want iron and steel for their equipment and rolling-stock, and coal to generate steam power. And with railroads and steamboats connecting the cotton plantations with the cotton mills of America and Europe, and then moving the finished products with higher speed to the world-wide markets, there would be realized another step in the international industrial revolution. Patents on new tools, machines, and devices had more than doubled in ten years; in 1830 there were 544 patents granted. The pilgrim people who came to the North Atlantic coast with Milton and Bunyan in their veins, with Bibles and prayer-books in their hands, were to gain a world name for a figure known as the Inventive Yankee, making breech-loading firearms, air pumps, rock drills, lathes, planing machines, pile drivers, truss frames, harvesters and reapers, sewing machines. Edward Everett issued an essay on "The Inevitable March of Improvement."

Three thousand prisoners were in jail for debt in Massachusetts, 10,000 in New York, 7,000 in Pennsylvania, and 3,000 in Maryland. In one city forty cases were recorded in which the sum total of the debt was $23.40, an average of less than sixty cents for each prisoner.

An industrial civilization was coming over the Middle States and New England. It covered less than 175,000 square miles and held a little more than 6,000,000 people, elements of Dutch blood in New York, Germans and Scotch-Irish in Pennsylvania, Swedes in Delaware and Philadelphia. And there were Irish in New York; one of their kith and kin had put through the Erie Canal project against the opposition of the Irish in the Tammany Society; they toiled on canals in Massachusetts.

The proudest, most cohesive unit in the North was New England; she had dialect, religion, law, climate, and regional personality enough to set up as a nation by herself, if there had been enough salt water or steep mountains to isolate her; geography and history were her enemies in that respect; when her shipping and trade were shot to pieces in the War of 1812, and she was ready and set for secession from the Union of states, events shifted.

And so, over New England and the Middle States had sprung up, without forewarning or foretelling, the beginnings of a civilization of power-driven looms, wage-earning labor, of iron, coal, and fast transport. The controlling men sat in office chairs, accustomed to add and subtract, measure and multiply, with maps, statistics, diagrams and designs before their eyes. The fabric and structure of the basic system of life at the North was in high contrast to that of the South. The big word in the South was Chivalry. In the North it was Improvements.

In the West, if there was a big word, it was something like "Freedom" or "Independence," or a slogan, "Hands Off." Its reckonings were under large skies and in spreading numbers. For the West was a stretch of country with the Great Lakes at the north, the Gulf of Mexico to the south, the Allegheny Mountains to the east, and a ragged-edged, shifty frontier on the west, moving its line farther west every year out into the Great Plains and beyond toward the Rocky Mountains. Its controlling physical feature was the Mississippi River waterway system, branching with tireless streams fed by regular rainfalls, into a region covering one and a quarter million square miles.

Pioneers in waves were crossing this stretch of country; there was an element of movers always selling out, packing up, and passing on, some saying, "It's time to move if you can hear your neighbor's shotgun." The early settlers had clung to rivers and timbers; now they were locating on prairie land and learning to farm it. Each wave of settlers made it easier for more to come. The young Frenchman, De Tocqueville, was writing: "This gradual and continuous progress of the European race toward the Rocky Mountains has the solemnity of a providential event; it is like a deluge of men rising unabatedly and daily driven onward by the hand of God!"

The New York millionaire fur-trader, Astor, was buying thousand-acre tracts in Illinois, Missouri, Wisconsin. For De Tocqueville had noted also: "The Valley of the Mississippi is, upon the whole, the most magnificent dwelling-place prepared by God for man's abode; and yet it may be said that at present it is but a mighty desert." Wild horses roamed in grass taller than their heads, occasionally roped and broken by white men. Buffaloes were killed by thousands, the skins sold in St. Louis or New Orleans, the carcasses left on the open plains for the wolves and crows. Little populations were pocketed in corners where European races were intermingled with Indians and negroes. Off southwest Texas was calling; cabins were empty in Kentucky and Tennessee with a scribble on the doors, "Gone to Texas"; a boom was on; men and women slanged each other, "Go to Texas";

six years had seen over 20,000 settlers, rustlers, horsemen, enter Texas. And a restless pioneer breed swarmed overland by wagon, horse, and afoot, across the Allegheny Mountains; in ten years the West had added a million and a half people; its population was one-third of the United States.

Connecting products with market, they took horses, mules, cattle, and hogs across country on foot, sometimes four and five thousand hogs in a drove; the turnpike gate at Cumberland Gap saw live stock worth a million dollars in the year 1828; tobacco and whisky worth another million dollars passed over the Falls of the Ohio at Louisville in one year; aggregates of a million dollars were getting common. Corn, oats, barley, hay were fed to cattle and hogs that walked to market, or the grain was distilled into whisky for concentrated transport. Three thousand wagons were making hauls east from Pittsburgh to traders in Baltimore, Philadelphia, and New York; feeding grounds for live stock had been located on plantations along the Potomac River where cattle were fattened for the eastern markets. Cincinnati had the nickname of "Porkopolis" and was packing hams, bacon, and salt pork. Exports from the West had mounted in 1830 to $17,800,000.

The West had become a granary sending food supplies to the factory and textile-mill towns of New England and the Middle States, to Great Britain and France, as well as corn, horses, and mules to the big cotton planters of the South. It was of immense importance, then, that in the year 1831, for the first time, goods were shipped from the Atlantic seaboard to St. Louis by way of Chicago at one-third lower cost than by the New Orleans route. History was in the reckoning. Cheaper and quicker movement of corn and cattle going east, and of textiles, iron, hardware, and human passengers coming west, would set up new connections west, east, south, and overseas.

Over the earth were many little dramas of personal struggle and hope in that year 1831. A cadet named Edgar Allan Poe, guilty of "neglect" and "disobedience," had been thrown out of the West Point military academy and was writing poetry, drinking whisky, toiling with black bats in the belfries. A young English doctor named Charles Darwin, just twenty-one years old, was starting on a five-year trip in a ship, the *Beagle;* he was taking along thick pads of writing-paper to put down notes about plants, animals, rocks, weather.

An Englishman, Michael Faraday, had been working in a partnership of international scientists, with facts and principles handed him by the Italian, Alessandro Volta, the Dane, Hans Christian Oersted, the Frenchman, A. M. Ampère, the German, G. S. Ohm, toilers on the borderland of fact and speculation; proud, conjectural fools in the realms of wire, plates, pivoted magnets, currents, circuits, attractions, and repulsions; they had identified, caged, captured, and measured that lightning terror, electrodynamic force; hitherto "electricity" had been a useless, mysterious juice; Faraday was making a dynamo; he was going to harness, drive and use the power of electromagnetism.

Such were a few of the things the white moon in its high riding over the sky might have told Abraham Lincoln that spring night in 1831. He would have listened with an understanding head and heart because he was blood and bone of North, South, and West, because there were in him the branched veins of New England emigrant, Middle State Quaker, Virginia planter, and Kentucky pioneer. As the regions of America grew and struggled, he might understand their growth and struggle.

In ten years there had been other little dramas of personal struggle and hope besides the one of Abraham Lincoln. John Keats, the poet, had died at twenty-five years of age among the ivies, marbles, and lizards of Rome, buried with his own epitaph on the gravestone: "Here lies one whose name was writ in water." In the same year passed out Napoleon with the declaration: "I die in the Apostolical and Roman religion, in the bosom of which I was born; it is my wish that my ashes may repose on the banks of the Seine, in the midst of the French people whom I have loved so well." The next year had seen the poet Shelley drowned in the Mediterranean and his body burned and its ashes placed next to the burial urn of Keats; only the year before he had written of Keats, "I weep for Adonais—he is dead." Two years more and the poet Lord Byron, fighting in Greece and far from home, in so far as he had a home, died of fever; of him Shelley had written, "Space wondered less at the swift and fair creations of God when he grew weary of vacancy, than I at this spirit of an angel in the mortal paradise of a decaying body"; while Symonds, a critic, was to write, "It was his misfortune to be well born, but ill bred." Beethoven, too, stepped out of his mortal frame, having been deaf twelve years so that the finest music he knew was in the inner arrangements of sound and silence known only to his own imagination; an escort of 20,000 music lovers swarmed to his grave the day he was laid away. In London town, the mad, sweet, colossal poet, William Blake, had died; "he wandered up and he wandered down, Ever alone with God."

Out of them all, a little flame blue, from the gray of their ashes, lived on.

Each had sung in his own way that line young Abraham Lincoln had written with a turkey-feather pen at Pigeon Creek: "Time! What an empty vapor 'tis!"

Chapter 29

IN the summer of the year 1831, Abraham Lincoln, twenty-two years old, floated a canoe down the Sangamon River, going to a new home, laughter and youth in his bones, in his heart a few pennies of dreams, in his head a ragbag of thoughts he could never expect to sell.

Catfish and bass, perch and pike, flipped in the still waters at the edge of the stream; they could be taken with a hook. The shadows of a bluejay, a kingfisher, moved flying over the water of the Sangamon, and once the silhouette of a bald eagle moved up a slope of bottom land away from the river—and these shadows were the same as air.

Crows went by, leaving the hoarse hawk of their caw-cry in the air. Long willows drowsed with hung-down branches in the green scum of muddy by-waters at a standstill. A slippery musk-rat might swim out of the hole of a rotten log to look at the weather of the day. Seldom—and yet once or twice—a bullfrog croaked his basso profundo croak.

Glimpses of landscape flitted by where the bee and dragonfly were going amid Indian pink and the bluebell and running wild rose. Red haw and the bitter fox-grape had intimations of fall-time to come. Behind the bumblebees buzzing in the yellow dust of goldenrod leaves, and behind the streamers of haze around the river curves, were hints, almost statements, of a future to follow the present, the intertwining of hours to come with hours that are.

New Salem, the town on a hill, to which Abraham Lincoln was shunting his canoe, was a place of promise there in the year 1831, just as all towns in Illinois then were places of promise. New Salem then had a dozen families as its population, just as Chicago in the same year reckoned a dozen families and no more. Both had water transportation, outlets, tributary territory, yet one was to be only a phantom hamlet of memories and ghosts, a wind-swept hilltop kept as cherished haunts are kept.

New Salem stood on a hill, a wrinkle of earth crust, a con-vulsive knob of rock and sod. The Sangamon River takes a curve as it comes to the foot of that bluff and looks up. It is almost as though the river said, "For such a proud standing hill as this I must make a proud winding curve for it to look at."

Up on the ridge level of that bluff, the buffalo, the wild horse, the wild hog and the Red Indian had competed for occupation a thousand years and more. Herds of shaggy-whiskered buffalo had roamed the Sangamon Valley; deer antlers had been plowed up and arched above doorways where men six feet tall walked under without stooping. Plows had turned up brown and white flint arrowheads of Indian hunters, red men whose learning had included buffalo and snake dances, and a necromancy of animal life unknown to men of the white race. Before the rifle and plow of the white man, the red man in that particular southern region of Illinois had moved off, had, in the words of some who followed, "gone and skedaddled." Yet the red man was still a near enough presence to be spoken of as more than a ghost who had just passed.

At the foot of a bluff where the Sangamon begins its curve, a thousand wagon-loads of gravel had been hauled and packed into the river to make a power-dam and mill-grind. The Rutledges and Camerons who started the mill bought the ridge of land on the bluff above and in 1829 laid out a town, sold lots, put up a log tavern with four rooms, and named the place New Salem.

Farmers came from fifty miles away to have their grain turned into flour and to buy salt, sugar, coffee, handkerchiefs, hardware, and calico prints and bonnets. If people asked, "Has the mud wagon come in?" they referred to the stagecoach driving from Havana to Springfield once a week, and carrying mail to the New Salem post office. The town in its time had a sawmill, fifteen houses, a hundred people, two doctors, a school, a church and Sunday school, a saloon, and a squire and two constables. The Herndon brothers, Rowan and James, kept a store; so did the partnership of Samuel Hill and James McNamar; also one Reuben Radford had a grocery.

And Denton Offut, who had rented the Rutledge and Cameron gristmill, had ordered a stock of goods and was going to open a new store, with A. Lincoln as clerk in charge. When Offut had seen Lincoln handle his flatboat on the New Salem mill-dam so masterfully, Offut had told people he would soon have a regular steamboat running up and down the Sangamon with Lincoln as captain; the boat would run the year round, in all weathers, with rollers for shoals and dams, runners for ice; Offut said that with Lincoln in charge, "By thunder, she'd have to go!" A hustler, a boomer, and a booster was Offut; nips from a bottle of corn juice doubled his natural enthusiasms; his vision took in wide empires of business, though he was blind to the barriers.

Election Day was on when Lincoln arrived in New Salem and

loafed along the main street. At the voting-place they told him a clerk was wanted and asked if he could write. Of course, he might have answered that where he came from in Indiana he used to write letters for the whole township; instead he answered with an up-and-down of careless inflections, "Oh, I guess I can make a few rabbit tracks." So, with a goose quill he sat registering ballots that first day in New Salem; and he felt as much at home with the goose quill as he had felt with the ax, the hoe, the flatboat oars, and other instruments he had handled.

The voting was by word of mouth. Each voter told the election judges which candidates he wanted to vote for. Then a judge would bawl out the voter's name and his candidates, which names would be written down by the clerks. Lincoln got acquainted with names and faces of nearly all the men in New Salem on his first day there.

Offut's stock for the new store had not come as yet, so when Dr. Nelson, who was leaving New Salem for Texas, said he wanted a pilot to take his flatboat through the channels of the Sangamon to Beardstown on the Illinois River, Lincoln was willing. When he came back from that little job, he said there were times he ran the flatboat three miles off onto the prairies, but always got back to the main channel of the Sangamon. A genius of drollery was recognized by the New Salem folks as having come among them to live with and be one of them. They were already passing along the lizard story, a yarn spun by the newcomer the first day he arrived. He had said it happened in Indiana and was as strange as many other things that had happened in Indiana.

In a meeting-house far and deep in the tall timbers, a preacher was delivering a sermon, wearing old-fashioned baggy pantaloons fastened with one button and no suspenders, while his shirt was fastened at the collar with one button. In a loud voice he announced his text for the day, "I am the Christ, whom I shall represent today." And about that time a little blue lizard ran up under one of the baggy pantaloons. The preacher went ahead with his sermon, slapping his legs. After a while the lizard came so high that the preacher was desperate, and, going on with his sermon, unbuttoned the one button that held his pantaloons; they dropped down and with a kick were off. By this time the lizard had changed his route and circled around under the shirt at the back, and the preacher, repeating his text, "I am the Christ, whom I shall represent today," loosened his one collar button and with one sweeping movement off came the shirt. The congregation sat in the pews dazed and dazzled; everything was still for a minute; then a dignified elderly lady stood up slowly and, pointing a finger toward the pulpit, called out at the top of her voice, "I just want to say that if you represent Jesus Christ, sir, then I'm done with the Bible."

Men were telling of Lincoln and a crew loading Squire Godbey's hogs onto a flatboat down at Blue Banks; the hogs were slippery and stubborn and the crew couldn't chase them on board. The gossip was that Lincoln said, "Sew their eyes shut." And farmers were "argufyin'" as to whether a hog is easier handled when his eyes are sewed shut.

On a lot Offut bought for ten dollars, he and Lincoln built a cabin of logs; this was to be the new store, and Lincoln started boarding at the home of the Reverend John Cameron, whose eleven daughters ran the house.

Offut's goods arrived; Lincoln stacked shelves and corners with salt, sugar, tea, coffee, molasses, butter and eggs, whisky, tobacco, hardware, stoneware, cups and saucers, plates, dishes, calico prints, hats, bonnets, gloves, socks, shoes. Bill Green, the eighteen-year-old son of Squire Bowling Green, was put in as a helper mainly to tell Lincoln which of the customers were good pay. Offut's enthusiasm about his new clerk ran high: "He knows more than any man in the United States. . . . Some day he will be President of the United States. . . . He can outrun, outlift, outwrestle, and throw down any man in Sangamon County."

And the Clary's Grove Boys, just four miles away, began talking about these claims; what they said mostly was, "Is that so?" Bill Clary, who ran a saloon thirty steps north of the

Offut store, put up a bet of ten dollars with Offut that Lincoln couldn't throw Jack Armstrong, the Clary's Grove champion.

Sports from fifty miles around came to a level square next to Offut's store to see the match; bets ran high, from money to jackknives and treats of whisky. Armstrong was short and powerful in build with the muscle haunches of a wild steer; his aim from the first was to get in close on his man where he would have the advantage of his thick muscular strength.

Lincoln held him off with long arms, wore down his strength, got him out of breath and out of temper. Armstrong then fouled by stamping on Lincoln's right foot and instep with his boot heel. This exasperated Lincoln so that he lost his temper, lifted Armstrong up by the throat and off the ground, shook him like a rag, and then slammed him to a hard fall, flat on his back.

As Armstrong lay on the ground, a champion in the dust of defeat, his gang from Clary's Grove started to swarm toward Lincoln, with hot Kentucky and Irish epithets on their lips. Lincoln stepped to where his back was against a wall, braced himself, and told the gang he was ready for 'em.

Then Jack Armstrong broke through the front line of the gang, shook Lincoln's hand and told the gang Lincoln was "fair," had won the match, and, "He's the best feller that ever broke into this settlement."

As the Clary's Grove Boys looked Lincoln over they decided he was one of them; he weighed 180 pounds; he was hard as nails; he outran the footracers of Sangamon County; he threw the maul and crowbar farthest; he told the lizard story; he saved a flatboat that looked like a wreck on the Cameron mill-dam. Yes, he belonged; even though he didn't drink whisky nor play cards, he belonged. They called on him to judge their horse-races and chicken fights, umpire their matches, and settle disputes. Their homes were open to him. He was adopted.

Chapter 30

Counting the money a woman paid for dry goods one day, Lincoln found she had paid six and a quarter cents more than her bill; that night he walked six miles to pay it back. Once, finding he weighed tea with a four-ounce weight instead of an eight, he wrapped up another quarter of a pound of tea, took a long walk and delivered to the woman the full order of tea she had paid for. A loafer used the wrong kind of language when women customers were in the store one day; Lincoln had warned him to stop; he talked back. Lincoln took him in front of the store, threw him on the ground and rubbed smartweed in his face. When trade was slack he split rails for Offut and built a pen to hold a thousand hogs.

The two clerks, Lincoln and young Bill Green, slept together on a narrow cot in the back of the store; "when one turned over, the other had to." When a small gambler tricked Bill, Lincoln told Bill to bet him the best fur hat in the store that he (Lincoln) could lift a barrel of whisky from the floor and hold it while he took a drink from the bunghole. Bill hunted up the gambler, made the bet and won it; Lincoln lifted the barrel off the floor, sat squatting on the floor, rolled the barrel on his knees till the bunghole reached his mouth, drank a mouthful, let the barrel down—and stood up and spat out the whisky.

Wildcat money, "rag money," "shinplasters," came across the counter sometimes. The clerk asked a customer, "What kind of money have you?" Once in a while he told about a Mississippi steamboat captain, short of firewood, who steered to a landing-place and offered the man in charge wildcat money for wood; but the owner of the wood said he could only trade "cord for cord," a cord of money for a cord of wood.

Lincoln and John Brewer acted as seconds for Henry Clark and Ben Wilcox when those two settled a dispute with a stand-up and knockdown fight with bare fists. The seconds had washed the blood off the faces and shoulders of the two fighters, when John Brewer, whose head came about as high as Lincoln's elbows, strutted like a bantam rooster up to Lincoln and broke out, "Abe, my man licked yours and I can lick you." Lincoln searched his challenger with a quizzical look and drawled: "I'll fight you, John, if you'll chalk your size on me. And every blow outside counts foul." In the laugh of the crowd even Brewer joined.

Between times, in spare hours, and in watches of the night when sleep came to the town and river, Lincoln toiled and quested for the inner lights of what was known as education and knowledge. Mentor Graham, the schoolmaster, told him there was a grammar at Vaner's house, six miles off; he walked the six miles, brought back the book, burned pine shavings in the blacksmith shop to light a book with a title page saying it held, "English Grammar in Familiar Lectures accompanied by a Compendium embracing a New Systematick Order of Parsing, a New System of Punctuation, Exercises in False Syntax, and a Key to the Exercises, designed for the Use of Schools and Private Learners. By Samuel Kirkham." As he got farther into the book, he had Bill Green at the store hold it and ask him questions. When Bill asked what adverbs qualify, Lincoln replied, "Adverbs qualify verbs, adjectives and other adverbs." When Bill asked "What is a phrase?" the answer came, "A phrase is an assemblage of words, not constituting an entire proposition, but performing a distinct office in the structure of a sentence or of another phrase."

Geography he studied without knowing he was studying geography. The store had calico prints from Massachusetts, tea from China, coffee from Brazil, hardware and stoneware from New York and Pennsylvania, products and utensils from the hands and machines of men hundreds and thousands of miles away. The feel of other human zones, and a large world to live in, connected with the Offut grocery stock.

A literary and debating society was formed in New Salem, with the educated and accomplished people as members, and all others who wished to "advance" themselves. Lincoln stood up for his first speech one evening. And there was close attention. For they all knew this was a joker, the young husky who brought the lizard story to their town, the lusty buck who grappled Jack Armstrong and slammed him for a fall, the pleasant spinner of yarns. He opened his address in a tone of apology, as though he had been thinking over what he was going to say, but he wasn't sure he could put on the end of his tongue the ideas operating in his head. He went on with facts, traced back and picked up essential facts and wove them into an argument, apologized again and said he hoped the argument would stand on its own legs and command respect. His hands wandered out of the pockets of his pantaloons and punctuated with loose gestures some of the decisive propositions, after which his hands slowly and easily slid back into the pantaloons pockets.

Then it came to Lincoln through the talk of friends that James Rutledge, the president of the society, was saying there was "more than wit and fun" in Abe's head; he was already a fine speaker; all he lacked was "culture to enable him to reach a high destiny which was in store for him." Lincoln noticed that Mr. Rutledge looked more keenly into his face and was more kindly in manner.

This had a double interest for the young store-clerk, because he had spent afternoon and evenings in the Rutledge tavern, and he had almost trembled and dark waves ran through him as he had looked wholly and surely into the face of the slim girl with corn-silk hair, Ann Rutledge, the eighteen-year-old daughter of James Rutledge.

When all New Salem laughed and wondered at the way he saved his flatboat when it hung over the dam the spring before, he had glimpsed this slim girl with light corn-silk hair, blue-eyed, pink-fair. Since then he had spoken with her as she sat sewing in a hickory splint chair, a quiet soft bud of a woman.

Some mentioned her as "beautiful"; the Clary's Grove Boys said she "wasn't hard to look at." While her two sisters, Nancy and Margaret, helped their mother with the dishes and the baby, Sarah, Ann did the sewing for all the women and showed new stitches to other New Salem girls who came in.

After the first evening in which Lincoln had sat next to her and found that bashful words tumbling from his tongue's end really spelled themselves out into sensible talk, her face, as he went away, kept coming back. So often all else would fade out of his mind and there would be only this riddle of a pink-fair face, a mouth and eyes in a frame of light corn-silk hair. He could ask himself what it meant and search his heart for an answer and no answer would come. A trembling took his body and dark waves ran through him sometimes when she spoke so simple a thing as, "The corn is getting high, isn't it?"

The name "Ann Rutledge" would come to him and he would pronounce it softly to the shadows in the blacksmith shop where he lay burning wood shavings to light the pages of Kirkham's Grammar. He knew the Rutledges branched back out of South Carolina and the Revolutionary War Rutledges, one of whom signed the Declaration of Independence; their names were in high places; her father was a southern gentleman of the old school; and he, Abe Lincoln, was from the Kentucky "Linkerns" who had a hard time to read and write. His heart would be hurting if he hadn't learned long ago to laugh at himself with a horse laugh.

The Cameron girls, where he boarded, tried to tease him about his long legs, long arms, his horsy ways; and he was always ready to admit he "wasn't much to look at." And as the blue spray from one young woman's eyes haunted him, he felt it was enough to have looked into such a face and to have learned that such an earthly frame as that of Ann Rutledge had been raised out of the breathing dust. He could say, and it was easy to say, "It can't happen that a sucker like me can have a gal like her."

During the winter of 1832, as Abe Lincoln took down calico prints from the shelves of the Offut store and measured off as many yards as the women customers asked for, or as he stepped to the whisky barrels and measured out as many quarts or gallons as the men customers asked for, he had warnings that the business of Denton Offut in New Salem was going to pieces. Offut was often filling his personal pocket-flask at his own barrels of pure and unsurpassed Kentucky rye whisky; he was more often loose with his tongue and its descriptions and predictions. Once it was said, "He talks too much with his mouth." As his cash dwindled and his prospects faded, his eyes became more red, his face more bleary and it was harder for his tongue to persuade men of the rainbow empires he saw beyond the horizon; it was said, "Offut is petering out."

Chapter 31

THE sawmill, the gristmill, the stores, and the post office of New Salem drew customers from different localities, such as Rock Creek, Clary's Grove, Little Grove, Concord, Sand Ridge, Indian Point, New Market, and Athens. The people mostly traced back to Kentucky and Virginia families, but Yankees from New England, Down-easters from New York, Pennsylvania Dutch, and emigrants from the British Isles and from Germany were sprinkled through. From the east of New Salem came the Smoots, Godbys, Rigginses, Watkinses, Whites, Wilcoxes, Clarks, Straders, Baxters; from the north came the Pantiers, Clarys, Armstrongs, Wagoners; from the west the Berrys, Bones, Greens, Potters, Armstrongs, Clarks, Summerses, Grahams, Gums, Spearses, Conovers, Whites, Joneses; from the south the Tibbses, Wisemans, Hoheimers, Hornbuckles, Purkapiles, Mattlings, Goldbys, Wynns, Cogdals.

They were corn-fed. The grain that came in sacks, slung over horses riding to the mill at New Salem dam, was nearly all corn, seldom wheat or rye. The mill ran all the year, and the people ate corn six days in the week and usually on Sunday. Milk and mush, or milk with corn-bread crumbled in it, was the baby food. For the grown-ups there were corndodgers. Two quarts of corn meal were mixed with cold water, a finger of salt thrown in, and into a well-greased skillet the cook put three pones (cakes), giving each pone a pat so as to leave the print of her hand on the bread; the skillet lid was fastened tight and a shovel of coals put on top; then, with hot charcoal over and under, the skillet was put in the fireplace. Sometimes, it was said, the cake came out "so hard that you could knock a Texas steer down with a chunk of it or split a board forty yards off."

On Saturdays young men off the farms came riding in. Horse races, with Abe Lincoln for judge, were run off between the river and Jacob Bale's place. There, too, were the gander pullings. An old tough gander was swung head down from the limb of a tree, with his neck greased slippery. Riders, who paid ten cents for the chance, rode full-speed, and the one who grabbed the gander's neck and pulled the head off, got the bird.

Up the river the boys sometimes took colts to break. They had found that a horse in water over his depth is helpless and will learn to obey. The boys would take one in, several would get onto his back, others would cling to his mane and tail, and by the time they let him come out, he could understand better the language of men speaking to horses.

Some Saturdays, when there were no strangers to pick a fight with, they fought among themselves. A gang of Wolverines from Wolf had taken on drinks in Petersburg one day and were on their horses pulling at each other's shirts, when little Johnny Wiseman called out to Greasy George Miller, "George, you have torn my shirt." "Yes," said George, "and I can tear your hide, too." And the gang got off their horses, formed a ring, and watched Wiseman and Miller fight it out till one had enough.

Between some families there was bitter hate year on year; they called it a "feud" between the families. Once two men met on the New Salem side of the river, spat hate at each other before a crowd of men, and then decided to go alone across the river and fight it out. They crossed over, stripped their clothes, and fought as wolves fight, with claw, tooth, and fang, till men came from over the river, parted them, and made them shake hands. One of the fighters was sick for a year and then died of his wounds and gouges.

And there were people who tried to stop the fighting, horse racing, gambling, and drinking. Through churches, schools, books, temperance societies, and the Government, they tried to correct these habits, and institute industry, thrift, sobriety, and bring into favor the admonition of St. Paul, "Let all things be done decently and in order." As many as fifty men, women, and children on one Sunday were baptized in the Sangamon River. The Methodists, Campbellites, Presbyterians, kept growing; at first the members of a faith met in a dwelling-house; then they had grove camp-meetings, and as they grew in membership they erected churches and sent delegates to state and national conferences, synods, presbyteries.

The most famous of all preachers in southern Illinois then was Peter Cartwright, a Jackson Democrat, a fighting Methodist, a scorner of Baptists, and an enemy of whisky, gambling, jewelry, fine clothes, and higher learning. As he visited along the Sanga-mon River, he would tell anecdotes. "I recollect once to have come across one of these Latin and Greek scholars, a regular graduate in theology. In order to bring me into contempt in a public company he addressed me in Greek. In my younger days I had learned considerable of German. I listened to him as if I understood it all, and then replied in Dutch. This he knew nothing about, neither did he understand Hebrew. He concluded that I had answered him in Hebrew, and immediately caved in, and stated to the company that I was the first educated Methodist preacher he ever saw."

And taking dinner with the governor of the State of Illinois, Cartwright stopped the serving of victuals by saying, "Hold on, Governor, ask the blessing." The governor said he couldn't, he didn't know how. So Cartwright pronounced the blessing—and afterward rebuked the governor for not being a practicing Christian.

One of the oldest and best loved of the Cumberland Presbyterians was Uncle Jimmy Pantier. He was a faith healer said to have cured cases of snake bite and of the bite of a mad dog; he took the patient into a room, rubbed the wound, mumbled unknown words, and sometimes the patient stood up and walked free from evil. Uncle Jimmy took a front seat at church services and would repeat the sermon as fast as the preacher preached it;

Left. A railsplitter's homestead. *Upper.* Store of John McNamar alias McNeil, New Salem, as restored. *Lower.* Lincoln and Berry store, New Salem, as restored.

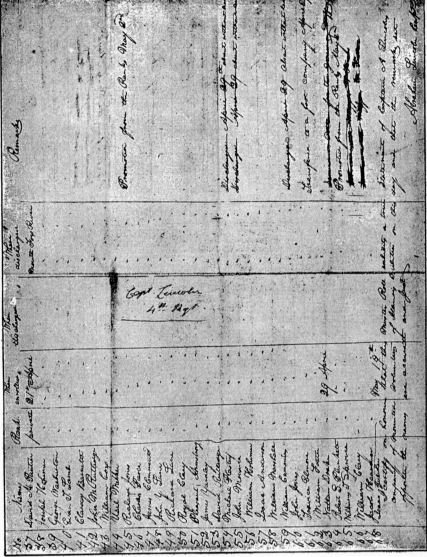

Captain Abraham Lincoln writes the muster roll of his Black Hawk War company in 1832.

he would nod approval or again shake a finger at the preacher and say in an undertone, "You are mistaken," or "That is not so, brother." He had hunted all manner of wild beasts, owned large tracts of land, wore a buckskin fringed shirt, and was a friend and neighbor to all men in the Sangamon River country.

Out around the New Salem neighborhood were men and women known to everybody. The father of James Short, for instance, was pointed out at the Fourth of July picnics as a soldier who had fought in the Revolutionary War; he had become a wild-turkey hunter, and once in blazing away at fifty had killed sixteen turkeys. Another veteran who had served under the Commander-in-Chief George Washington was Daddy Boger, who lived in Wolf and wove bushel baskets out of white oak splints; he would go to town with a basket under each arm, trade his baskets, rest awhile, and then start home.

Farmers who had taken beef hides to the tanyard would bring hides to Alex Ferguson in New Salem, and give Alex the foot measures of the family; William Sampson, a farmer with a big family, used to come after his shoes with a two-bushel sack and take a dozen pairs home. There was Granny Spears of Clary's Grove, who was so often seen helping at houses where a new baby had come; she had been stolen by Indians when a girl and living with them had heard from them how to use herbs and salves; she was a little dried-up woman whose chin and nose pointed out and curved out till they nearly touched each other.

Uncle Johnny Watkins had a flat stone the size of a dollar, given him by a friend in Pennsylvania. The stone was to cure snake bite. It was laid on the place where the snake had bitten, and clung there soaking the poison out. Then the stone was dropped into sweet milk, which soaked the poison out of the stone, and then again the stone was put on the snake bite; this was kept up till all the poison was drawn out. Some said Uncle Johnny's stone was a sure cure for snake bite; others said corn whisky was better.

Here and there the question was asked, "Who is this Abe Lincoln?" In Menard County one story was told about how

Lincoln came to New Salem and what happened. The boys in and around New Salem had sized up Abe, as they called him, and decided to see what stuff he had in him. First, he was to run a foot race with a man from Wolf. "Trot him out," said Abe. Second, he was to wrestle with a man from Little Grove. "All right," said Abe. Third, he must fight a man from Sand Ridge. "Nothing wrong about that," said Abe. The foot-racer from Wolf couldn't pass Abe. The man from Little Grove, short and heavy, stripped for action, ran at Abe like a battering-ram. Abe stepped aside, caught his man by the nape of the neck, threw him heels over head, and gave him a fall that nearly broke the bones. Abe was now getting mad. "Bring on your man from Sand Ridge," he hooted. "I can do him up in three shakes of a sheep's tail, and I can whip the whole pack of you if you give me ten minutes between fights." But a committee from the boys came up, gave him the right hand of fellowship and told him, "You have sand in your craw and we will take you into our crowd."

Thus one story was beginning to be told of how Lincoln had arrived in Illinois and what manner of man he was. Henry Onstott and others were telling the story, just like that.

Chapter 32

IN the winter of 1832, a steamboat was advertised to leave Cincinnati and sail on the four rivers necessary to reach New Salem by water route. Her name was classical, the *Talisman;* her owners hoped she had a magic charm. At the post office in New Salem, at the gristmill and the sawmill, at the wrestling matches, hoedowns, shindigs and chicken fights, the big talk was about that steamboat coming from Cincinnati. She had started down the Ohio going west, she had turned up the Mississippi running north, and in spite of fogs, rain, and floating ice-jams, she had twisted into the channel of the Illinois River and arrived at Beardstown in April.

As a sporting event it was interesting that she came through that far as a winner. As a business event it was important; after she turned into the Sangamon River and unloaded part of a cargo at Springfield, the stores there advertised arrival of goods "direct from the East per steamer *Talisman.*" Store-keepers and land-buyers along the Sangamon were excited; if the steamer made all its connections and its plans worked out, then the Sangamon prairie valley would have direct water-route connections with Cincinnati and Pittsburgh; land and business values would go booming. It was a matter aside that the steamer captain, Bogue, had sent a dude captain to command the boat and this deck officer had worried the women of Springfield by bringing along a flashily dressed woman not his wife, and both of them were drunk and loose-tongued at a reception and dance in the county courthouse tendered by the ladies and gentlemen of Springfield. A lawyer in Springfield wrote in the *Sangamo Journal*, getting some of the atmosphere of the river events in these two verses to be sung to the tune of "Clar de Kitchen":

> Now we are up the Sangamo,
> And here we'll have a grand hurra,
> So fill your glasses to the brim,
> Of whisky, brandy, wine, and gin.
>
> Illinois suckers, young and raw,
> Were strung along the Sangamo,
> To see a boat come up by steam,
> They sure thought it was a dream.

She steamed up the river past New Salem, and tied up at Bogue's Mill. After the high waters of spring had gone down, making a narrower river and shallower channel, she started on her trip downstream. In charge as pilot the boat officers had put Abe Lincoln; he sat by and listened as the boat was stopped at the New Salem dam and the boat officers quarreled with the dam owners, Cameron and Rutledge, about whether they could tear a hole so as to run the boat through. At last a rip was made through the dam, the boat made the passage downstream, and everybody concerned said it must happen never again. The lawyer, writing verses down at Springfield, tried to cover it with this rhyme:

> And when we came to Salem dam,
> Up we went against it jam.
> We tried to cross with all our might,
> But found we couldn't and staid all night.

It was a serio-comic chapter, one of many, in the struggles of western pioneer communities for outlets, transportation, connections with the big outside world, to bring more people to the prairies, and to sell crops and produce to the East in exchange for hardware and nails; there were as yet more houses and wagons held together by wooden pegs and cleats than by iron nails and spikes.

On a ridge the other side of Green's Rocky Branch, a creek south of New Salem, stood a log schoolhouse, where Lincoln occasionally dropped in to sit on a bench and listen to the children reciting their lessons to Mentor Graham, the tall, intellectual, slant-jawed school-teacher. He wanted to find out how much he already knew of what they were teaching in the schools. And he spent hours with Mentor Graham going over points in mathematics, geography, grammar, and correct language. The words "education" and "knowledge" were often on his lips when he talked with thoughtful people; they referred to him as "a learner." He called himself that, "a learner." The gift of asking questions intelligently, listening to the answers, and then pushing quietly on with more questions, until he knew all that could be told to him, or all there was time for—this gift was his. "He could pump a man dry on any subject he was interested in."

In the month of March, 1832, he launched forth into an action that took as much nerve as wrestling Jack Armstrong the year before. He had just passed his twenty-third year, had for the first time in his life read through a grammar, was out of a job, and, except for a few months as a grocery clerk, he still classified as a workingman or a propertyless manual laborer. And he an-

nounced that he was going to run for the office of member of the
legislature of the state of Illinois, to represent the people of
Sangamon County in the chief law-making body of the state.
He told friends he didn't expect to be elected; it was understood
that James Rutledge and others had told him to make the run;
it "would bring him prominently before the people, and in time
would do him good." So he took his first big plunge into politics.

In a long speech, later printed as a handbill, he expressed his
views about navigation of the Sangamon River and railroad
transportation as compared with rivers and canals. Having
floated boats and cargoes some four thousand miles in four years,
he felt at home in discussing water transportation. A railroad
connecting Sangamon County with other parts of Illinois, was, he
said, "indeed, a very desirable object," but the cost, $290,000,
he pointed out, "forces us to shrink from our pleasing anticipa-
tions." Then he analyzed the geography of the Sangamon River,
argued for improvements in its channel, and pledged himself to
support all measures for such improvements.

He declared, "I think I may say, without the fear of being
successfully contradicted, that its navigation may be rendered
completely practicable as high as the mouth of the South Fork."
Next, he called for a strong law to stop "the practice of loaning
money at exorbitant rates of interest," and declared that cases
of greatest necessity may arise when the evasion of laws is jus-
tifiable. His four closing sentences on this subject were: "A law
for this purpose [fixing the limits of usury], I am of the opinion,
may be made without materially injuring any class of people.
In cases of extreme necessity, there could always be means found
to cheat the law; while in all other cases it would have its intended effect. I would favor the passage of a law on this subject
which might not very easily be evaded. Let it be such that the
labor and difficulty of evading it could only be justified in cases
of greatest necessity."

Some of the wishes of his heart were spoken in a paragraph
saying: "Upon the subject of education, not presuming to dictate
any plan or system respecting it, I can only say that I view it

as the most important subject which we as a people can be engaged in. That every man may receive at least a moderate education, and thereby be enabled to read the histories of his own and other countries, by which he may duly appreciate the value of our free institutions, appears to be an object of vital importance, even on this account alone, to say nothing of the advantages and satisfaction to be derived from all being able to read the Scriptures, and other works both of a religious and moral nature, for themselves."

And as connected therewith, he added, "For my part, I desire to see the time when education—and by its means, morality, sobriety, enterprise, and industry—shall become much more general than at present." He closed in a manner having the gray glint of his eyes and the loose hang of his long arms, "If the good people in their wisdom shall see fit to keep me in the background, I have been too familiar with disappointments to be very much chagrined."

Chapter 33

ONE morning in April, when the redbud was speaking its first pink whispers, and the dandelions scattered butter colors in long handfuls over the upland bull-grass, a rider on a muddy, sweating horse stopped in New Salem and gave out handbills signed by the governor of the state calling for volunteer soldiers to fight Indians. The famous old red man, Black Hawk, had crossed the Mississippi River with the best fighters in the Sac tribe, to have a look at land where they and theirs had planted corn, also a burying-ground at the mouth of the Rock River where their fathers and mothers of far back were buried.

For hundreds of years, the Sac tribe had hunted and fished in the rich prairie valley of the Rock River, and among the rocky hills and bluffs of northwestern Illinois; in the time of the falling leaves and the ghost shapes of the hazes of Indian summer, they had piled harvest corn in their little villages, and told the Great

Spirit, Man-ee-do, with songs, dances, and prayers, they were thankful it was a good corn year. After they had seen the frost and wind take the last of the yellow leaves off the haw trees and hazel bushes, they sat around winter fires in their deerskin shelters with buffalo robes to cover them if the blizzard winds blew snow inside; they heard their fathers and mothers tell why the rabbit has a short tail, where the rattlesnake got its rattles and the gopher its stripes, how the first corn and beans came, when and how the wind was first let loose into the sky and sent roaming, who made the foot tracks of that thin snowdrift trail of the Milky Way of stars shining on the winter sky, who makes the war drums of the sky thunderstorms, who the strong and watchful spirits are in other worlds up over and down under the prairie world.

The land of their stories, their corn-planting and harvest, their hunting and fishing places, the burying ground of their fathers who had fought for its possession as against other tribes, had passed from under their feet. In the year 1804, they sold their corner in northwestern Illinois to the United States Government, with the promise on paper, a sheet of writing, saying that they could hunt and could plant corn in Illinois till the lands were surveyed and opened up for settlers.

Then they had taken their horses, women, children, and dogs across the Mississippi River. And now they were saying the white men had broken the written promises; white squatters had come fifty miles past the line of settlement; and more than that, the United States Government could not buy land because land cannot be sold. "My reason teaches me," wrote Black Hawk, "that land cannot be sold. The Great Spirit gave it to his children to live upon. So long as they occupy and cultivate it they have the right to the soil. Nothing can be sold but such things as can be carried away."

Black Hawk was now sixty-seven years old and could look back on forty years as a chief of the Sac tribe. On his blanket was a blood-red hand, the sign that he had killed and scalped an enemy when he was a fifteen-year-old boy. In his time he had straddled his pony and helped other Indian tribes and had joined hands with British soldiers in fighting back the tide of American settlers; he had seen the red man drink the fire water of the white man and then sign papers selling land. Now he felt the Great Spirit, "Man-ee-do! Man-ee-do!" telling him to cross the Mississippi River, scare and scatter the squatters and settlers, and then ambush and kill off all the pale-faced soldiers who came against him.

The voices of his fathers said, "Go." The Fox, Winnebago, Sioux, Kickapoo, and other tribes had sent word they would join him in driving out the palefaces. Already his young men on fast ponies had circled among settlers around Rock Island and along the Rock River, leaving cabins in ashes and white men and women with their scalps torn out. And Black Hawk himself was leading his paint-face warriors, with strings of eagle feathers down their heads and shoulders, with rifles and toma-hawks, up the Rock River valley, telling settlers, "We come to plant corn," saying also, "Land cannot be sold." Copper-faced men had tumbled off their horses with the rifle bullets of white men in their vitals; white men had wakened in their cabins at night to hear yells, to see fire and knives and war-axes burn and butcher.

Across all northern Illinois any strange cry in the night sent shivers of terror to the white people in their lonely cabins. Men on horses picked for speed rode to the governor at Springfield and asked for help.

The Washington government, a thousand miles away, was send-ing the pick of its young regulars to handle the revolt of the Indian chief who would sell land and afterward raise the point that land cannot be sold. Sons of Alexander Hamilton and Daniel Boone were helping young commanders named Albert Sidney Johnston, Zachary Taylor, and Winfield Scott. The white civilization of firearms, printed books, plows, and power-looms was resolved on a no-compromise war with the redskin civiliza-tion of spears, eagle feathers, buffalo dances, and the art and tradition of the ambush.

And now over the rolling prairie and the slopes of timber bottoms along the Rock River, with a measureless blue sky arching over them, the red man and the white man hunted each other, trying to hand crimson death to each other. As they hunted they measured small and were hard to see, each trying to hide from the other till the instant of clash, combat, and death— bipeds stalking each other; only keen eyes could spot the pieces of the action and put together the collective human movement that swerved, struck, faded, came again, and struck, in the reaches of rolling prairie and slopes of timber bottom where the green, rain-washed bushes and trees stood so far, so deep under the arch of a measureless blue sky.

The Indians shaped and reshaped their army as a shadow, came and faded as a phantom, spread out false trails, mocked their enemy with being gone from horizons they had just filled. An ambush was their hope. They tried for it and couldn't get it. The white men had fought Indians before and had solved the theory of warfare by ambush.

By zigzag and crisscross paths, with the Sacs and Foxes the only tribes fighting, Black Hawk was driven north out of Illinois and, in swamp and island battles on the Wisconsin and Bad Axe rivers, his armies were beaten and his last chance taken. On a willow island in the Bad Axe River, his men tried to hold off the whites who came wading in muddy water to their armpits, who took the island and shot the swimming Indians trying to get away to a west shore. Fifty prisoners only were taken, mostly squaws and children.

Black Hawk did not know then that the white men had ambushed him by a white man's way of ambush, that Sioux and Winnebago Indians acting as guides for his army were in the pay of the whites and had led his army on wrong roads. It was these same red men who were paid by the whites to bring him in as a prisoner after he escaped from the battle on the Bad Axe.

And Black Hawk was taken a thousand miles to Washington, where at the White House he met President Andrew Jackson.

They faced each other, a white chief and red chief; both had killed men and known terrible angers, hard griefs, high dangers, and scars; each was nearly seventy years old; and Black Hawk said to Jackson, "I—am—a man—and you—are—another."

And he explained himself: "I took up the hatchet to avenge injuries which could no longer be born. Had I borne them longer my people would have said, 'Black Hawk is a squaw; he is too old to be a chief; he is no Sac.' This caused me to raise the war-whoop. I say no more of it; all is known to you."

Abraham Lincoln had two reasons, if no more, for going into the Black Hawk War as a volunteer soldier. His job as a clerk would soon be gone, with no Offut store to clerk in. And he was running for the legislature; a war record, in any kind of war, would count in politics. He enlisted, and Jack Armstrong and the Clary's Grove Boys said they were going to elect him captain of the company. They ran him against a sawmill owner named Kirkpatrick, who had one time cheated Lincoln out of two dollars.

Kirkpatrick had hired Lincoln to move logs, and agreed that because he didn't supply a tool known as a cant hook, he would pay Lincoln an extra two dollars for doing the heavier work without a cant hook. On pay day the two dollars wasn't paid. Now the Clary's Grove boys said, "We'll fix Kirkpatrick."

The two candidates, Lincoln and Kirkpatrick, stood facing the company of recruited soldiers, and each soldier walked out and stood behind the man he wanted for captain. Lincoln's line was twice as long as Kirkpatrick's.

He was now Captain Lincoln, and made a speech thanking the men for the honor, saying the honor was unexpected, the honor was undeserved, but he would do his best to merit the confidence placed in him. After that he appointed Jack Armstrong first sergeant, with plenty of other sergeants and corporals from among the Clary's Grove boys.

But Kirkpatrick, too, was promoted from the ranks, just nine days after the company was enrolled.

On the muster roll were such names as Obadiah Morgan, Royal Potter, Pleasant Armstrong, Michael Plaster, Isaac Guliher, Robert S. Plunkett, Travice Elmore, Usil Meeker, and Joseph Hoheimer.

Their military unit was officially designated as "Captain Abraham Lincoln's Company of the First Regiment of the Brigade of Mounted Volunteers commanded by Brigadier-General Samuel Whiteside." And though officially they were mounted volunteers, they had no mounts as yet. All were afoot, including Captain Lincoln.

The first military order he gave as captain got the reply, "Go to hell." He knew his company could fight like wildcats but would never understand so-called discipline. Other volunteer companies, also the regular army soldiers and officers, said they were "a hard set of men."

As their captain was drilling them one day with two platoons advancing toward a gate, he couldn't think of the order that would get them endwise, two by two, for passing through the gate. So he commanded, "This company is dismissed for two minutes, when it will fall in again on the other side of the gate." At Henderson River, with horses swimming the stream, it was a camp rule that no firearms should be discharged within fifty yards of the camp. Somebody shot off a pistol inside the camp; the authorities found it was Captain Lincoln; he was arrested, his sword taken away, and he was held under arrest for one day.

At another time his men opened officers' supplies and found a lot of whisky; on the morning after, the captain and his sergeants had a hard time rousing the men out of their blankets; some were dead drunk, others straggled on the march. A court-martial ordered Captain Lincoln to carry a wooden sword two days.

An old Indian rambled into camp one day. The men rushed at him; they were out in an Indian war, to kill Indians. Lincoln jumped to the side of the Indian, showed the men that the old copper-face had a military pass, and said with a hard gleam, "Men, this must not be done; he must not be shot and killed by us." One of the men called Lincoln a coward, as though he were taking advantage of his men as captain. The gleam in his eyes blazed as he stood by the old Indian and quietly told the mob, "If any man thinks I am a coward, let him test it." There was a cry, "Lincoln, you're bigger and heavier than we are," and the answer came like a shot, "You can guard against that—choose your weapons!" And the hot tempers cooled down and came to an understanding that they had an elemental captain who didn't presume on his authority.

The Sangamon County volunteers were part of an army of 1,600 soldiers mobilized at Beardstown, and marched in cold and drizzly weather across muddy roads to Yellow Banks on the Mississippi, then to Dixon on the Rock River. Sometimes the company cooks had nothing to cook and there was growling from the volunteers; one company refused to cross the line out of Illinois toward the north; Colonel Zachary Taylor, in command, made them a speech saying that some of them would probably be congressmen and go to Washington; they were important citizens of Illinois; but he had his orders from Washington to follow Black Hawk and take the Illinois troops along; behind them he had drawn up lines of regular soldiers; ahead of them were the flatboats to cross the river and leave Illinois; they could take their choice. They decided to get into the flatboats and fight Indians rather than the regular soldiers.

About this same time Captain Lincoln went to the regular army officers of his brigade and told them that, representing his men, he had to say that there would be trouble if his men didn't get the same rations and treatment as the regulars. Bill Green remembered Lincoln saying to a regular army officer: "Sir, you forget that we are not under the rules and regulations of the War Department at Washington; we are only volunteers under the orders and regulations of Illinois. Keep in your own sphere and there will be no difficulty, but resistance will hereafter be made to unjust orders. My men must be equal in all particulars—in rations, arms, camps—to the regular army." And this threat of mutiny, voiced by the leader of the Clary's

Grove Boys, resulted in better treatment, so that no mutiny followed.

Marching from Dixon to the Fox River, the little army camped one night, put its horses to grass, ate bread and fried salt pork, and a short hour after dark was ready for sleep. Suddenly the whole army shook with terror, fire streaked the air, drums and fifes sounded, hoots and yells were on all sides—and running horses. A scare had hit the horses as they cropped the prairie summer grass, some unknown fear, and they had broken in a run across the camp, snorting and cavorting, stepping on corporals and privates stretched out for the night sleep. No enemy Indians were in sight or hearing; but a battle-line was formed, every man clutched his gun—and nothing happened, only they lost a night's sleep.

While they were marching across Knox County, a young white sow joined Lincoln's company as a mascot, marched, swam the creeks, foraged for food, and, when greased by the company cook, slipped loose from those who tried to catch and hold her; she stayed through past Paw Paw Grove to the mouth of the Fox River, where she was butchered to make a Clary's Grove holiday.

While Lincoln's company was quartered near a fort, his men noticed that the officers had plenty of milk from two cows, one stub-tailed. And the men planned to borrow or steal one of the cows, and see what the taste of milk was like. One man rode to a slaughterhouse and came back with a long red cow's tail to match the color of the stub-tailed cow, and it was fastened to the stub-tailed cow, which had been taken from the officers. Then along came the fort commander, saying, "If that cow of yours had a stub tail, I should say it was ours." "But she hasn't got a stub tail, has she?" "No, she certainly has not a stub tail." "Well, she isn't yours then."

The lizard story and all the other stories Lincoln could remember were told around the camp-fires. "That reminds me of a feller down in Indianny," he would open up—and go on. At his hip was the wrestler's handkerchief; champions from neighborhoods in all parts of Illinois tried him out. The Clary's Grove Boys said no man in the army could throw him. This reached the ears of a wrestler named Thompson, who had friends.

A championship match was arranged, and Lincoln's friends bet money, hats, whisky, knives, blankets, and tomahawks. On the day of the match, as the two wrestlers tussled in their first feel-outs of each other, Lincoln turned to his friends and said, "Boys, this is the most powerful man I ever had hold of." For a while Lincoln held him off; then Thompson got the "crotch hoist" on him, and he went under, fairly thrown. The match was for the best two out of three falls.

In the second grapple, Lincoln went to the ground pulling Thompson down with him. It looked like a "dog-fall"; the boys from Clary's Grove swarmed around; an all-round fight seemed next on the program of the day's events, when Lincoln raised his head over the crowd, "Boys"; and in the silence that followed, he said: "Boys, give up your bets. If this man hasn't thrown me fairly, he could."

And his men paid their bets to the last dollar or jackknife or blanket—but still went on claiming it was a dog-fall wrestle, and Lincoln could throw any man in the army. At a later time Lincoln told friends about Thompson: "I never had been thrown in a wrestling match until the man from that company did it. He could have thrown a grizzly bear."

Near Kellogg's Grove Lincoln helped bury five men killed in a skirmish the day before. This was the nearest to actual war combat that he came. He and his men rode up a little hill as the red light of the morning sun streamed over the five corpses. Telling about it afterward, he said each of the dead men "had a round spot on the top of his head about as big as a dollar, where the redskins had taken his scalp." He said it was frightful, grotesque, "and the red sunlight seemed to paint everything all over."

When his company of volunteers was mustered out, he enlisted again, serving as a private till his term was up. At Whitewater, Wisconsin, his horse was stolen and he walked to Peoria.

Illinois, resting his long shanks if a comrade on a horse let him ride a mile.

Crops had gone to waste that year of Indian fighting in northern Illinois; food was scarce; Lincoln and the returning soldiers lived on corn meal mixed with water baked over a fire in rolls of bark.

They bought a canoe at Peoria, paddled the Illinois River to Havana, sold the canoe, and walked back to good old New Salem, where there was a dry place to sleep.

So, Abe Lincoln had been through an Indian war without killing an Indian, and having saved the life of one Indian. He had seen deep into the heart of the American volunteer soldier; he had fathomed a thousand reasons why men go to war, march in the mud, sleep in cold rain, and kill when the killing is good. In the depths of his own heart there were slow changes at work; a slant of light had opened when he was elected captain; it had made him glad; it had softened and lit up shadows that floated around him sometimes in a big dark room alone with his thoughts, alone with ghosts and faded dreams that went as far back as Nancy Hanks and the lonely grave where they laid her in early winter so long ago; and, if he could be a captain of men who chose him for captain as they were going to war, he might perhaps have two hopes where before he had had only one or none at all; he might perhaps make a less desperate figure at the door of the house where the girl lived with light corn-silk hair framing a pink-fair face.

He had spent long hours talking with a volunteer from Springfield, Major John T. Stuart, who was a lawyer and had told him he could be a lawyer. Reading a tough grammar through hadn't stumped him; maybe reading law would be the same; maybe he would suddenly find himself a lawyer making speeches to the court and jury, just as he suddenly had found himself captain of a company of Sangamon County volunteers going to an Indian war.

Life seemed to be a series of doors that open and shut and with no telling beforehand which door is to be shut with its

"No! No!" and which door is to swing open with a "Welcome!
I was waiting for you!" .

Chapter 34

ELECTION Day was to be August 6, and, after reaching New
Salem and washing off the Black Hawk War mud from his rawhide boots, Lincoln started electioneering and kept it up till the
ballots were counted. He traveled over Sangamon County with
his long frame wrapped in flax and tow-linen pantaloons, a mixed
jean coat, claw-hammer style, short in the sleeves, and bobtail,
"so short in the tail he could not sit on it"; a straw hat topped
the long frame. To the reading and educated public, a small
fraction, he gave the arguments in his long address, written in
the spring, on Sangamon River navigation, a usury law, and
education.

Mixing with the voters known as "the butcher-knife boys,"
who carried long knives in the belts of their hunting-shirts, he
had the lizard story and others to tell, besides all the fresh
jokes and horsy adventures by night and day in the Black
Hawk War. His first stump speech was at Pappville, when the
auctioneers, Poog & Knap, were selling hogs, bulls, and steers
to the highest bidders.

As Lincoln stepped on a box, ready to say "Gentlemen and
fellow citizens," and make his speech, he saw several fellow
citizens on the edge of the crowd planting their fists in each
other's faces, rushing and mauling. He noticed one of his own
friends getting the worst of it, stepped off the box, shouldered
his way to the fight, picked a man by the scruff of the neck and
the seat of the breeches, and threw him ten feet for a fall. Then
he walked back to his box, stepped up, swept the crowd with
his eyes in a cool way as though what had happened sort of
happened every day, and then made a speech, which Bill Green
recalled afterward in these words:

"Gentlemen and fellow citizens: I presume you all know who

I am. I am humble Abraham Lincoln. I have been solicited by many friends to become a candidate for the legislature. My politics are short and sweet, like the old woman's dance. I am in favor of a national bank. I am in favor of the internal-improvements system and a high protective tariff. These are my sentiments and political principles. If elected, I shall be thankful; if not, it will be all the same."

This was speech as plain and straight as if he were telling a horse-race or chicken-fight crowd which way to pay their bets. In standing for a national bank, high tariff, and internal improvements, he was lining up with the Henry Clay crowd rather than the Jackson men. At that hour in Illinois politics, the large majority of voters were Jackson men, either "whole-hog" or "nominal"; the real regular, hot whole-hog Jackson men said, "All Whigs ought to be whipped out of office like dogs out of a meat house."

In campaigning among farmers, Lincoln pitched hay at the barns and cradled wheat in the fields to show the gang he was one of 'em; at various crossroads he threw the crowbar and let the local wrestlers try to get the crotch hoist on him. At one town a doctor, who had heard about Lincoln, asked Row Herndon, "Can't the party raise no better material than that?" but after hearing a stump speech from the young candidate, he told Herndon, "He is a take-in, knows more than all of them put together."

A judge, Stephen T. Logan, heard his Springfield speech and commented: "He was tall, gawky, rough-looking; his pantaloons didn't meet his shoes by six inches. But I became very much interested in him; he made a very sensible speech. He had novelty and peculiarity in presenting his ideas; he had individuality."

On Election Day Lincoln lost, standing seventh from the highest of twelve candidates.

But in his own neighborhood, the New Salem precinct where the poll-books showed 300 votes cast, he got 277 of those votes.

Chapter 35

LINCOLN was now out of a job, and had his choice of learning the blacksmith trade or going into business. He drifted into business; friends took his promissory notes.

Five stores were running in New Salem, and somehow, after a time, three of the stores, or the wrecks and debts of them, passed into Lincoln's hands.

He and William F. Berry, the son of a Presbyterian minister, bought out the Herndon Brothers and hung up the sign Berry & Lincoln. Also they bought the stock of Reuben Radford's store.

It happened Radford passed threatening words with the Clary's Grove Boys, and one day went away from the store telling his younger brother that if the Clary's Grove Boys came in they should have two drinks apiece and no more. The boys came, took their two drinks, stood the young clerk on his head, helped themselves at the jugs and barrels, wrecked the store, broke the windows, and rode away yelling on their ponies.

When Radford came back and looked the store over, he was discouraged, and sold the stock to Bill Green, who sold it at a profit to Berry & Lincoln. On top of these stocks, they bought out the little grocery of James Rutledge.

As the store of Berry & Lincoln ran on through the fall and winter, business didn't pick up much, and nobody cared much. Berry was drinking and playing poker; Lincoln was reading law and learning Shakespeare and Burns.

Early harvest days came; the oat straw ripened to cream and gold; the farmers bundled the grain in the russet fields. From the Salem hilltop, the prairie off toward Springfield lifted itself in a lazy half-world of harvest haze; the valley of the Sangamon River loitered off in a long stretch of lazy, dreamy haze.

The tawny and crimson sunsets faded off into purple lines of prairie haze; the harvest moon, in a wash of pumpkin colors,

lifted its balloon float over silver prairie haze; in the harvest
days the prairie kept its horizons in haze.

For Abraham Lincoln these were haze and horizon days.
Mornings and afternoons went by with few customers to bother
him. He had never in his life sat so free with so many uninterrupted thoughts, so footloose day after day to turn and look
into himself and find the measure of his personal horizons, to
let dark, vivid roots take deeper root in their clutch and climb
for the sun.

All the insides of him that could be nourished by hard work
and steady chores had seen their days in plenty. Now he was
having, for once, the days that might nourish by letting him sit
still and get at himself, by letting him lean a moment at his door
lintels and feel the flow and the slow drive of his deeper channels.

He had a keen, tenacious memory; he could review, with im-
mensity of fact and impression, all the panoramas and sketches
of his past years; and on this record he could turn the scrutiny
of a developing and sharpening eye of analysis. He was growing
as inevitably as summer corn in Illinois loam, when its stalks
thicken as it lifts ears heavier with juices, and longer with its
dripping tassels of brown silk. Leaning at the porch-posts of a
store to which fewer customers were coming, he was growing,
in silence, as corn grows.

A mover came by, heading west in a covered wagon. He
sold Lincoln a barrel. Lincoln afterward explained, "I did not
want it, but to oblige him I bought it, and paid him half a dollar
for it." Later, emptying rubbish out of the barrel, he found
books at the bottom, Blackstone's "Commentaries on the Laws
of England."

By accident, by a streak of luck, he was owner of the one
famous book that young men studying law had to read first of
all; it had sneaked into his hands without his expecting it; he
remembered his Springfield lawyer-friend, John T. Stuart, saying
the law student should read Blackstone first.

He remembered how he walked barefoot to the courthouse at
Booneville down in Indiana and heard a "distinguished" lawyer

make a speech to a jury with logic, sarcasm, and tears, and how he wished deep wishes he might some day be a lawyer like that. And now the book, Blackstone's Commentaries, had jumped into his hands out of an empty barrel, as if to say, "Take me and read me; you were made for a lawyer."

So he read Blackstone, the book of lectures delivered by Sir William Blackstone at Oxford, England, in 1753. Laws derive their validity from their conformity to the so-called law of nature or law of God. The objects of law are rights and wrongs. Rights are either rights of persons or rights of things. Wrongs are either public or private. And so on, read Lincoln, on the flat of his back on the grocery-store counter, or under the shade of a tree with his feet up the side of the tree. One morning he sat barefoot on a woodpile, with a book. "What are you reading?" asked Squire Godby. "I ain't reading; I'm studying." "Studying what?" "Law." "Good God Almighty!"

Jack Kelso came with gypsy ways, and Shakespeare and Burns on his tongue. He drew Lincoln to him with talk; they were chums. Lincoln hated fishing, yet he went to the river and spent hours listening while Kelso talked and fished. It was said that when other men in New Salem got drunk they wanted to fight, but Jack Kelso recited Shakespeare and Burns. To Kelso those poets were not books so much as faces, breaths of life; their meanings could be found in Sangamon County. Some of Clary's Grove was in the verse of Burns:

> "O Willie, come sell your fiddle,
>   O sell your fiddle sae fine;
> O Willie, come sell your fiddle,
>   And buy a pint o' wine!"

> "If I should sell my fiddle,
>   The warld would think I was mad;
> For monie a rantin' day
>   My fiddle and I hae had."

They sat along quiet river-banks where the waters were living and the fish bit; they asked: "Who am I? What is a man or a woman? Who is God? Where do we go from here?" Kelso watched his bobber and line, and discussed such things from Shakespeare as a king's skull at the bottom of the sea with pearls grown in its green eyesockets, or a queen haunted by a murder, trying to wash a blood-spot off her hand, moaning, "Out, out, damned spot."

And Lincoln, with his heart drawn to this vagabond who fished and drank corn whisky, went his own way; he couldn't see any sport in fishing nor any health, for him, in whisky. Across the road from the store of Berry & Lincoln was the house of Dr. John Allen, a Presbyterian elder who started the first Sunday school in the village, spoke strong words against negro slavery, and organized the Washingtonian Society, whose members pledged themselves to drink no intoxicating liquors.

He was an earnest, obstinate, quiet man, was Dr. Allen; and he drew Lincoln to him, by the way he practiced his religion. On Sundays, the doctor had his horse tied in front of the church, with large double-pocketed medicine saddlebags in his church pew, ready for any sick call. In sleet or snow of winter or in the sweltering dog-days of late summer, he went when his patients called; but all money collected for Sunday visits was put in a separate fund to be given to the church or to poor or sick people; house servants or hired hands on farms, he charged only for the price of the medicine. Other towns knew him as a skilled physician; doctors in Springfield and Jacksonville called him into consultations. Unless a patient was well off with property, Dr. Allen never sent a bill. His smoke-house cured hams and bacons with which farmers had paid their doctor's bills; ox-teams hauled the cured meat to Beardstown to be sent by flatboat to St. Louis and New Orleans. He was scorned, hated, and laughed at by some settlers along the Sangamon because he never let up on his steady, quiet arguments against slavery and whisky.

Even the Hard-shell Baptist church was not then ready to take a stand against whisky. When Mentor Graham, the schoolmaster, joined the temperance reform movement, the church trustees suspended him. Then, to hold a balance and hand out even justice all around, the trustees suspended another church member who had gone blind drunk. This action puzzled one member, who stood up and took from his pocket a quart bottle half full, which he shook till it bubbled, as he drawled: "Brethering, you have turned one member out beca'se he would not drink, and another beca'se he got drunk, and now I wants to ask a question. How much of this 'ere critter does a man have to drink to remain in full fellership in this church?"

Dr. Allen had a close friend in John Berry, the Cumberland Presbyterian preacher, and father of Lincoln's partner in the firm of Berry & Lincoln. Rev. Mr. Berry's arguments against whisky reached deep into Lincoln's life. At this time he was watching what whisky could do in the case of his business partner, who was physicially going to wreck. He could name homes where the children were afraid of the father coming home, where crops had been lost, where the mothers had learned to take comfort from the bottle, and babies were put to sleep with wild corn-juice. Lincoln came to understand why earnest, obstinate men like Dr. Allen and Rev. Mr. Berry should go on as they did, never letting up on their argument against whisky.

Whisky seemed to be making his business partner useless. Lincoln ran the store alone. The name of "Honest Abe" was sticking. One winter morning a farmer, Harvey Ross, asked for a pair of buckskin gloves. Lincoln threw him a pair of gloves and said they were dogskin, good gloves, and 75 cents for the pair. Ross said he never had heard of dogskin gloves; they had always been deerskin. He asked if Lincoln was sure they were dogskin. The answer was: "I'll tell you how I know. Jack Clary's dog killed Tom Watkins's sheep, and Tom Watkins's boy killed the dog; old John Mounts tanned the dogskin, and Sally Spears made the gloves. That's the way I know they're dogskin."

Business dropped off; customers got scarcer. Berry & Lincoln took out a license in March, 1833, to keep a tavern and sell retail liquors. Their license specified that they could sell whisky at 12½ cents a pint, and French brandy, peach and apple brandies,

Holland and domestic gins, and wine and rum, at various other prices.

He was learning to be careful about signing notes to pay stipulated sums at future dates. While he was jingling in his jeans the forty dollars paid him for piloting the steamer *Talisman*, he signed with Nelson Alley a note for $104.87½—"for the benefit of the creditors of V. A. Bogue," the note read. A Springfield lawyer, George Forquer, sued and won judgment against Lincoln and Alley that year of 1833.

In May, Lincoln was appointed postmaster; no Democrat cared for the office; but Lincoln wanted to read the newspapers. The four-horse "mud-wagon" brought most of the mail; the postmaster carried all the letters in his hat till they were called for. He came to know people always asking for a letter, and acting as though the Government was holding back a letter from them. It was here, a report ran, he met the Irishman who asked, "Is there a letter for me?" "What is the name?" "Oh, begorry, an' ye'll find the name on the letter!" He read the newspapers, kept in touch with St. Louis and Louisville and Cincinnati. "Howdy, Jack?" he would say to Jack Kelso, tell him the news, and then hear Kelso talk about Shakespeare and Burns. Some days he locked up the store for a couple of hours on an afternoon to go down to the river and listen while Kelso fished and talked.

He read in newspapers such oddities as why Lieutenant-governor William Kinney had used the little "i" in his writings; Kinney said that Governor Edwards had used up all the capital "I's," leaving him only the small "i's." And when Kinney ran for governor and his friends were mentioning his humble beginnings, the *Kaskaskia Democrat* queried and replied, "Why should Mr. Kinney be elected governor? Because he plowed in his shirt-tail."

As postmaster of New Salem Lincoln either was too careless or didn't have the heart to force newspaper subscribers to pay postage in advance, as the Government regulations required. And when George Spears sent postage money to Lincoln by a

messenger somewhat loaded with corn juice, he wrote a note
telling Lincoln he wanted a receipt. Lincoln replied he was
"surprised" at the request. "The law requires Newspaper postage to be paid in advance and now that I have waited a full
year you choose to wound my feelings by intimating that unless
you get a receipt I will probably make you pay again."

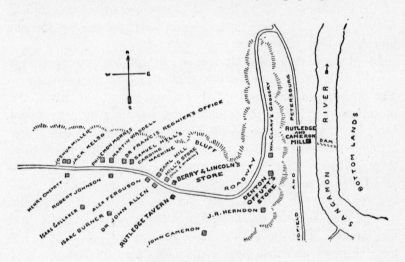

Map of New Salem.

Drawn by J. McCann Davis and loaned by Ida M. Tarbell

Chapter 36

MORE and more often it happened the store of Berry & Lincoln
was locked for the day; customers went to other stores; Lincoln
took jobs splitting fence-rails, worked at the sawmill, harvested
hay and oats, and helped out when there was a rush of customers at the store of Samuel Hill. He now saw that honesty
and hard work are not enough in order to win respect as a merchant; he didn't have the trader's nose for business; he lacked
the gumption to locate where trade had to come and then to
use customers so they would come back. The store was a goner.
"It winked out."

And Lincoln was reading books about famous ruins of large enterprises, Volney's "The Ruins of Empire" and Gibbon's "The Decline and Fall of the Roman Empire." Also, Thomas Paine's "The Age of Reason." He was out of a job, with debts. Misery and melancholy he had learned to stand against; he could chase them away with a few comic stories told to the boys. But debts —they wouldn't laugh away.

No matter how he forgot himself and laughed through his lean ribs with the ins and outs of new gay stories—after all was over and he was alone, there were the debts. They were little rats, a rat for every dollar, and he could hear them gnawing in the night when he wanted to sleep.

He had one possession: many friends. One of them was John Calhoun, a Jackson Democrat, surveyor of Sangamon County, who sent word he would like to appoint Lincoln his deputy. Lincoln walked twenty miles to Springfield, and fixed the point clear with Calhoun that he could speak as he pleased, and was not tied up politically, if he took the job.

As he walked back to New Salem he saw ahead of him a tough piece of work to husk out; he had to transform his blank ignorance of the science and art of surveying into a thorough working knowledge and skill.

As he hiked along the low hills of prairie overlooking the Sangamon, it happened that Mrs. Calhoun, back in Springfield, was telling her husband she had never seen such an ungodly-looking gawk as the caller that day. He puzzled her. To which her husband offered the reply, "For all that, he is no common man."

With a copy of "The Theory and Practice of Surveying," by Robert Gibson, published in 1814, Lincoln hunted up Mentor Graham, the schoolmaster, and settled down to gain the knack of surveying. Many nights Graham's daughter woke up at midnight, she told friends, and saw Lincoln and her father by the fire, figuring and explaining.

On some nights Lincoln worked alone till daylight. The sleep he took was in short stretches. The work wore him down.

Bowling Green and Jack Armstrong told him to take care of himself.

From decimal fractions the book ran on into logarithms, the use of mathematical instruments, trigonometry, operating the chain, circumferentor, surveying by intersections, changing the scale of maps, leveling, and the General Method, also the Pennsylvania Method, for mensuration of areas.

Lincoln was fagged, with sunken cheeks and bleary, red eyes; friends said he looked exactly like a hard drinker on a spree that has lasted two or three weeks.

On page 300, the book said, "There are three different Horizons, the apparent, the sensible, and the true. The apparent or visible Horizon is the utmost apparent view of the sea or land. The sensible is a plane passing through the eye of an observer, perpendicular to a plumb line hanging freely. And the true or rational Horizon is a plane passing through the center of the Earth, parallel to the sensible Horizon." Also, "The Ecliptic is that great circle in which the annual revolution of the Earth round the Sun is performed."

"You're killing yourself," good people told Lincoln; and among themselves they whispered it was too sad; he would break under the load and come forth shattered.

In six weeks' time, however, Lincoln had mastered his books, the chain, the circumferentor, the three Horizons, and Calhoun put him to work on the north end of Sangamon County. The taste of open air and sun healed him as he worked in field and timberland with compass and measurements. Winter came on and his fibers toughened.

In January, 1834, Russel Godbey paid him two buckskins for work done. As there was no other job ahead then, he took them to Hannah Armstrong, the wife of Jack, and while Lincoln rocked the baby's cradle and told the Armstrong children stories to chuckle over, Hannah sewed the buckskins on the inner, lower part of his trousers, "foxed his pants," as the saying was, so that between ankles and knees he would have leather protection in briers and brush. He and Hannah sort of adopted each other;

he was one of her boys; she talked to him with snapping lights
in her eyes; she reminded him of Sally Bush, though she had
a different religion. Jack Armstrong and Jack Kelso went along
as helpers on surveying trips; one of the Jacks could tell about
all the fights and wrestling matches for years back in that part
of Illinois; the other Jack was full of Shakespeare and Burns.

For his surveying Lincoln was paid three dollars a day—when
he worked. Yet he saw that even with the best of luck it would
be a long time before he could pay the $1,100.00 he was owing.
Berry, his store partner, was dead, was through battling with
whisky; a Rock Creek farmer rode in one day with the news.
And the Trent brothers, who had bought with promissory notes
what was left of the Berry & Lincoln store, had gone away without leaving their next address; the few groceries in the store were
taken by constables in behalf of creditors. So Lincoln at twenty-
four years of age had on his hands the airy wrecks and the cold,
real debts of three bankrupt stores.

He could go away from New Salem by night, leaving no future
address, as the Trent brothers did, as Offut had done, as many
others did on the frontier. Or he could stay and stick it out.

He was sued for ten dollars owing on his horse; a friend let
him have the ten dollars; the horse was saved. He was sued
again, and his horse, saddle, bridle, surveying instruments were
taken away. James Short, a Sand Ridge farmer, heard about
it; he liked Lincoln as a serious student, a pleasant joker, and a
swift cornhusker; he had told people, when Lincoln worked for
him, "He husks two loads of corn to my one."

Short went to the auction, bought in the horse and outfit for
$125.00, and gave them back to Lincoln, who said, "Uncle
Jimmy, I'll do as much for you sometime." Lincoln had stayed
away from the auction, too sad to show up. And when Short
came along with his horse, saddle, bridle, compass, and all, it
hit him as another surprise in his life.

He noticed these surprises kept coming regularly into his
young life. It was a surprise when Gentry asked him to take
a flatboat down the Ohio and Mississippi rivers, when Offut

picked him to clerk in a new store, when the Sangamon River boys elected him captain for the Black Hawk War, when James Rutledge and others told him he ought to run for the legislature, when New Salem voted for him and it was nearly unanimous, and again now when Uncle Jimmy Short, without saying anything about it beforehand, came in at the last dark moment with his horse and surveying outfit.

It seemed as though he planned pieces of his life to fit together into personal designs as he wanted. Then shapes and events stepped out of the unknown and kicked his plans into other lines than he expected, and he was left holding a sack, wondering just what it was he wanted.

When dreams came in sleep, he tried to fathom their shapes and reckon out events in the days to come. Beyond the walls and handles of his eyesight and touch, he felt other regions, out and away in the stuff of stars and dreams.

If a blizzard stopped blowing and the wind went down, with the white curve of a snow floor over Salem Hill looking up to a far blue scoop of winter stars blinking white and gold, with loneliness whispering to loneliness, a man might look on it and feel organization and testimony in the movement of the immense, relentless hubs and sprockets on the sky.

Chapter 37

As Lincoln boarded round here and there in New Salem, his days and hours were filled with many different occupations besides the work of surveying and politics. As postmaster he was the first in the village to receive and to read the *Sangamo Journal*, published at Springfield, the *Louisville Journal*, the *St. Louis Republican*, and the *Cincinnati Gazette*. He wrote to a firm of publishers: "Your subscriber at this place, John C. Vance, is dead; and no person takes the paper from the office."

He dipped into popular and trashy fiction such as Mrs. Lee Hentz's novels, and stories having such titles as "Cousin Sally

Dillard," "Becky Williams' Courtship," "The Down-Easter and the Bull." He was at the barbecue pit when there were roastings, at the ridge south of the old Offut store when there were

New Salem Ills
Nov 3 1835

Messrs
Your subscriber at this place
John C Vance, is dead; and no
person takes the paper from the
office
Respectfully,
A. Lincoln P.M

Blair & Rives. 3

Postmaster Lincoln notifies publishers their subscriber is dead and no person takes the paper.

gander pullings, at the horse races at the west end of the main street, the horses starting or finishing in front of the Berry & Lincoln store. He played marbles with boys and took a hand often at pitching big round flat stones in a game played like quoits or horseshoes.

He worked in cornfields and timbers to earn money needed on top of his surveyor's fees and postmaster's pay. In an off hour one day he took his jackknife and cut on one side of his ax handle "A. Lincoln" and on the other side "New Salem 1834."

He saw Bab McNab's fancy red rooster get scared of another cock it was pitted against and run rings around the pit, till Bab got so disgusted he jumped in, grabbed the bird by the neck, and threw it off into the air so it lit on a pile of fresh-cut saplings. There the rooster stood up, stretched its neck, flapped its wings, and let out a long cock-a-doodle-doo. And Bab McNab yelled, "Yes, you little son of a gun, you're great on dress parade, but you're not worth a damn in a fight." Surveying near Bobtown, Lincoln put up one evening at the McHenry home, Mrs. McHenry being Nancy, a sister of Jack Armstrong. Her three-year-old girl climbed Lincoln's knee; he asked the mother what was the girl's name; the mother said she hadn't been named yet, and Lincoln could name her, if he pleased. He said, "I name you Parthenia Jane."

When called on, and at times without being called on, Lincoln recited for a crowd of men drying their mittens at the fireplace in the store on a winter afternoon, the ballad of "How St. Patrick Came to Be Born on the Seventeenth of March." Two of its verses were:

> On the eighth day of March, as some people say,
> St. Patrick at midnight he first saw the day;
> While others assert 'twas the ninth he was born—
> 'Twas all a mistake—between midnight and morn.
>
> Some blamed the baby, some blamed the clock;
> Some blamed the doctor, some the crowing cock,
> With all these close questions sure no one could know
> Whether the babe was too fast or the clock was too slow.

One winter morning he saw the boy, Ab Trent, chopping up the logs of an old stable that had been pulled down. Rags wrapped around Ab's feet took the place of shoes; he told Lincoln he was earning a dollar to buy shoes. Lincoln told him to run to the store and warm his feet. And after a while Lincoln came to the store, handed the boy his ax, and told him to collect the dollar and buy shoes; the wood was chopped. And it happened later that Ab, who was a Democrat, told his friends he was going to vote for Abe Lincoln for the legislature.

And when the poll-books showed that Ab Trent had voted against Lincoln, Ab came to Lincoln with tears in his eyes and said his friends got him drunk and he voted against the way he intended.

One of his best friends was the justice of the peace, Bowling Green, who carried a little round paunch of a stomach in front of him, and was nicknamed "Pot." The squire had a smooth, translucent, fair skin, and an original sense of justice. When John Ferguson sued Jack Kelso, claiming a hog, Ferguson put on the stand two witnesses who swore the hog belonged to him, while Kelso swore it was his. Squire Green gave his decision in favor of Kelso, saying: "The two witnesses we have heard have sworn to a damned lie. I know this shote, and I know he belongs to Jack Kelso."

Bowling Green was acquainted with the statutes and Lincoln spent hours in the Green home talking about the statutes. Nancy Green, the squire's wife, cooked hot biscuit smothered in butter and honey, doughnuts, and cookies, to eat with buttermilk, apples, and sweet cider.

Another friend was Dr. Charles Chandler, who was so busy practicing medicine and stocking his farm that he didn't have time to register a Government title to his land over where he had a cabin and horses in Cass County. A stranger named English, buying land tracts for a Philadelphia capitalist, took dinner with Dr. Chandler and made himself at home.

Late in the afternoon, a few hours after English had gone away, word came to Chandler that English was heading for Springfield to register for himself Dr. Chandler's two 80-acre tracts. Dr. Chandler got on a horse, skirmished among neighbors and raised the cash needed to file his land claims, and started about midnight for Springfield.

In the morning he was twelve miles from Springfield and his horse played out. He was afoot leading the nag when Abe Lincoln on a fresh fast horse came along, listened to a few words from the doctor, jumped off his horse, shortened his stirrups, changed saddlebags on the two horses, and cried: "There, doctor, mount my horse, and leave me yours, and don't let any grass grow under his feet on the way. Leave him at Herndon's stables, where I will have yours sometime today and we'll swap back. I want to get you and your pill-bags and the specie into the land office ahead of that shark. No thanks—just go." So Chandler's title to two 80-acre tracts of land was saved.

A case came up before Squire Samuel Berry at Concord one afternoon which Lincoln heard about, so that he left his surveying and acted as the lawyer for a girl in a bastardy case. Several elderly women whom he knew were put on the witness stand and felt awkward and flustered till Lincoln put them at ease by calling them "Aunt Polly" or "Aunt Sally" and the given names their homefolks used. In his address to the court, Lincoln's speech likened a man's character in such a case to a piece of white cloth, which, though it became soiled, yet could be washed and hung out in the sun, and by the aid of water, sun, and air would become white again; whereas the character of the girl, who was no more to blame, and in most instances not nearly so much to blame as the man, was like a broken and shattered bottle or glass vase, which could not be restored or made whole again.

Surveying the town of Petersburg, he laid out one street crooked. If he had run it straight and regular, the house of a Jemima Elmore and her family would have been in the street. She was the widow of an old friend who had been a private in Lincoln's company during the Black Hawk War and was farming on a little tract of land with her children.

In those New Salem days of Abraham Lincoln there were some who said he would be a great man, maybe governor of the

Flat stone found by William Green near Lincoln's store in New Salem. The lettering chipped in reads, "A. Lincoln and Ann Rutledge were betrothed here July 4, 1833."

From the Barrett Collection

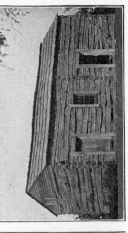

Left. Down the Sangamon River from New Salem hilltop; Lincoln arrived here in a canoe, took a flatboat from here to New Orleans, and twice piloted a steamboat around this bend. *Upper.* Ravine where old-time road led past Lincoln and Berry store. *Center.* Offut store, where Lincoln clerked; he outwrestled Jack Armstrong on a level green alongside. *Right.* Rutledge Tavern, where he came to know Ann Rutledge.

Photographs by Herbert Georg of Springfield, Ill.

state, anyhow a great lawyer. And there were others who looked on him as an athlete, an ordinary man, and a homely, awkward joker who felt sad sometimes and showed it.

When he kept store he often held an open book in his hand, reading five or ten minutes, closing the book to wait on a customer or to tell a story, then opening the book and reading in spite of the babblings of the men drying their mittens by the fire. He was seen walking the main street of New Salem reading a book, and, if attracted by a page or paragraph, shuffling slowly to a standstill, pausing for contemplation.

And whereas in former days in Indiana he had hunted company, hungry for human talk and thought of any kind, he found himself now drifting away from people; days came oftener when he wanted hours alone to think his way through the circles and meshes around him. The look on his face, "solemn as a papoose," held in these moods. Part of its tone was in the line of his early verse, "Time, what an empty vapor 'tis!" It was noticed among men that he had two shifting moods, the one of the rollicking, droll story and the one when he lapsed into a gravity beyond any bystander to penetrate.

At one time, while storekeeping, he slept on the counter of the store because the Rutledge tavern was overcrowded. He wore flax and tow-linen pantaloons, no vest, no coat, and one suspender, a calico shirt, tan brogans, blue yarn socks, and a straw hat bound round with no string or band.

The Onstotts took over the Rutledge tavern and had Lincoln for a boarder a year or two. And one of the Onstotts said Lincoln never drank liquor of any kind, never smoked nor chewed tobacco, and the nearest he came to swearing was when, excited, one time he had blurted out, "By Jing!" That was his behavior in the Onstott tavern. He didn't fish or shoot. Though he was the champion wrestler and crowbar thrower, one of his favorite sports was playing marbles with boys.

One morning Lincoln asked Mentor Graham, the schoolteacher, "Graham, what do you think of the anger of the Lord?" to which Graham replied, "I believe the Lord never was angry and never will be; His loving-kindness endures forever; He never changes." Lincoln then brought out a manuscript, carefully written, arguing that God never gets excited, mad, or angry. It quoted from the Bible, "As in Adam all men die, even so in Christ shall all be made alive," and defended the idea of universal salvation.

At that time it was preached from nearly all pulpits that the earth is flat, and below the earth is a pit of fire and brimstone into which an angry God will cast sinners. Against this doctrine of eternal punishment by a God of wrath Lincoln directed the argument of his manuscript. To friends he quoted the line from Burns's "Holy Willie's Prayer": "What! Send one to heaven and ten to hell?" And he had a clear memory of an old man named Glenn over in Indiana who used to say, "When I do good, I feel good; when I do bad, I feel bad."

His voice was tenor in pitch, and managed tunes in a reciting, singsong tone. A song titled "Legacy" was a favorite with groups who heard him substitute his own words "old gray" for the regular words "red grape" in the hymn. The lines were:

> When in death I shall calm recline,
>   Oh, bear my heart to my mistress dear.
> Tell her it lived on smiles and wine,
>   Of brightest hue while it lingered here.
>
> Bid her not shed one tear of sorrow
>   To sully a heart so brilliant and light;
> But balmy drops of the red grape borrow,
>   To bathe the relict from morn till night.

Jack and Hannah Armstrong, out at Clary's Grove, took him in two and three weeks at a time when he needed a place to eat and sleep. Hannah said, "Abe would come out to our house, drink milk, eat mush, corn-bread and butter, bring the children candy, and rock the cradle while I got him something to eat. I foxed his pants, made his shirts. He would tell stories, joke people, boys and girls at parties. He would nurse babies—do anything to accommodate anybody."

Jack once nailed up a man in a barrel and set the barrel rolling from the top of Salem Hill to the river bank three hundred yards down; and once he nailed up two men, the barrel ran crooked, jumped off an embankment and nearly killed the two men inside. Another time, as he was nailing up old man Jordan, a hard drinker, he explained to Abe Lincoln, "Old man Jordan *agreed* to be rolled down the hill for a gallon of whisky."

Sometimes, Lincoln could tease or coax Jack into another line of fun. When a stranger backed up to a woodpile, took a club and knocked Jack to the ground, there seemed to be a mean fight on hand between the two men. Jack told Lincoln he had called the man a liar and a coward, and Lincoln asked, "If you were a stranger in a strange place and a man called you a liar and a coward, what would you do?" "Whip him, by God!" "Then this man has done no more to you than you would have done to him," Lincoln explained. And Jack insisted on the stranger having a drink with him.

A little frontier drama took place one day which A. Y. Ellis told about in this way: "I remember of seeing Mr. Lincoln out of temper and laughing at the same time. It was at New Salem. The boys were having a jollification after an election. They had a large fire made of shavings and hemp stalks; and some of the boys made a bet with a fellow I shall call 'Ike,' that he couldn't run his bobtail pony through the fire. Ike took them up, and trotted his pony back about one hundred yards, to give him a good start, as he said. The boys all formed a line on either side, to make way for Ike and his pony. Presently here he come, full tilt, with his hat off; and just as he reached the blazing fire, Ike raised in his saddle for the jump straight ahead; but pony was not of the same opinion, so he flew the track, and pitched poor Ike into the flames. Lincoln saw it and ran to help, saying, 'You have carried this thing far enough.' I could see he was mad, though he could not help laughing himself. The poor fellow was considerably scorched about the head and face. Jack Armstrong took him to the doctor, who shaved his head to fix him up, and put salve on the burn. I think Lincoln

was a little mad at Armstrong, and Jack himself was very sorry
for it. Jack gave Ike next morning a dram, his breakfast, and
a skin cap, and sent him home."

Ellis kept a store where Lincoln helped out on busy days.
"He always disliked to wait on the ladies," said Ellis. "He
preferred trading with the men and boys, as he used to say.
He was a very shy man of ladies. On one occasion, when we
boarded at the same log tavern, there came an old lady and her
son and three stylish daughters, from the state of Virginia, and
stopped there for two or three weeks; and during their stay, I
do not remember of Mr. Lincoln ever eating at the same table
when they did. I thought it was on account of his awkward
appearance and his wearing apparel."

When Ellis was asked about the first time he saw Lincoln, he
said, "I was out collecting back tax for General James D. Henry.
I went from the tavern down to Jacob Bale's old mill, and then
I first saw Lincoln. He was sitting on a saw log talking to Jack
and Rial Armstrong and a man by the name of Hoheimer. I
shook hands with the Armstrongs and Hoheimer, and was conversing with them a few minutes, when we were joined by my
old friend, George Warburton, pretty tight as usual; and he
asked me to tell him the old story about Ben Johnson and Mrs.
Dale's blue dye, and so on, which I did. And then Jack Armstrong said, 'Lincoln, tell Ellis the story about Governor Sichner,
his city-bred son, and his nigger Bob,' which he did, with several
others, by Jack's calling for them. I found out then that Lincoln was a cousin of Charley Hanks of Island Grove. I told
him I knew his uncle, old Billy Hanks, who lived up on the
North Fork of the Sangamon River. He was a very sensible
old man; he was father to Mrs. Dillon on Spring Creek; and
Charley, Billy, and John were his sons; they were all low-flung,
could neither read nor write."

Chapter 38

THE Rutledge family was serious, pious, though they lived in
a tavern, where travelers and strangers ate and talked around
a big table, and gathered afterward around the big fireplace
with talk not always serious nor pious. In the big loft of the
cabin they had stowed away a dozen sleepers of a night. The
Rutledges were not isolated people. They had plenty of company. Yet they were earnest, sober, a little somber.

They sang from a book, "The Missouri Harmony," printed
and published by Morgan and Sanxay in Cincinnati. It was
"a collection of psalm and hymn tunes, and anthems, from
eminent authors: with an introduction to the grounds and rudi-
ments of music," and a supplement of "admired tunes and
choice pieces of sacred music."

The preface to the book declared, "Too often does a disgraceful silence prevail in our churches; too often are dissonants and
discords substituted for the charms of melody and harmony."
It rebuked those who come "into the house of God and sit either
with their mouths shut, or grinning at some vain and idle speculation, while the devout worshipers are singing the praises of
their Redeemer." An eminent writer was quoted, "The worship in which we most resemble the inhabitants of heaven, is the
worst performed on earth."

Learners were instructed: "Each one should sing so soft, as
not to drown the teacher's voice; if the teacher's voice cannot
be heard, it cannot be imitated." A good voice may be "soon
much injured by singing too loud." The advice was italicized:
"A cold or cough, all kinds of spirituous liquors, violent exercise,
bile upon the stomach, long fasting, the veins overcharged with
impure blood, &c., &c., are destructive to the voice; a frequent
use of spirituous liquors will speedily ruin the best voice."

Lincoln and Ann Rutledge could read the learned admonition:
"There should not be any noise indulged while singing (except

the music) as it destroys entirely the beauty of the harmony, and renders the performance (especially to learners) very difficult; and if it is designedly promoted, is nothing less than a proof of disrespect in the singers to the exercise, to themselves who occasion it, and to the Author of our existence."

A dark and moving poetry and music from the religion of the people of Europe two and three hundred years back reached out to take the hearts of the pioneers in the log-cabin tavern, singing by candlelight there in New Salem. They could actually turn to page 65 and find the hymn named "New Salem," with its words:

> O Thou in whose presence my soul takes delight,
>   On whom in affliction I call,
> My comfort by day, and my song in the night,
>   My hope, my salvation, my all.

The human family has a heavy load, "hills of guilt" to carry, during tedious rounds of sluggish years, said the lines of songs. Man is a pilgrim across scorching sands, longing for a cooling stream; a wandering sheep in a howling wilderness, seeking rivers of salvation and pleasant fields of paradise. Shaped in a case of clay, man lives in a babel of loose tongues till the case falls off him, the captive is free, and he is ready to go to hell or to Zion. "In the worship of my God I'll spend my breath," ran one line, and a couplet:

> The Jewish wintry state is gone,
> The mists are fled, the spring comes on.

There was a promise in the tone of Abe Lincoln telling **Ann** Rutledge of one attribute of God. It was sung:

> While the lamp holds out to burn,
> The vilest sinner may return.

Englishmen who knew the sea and had been fascinated in contemplating the sea, had written the hymn, "Judgment," of how on the Last Day,

> The earth was from her center tossed
> And mountains in the ocean lost,
> Torn piecemeal by the roaring tide.

"To spend one day with God on earth exceeds a thousand days of mirth." The sky, the unfathom'd deep, the boisterous sea, were a stage whereon man saw the lighted clouds of chariots, storms moving with wings; the heavens had curtains, in the spacious arrangements of the Lord.

In the presence of God's great and terrible panoramas, man was a little trembling shadow who should sing softly:

> Teach me the measure of my days,
>   Thou Maker of my frame,
> I would survey life's narrow space,
>   And learn how frail I am.

A time would come when "the rolling years shall cease to move," when the sky would be taken apart and wrapped as a parchment. In the Worthington hymn on page 62, the recurring lines were, "How feeble is our mortal frame!" and "What dying worms are we, what dying worms are we!" The Windsor hymn on page 66 struck a shrill note:

> My God, how many are my fears,
>   How fast my foes increase!
> Their number how it multiplies!
>   How fatal to my peace.

Flashes of eloquence jutted forth, as in the line, "Teach me some melodious sonnet, sung by flaming tongues above." Many of the pieces were occupied with the fact that man's life is a short and momentary breath in the world of flesh.

> Death, like an overflowing stream,
>   Sweeps us away; our life's a dream,
> An empty tale, a morning flow'r,
>   Cut down and withered in an hour.

Beauty, youth, wealth are phantoms of folly. They become ripe corn that an inevitable later phantom cuts down with a sickle. "Let us live so in youth that we blush not in age." The body is feeble, wanders, faints, dies, is released from this vale of tears. "Vain, delusive world, adieu!" So soon will death disrobe us all.

There was occasional jubilation, joy over moments to come when life was over on earth, when the scroll of time was rolled and the region of the timeless, the eternal, was entered. Many a line in "The Missouri Harmony" songbook had the testimony of hands strengthened for living through reverence and humility toward the regions of the invisible, the inscrutable. "Through faith, the glorious telescope, I viewed the worlds above," ran one extravagant metaphor. And there was something to think about in the line, "Not to our worthless names is glory due."

And though Abraham Lincoln had found it easy to master Kirkham's Grammar, saying it wasn't much of a science, and he would like to tackle another one as easy, he made no comment about having mastered "The Missouri Harmony Songbook." Many a line in it, as he held it in his hands at the Rutledge place, had more than a casual reading, lines singing of world illusions, of the dissolving of strong frameworks, of proud men to be "light as a puff of empty air," of the "dear sov'reign whirl of seasons," the melting phantasmagoria of the years. Of these he was kith and kin.

Chapter 39

WHEN the Illinois legislature met at Vandalia in 1834, one of the sitting members was Abraham Lincoln. He was twenty-five years old, holding his first elective political office, and drawing three dollars a day pay, with privileges of ink, quills, and stationery. The four highest candidates from Sangamon County in the voting had stood: Dawson, 1,390; Lincoln, 1,376; Carpenter, 1,170; Stuart, 1,164. On being elected Lincoln went to a friend, Coleman Smoot, who was farming near New Salem, and asked Smoot, "Did you vote for me?" and on Smoot answering "Yes," he said, "I want to buy some clothes and fix up a little, and I want you to loan me $200.00." Therefore he sat at his desk in the state capitol wearing bran-new blue jeans.

He was now away from New Salem and Ann Rutledge. And the girl Ann Rutledge had been engaged to marry John McNeil, the storekeeper and farmer who had come to New Salem and in five years acquired property worth $12,000.00. In money and looks McNeil was considered a "good catch"; and he and Ann Rutledge were known as betrothed, when McNeil started on a trip East. In a short time, as soon as he could visit his father and relatives in New York, he would come back and claim his bride. This was the promise and understanding.

And it was known to Lincoln, who had helped McNeil on deeds to land holdings, that McNeil's real name was McNamar. This was the name put in the deeds. He said he had come West taking another name in order that he might make his fortune without interference from his family back East. He had, for convenience, kept his name off election poll books, and never voted.

McNamar had been away for months and sent few letters, writing from Ohio that he was delayed by an attack of fever, writing again from New York that his father had died and he could not come West till the estate was settled. Thus letters came, with excuses, from far off. Whisperers talked about it in New Salem. Had his love died down? Or was a truthful love to be expected from a man who would live under a false name?

Days were going hard for the little heart under the face framed in auburn hair over in New Salem, as Lincoln had his thoughts at his desk in the capitol at Vandalia. She had sung to him, clear-voiced, a hymn he liked with a line, "Vain man, thy fond pursuits forbear."

He introduced a bill limiting the jurisdiction of justices of the peace; he introduced a bill to authorize Samuel Musick to build

a toll bridge across Salt Creek; he moved to change the rules
so that it should not be in order to offer amendments to any
bill after the third reading; he offered a resolution relating to
a state revenue to be derived from the sale of public lands; he
moved to take from the table a report submitted by his committee on public accounts. And he had his thoughts. The line
had been sung for him clear-voiced, "Vain man, thy fond pursuits forbear."

Back to New Salem he came in the spring of 1835. And there
was refuge for Ann Rutledge, with her hand in a long-fingered
hand whose bones told of understanding and a quiet security.
She had written McNamar that she expected release from her
pledge to him. And no answer had come; letters had stopped
coming. Her way was clear. In the fall she was to go to a
young ladies' academy in Jacksonville; and Abraham Lincoln,
poor in goods and deep in debts, was to get from under his
poverty; and they were to marry. They would believe in the
days to come; for the present time they had understanding and
security.

The cry and the answer of one yellowhammer to another, the
wing flash of one bluejay on a home flight to another, the drowsy
dreaming of grass and grain coming up with its early green
over the moist rolling prairie, these were to be felt that spring
together, with the whisper, "Always together."

He was twenty-six, she was twenty-two; the earth was their
footstool; the sky was a sheaf of blue dreams; the rise of the
blood-gold rim of a full moon in the evening was almost too
much to live, see, and remember.

Chapter 40

JAMES RUTLEDGE had sold his New Salem tavern to the Onstotts,
and taken his family to a farm near Sand Ridge. Lincoln rode
back and forth between New Salem and the Rutledge farm when
he paid Ann a call. They were talking over their plans. Ann

was proud of Lincoln, and believed he had a future and would make a name as a great man. In her father's tavern at New Salem she had heard men say Abe Lincoln was considerable of a thinker and a politician; he had a way with people; he had an independent mind and yet he wanted to learn. He would go far and she would go with him; she would be to him what other women had been to other men in days gone by, women who were the wives of Rutledges, among whom there had been a signer of the Declaration of Independence, a governor, judges of courts, and other holders of high place.

For a time Ann worked at the farm of James Short and Lincoln rode over there to see her. He could laugh with her over Parthenia Hill, who had married a man who once wanted to marry Ann, saying, "Ann isn't beautiful—to begin with she has red hair."

She and Lincoln talked over the plan for her to go in the following autumn to the Jacksonville Female Academy, while he would register in the Illinois College at Jacksonville. A brother of Bill Green was a student there, some of the school-teachers around Sangamon County had been Illinois College students, and Ann's own brother David was studying there in that spring of 1835. Out of his companionship with Ann Rutledge, Lincoln had taken seriously to plans for a college education. He would have to leave college to sit in legislative sessions, but that could be arranged.

He was a witness to the wedding of William Taylor and Emaline Johnson in May, signed their "Bans of Matrimony," and believed that with luck he would in another year be married himself.

In the summer of 1835, the brother of Lincoln's betrothed woman wrote three letters, all on one sheet of paper, and saved postage by having a fellow-student carry the three-in-one letter from Jacksonville to the Rutledge farm near Sand Ridge. This letter of young David Rutledge to his father explained that the carrier of the letter, Mr. Blood, should be invited to stay all night free of cost; also that an editor, Brooks, could not pay

money owing to James Rutledge and therefore David had sub-
scribed for the editor's paper; and furthermore that David had
planned to come home, but that the college wouldn't pay him
back his tuition money for the term, and therefore he was
staying on.

The letters were quaint, as in David addressing Anna Rutledge as "Valued Sister," and in closing each of the letters with
the formal expression, "I add nomore," the word "nomore" being
used then in letters, speeches, and sermons as one word, with
the accent on the second syllable. Also in the missive, the ideals
of courtesy and the aspirations for higher life, among the Rutledges, were reflected. The letter to the father read:

College Hill, July 27, 1835.

Dear Father:—

The passing of Mr. Blood from this place to that affords me an
opportunity of writing you a few lines. I have thus far enjoyed good
health, and the students generally are well. I have not collected anything of Brooks, except that I agreed to take his paper as I thought
that would be better than nothing at all, though he says he could pay
the order in about two months. L. M. Greene is up at home at this
time trying to get a school, and I had concluded to quit this place and
go to him untill the commencement of the next term, but I could not
get off without paying for the whole term, therefore I concluded to
stay here.

If Mr. Blood calls on you to stay all night, please to entertain him
free of cost, as he is one of my fellow students and I believe him
to be a good religious young man. I add nomore, but remain yours
with respect until death.

D. H. Rutledge.

To James Rutledge.

The second letter was to James Kittridge about school-teaching
on Sand Ridge, the letter closing: "I want intelligence to come
the next mail concerning it. I add nomore." Then came advice
and hopes for his sister, in the following letter:

To Anna Rutledge:

Valued Sister. So far as I can understand Miss Graves will teach
another school in the Diamond Grove. I am glad to hear that you

have a notion of coming to school, and I earnestly recommend to you that you would spare no time from improving your education and mind. Remember that Time is worth more than all gold therefore throw away none of your golden moments. I add nomore, but &c.

                                                    D. H. RUTLEDGE.

Anna Rutledge.

And Ann might have remarked to herself that some of the golden moments of that year had been snatched and counted, and measured over again in memories afterward.

Chapter 41

AUGUST of that summer came. Corn and grass, fed by rich rains in May and June, stood up stunted of growth, for want of more rain. The red berries on the honeysuckles refused to be glad. The swallows and martins came fewer.

To the homes of the settlers came chills and fever of malaria. Lincoln had been down, and up, and down again with aching bones, taking large spoons of Peruvian bark, boneset tea, jalap, and calomel. One and another of his friends had died; for some, he had helped nail together the burial boxes.

Ann Rutledge lay fever-burned. Days passed; help arrived and was helpless. Moans came from her for the one man of her thoughts They sent for him. He rode out from New Salem to the Sand Ridge farm. They let him in; they left the two together and alone a last hour in the log house, with slants of light on her face from an open clapboard door. It was two days later that death came.

There was what they called a funeral, a decent burial of the body in the Concord burying ground seven miles away. And Lincoln sat for hours with no words for those who asked him to speak to them. They went away from him knowing he would be alone whether they stayed or went away.

A week after the burial of Ann Rutledge, Bill Green found him rambling in the woods along the Sangamon River, mumbling sentences Bill couldn't make out. They watched him and tried to keep him safe among friends at New Salem. And he rambled darkly and idly past their circle to the burying ground seven miles away, where he lay with an arm across the one grave.

"Vain man, thy fond pursuits forbear." As the autumn weeks passed, and the scarlet runners sent out signals across the honey locust and the sycamore tree where they had sat together on the Salem hilltop, and the sunsets flamed earlier in the shortening afternoons, the watchers saw a man struggling on a brink; he needed help. Dr. Allen said rest would help. They took him to the home of Bowling and Nancy Green, at the foot of a bluff climbed by oak-timber growths. A few days he helped in the field at cornhusking; most of the time Nancy had him cutting wood, picking apples, digging potatoes, doing light chores around the house, once holding the yarn for her as she spun.

In the evenings it was useless to try to talk with him. They asked their questions and then had to go away. He sat by the fire one night as the flames licked up the cordwood and swept up the chimney to pass out into a driving storm-wind. The blowing weather woke some sort of lights in him and he went to the door and looked out into a night of fierce tumbling wind and black horizons. And he came back saying, "I can't bear to think of her out there alone." And he clenched his hands, mumbling, "The rain and the storm shan't beat on her grave."

Slowly, as the weeks passed, an old-time order of control came back to him—only it was said that the shadows of a burning he had been through were fixed in the depths of his eyes, and he was a changed man keeping to himself the gray mystery of the change.

Chapter 42

AGAIN Lincoln was in Vandalia as a lawmaker, and, his term over, again he was back surveying in Sangamon County. On

June 13, 1836, he had announced himself as a candidate again, declaring he was for internal improvements, that he would vote for Hugh L. White, the Tennessee Whig, for President in November, and declaring that women ought to have the vote. "I go for admitting all whites to the right of suffrage who pay taxes or bear arms (by no means excluding females)."

Bob Allen, a Democratic candidate, came through New Salem, and sort of allowed he could tell a few things about Abe Lincoln and Ninian W. Edwards, only it wouldn't be fair to tell 'em.

Lincoln wrote him: "I am told that during my absence last week you stated publicly that you were in possession of a fact or facts, which if known to the public would entirely destroy the prospects of N. W. Edwards and myself at the ensuing election, but that through favor to us you would forbear to divulge them. No one has needed favors more than I, and generally few have been less unwilling to accept them, but in this case favor to me would be injustice to the public, and therefore I must beg your pardon for declining it. That I once had the confidence of the people of Sangamon County is sufficiently evident; and if I have done anything, either by design or misadventure, which if known would subject me to a forfeiture of that confidence, he that knows of that thing and conceals it, is a traitor to his country's interest. I find myself wholly unable to form any conjecture of what fact or facts, real or supposed, you spoke; but my opinion of your veracity will not permit me for a moment to doubt that you at least believed what you said. I am flattered with the personal regard you manifested for me; but I hope that on mature reflection you will view the public interest as a paramount consideration and therefore let the worst come. I assure you that the candid statement of fact on your part, however low it may sink me, shall never break the ties of personal friendship between us. I wish an answer to this, and you are at liberty to publish both if you choose."

No reply came from Allen; Lincoln's mention of "personal friendship" between himself and Allen was sarcasm; his friends alluded to Allen as "a bag of wind."

On the stump in Springfield, speaking in the courthouse, Lincoln was challenged by George Forquer, a lawyer who had switched from Whig to Democrat and after the switch was named by the Democratic administration at Washington as register of the land-office. Forquer had just finished building a frame house, the finest in Springfield, and put up a lightning-rod on it. Farmers and their wives hitched the horses at the public square and went to have a look at Forquer's lightning-rod before buying calico, sugar and coffee, or harness buckles; it was the first lightning-rod in that part of Illinois. Forquer was a prominent citizen.

The crowd was starting to leave after a speech by Lincoln. Forquer took the platform and said the young man who had just spoken was sailing too high and would have to be "taken down"; and he was sorry the task devolved on him. Then he made what Josh Speed called "a slasher-gaff speech," while Lincoln stood by with folded arms and measuring eyes.

When Forquer quit speaking, Lincoln stepped up quietly, apologized, offered his argument and closed as follows: "Mr. Forquer commenced his speech by announcing that the young man would have to be taken down. It is for you, fellow citizens, not for me, to say whether I am up or down. The gentleman has seen fit to allude to my being a young man; but he forgets that I am older in years than I am in the tricks and trades of politicians. I desire to live, and I desire place and distinction; but I would rather die now than, like the gentleman, live to see the day that I would change my politics for an office worth $3,000.00 a year, and then feel compelled to erect a lightning-rod to protect a guilty conscience from an offended God."

As a speech it held the audience screwed to the benches, and earned a reputation for Lincoln as a hard man to handle when he was stumping for the legislature. His friends carried him from the courthouse on their shoulders. There was a new feeling for him about being carried on men's shoulders. It was like wrestling, but different.

Once he rode to a meeting with a Democratic candidate in a

rig that belonged to the Democrat. At the meeting he told the farmers: "I am too poor to own a carriage, but my friend has generously invited me to ride with him. I want you to vote for me if you will; but, if not, then vote for my opponent, for he is a fine man."

The Whigs took Sangamon County away from the Democrats, by an average majority of four hundred votes, Lincoln in the lead. The famous "Long Nine" went to Vandalia, nine Whigs averaging six feet in height and over 200 pounds weight. They were for big schemes "commensurate with the wants of the people," a railroad from Galena to the mouth of the Ohio River, running the north-and-south length of the state; a railroad from Alton to Shawneetown; from Alton to Mt. Carmel; from Alton to the eastern state line, running the east and west breadth of the state; from Quincy to the Wabash River; from Bloomington to Pekin; from Peoria to Warsaw; in all about 1,350 miles of railroad. They would spend $100,000.00 to improve the Rock River; $4,000,000.00 to complete the Illinois and Michigan Canal; $250,000.00 for the Western Mail Route.

Altogether, the scheme would cost $12,000,000.00. Lincoln was among the leaders arguing for it. They would sell bonds to raise the $12,000,000.00; they would raise the money in the same way Lincoln and Berry bought their stores in New Salem, by promises on paper. The bonds would sell like hot cakes; the Rothschilds and the Baring Brothers over in London would snap up the bargains.

The scheme won out in the legislature. And the legislature was in close touch with the people of the state, who as a mass were silent and had their silence taken for consent. The Black Hawk War had put $4,000,000.00 in circulation. Land speculators and real-estate dealers were busy; on open prairies many towns and cities were laid out in lots; men joked each other that soon no land would be left for farming.

The governor of the state had officially declared: "Under the blessing of a bountiful Providence, Illinois is fast ascending in the scale of importance and will in a short time take her station among the first States in the Union; the steadiness and grandeur of her outward march, will however, in a great degree, depend on her future legislation."

A boom was on, overloaded and sure to collapse. It was the pioneer stock, taking its chances, believing in the future, and believing that future would come sooner if boomed.

That Lincoln, who could not finance himself, should show no ability in financing the state of Illinois in a vast economic project was to have been expected. And yet he had a vision of himself at this time as a constructive statesman, pushing through plans in Illinois for transportation ways, schools, and education. He told his friend, Joshua Speed, at Springfield that he aimed at being called "the De Witt Clinton of Illinois," achieving for his state what a constructive Irishman had done for New York in getting the Erie Canal built and in bringing school improvements.

Lincoln led the "Long Nine" in finding the votes in the legislature to pass a bill moving the capital of the state from Vandalia to Springfield. Other counties besides Sangamon were hustling for the location; it went to Springfield mainly because of the patient and skilled manipulation of Lincoln. A few members voted for the bill because they liked Lincoln, but most of the voters came through trades, deals, "log-rolling." "You scratch my back and I'll scratch yours."

And yet as a manipulator, trading, fixing, coaxing, Lincoln operated by a code of his own. An all-night session was held by the members favoring Springfield for the state capital; and Lincoln was told of a block of votes he could have if he would give his vote for a certain measure that he considered against his principles; the members went home at daybreak without having brought him their way.

A second meeting was called; again they tried to ride down Lincoln's objections; midnight came, the candles burned low, all were tired. Lincoln began speaking amid silence, seriously and with feeling, telling why he couldn't in such a case trade his vote.

As old man Henderson remembered the speech, it ended:

"You may burn my body to ashes, and scatter them to the winds of heaven; you may drag my soul down to the regions of darkness and despair to be tormented forever; but you will never get me to support a measure which I believe to be wrong, although by doing so I may accomplish that which I believe to be right."

After the bill passed and Springfield was named as the future capital city of the state, the Democrats charged the Sangamon County Whigs with "bargain and corruption." At an extra session General L. D. Ewing, who favored Vandalia, declared the Springfield crowd had "sold out to the internal improvements men." Lincoln then delivered a speech that bristled with keen thrusts. "He tore the hide off Ewing." And Ewing, who was an army general and a proud man, was ready for a duel. Friends stepped between and saved bloodshed.

With drawling and whimsical good nature, Lincoln opened his discussion of a resolution offered by Linder to investigate the state bank, saying: "It is not without a considerable degree of apprehension that I venture to cross the track of the gentleman from Coles [Mr. Linder]. Indeed, I do not believe I could muster a sufficiency of courage to come in contact with that gentleman, were it not for the fact that he, some days since, most graciously condescended to assure us that he would never be found wasting ammunition on small game. . . . Whenever I shall have occasion to allude to that gentleman I shall endeavor to adopt that kind of court language which I understand to be due to decided superiority. In one faculty, at least, there can be no dispute of the gentleman's superiority over me, and most other men; and that is, the faculty of entangling a subject so that neither himself, nor any other man, can find head or tail to it. . . . In the present case, if any gentlemen whose money is a burden to them choose to lead off a dance, I am decidedly opposed to the people's money being used to pay the fiddler. No one can doubt that the examination proposed must cost the State some ten or twelve thousand dollars; and all this to settle a question in which the people have no interest, and about which they care nothing. These capitalists generally act harmoniously and in concert to fleece the people; and now that they have got into a quarrel with themselves, we are called upon to appropriate the people's money to settle the quarrel."

Then he filed the declaration: "Mr. Chairman, this work is exclusively the work of politicians; a set of men who have interests aside from the interests of the people, and who, to say the most of them, are, taken as a mass, at least one long step removed from honest men. I say this with the greater freedom because, being a politician myself, none can regard it as personal."

He was now meeting men of importance from all parts of Illinois; they came from towns and counties wanting appropriations, from banks, railroads, contractors, seeking legislation for special interests. Lincoln, the story-teller, the whimsical, good-natured philosopher, was asked to their game suppers and banquets. It cost $600.00 to pay for the supper, wines, cigars, whisky, and damages, at a party given by the newly elected United States Senator, John M. Robinson.

Attending the party was a brother of William Cullen Bryant, the New York poet, one John Bryant, sent from Princeton to help legislation for Bureau County. He wrote that after the company had got noisy and mellow on rye and corn-juice, "Mr. Douglas and General Shields, to the consternation of the host and intense merriment of the guests, climbed up on the table at one end, encircled each other's waists, and, to the tune of a rollicking song, pirouetted down the whole length of the table, shouting, singing, and kicking dishes, glasses, and everything right and left, helter-skelter."

The Douglas referred to was a short, thick-set, blue-eyed man whose full name was Stephen Arnold Douglas, a young lawyer from Vermont. Neither he nor Lincoln took any special notice of each other, except that Lincoln remarked to others that Douglas was "the least man I have ever seen."

After a day of legislative sessions, committee meetings, conferences, study of bills and measures, and a game supper, Lincoln enjoyed sitting in a hotel room with friendly souls, sitting with his knees up to his chin, drawling out stories, talking about how they were beating the Democrats, emphasizing a good point by drawing his knees again up to his chin and letting both feet down on the floor with a slam.

Newton Walker had brought his fiddle from Lewistown. Lincoln would go over to where Walker was boarding and ask him for a tune. Then Lincoln would tell a story, and it would be a story and a tune till late hours. Walker said, "When he grew weary of telling stories he would ask me to give him a tune, which I never refused to do."

Each of several taverns in Vandalia called itself a "House of Entertainment." Willis & Maddox issued a card "to respectfully inform the public" they were located two doors from the post office, and, "They will serve up at any hour of the day or the night Fried Ham, Turkeys, Grouse, or Prairie Chicken, Partridges, Venison, Pigs' Feet, Tripe, Sausages, Oysters, Mackerel, Herrings, and Crackers: Coffee, Tea, and Soups, together with many other nicknacks unmentionable: Hot Punch, Egg Nogg &c. at any time: all of which will be afforded with great goodwill and on the most accomodating terms. They have also on hand and for sale Best Teas, Loaf and Brown Sugars, Tobacco, Oranges, Lemons, Figs; Lobsters, Olives, Mushrooms, Walnut and Tomato Pickles, Ketchups, Rochelle, Cherry, Champaign, Cogniac, Peach, American and other Brandies; Claret, Teneriffe, Sherry, Dry, Brown, Port, Malaga, and Madeira Wines; Seidlitz and Soda Powders; Fire Crackers, &c., &c."

There were yarns, true to fact, told among people then, to pass the time. One was about Governor Duncan, who had a misunderstanding with the Jackson administration and switched his politics from Democrat to Whig. One plain old henchman came to him and spoke the regrets: "You was young, poor, friendless; we put you into high office and enabled you to make a fortune. You was like a poor colt. We caught you up out of the thicket, fed you on the best, combed the burrs out of your mane and tail, and made a fine horse of you. And now you have strayed away from your owners."

Among politicians there was a tradition of a legislature which passed a law forbidding small bulls to roam at large. Owners of such small stray bulls would get heavy fines, under the law. The small farmers rose in anger, claiming that the law was all in favor of the rich farmers who had only big bulls, and the law let the big bulls roam as they pleased. At the next election the small farmers revolted and threw out of office every politician who had voted against small bulls.

Quaint tales out of green, moist solitudes passed around. One was of James Lemon, an old-time Baptist preacher and farmer in Monroe County, who made his own horse-collars, of straw or corn-husks plaited together. While breaking stubble, with his wild son helping, he left the harness on the beam of the plow at dinner-time. The son hid the horse-collar, so as to have a longer rest at dinner in the hours his father would plait a new horse-collar of corn-husks. But when, after dinner, the old man saw the horse-collar gone, he pulled off his leather breeches, stuffed the pant-legs with stubble, straddled them across the neck of the horse for a collar, and so plowed the rest of the afternoon, "as bare-legged as when he came into the world."

There was William Meharry, herding cattle in Champaign County. He rode horseback, snapping off rattlesnake heads with a long cattle whip, sometimes killing twenty-five in a day.

There was talk of farmers like Andrew McCorkle, not far from Springfield, who was afraid the railroads would scare his cows so they wouldn't give milk.

Shooting matches, rifles and marksmanship commanded attention. In the part of Indiana that Lincoln came from, hunters aimed for the head of the gray squirrel; a shot in the body was wide of the target. Some keen riflemen were known to the coons in the woods; one famous dead-shot had a coon up the top of a tree; the coon hesitated and said, "Don't shoot; I'll come down." Friends of a hunter with a big reputation bragged that he could put a panther under one arm, a hedgehog under the other, and climb a thorn-tree without a scratch.

A topic discussed at many a tavern was whether or not the skin of the Indian chief Tecumseh had been taken off and used for razor-strops, whether such material made a good razor-strop, and if so why.

There had been weather to talk about one rainy day in December of 1836, when soft mud turned hard in an hour, and Washington Crowder, riding to Springfield, froze to his saddle and had to be carried into a house, saddle and all, to be thawed out.

And it was told of various communities that a mob went to the house of a man and took him away and hanged him to a tree. It was a dark night and when morning came they saw they had hanged the wrong man. And they went and told the widow, "The laugh is on us."

The end of the legislative session at Vandalia came on March 6, 1837, and the "Long Nine," with their long legs and 200 pounds weight apiece, started home on their horses, with the exception of Lincoln, whose horse had been stolen, leaving him without cash to buy another. As Lincoln walked, the others pointed to the size of his feet; when he shivered, "Boys, I'm cold," another noticed, "No wonder—there's so much of you on the ground."

Arrived at Springfield, the "Long Nine" sat down to a game supper while spokesmen for Springfield expressed gratitude to those who had arranged to move the state capital from Vandalia to their own city. One toast ran, "Abraham Lincoln: he has fulfilled the expectations of his friends, and disappointed the hopes of his enemies," and Lincoln offered the toast, "All our friends: they are too numerous to mention now individually, while there is no one of them who is not too dear to be forgotten or neglected."

On the way to New Salem he stopped at the village of Athens, the home of his colleague, Robert L. Wilson of the "Long Nine." At a banquet he was toasted, "Abraham Lincoln: one of nature's noblemen." And Wilson gave people this size-up of Lincoln, "He was as much at home in the legislature as at New Salem; he had a quaint and peculiar way, all his own, of treating a subject, and he frequently startled us. He seemed to be a born politician. We followed his lead; but he followed nobody's lead. It may almost be said that he did our thinking for us. He inspired respect, although he was careless and negligent. We would ride while he would walk, but we recognized him as a master in logic. He was poverty itself, but independent. He seemed to glide along in life without any friction or effort."

Wilson had spent many hours with Lincoln during the years they were together in the legislature, and with Athens and Wilson's home so near New Salem they had seen a good deal of each other in action. When Wilson had occasion to tell later what he knew about Lincoln, he said: "I made a canvass through Sand Ridge; Mr. Lincoln accompanied me, and we called at nearly every house. At that time it was the custom to keep whisky in the house. The subject was always mentioned, but with the remark to Mr. Lincoln, 'You never drink, but maybe your friend would like to take a little.'"

"In a conversation about that time," Wilson said, "Lincoln told me that although he appeared to enjoy life rapturously, still he was the victim of terrible melancholy. He sought company, and indulged in fun and hilarity without restraint or stint as to time; but, when by himself, he told me that he was so overcome by mental depression that he never dared carry a knife in his pocket; and as long as I was intimately acquainted with him, previous to his commencement of the practice of law, he never carried a pocketknife."

When people talked about Lincoln, it was nearly always about one or more of these five things: (1) how long, tall, quick, strong, or awkward in looks he was; (2) how he told stories and jokes, how he was comical or pleasant or kindly; (3) how he could be silent, melancholy, sad; (4) how he was ready to learn and looking for chances to learn; (5) how he was ready to help a friend, a stranger, or even a dumb animal in distress.

Henry E. Dummer, a lawyer in Springfield, remarked: "Lincoln used to come to our office—Stuart's and mine—in Springfield from New Salem and borrow law books. Sometimes he walked but generally rode. He was the most uncouth-looking young man I ever saw. He seemed to have but little to say, seemed to feel timid, with a tinge of sadness visible in the countenance, but when he did talk all this disappeared for the time, and he demonstrated that he was both strong and acute. He surprised us more and more at every visit."

Chapter 43

DURING the winter at Vandalia, Lincoln had written a drawling and half-bashful love letter to the daughter of a rich farmer in Green County, Kentucky. She was Miss Mary Owens, one year older than Lincoln, with a head of dark curly hair, large blue eyes, standing five feet five inches high, and, on her first visit to New Salem three years before, weighing about one hundred and fifty pounds.

Her sister, Mrs. Bennet Able, was anxious for the two to get married. But Mary Owens held off; she had been trained in Kentucky schools for refined young ladies; she dressed in what one of the Greens called "the finest trimmings I ever saw"; and she took note in the case of Lincoln, "His training had been different from mine; there was not congeniality; he was deficient in those little links which make up a woman's happiness."

Once when a party were riding to Uncle Billy Green's, they came to a branch of the creek which was a bad crossing. Miss Owens noticed the other men helping their partners, while Lincoln rode ahead of her without looking back. "You are a nice fellow!" she remarked when she caught up with him. "I suppose you did not care whether my neck was broken or not." And he had laughed back a defense that was a compliment, telling her he knew she was plenty smart enough to take care of herself.

She climbed a steep hill with Lincoln and Mrs. Bowling Green.

And Lincoln kept on joking and talking to her, not once offering to help carry the fat baby Mrs. Green had in her arms. It seemed to Miss Owens to be "neglect" on Lincoln's part.

She was puzzled by him; in some things he was so soft-hearted; he told her he saw "a hog mired down" one day when he was crossing a prairie and, as he had a new suit of blue jeans on and was "fixed up" in his best clothes, he said to himself he would pass by and pass on without looking again at the struggling shote in the mud. But after he had passed on, the hog haunted him and seemed to be saying, "There, now, my last hope is gone," and he had turned around, gone back, and got the hog loose from the mire. It was puzzling to Miss Owens's ideas about chivalry that a man could be so thoughtful about a hog in that way and at another time be so abstracted and lost in his own feelings that he couldn't stay alongside his woman partner when riding across a dangerous creek.

They had parted without any particular understanding except that they were good friends. She had gone home to Green County, Kentucky, and talked with her father, of whom she said, "Few persons placed a higher estimate on education than he did." And if she told her father about Lincoln's personal speech she included such information as the fact that Lincoln said "ain't" as often as "isn't" and that sometimes his pronunciation of "such" sounded like "sich."

Lincoln, at Vandalia, making laws for the commonwealth of Illinois, one cold, lonesome winter night, wrote her a letter which he called dry and stupid, which he said he was ashamed to send. The letter read:

VANDALIA, December 13, 1836.
MARY:

I have been sick ever since my arrival, or I should have written sooner. It is but little difference, however, as I have very little even yet to write. And more, the longer I can avoid the mortification of looking in the post-office for your letter and not finding it, the better. You see I am mad about that old letter yet. I don't like very well to risk you again. I'll try you once more, anyhow.

The new State House is not yet finished, and consequently the legislature is doing little or nothing. The governor delivered an inflammatory political message, and it is expected there will be some sparring between the parties about it as soon as the two Houses get to business. Taylor delivered up his petition for the new county to one of our members this morning. I am told he despairs of its success, on account of all the members from Morgan County opposing it. There are names enough on the petition, I think, to justify the members from our county in going for it; but if the new members from Morgan oppose it, which they say they will, the chances will be bad.

Our chance to take the seat of government to Springfield is better than I expected. An internal-improvement convention was held here since we met, which recommended a loan of several millions of dollars, on the faith of the State, to construct railroads. Some of the legislature are for it, and some against it; which has the majority I cannot tell. There is great strife and struggling for the office of the United States Senator here at this time. It is probable we shall ease their pains in a few days. The opposition men have no candidate of their own, and consequently they will smile as complacently at the angry snarls of the contending Van Buren candidates and their respective friends as the Christian does at Satan's rage. You recollect that I mentioned at the outset of this letter that I had been unwell. That is the fact, though I believe I am about well now; but that, with other things I cannot account for, have conspired, and have gotten my spirits so low that I feel I would rather be any place in the world than here. I really cannot endure the thought of staying here ten weeks. Write back as soon as you get this, and, if possible, say something that will please me, for really I have not been pleased since I left you. This letter is so dry and stupid that I am ashamed to send it, but with my present feelings I cannot do any better.

Give my best respects to Mr. and Mrs. Able and family.

Your friend,
LINCOLN.

Chapter 44

ONE day in March of that year of 1837, Lincoln visited the home of Bowling and Nancy Green at the foot of the bluff with its timber of oak-growth climbing. And he and Squire Bowling Green talked about politics—and about Lincoln going to Springfield to be a lawyer, practicing law in the law firm of Stuart & Lincoln. Like all lawyers, he had been certified to the supreme court as having good moral character; he was licensed to write his name, "Abraham Lincoln, Attorney-at-Law."

So he was leaving the town of the hilltop at the curve of the Sangamon River, with its memories of the flatboat stuck on the dam, of the trip as pilot on the *Talisman,* of the Offut store that petered out, of the Black Hawk War and the boys that stepped to the front and elected him a captain, the wrestling match with Jack Armstrong, the horse races and rooster fights of the boys from Clary's Grove and Wolf Creek and Sand Ridge, the mastery of Kirkham's Grammar and surveying, the store of Berry & Lincoln that winked out and left him struggling under debts it would take years to pay off, the winning of the girl with the wavy corn-silk hair and the folding of her hands and the taking her away, shadows speaking in thin whispers.

Men talked about John McNamar, the first betrothed of Ann Rutledge, coming back, buying more land to raise more corn to feed more hogs to buy more land, how quick McNamar was at figuring fractions and decimals, how sharp he was at reading mortgages and deeds, and one woman saying he was cold as the multiplication table.

James Rutledge had died the same year as his daughter Ann. The new owner of the farm at Sand Ridge was John McNamar, and he told the Widow Rutledge she would have to move; he couldn't use promises or hopes and would have to have rent money. And the daughters had told friends, "Mother is having a hard time. We're turned out, moving to Iowa, to begin all over again."

One morning Lincoln saddled a horse borrowed from Bowling Green, threw across its back saddlebags containing his copies of Blackstone and a change of underwear, and started on the twenty-mile ride to Springfield. On this ride his thoughts were different from the time when he moved from Kentucky up into Indiana at eight years of age, and again when he moved from Indiana to Illinois at twenty-one. Now he was twenty-eight years old; he had talked with men on main-traveled roads, ever-lastingly asking questions; he had read newspapers and heard public speakers; he was watching civilization.

In the legislature that winter just passed, he had done a thing as independent as the way he wore his hat. He had stood almost alone against the whole legislature; he had found only one other man to stand with him.

Over the nation the question had come up whether the slavery of the negro race under the white race was right or wrong, and whether any man or woman, believing it wrong, should be free to say so.

Forty peculiar and solemn men and women meeting in a house in Philadelphia four years previous had organized the American Antislavery Society, calling on the free states to remove slavery "by moral and political action, as prescribed in the Constitution of the United States," and announcing, "With entire confidence in the overruling justice of God, we plant ourselves upon the Declaration of Independence and the truths of divine revelation as upon the everlasting rock. We shall organize antislavery societies, if possible, in every city, town, and village in the land. We shall send forth agents to lift up the voice of remonstrance, of warning, of entreaty, and of rebuke. We shall circulate un-sparingly and extensively antislavery tracts and periodicals."

In the southern states it was no longer lawful to speak against slavery; any person found guilty of an agitation that might cause an insurrection of slaves would be hanged, in accordance with the statutes. Governor Lumpkin and the legislature of the state of Georgia offered $5,000.00 for the person of one Boston agi-tator to be brought to Georgia for trial. The three million negro workers in the southern states were property, live stock valued by tax assessors at more than one thousand million dollars; in the Senate at Washington Henry Clay had named the total slave property value as twelve hundred million dollars; the cotton belt was spreading westward, adding thousands of acres every month.

The *Richmond Whig* of Virginia urged: "The people of the

North must go to hanging these fanatics if they would not lose the benefit of the Southern trade, and they will do it. Depend upon it, the Northern people will never sacrifice their present lucrative trade with the South, so long as the hanging of a few thousands will prevent it." The New York *Courier and Enquirer* declared, "They (the Abolitionists) have no right to demand protection of the people they insult. Ought not, we ask, our city authorities to make them understand this—to tell them that they prosecute their treasonable and beastly designs at their own peril?"

President Jackson had told Congress: "I would respectfully suggest the propriety of passing such a law as will prohibit, under severe penalties, the circulation in the Southern States, through the mail, of incendiary publications intended to instigate the slaves to insurrection." The *Augusta Chronicle* of Georgia offered the prophecy: "We do firmly believe that, if the Southern States do not quickly unite, and declare to the North, if the question of slavery be longer discussed in any shape, they will instantly secede from the Union, that the question must be settled, and very soon, by the sword, as the only possible means of self-preservation." Riots in Philadelphia lasted three nights, ending with forty-four houses smashed, a colored Presbyterian church battered, one negro beaten to death, another drowned in the Schuylkill River.

In Boston an agitator who came to a meeting of the Female Antislavery Society had his clothes torn off, was dragged at a rope's end through the streets, and, after being rescued by the police, had to borrow coat, hat, and pantaloons to go to jail for further safety from those hunting him, who were respectable, well-to-do citizens of Boston. When Miss Prudence Crandall opened a school for negro children at Canterbury, Connecticut, she was sent to jail for violation of the state law forbidding the teaching of colored children from other states. At Concord, New Hampshire, an academy was wrecked where colored children were being taught reading and writing.

The meek, mild, soft-spoken little Quaker, Benjamin Lundy,

editing a paper with the meek, mild, soft-spoken title, "The Genius of Universal Emancipation," was beaten by a Baltimore mob. And James Gillespie Birney, Kentucky-born and raised, a brilliant young lawyer who had been an Alabama planter and had given all his slaves freedom papers, couldn't get a paper printed nor hire a hall for a speech in Owensville, Kentucky; the *Philanthropist,* which he was publishing in Cincinnati, was refused delivery by postmasters in the states South. He had traveled southwest and met dreams of southern empire while listening to planters talking about the big land stretches west of the Mississippi River and how to make them slave territory. He wrote: "There will be no cessation of conflict until slavery shall be exterminated or liberty destroyed. Liberty and slavery cannot live in juxtaposition." And while Birney and his group tried to bring gradual emancipation by lawful and constitutional methods, the Garrison group demanded immediate emancipation by moral suasion and Christian wisdom, or somehow otherwise, maintaining that the United States Constitution in its silent assent to slavery was "a compact with Hell."

From week to week the Abolitionist papers published articles and items about mobs North and South, about auctioneers of slaves calling for bids near the steps of the Capitol in Washington, the tactics of John Quincy Adams in Congress against the so-called "Gag Rule," a resolution passed by Congress providing that all petitions relating to slavery should be laid on the table without being referred to a committee or printed. Events were splitting the churches into northern and southern divisions.

Far down in Texas men of southern kin were fighting, the Alamo garrison of 187 men dying to the last man in trying to hold out against a Mexican army of 5,000; it was part of the march of the South, or the southern planters, to wider regions, more cotton-planted land. Sam Houston's men took victory from a Mexican army at San Jacinto and won independence for Texas; planters had come; slave ships had arrived at the coast line of Texas direct from Africa; a woman wrote of fresh arrivals, shipwrecked near Galveston Bay: "As soon as the beeves were skinned the negroes acted like dogs, they were so hungry; they laughed and chattered like monkeys; they did not understand a word of English; all the men and boys in the neighborhood came to see the wild Africans."

So, windy and clamorous forces blew across America. The future held unknown cross-paths. While the hot blood of the South tingled to the sneers and curses of the Abolitionists, and while the South was now openly phrasing its defense of slavery as an inevitable institution and a necessary practice, there had not yet come a clear vision of a southern empire. The nearest to that was the attempt of South Carolina to break out of the Union of states in 1832; medals were struck reading, "John C. Calhoun, First President of the Southern Confederacy"; the flag was ready, a palmetto tree coiled with a rattlesnake, "Don't tread on me"; arrangements for troops, and defense operations were under way; Governor Hayne proclaimed: "I recognize no allegiance as paramount to that which the citizens of South Carolina owe to the State of their birth or their adoption. If the sacred soil of Carolina should be polluted by the footsteps of an invader, or be stained with the blood of her citizens, shed in her defense, I trust in Almighty God that no son of hers, native or adopted, who has been nourished at her bosom, or been cherished by her bounty, will be found raising a parricidal arm against our common mother."

This, while President Andrew Jackson publicly appealed: "To say that any State may at pleasure secede from the Union, is to say that the United States are not a nation. Fellow-citizens of my native State, let me not only admonish you, as the First Magistrate of our common country, not to incur the penalty of its laws, but use the influence that a father would over his children whom he saw rushing to a certain ruin. In that paternal language, with that paternal feeling, let me tell you, my countrymen, that you are deluded by men who are either deceived themselves or wish to deceive you."

And privately, Jackson said to a go-between from South Carolina: "Tell them, if one South Carolina finger be raised in defiance

The famous Methodist preacher and circuit rider, Peter Cartwright. A Democrat beaten by Lincoln in the run for Congress in 1846. He personally threw scoffers out of church when they interrupted sermons. He once told a cold deacon who had prayed, "Brother, three prayers like that would freeze hell over."

Daguerreotype presented by Mrs. B. C. Keene to Bloomington (Ill.) Historical Society

Mary Owens, with whom Lincoln seriously considered marriage
(lower left). The Rutledge family coffee pot (lower right). William
G. Green, who clerked in the Lincoln & Berry store and studied
grammar with Lincoln (upper left). Mentor Graham, the New
Salem schoolmaster who helped Lincoln to learn surveying (upper
right).

of this Government, that I shall come down there; and once I'm there, I'll hang the first man I lay hands on to the first tree I can reach."

As that small yet significant storm died down, Andrew Jackson wrote a letter to his friend, the Rev. A. J. Crawford of Georgia, reading, "Nullification is dead, and its actors and courtiers will only be remembered by the people to be execrated for their wicked designs to sever and destroy the only good Government on the globe. Haman's gallows ought to be the fate of all such ambitious men who would involve the country in a civil war, and all the evils in its trains, that they might ride on its whirlwinds and direct the storm. The free people of the United States have spoken, and consigned these demagogues to their proper doom. The tariff, it is now well known, was a mere pretext, and disunion and a Southern confederacy the real object. The next pretext will be the negro or slavery question."

By the ballots of voters North and South, a New York Tammany Democrat, Martin Van Buren, took office as President of the nation on March 4, 1837, telling the country he was an "inflexible and uncompromising opponent of every attempt on the part of Congress to abolish slavery in the District of Columbia against the wishes of the slaveholding states," saying he was determined "to resist the slightest interference with it in the states where it exists," and without mentioning Abolitionists or mobs, he took notice that a "reckless disregard of the consequences of their conduct has exposed individuals to popular indignation."

From the Government at Washington and the national church organizations on down to business partnerships and families, the slavery question was beginning to split the country in two. At one far end was the Abolitionist agitator who wanted to take away a billion dollars' worth of property from the Southerners; and at the other far end was the Southerner who cried, "The people of the North must go to hanging these fanatics."

At two far opposite ends of an issue were passionate, reckless, stubborn men whose grandfathers had fought side by side in open combat to overthrow by violent revolution the government of the British Empire over the American colonies.

Aggravations between people South and North were getting worse. Across the northern states had been organized "The Underground Railway," a series of routes from the slave states across the free states and over the line into Canada. An anti-slavery man would keep a runaway slave in his house, cellar, or barn, and drive him to the next house or tell him the way. Officers of the law and slave owners came North with warrants hunting their runaway property; Illinois was seeing them often. Also there were bogus slave hunters scattered through southern Illinois; they kidnaped free negroes, took them to St. Louis or across the Ohio River into Kentucky and sold them.

Wagons from Tennessee and Kentucky drove across southern Illinois with movers who called out from the wagon seat that they were driving to Missouri, where a man "had a right to own a nigger if he wanted to." Hostile feeling developed between Illinois and Missouri people; the Missourians called Illinois land a suckhole and its people "Suckers" while the Illinoisans let it pass by alluding to Missouri residents as "Pukes."

In St. Louis a negro, McIntosh, killed a deputy sheriff, and a large mob took and burned him one night and the next morning boys threw stones to see who could hit the skull most often. At the trial of the mob leaders before Judge Lawless, he charged the jury: "If the destruction of the murderer was the act of congregated thousands, seized upon and impelled by that mysterious, metaphysical, and almost electric frenzy which, in all ages and nations, has hurried on infatuated multitudes to deeds of death and destruction—then I say the case transcends your jurisdiction—it is beyond the reach of human law."

A young Presbyterian minister, Elijah P. Lovejoy, a halfway Abolitionist editing a paper in St. Louis, had written: "Today a public meeting declares you shall not discuss slavery. Tomorrow another meeting decides it is against the peace of society that popery be discussed. The next day a decree is issued speaking against distilleries, dramshops, or drunkenness. And so on.

The truth is, if you give ground a single inch, there is no stopping place. I deem it, therefore, my duty to take my stand upon the Constitution, and declare my fixed determination to maintain this ground."

The editorial which discussed Judge Lawless, was answered by a mob that smashed his press and threw his type out of the window. Lovejoy got the press repaired, decided to move up the river to Alton, Illinois, loaded the press on a boat, and was met at Alton by a mob that threw the press into the river.

Events slowly changed Lovejoy to an "immediate emancipationist"; he wrote: "As well might a lady think to bail out the Atlantic Ocean with her thimble, as the Colonization Society to remove slavery by colonizing the slaves in Africa."

These drifts were known to Abraham Lincoln, as he had spent the past winter months in Vandalia. He knew the legislature was mostly of southern blood and point of view. In the first legislature in which he had served there were 58 members from Kentucky and Tennessee or south of the Ohio River, 19 from the middle Atlantic states, and only 4 from New England. He knew that there was this crimson kinship of like blood between populations in southern Illinois, Indiana, Ohio, and in states south of the Ohio River; and that beyond blood kinship there were the closely interlocking interests of the southern planters buying immense quantities of pork, corn, and produce from the northern frontier states, and the New England power-loom mills buying increasing millions of bales of cotton each year.

Legislatures of four southern states were asking that states North "effectually suppress all associations purporting to be abolition societies"; governors of New York and Massachusetts had asked their legislatures to take such action; a mass meeting of 1,800 of the wealthiest, influential citizens of Boston had declared the Abolitionists to be dangerous meddlers; the years were short and few since John Randolph of Virginia had pronounced slavery "a volcano in full operation."

Amid this welter, Lincoln could understand his fellow members of the legislature when they passed resolutions declaring: "We

highly disapprove of the formation of Abolition Societies; . . .
the right of property in slaves is sacred to the slaveholding States
by the Federal Constitution, and . . . they cannot be deprived
of that right without their consent. . . ."

Lincoln voted against these resolutions, and was joined by
only one other member. Dan Stone and he recorded a protest
spread on the Journal of Proceedings as follows:

Resolutions upon the subject of domestic slavery having passed both
branches of the General Assembly at its present session, the undersigned hereby protest against the passage of the same.

They believe that the institution of slavery is founded on both injustice and bad policy, but that the promulgation of abolition doctrines
tends rather to increase than abate its evils.

They believe that the Congress of the United States has no power
under the Constitution to interfere with the institution of slavery in
the different States.

They believe that the Congress of the United States has the power
under the Constitution to abolish slavery in the District of Columbia,
but that the power ought not to be exercised unless at the request of
the people of the district.

The difference between these opinions and those contained in the
resolutions is their reason for entering this protest.

Just five weeks before filing this protest, Lincoln had delivered an address before the Young Men's Lyceum at Springfield,
taking as his subject "The Perpetuation of Our Political Institutions." He had spoken windy sentences such as: "Shall we
expect some transatlantic military giant to step the ocean and
crush us at a blow? Never! All the armies of Europe, Asia,
and Africa combined, with all the treasure of the earth (our own
excepted) in their military chest, with a Bonaparte for a commander, could not by force take a drink from the Ohio or make
a track on the Blue Ridge in a trial of a thousand years."

With this he connected the solemn, quiet murmur: "At what
point then is the approach of danger to be expected? I answer,
If it ever reach us it must spring up amongst us; it cannot come
from abroad. If destruction be our lot we must ourselves be its

author and finisher. As a nation of freemen we must live through all time or die by suicide."

He went on: "Accounts of outrages committed by mobs form the everyday news of the times, from New England to Louisiana. In Mississippi they first commenced by hanging the regular gamblers—a set of men certainly not following for a livelihood a very useful or honest occupation, but one which, so far from being forbidden by the laws, was actually licensed by an act of the legislature passed but a single year before. Next, negroes suspected of conspiring to raise an insurrection were caught up and hanged in all parts of the state; then, white men supposed to be leagued with the negroes; and finally strangers from neighboring states, going thither on business, were in many instances subjected to the same fate. Thus went on this process of hanging, from gamblers to negroes, from negroes to white citizens, and from these to strangers, till dead men were seen literally dangling from the boughs of trees upon every roadside, and in numbers that were almost sufficient to rival the native Spanish moss of the country as a drapery of the forest.

"When men take it into their heads today to hang gamblers or burn murderers, they should recollect that in the confusion usually attending such transactions they will be as likely to hang or burn some one who is neither a gambler nor a murderer as one who is, and that, acting upon the example they set, the mob of tomorrow may, and probably will, hang or burn some of them by the very same mistake. And not only so; the innocent, those who have ever set their faces against violations of law in every shape, alike with the guilty fall victims to the ravages of mob law; and thus it goes on, step by step, till all the walls erected for the defense of the persons and property of individuals are trodden down and disregarded. . . .

"Good men, who love tranquillity, who desire to abide by the laws and enjoy their benefits, who would gladly spill their blood in the defense of their country, become tired and disgusted with a government that offers them no protection. . . . Whenever the vicious portion of population shall be permitted to gather in bands of hundreds and thousands, and burn churches, ravage and rob provision stores, throw printing-presses into rivers, shoot editors, and hang and burn obnoxious persons at pleasure and with impunity, depend upon it, this government cannot last."

He touched on the topic of human glory, how men of ambition spring up, with towering genius. "It thirsts and burns for distinction," he said, "and if possible, it will have it whether at the expense of emancipating slaves or enslaving freemen. Is it unreasonable, then, to expect that some man possessed of the loftiest genius, coupled with ambition to push it to its utmost stretch, will at some time spring up among us? And when such a one does, it will require the people to be united with each other, attached to the government and laws, and generally intelligent, to successfully frustrate his designs."

Sprinkled through the address were sentences imitating the famous orator, Daniel Webster of Massachusetts, and the other famous orator, Henry Clay of Kentucky, besides still other famous orators of that day. He closed in a manner modeled on Webster, saying: "Upon these let the proud fabric of free- dom rest, as the rock of its basis; and as truly as has been said of the only greater institution, 'The gates of hell shall not prevail against it.'"

An honest poetry of his own heart, an inevitable, mournful rhythm from the shadows of his own melancholy, stood forth in a passage where he had spoken of "the generation just gone to rest" and how near that generation was to the passionate, fight- ing men who accomplished the American Revolution. Each scarred and mutilated form that lived through the Revolution was himself a living history. "But those histories are gone. They can be read no more forever. They were a fortress of strength; but what invading foeman could never do, the silent artillery of time has done—the leveling of its walls. They are gone. They were a forest of giant oaks; but the all-restless hurricane has swept over them, and left only here and there a lonely trunk, despoiled of its verdure, shorn of its foliage, un- shading and unshaded, to murmur in a few more gentle breezes, and to combat with its mutilated limbs a few more ruder storms, then to sink and be no more."

He was growing, young Abraham Lincoln. He was a learner, calling himself, and called by others, "a learner always."

As he rode with his long legs straddling a borrowed horse that day in March, 1837, toward Springfield, where his name would be put on a lawyer's shingle, he had seven dollars in cash in his pockets, and he was more than a thousand dollars in debt.

On certain March days in Illinois, the sky is a ragbag of whimsies. It may whisper of spring to come with soft slants of sun, while baby pearl-shell clouds dimple and drift, and then let blusters of wind blow up followed with flurries of snow, a little sleet, a drizzle of rain, then sunshine again and baby pearl-shell clouds dimpling and drifting.

Chapter 45

SPRINGFIELD with its 1,500 inhabitants in 1837 was the big town of Sangamon County, selling to the 18,000 people of the county a large part of their supplies, tools, groceries, handling grain, pork, beef, and produce, with stores, churches, schools, banks, newspapers, courts, lawyers, offices of government, taverns, saloons, places of entertainment. It was a city, its people ready to say there was no more wilderness in that part of the country; the land had been surveyed and allotted.

The farm women who came to town wore shoes where they used to go barefooted; the men had changed from moccasins to rawhide boots and shoes. Farmers no longer spent time killing deer, tanning the hide and making leather breeches to tie at the ankles: it was cheaper and quicker to raise corn and buy pantaloons which had come from Massachusetts over the Ohio or the Mississippi River or the Great Lakes. Stores advertised "velvets, silk, satin, and Marseilles vestings, fine calf boots, seal and morocco pumps, for gentlemen," and for ladies "silks, bareges, crepe lisse, lace veils, thread lace, Thibet shawls lace handkerchiefs, fine prunella shoes."

Carriages held men riding in top-boots and ruffled silk shirts, and women in silks and laces. It was civilization which Abraham Lincoln, twenty-eight years old, saw as he rode into Springfield that March day in 1837—to be a lawyer. Its people were mostly from Kentucky, coming by horse, wagon, and boat across country not yet cleared of wolves, wildcats, and horse thieves. And there were in Sangamon County 78 free negroes, 20 registered indentured servants, and 6 slaves.

The centre of the town was a public square, with the court-house, jail, stores, churches, banks, harness-makers, and black-smiths lined about the square. The streets and sidewalks were plain black Illinois soil underfoot, except for gravel here and there for dry footing in rain or snow, and stones and sticks for street crossings.

Lincoln pulled in his horse at the general store of Joshua Speed. He asked the price of bedclothes for a single bedstead, which Speed figured at $17.00. "Cheap as it is, I have not the money to pay," he told Speed. "But if you will credit me until Christmas, and my experiment as a lawyer here is a success, I will pay you then. If I fail in that I will probably never pay you at all." Speed said afterward: "The tone of his voice was so melancholy that I felt for him. I looked up at him and thought that I never saw so gloomy and melancholy a face in my life." Speed offered to share his own big double bed upstairs over the store. Lincoln took his saddlebags upstairs, came down with his face lit up and said, "Well, Speed, I'm moved."

His meals he had arranged to take with Bill Butler, one of the "Long Nine," who said Lincoln could put his feet under the table at the Butler home as long as he wanted to; they wouldn't worry about the board bill. He joined Stuart, and their professional card read, "J. T. Stuart and A. Lincoln, Attorneys and Counsellors at Law, will practice conjointly, in the Courts of this Judicial Circuit—Office No. 4 Hoffman's Row upstairs. Springfield, April 12, 1837."

In his new copy of Webster's dictionary, he wrote, to see how it would look, on the flyleaf, "A. Lincoln, Esq., Attorney and Counselor-at-Law."

The county courtroom was on the lower floor of a two-story building in Hoffman's Row. Upstairs, over the courtroom, was the law office of the new firm of Stuart & Lincoln: a little room with a few loose boards for bookshelves, an old wood stove, a table, a chair, a bench, a buffalo robe, and a small bed.

Stuart was running for Congress, so Lincoln handled all of the law practice in range of his ability. His first case was one he had helped work on during the previous year, defending David Wooldridge, in a suit brought by James P. Hawthorn. Hawthorn claimed Wooldridge was to furnish him two yoke of oxen to break up twenty acres of prairie sod-ground; also he claimed Wooldridge was to allow him to raise a crop of corn or wheat on a certain piece of ground; and Wooldridge had failed him in both cases.

Furthermore, Hawthorn claimed damages because Wooldridge struck, beat, bruised, and knocked him (Hawthorn) down; plucked, pulled, and tore large quantities of hair from his head. Also because with a stick and his fists he struck Hawthorn many violent blows and strokes on or about the face, head, breast, back, shoulders, hips, legs, and divers other parts of the body, and because he had with violence forced, pushed, thrust, and gouged his fingers into Hawthorn's eyes.

Such were the allegations on assumpsit and trespass vi et armis, including also replevin action demanding return of a black and white yoke of steers, one black cow and calf, and one prairie plow. Lincoln's first move was to bring up a board bill for eight months which Hawthorn owed Wooldridge, amounting at $1.50 a week to $45.75. Also, for the same eight months, he had used a wagon and team for which he should pay $90.00 besides a cash loan of $100.00. The case never came to trial. Peacemakers settled it out of court. The plaintiff and defendant divided the court costs. In the record Lincoln spelled wagon "waggon" and prairie "prairy."

Between law cases he kept up his political fences, writing such letters as this to John Bennett at Petersburg:

SPRINGFIELD, August 5, 1837.

DEAR SIR:

Mr. Edwards tells me you wish to know whether the act to which your town incorporation provision was attached, passed into a law. It did. You can organize under the general incorporation law as soon as you choose.

I also tacked a provision on to a fellow's bill to authorize a relocation of the road from Salem down to your town; but I am not certain whether or not the bill passed; neither do I suppose I can ascertain before the laws will be published. If it is a law, Bowling Green, Bennet Abell, and yourself are appointed to make the change.

No news. No excitement except a little about the election of Monday next. I suppose, of course, our friend, Dr. Henry, stands no chance in your "diggings."

Your friend and humble servant,

A. LINCOLN.

Mrs. Joseph Anderson, a widow, came into the office of Stuart & Lincoln, to ask if they could help her. She had come to Springfield to sell ten acres of land left by her husband, but she found that General James Adams claimed the ten acres had been signed over to him by her husband for a debt he owed General Adams as a lawyer. Lincoln worked on the case, searched the records, and then published a handbill opening with the statement: "It is well known to most of you, that there is existing at this time, considerable excitement in regard to Gen. Adams's titles to certain tracts of land, and the manner in which he acquired them."

He then went into a tissue of facts to show that Adams had falsified documents in order to swindle "a widow woman" out of ten acres of land. General Adams wrote a reply which filled six newspaper columns, and Lincoln returned with a one-column answer analyzing affidavits offered by Adams, saying they were "all false as hell," and adding: "In conclusion I will only say that I have a character to defend as well as Gen. Adams, but I disdain to whine about it as he does."

When Adams again filled six newspaper columns with his defense, Lincoln commented: "Let it be remembered that when he first came to this country he attempted to impose himself upon the community as a lawyer, and actually carried the attempt so far, as to induce a man who was under a charge of murder to entrust the defense of his life in his hands, and finally took his money and got him hanged. Is this the man that is to raise a breeze in his favor by abusing lawyers? If he is not himself a lawyer, it is for the lack of sense, and not of inclination. If he is not a lawyer, he *is* a liar, for he proclaimed himself a lawyer, and got a man hanged by depending on him."

His scorn of Adams was put into a clear lingo. "It is true I have no children nor *kitchen boys;* and if I had, I should scorn to lug them in to make affidavits for me."

He declared further newspaper argument closed. "Farewell, General. I will see you again at Court, if not before—when and where we will settle the question whether you or the widow shall have the land."

In the trial he won for Mrs. Anderson her ten acres of land, shortly after which an editorial supposed to have been written by Lincoln was published in the *Sangamo Journal,* containing a copy of an indictment found against Gen. Adams in Oswego County, New York, in 1818, the crime charged being forgery of a deed. "A person of evil name and fame and of a wicked disposition," was the *Journal's* allusion to Adams, who at the August election had been chosen probate justice of the peace.

The affair with General Adams was taken by some people as a noisy rumpus that could have been conducted more decently by Lincoln, while others held it as a sign that chivalry was alive, even if it came in drab blue jeans, with a grin.

Veiled accusations were published in the *Illinois Republican,* a Democratic newspaper, that Lincoln's friend, Dr. A. G. Henry, the acting commissioner in charge of the construction work on the new Statehouse, was hornswoggling the taxpayers; a committee of Whigs marched on the editorial rooms of the newspaper; warnings and threats were exchanged; it was said that among the Democratic leaders who got their hair mussed was Stephen A. Douglas, reported to be the writer of the unsigned articles attacking Dr. Henry.

Lincoln helped organize a mass meeting where he offered a resolution pointing at Dr. Henry as being accused of "squandering uselessly and wastefully the public money" appropriated for the Statehouse. Therefore, said Lincoln's resolution, a committee of seven should be appointed to investigate whether the work under Dr. Henry was "progressing in the most economical and judicious manner." The committee was appointed and did its duty in a report vindicating the Whig commissioner, Lincoln's friend.

It was a year with branches thickening out into the air, struggling for fresh lines for the run of the sap.

The young lawyer and politician could look out from the office window on the main street and the public square, with freedom to read what could be read in the passers-by, the forms and faces, the doctor going to a birth, the hearse leading a burial party, children going to school, the town drunkard dragged by the town constable, bankers, landowners, squatters, carpenters, well-diggers, washerwomen, Kentuckians, Virginians, Yankees, French-Canadians, Pennsylvania Dutch, Irish, and Germans— passers-by.

Past the window of the law office of Stuart & Lincoln came farmers hauling corn, wheat, potatoes, and turnips, in wagons; the axles creaked; husky voices bawled at the yokes of steers while the whip thongs lashed and cracked.

Droves of hogs came past, in muddy weather wallowing over their knees, the hair of their flanks spattered, their curls of tails flipping as they grunted onward to sale and slaughter.

And there were horses, and men riding and driving who loved horses. It was a horse country. They too were passers-by— roans, grays, whites, black horses with white stockings, sorrels with a sorrel forelock down a white face, bays with a white star in the forehead.

In a letter to Levi Davis. Esq., of Vandalia, Lincoln wrote

one April day, "We have generally in this Country, Peace, Health, and Plenty, and no News."

Chapter 46

ONE day Lincoln had dipped a pen in an ink-bottle and written the words, "State of Illinois, Sangamon County and Circuit— of the July term of the Sangamon Circuit Court in the Year of Our Lord One Thousand Eight Hundred and Thirty-Nine." And he had since dipped his pen and written the same words, changing only the date, dozens of times, and he knew if he lived he would write them thousands of times. He could almost write those words in his sleep. Likewise with the form he scratched off, reading, "I do hereby enter myself as security for costs in this cause, and acknowledge myself bound to pay, or cause to be paid, all costs which may accrue in this action either to the opposite party or to any of the officers of this court in pursuance of the laws of this state." He could repeat that, almost, backward.

Money came to his hands, fees, of which half must go to Stuart. He wrote a memorandum, such as "I have received five dollars from Deed of Macon, five from Lewis Keeling, five from Andrew Finley, one half of which belongs to Stuart and has not been entered on the books."

"Safety" was the anxious key word in one letter. "I am unwilling to make any conveyance until I see the assignments and original certificate. If Mr. Underhill will bring that certificate I will do all an honorable man should do. It is not money, but safety, I desire." And closing the letter he repeated, "If Mr. Underhill will come and bring the certificate I will do all in safety I can."

A caller came one day, representing the United States Government and its Post Office Department. The caller wanted to ask about a certain number of dollars and cents that had come into the hands of Lincoln as postmaster at New Salem. Lincoln stepped to a corner of the office, dug out a sack and counted the money in it, the exact amount asked for by the inspector, who took the money, gave a receipt, and went away satisfied.

His grocery days were an advantage to Lincoln in the case where the Hickox brothers had sold flour to the defendant as "good, merchantable, superfine flour," against which Lincoln pleaded that "twenty barrels were *not* at the time of sale, good, merchantable, superfine flour, but, on the contrary, greatly inferior in quality."

In one of his first murder cases, tried in Hancock County, Lincoln failed to save William Fraim, who was convicted on April 25, 1839, and, by court order, hanged by the neck till dead, just twenty-three days later.

Murderers, horse thieves, scandalmongers, and slanderers came at various times and poured out their stories amid the walls of the Stuart & Lincoln law office. There came bothered and puzzled people.

George Stockton walked in one day and told how a cooking-stove was spoiled a hundred dollars' worth, he guessed; and Lincoln brought suit against Tolby for that amount of damages to "a cooking-stove." But he had many quiet hours when there was little business, because there was little crime. In the office record of expenses he made an entry, "Lincoln paid for wood . . . $.50," and "Lincoln paid for saw . . . $2.25." If not busy at law practice, he was sawing wood.

A boatload of corn coming down the Sangamon River ran onto a fish-trap dam, and sprang a leak so that the corn was wet. On being unloaded the corn got rained on and further damaged. Lincoln brought suit for the owners of the boat and the corn against the fish-trappers for obstructing the navigation of the Sangamon River and unlawfully damaging the boat and the corn as property.

One hot summer day Harvey Ross came; in order to prove ownership of his farm at Macomb he had to have the testimony from a witness near Springfield. Court had closed for six months, Lincoln explained, but they would go out to Judge Thomas's farm a mile east and see what he could do. Lincoln took off his coat, laid it on a chair, and with a bundle of papers in one hand and a red handkerchief for wiping sweat off, in the other hand, he and the witness walked out to the Thomas farm, asking the way and taking the short cuts.

The judge's wife said the judge had gone to the north part of the farm, where he had a tenant house, to help his men put up a corncrib. If they went the main road it would be a half-mile, but if they cut across the cornfield it would be only a quarter-mile, Mrs. Thomas said; and on Lincoln asking her to show them the path she came out of the house and pointed to where the short cut led across the cornfield from their barn.

They struck out Indian-file, Lincoln with a bundle of papers in one hand and a red handkerchief in the other, till they came to where the judge and his men were raising logs to make a corn-crib and hogpen. Lincoln put the case to the judge, who looked over the papers, swore in the witness, and, with pen and ink from the tenant house, signed the documents.

All were in shirt-sleeves, and Lincoln remarked it was a kind of shirt-sleeve court they were holding. "Yes," laughed the judge, "a shirt-sleeve court in a cornfield."

The main business being over, Lincoln asked the judge if he didn't want some help in rolling up the logs. The judge guessed two of them were pretty heavy and he could stand a little help. So Lincoln and Ross pitched in and helped, and when Ross offered to pay the judge for his services the judge said he guessed the helping with the logs was pay enough.

On the road back to Springfield Lincoln could have told Ross some of the stories passing among lawyers and judges, of the man, for instance, charged with sheep-killing, who was asked by the court, "Are you guilty or not guilty?" And the man wouldn't answer. The court kept at him, and at last said, "You must do something—what do you do?" The man answered, "I stands mute," and, pushed further, would only answer, "I stands mute." On trial the case was decided against him, but he was told he could carry it higher up to the Court of Errors. And he murmured, "If this here ain't a court of errors, I'd like to know where you kin find one!"

In the case of a defendant charged with mistreating a livery-stable horse, a witness testified, "When his company rides fast he rides fast, and when his company rides slow he rides slow." "I want to know," said the important lawyer for the other side, "how he rides when he is alone. "W-e-l-l," said the witness, a slow talker, "I—never—was—with—him—when—he—was—alone; so—I don't know."

And there was a case told among lawyers of a defendant, losing, who stood up and called the court unjust, corrupt, and false. He was fined ten dollars for contempt of court, and handed the clerk a twenty-dollar bill. "I can't change this," said the clerk. "Never mind about the other ten dollars," came the hot reply, "I'll take it out in contempt!"

Chapter 47

ONE day early in May, when the stir of new grass was green over the prairie, and lazy winds came in the jack-oak brush and among the prongs of the oak and the shagbark in their spring coat of leaves, Lincoln took his pen and wrote a quaint letter out of an odd, lonely heart. It was another letter to Miss Mary Owens down in Green County, Kentucky. She would have to be poor and show her poverty, if she married him. He was willing to marry, if she so wished. His advice would be not to marry. The letter read:

SPRINGFIELD, May 7, 1837.

MISS MARY S. OWENS.

Friend Mary: I have commenced two letters to send you before this, both of which displeased me before I got half done, and so I tore them up. The first I thought was not serious enough, and the second was on the other extreme. I shall send this, turn out as it may.

This thing of living in Springfield is rather a dull business, after all; at least it is so to me. I am quite as lonesome here as I ever was anywhere in my life. I have been spoken to by but one woman since I have been here, and should not have been by her if she could have avoided it. I've never been to church yet, and probably shall not be soon. I stay away because I am conscious I should not know how to behave myself.

I am often thinking of what we said about your coming to live at Springfield. I am afraid you would not be satisfied. There is a great deal of flourishing about in carriages here, which it would be your doom to see without sharing it. You would have to be poor, without the means of hiding your poverty. Do you believe you could bear that patiently? Whatever woman may cast her lot with mine, should any ever do so, it is my intention to do all in my power to make her happy and contented; and there is nothing I can imagine that would make me more unhappy than to fail in the effort. I know I should be much happier with you than the way I am, provided I saw no signs of discontent in you. What you have said to me may have been in the way of jest, or I may have misunderstood it. If so, then let it be forgotten; if otherwise, I much wish you would think seriously before you decide. What I have said I will most positively abide by, provided you wish it. My opinion is that you had better not do it. You have not been accustomed to hardship, and it may be more severe than you now imagine. I know you are capable of thinking correctly on any subject, and if you deliberate maturely upon this before you decide, then I am willing to abide your decision.

You must write me a good long letter after you get this. You have nothing else to do, and though it might not seem interesting to you after you had written it, it would be a good deal of company to me in this "busy wilderness." Tell your sister I don't want to hear any more about selling out and moving. That gives me the "hypo" whenever I think of it.

Yours, etc.,
LINCOLN.

Mary Owens came on a visit to her sister near New Salem that summer. She and Lincoln saw each other and talked and came to no understanding. After they parted, and on the day that they parted, Lincoln wrote her another letter. It read:

SPRINGFIELD, August 16, 1837.

FRIEND MARY: You will no doubt think it rather strange that I should write you a letter on the same day on which we parted, and I can only account for it by supposing that seeing you lately makes me think of you more than usual; while at our late meeting we had but few expressions of thoughts. You must know that I cannot see you or think of you with entire indifference; and yet it may be that you are mistaken in regard to what my real feelings toward you are. If I knew you were not, I should not trouble you with this letter. Perhaps any other man would know enough without further information; but I consider it my peculiar right to plead ignorance, and your bounden duty to allow the plea. I want in all cases to do right, and most particularly so in all cases with women. I want at this particular time, more than anything else, to do right with you; and if I knew it would be doing right, as I rather suspect it would, to let you alone, I would do it. And for the purpose of making the matter as plain as possible, I now say that you can now drop the subject, dismiss your thoughts (if you ever had any) from me forever, and leave this letter unanswered, without calling forth one accusing murmur from me. And I will even go further, and say that if it will add anything to your comfort or peace of mind to do so, it is my sincere wish that you should. Do not understand by this that I wish to cut your acquaintance. I mean no such thing. What I do wish is that our further acquaintance shall depend upon yourself. If such further acquaintance would contribute nothing to your happiness, I am sure it would not to mine. If you feel yourself in any degree bound to me, I am now willing to release you, provided you wish it; while, on the other hand, I am willing and even anxious to bind you faster, if I can be convinced that it will, in any considerable degree, add to your happiness. This, indeed, is the whole question with me. Nothing would make me more miserable than to believe you miserable—nothing more happy than to know you were so.

In what I have now said, I think I cannot be misunderstood, and to make myself understood is the only object of this letter.

If it suits you best to not answer this, farewell. A long life and a merry one attend you. But if you conclude to write back, speak as plainly as I do. There can be neither harm nor danger in saying to me anything you think, just in the manner you think it.

My respects to your sister.

Your friend,
LINCOLN.

And the months passed by till the first day of April came in the next year. And the comedy of man, woman, and destiny, the fact that marriages are often accidents, was lighting up his brain as his imagination reviewed events. He wrote a letter filled with the chuckles and oddities of a story-teller telling a story with the laugh on himself. Among his men acquaintances and friends there was not one he could pour out the story to.

He chose a woman, Mrs. O. H. Browning, the wife of a fellow member of the legislature, to hear his confessions that he had vanity, that he had stupidity, that he had made a fool of himself, that he believed he had had a narrow escape from a marriage that would have been comic. The letter:

SPRINGFIELD, April 1, 1838.

DEAR MADAM:—

Without apologizing for being egotistical, I shall make the history of so much of my life as has elapsed since I saw you the subject of this letter. And, by the way, I now discover that, in order to give a full and intelligible account of the things I have done and suffered since I saw you, I shall necessarily have to relate some that happened before.

It was, then, in the autumn of 1836 that a married lady of my acquaintance and who was a great friend of mine, being about to pay a visit to her father and other relatives residing in Kentucky, proposed to me that on her return she would bring a sister of hers with her on condition that I would engage to become her brother-in-law with all convenient despatch. I, of course, accepted the proposal, for you know I could not have done otherwise, had I really been averse to it; but privately, between you and me, I was most confoundedly well pleased with the project. I had seen the said sister some three years before, thought her intelligent and agreeable, and saw no good objection to plodding life through hand in hand with her. Time passed on, the lady took her journey sure enough. This stomached me a little; for it appeared to me that her coming so readily showed that she was a trifle too willing; but, on reflection, it occurred to me that she might have been prevailed on by her married sister to come, without anything concerning me ever having been mentioned to her; and so I concluded that, if no other objection presented itself, I would consent to waive this. All this occurred to me on hearing of her arrival in the neighborhood; for, be it remembered, I had not yet seen her, except about three years previous, as above mentioned. In a few days we had an interview; and, although I had seen her before, she did not look as my imagination had pictured her. I knew she was over-size, but she now appeared a fair match for Falstaff. I knew she was called an "old maid," and I felt no doubt of the truth of at least half of the appellation; but now, when I beheld her, I could not for my life avoid thinking of my mother; and this, not from withered features, for her skin was too full of fat to permit of its contracting into wrinkles, but from her want of teeth, weather-beaten appearance in general, and from a kind of notion that ran in my head that nothing could have commenced at the size of infancy and reached her present bulk in less than thirty-five or forty years; and, in short, I was not at all pleased with her. But what could I do? I had told her sister I would take her for better or for worse; and I made a point of honor and conscience in all things to stick to my word, especially if others had been induced to act on it, which in this case I had no doubt they had; for I was now fairly convinced that no other man on earth would have her, and hence the conclusion that they were bent on holding me to my bargain. "Well," thought I, "I have said it, and, be the consequences what they may, it shall not be my fault if I fail to do it." At once I determined to consider her my wife; and, this done, all my powers of discovery were put to work in search of perfections in her which might be fairly set off against her defects. I tried to imagine her handsome, which, but for her unfortunate corpulency, was actually true. Exclusive of this, no woman that I have ever seen has a finer face. I also tried to convince myself that the mind was much more to be valued than the person; and in this she was not inferior, as I could discover, to any with whom I had been acquainted.

Shortly after this, without coming to any positive understanding with her, I set out for Vandalia, when and where you first saw me. During my stay there I had letters from her which did not change my opinion of either her intellect or intention, but on the contrary confirmed it in both.

All this while, although I was fixed, "firm as the surge-repelling rock," in my resolution, I found I was continually repenting the rash-ness which had led me to make it. Through life I have been in no bondage, either real or imaginary, from the thraldom of which I so much desired to be free. After my return home I saw nothing to change my opinions of her in any particular. She was the same, and so was I. I now spent my time in planning how I might get along through life after my contemplated change of circumstances should have taken place, and how I might procrastinate the evil day for a time, which I really dreaded as much, perhaps more, than an Irishman does the halter.

After all my suffering upon this deeply interesting subject, here I am, wholly, unexpectedly, completely, out of the "scrape"; and now I want to know if you can guess how I got out of it—out, clear, in every sense of the term; no violation of word, honor, or conscience. I don't believe you can guess, and so I might as well tell you at once. As the lawyer says, it was done in the manner following, to-wit: After I had delayed the matter as long as I thought I could in honor do

(which, by the way, had brought me round into the last fall), I concluded I might as well bring it to a consummation without further
delay; and so I mustered my resolution, and made the proposal to her
direct; but, shocking to relate, she answered, No. At first I supposed
she did it through an affectation of modesty, which I thought but ill
became her under the peculiar circumstances of her case; but on my
renewal of the charge, I found she repelled it with greater firmness than
before. I tried it again and again, but with the same success, or rather
with the same want of success.

I finally was forced to give it up; at which I very unexpectedly
found myself mortified almost beyond endurance. I was mortified, it
seemed to me, in a hundred different ways. My vanity was deeply
wounded by the reflection that I had been too stupid to discover her
intentions, and at the same time never doubting that I understood them
perfectly; and also that she, whom I had taught myself to believe
nobody else would have, had actually rejected me with all my fancied
greatness. And, to cap the whole, I then for the first time began to
suspect that I was really a little in love with her. But let it all go.
I'll try and outlive it. Others have been made fools of by the girls;
but this can never with truth be said of me. I most emphatically, in
this instance, made a fool of myself. I have now come to the conclusion never again to think of marrying, and for this reason: I can
never be satisfied with any one who would be blockhead enough to
have me.

When you receive this, write me a long yarn about something to
amuse me. Give my respects to Mr. Browning.

Your sincere friend,
A. LINCOLN.

And a few months later when Mrs. Bennet Able of New Salem,
Illinois, visited her sister Mary Owens in Green County, Kentucky, Miss Owens told neighbors that Abe Lincoln said to Mrs.
Able in Springfield, "Tell your sister that I think she was a
great fool, because she did not stay here, and marry me."

And when one of the Greens at New Salem was asked later
to write a letter telling what he knew about Miss Owens and
especially her looks, he wrote: "Bill, I am getting old; I have
seen too much trouble to give a lifelike picture of this woman.
I won't try it. None of the poets or romance writers has ever
given to us a picture of a heroine so beautiful as a good description of Miss Owens in 1836 would be."

Chapter 48

A SCHOOL for young ladies in Springfield was announcing that besides ordinary branches of education and training in "intellectual and moral science," it would conduct "a class in Mezzotint painting." A store was offering on sale "cloth, comb, tooth, hair, and nail brushes." Civilization and culture were stirring in Illinois. The Alton Literary Society met in the courthouse in that city and debated the question, "Was Brutus justified in killing Cæsar?"

Lincoln read newspapers, skirmished through exchanges in the *Sangamo Journal* office. He could read there in the year 1839 that the Northern Cross Railroad would pay cash for timber to make the grade from Springfield to Meredosia. Shipments of rifles had arrived in Illinois, "all lengths and sizes, mounted with brass, silver, and gold, single and double barrel, with shotguns to fit the same stock, some very fine in mahogany and leather cases."

Orchards were being planted with new kinds of apple trees, Winter Sweets, Red Streaks, Red Russets, Yellow Hearts, Rainbows. One January day the *Journal* announced, "Our farmers can now be supplied with Ruta Baga seed at Mr. Canedy's Drug Store. Now is the time to sow it. Select a piece of clean land, harrow in the seed well, keep the land clear of weeds, and thin the plants to six inches apart. The drill culture is better, but is more troublesome."

One, and often two, columns in a newspaper had the heading "Estrays," and told of lost horses, sorrels, bays, dapple bays, some "blaze-faced," some with saddle-marks or spots and scars, or "bit in the ear," or long-tailed or switch-tailed or with "a snip on the nose." Lincoln, on losing his horse, advertised:

Strayed or Stolen: From a stable in Springfield on Wednesday, 18th inst., a large bay horse, star in his forehead, plainly marked with harness; supposed to be eight years old; had been shod all around, but is believed to have lost some of his shoes, and trots and paces. Any person who will take up said horse and leave information at the Journal office or with the subscriber, shall be liberally paid for their trouble. A Lincoln.

One week in November of 1839, Lincoln saw two editorials which he read carefully more than once or twice in the *Illinois State Register*, the Democratic newspaper of Springfield. The articles were about him, aimed straight at him. It was the first time any attempt had been made through the public prints to improve his manners. His personal behavior was publicly discussed and he was advised how he should so act that he would appear to better advantage and win more general approval. He looked on the public platform like a clown, but in so looking he was a good deal of an actor, a sort of comedian, not a real clown, but one playing a part—thus the *State Register* pictured him.

Lincoln had spoken in the courthouse as a candidate for presidential elector on a Tuesday evening, in reply to Stephen A. Douglas, and the *State Register* commented:

"Mr. Lincoln's argument was truly ingenious. He has, however, a sort of *assumed clownishness* in his manner which does not become him, and which does not truly belong to him. It is *assumed*—assumed for effect. Mr. Lincoln will sometimes make his language correspond with this clownish manner, and he can thus frequently raise a loud laugh among his Whig hearers; but this entire game of buffoonery convinces the *mind* of no man, and is utterly lost on the majority of his audience. We seriously advise Mr. Lincoln to correct this clownish fault before it grows upon him."

In Tuesday's debating, Douglas was the loser, the *Register* acknowledged. "The main object of calling in Mr. Lincoln was to raise up Cyrus Walker, a Whig, who had been actually demolished by Mr. Douglas in the afternoon. Lincoln made out to get Walker rather unsteadily on his legs again and between the two Whig speakers, our Democratic 'little giant,' as Walker called him, had a rough time of it. Lincoln misrepresented Douglas, as was apparent to every man present. This brought a *warm* rejoinder from Mr. Douglas. Mr. Walker then rose, complained of Mr. D. for his *warmth* and went on for an hour starting new points. Thus a concerted plot of 'two pluck one' began to show itself."

On the Wednesday night following, Douglas argued against the United States Bank, and it seemed to the *State Register:* "There was a profound silence upon his conclusion and a settled gloom covered the Whigs. They saw how utterly hopeless must be the attempt to answer. Mr. Lincoln was, however, again put forward; but he commenced with embarrassment and continued without making the slightest impression. The Mr. Lincoln of Wednesday night was not the Mr. Lincoln of Tuesday. He could only meet the arguments of Mr. Douglas by relating stale anecdotes and old stories, and left the stump literally whipped off of it, even in the estimation of his own friends." Then, after declaring Lincoln and Walker were without measures or principles to advocate, the editorial closed, "The *men* are smart enough, but the *cause* they have espoused is rotten to the core."

The second editorial had the heading, "Mr. Lincoln and the Register," and opened: "On last Wednesday night, Mr. Lincoln, in the course of his reply to Mr. Douglas, traveled out of his way to attack the veracity of the editors of this paper. Under the rule agreed upon by a committee, governing the discussion, Mr. Lincoln could not be replied to by either of the editors of this paper. This Mr. Lincoln knew, and he has lowered himself in our estimation by his conduct on that occasion. He asserted that he did not advise the running of John Bennett for the Legislature, but was in favor of Bowling Green; and that the editors of the *Register* had lied in making such a statement. Mr. Lincoln said further that we had no *authority* for making the statement; and that having no authority even had we published the truth, we were still *liars!* Such was the language of the man selected by the Whig party to be an elector of the high office of President of the United States. To the indecorous language of Mr. Lincoln we make no reply."

Then followed the publication of an anonymous letter, which the *Register* said was written by "a highly respectable citizen of Petersburg." The letter set forth that two good candidates had been turned down by Lincoln and two other Whig bosses, who had handed the nomination to John Bennett, "a Nullifier, also a thorough aristocrat, an advocate for taking the election of Justices and Constables from the people."

The same letter had been published two weeks previous in the *Register,* and, neither Lincoln nor any other Whigs replying to it, the *Register* assumed it was true. "Before and since, we have heard several of the friends of Mr. Lincoln admit, on the streets, and undertake to justify, this party arrangement. Mr. Lincoln's allowing two weeks to pass by with the accusation resting on him, and making no effort to relieve himself from it, gave the public the right to look upon the accusation as true."

Also in the same issue of the *Register,* Lincoln could turn a page and read an advertisement of a sort common in all newspapers then. Usually such advertisements were scattered among the lost-horses and strayed-cattle notices. One read:

$50 Reward. Ran away from the subscriber, living in Lewis County, Mo., four miles from Tully, a slave named Charles, about 20 years of age, five feet six or seven inches high, well made, free spoken among whites, and pleasant in conversation, had a white speck in the ball of eye, a scar at the extremity of the left eyebrow, also a scar on the right wrist, and one between the neck and collar-bone; had also scars on his back.

Then followed particulars about the payment of the reward for the delivery of the property.

Chapter 49

LOOKING out through the little windowpanes of the law office overlooking the main street and the public square where the new capitol building was to stand, listening at the street corners in summer and at the circles around wood stoves in the grocery stores in winter, Lincoln came to know the haunts and tabernacles of politics, their passions and hatreds, their stormy laughter. It was precisely this period and these people that the young French philosopher, De Tocqueville, traveling north, south, and west over America, had in mind, when he sharpened a pencil and wrote:

"Almost the only pleasure of which any American has any idea is to take part in the government, and to discuss the part he has taken. An American cannot converse, but he can discuss . . . He speaks to you as if he were addressing a meeting; and if he should chance to warm in the course of the discussion, he will infallibly say, 'Gentlemen' to the person with whom he is conversing. If an American were condemned to confine his activity to his own affairs, he would be robbed of one-half of his existence."

And the shrewd Frenchman held a balance by also noting: "It is difficult to imagine the rapidity with which public opinion circulates in the midst of these deserts. I do not think that so much intellectual discourse takes place in the most enlightened and populous districts of France." So far as Sangamon County and Illinois were concerned, he sketched it.

Once more Lincoln carried an election to the legislature, also stumping for his law partner John T. Stuart, who was elected to Congress. Two years later, in 1840, he and Stuart were again elected to the same offices. Talk ran that he deserved a nomination to Congress for his efforts in behalf of the Whig party; he was pushed by his party for speaker of the house in the legislature.

Besides wit and personality, a man had to have bulldog courage and "a constitution like a horse" to stand up in the game. When Stuart was running against Steve Douglas for Congress in 1838 the two struck, grappled, and "fought like wildcats" back and forth over the floor of Herndon's grocery till each was too tired to hit another blow. When Stuart came to, he ordered a barrel of whisky for the crowd.

Lincoln, a while later, sending news to Stuart in Washington, wrote: "Yesterday Douglas having chosen to consider himself insulted by something in the *Journal,* undertook to cane Francis [the editor] in the street. Francis caught him by the hair and jammed him back against a market-cart, where the matter ended by Francis being pulled away from him. The whole affair was so ludicrous that Francis and everybody else, Douglas excepted, have been laughing about it ever since."

The Whigs rented the courthouse for a campaign meeting one day, and Edward D. Baker, speaking on the issues of the day, led up to the point where he declared that wherever there was a land office, there was a Democratic newspaper to defend its corruption. Democrats in the audience yelled, "Pull him down."

A riot was starting when Lincoln, who had been listening to the speech through a trapdoor looking from his office down into the courtroom, came dangling down with his long legs through the hole in the ceiling. He helped bring order by saying: "Hold on, gentlemen. This is a land of free speech. Baker has a right to speak, and if you take him off the stand you'll have to take me, too."

When a railroad contractor, Reuben Radford, brought in a construction gang to man the polls for the Democratic ticket one election day, Lincoln heard about it and went to the polling-place on a slow trot. In warning Radford, he remarked, "Radford, you'll spoil and blow if you live much longer." He told Speed in the evening that he wanted to hit Radford but couldn't get a chance. "I intended just to knock him down and leave him kicking."

At a political meeting in Springfield he replied to an attack on the "Long Nine" by Jesse B. Thomas; it was a furious and directly personal handling he gave Thomas, with jabs of sarcasm and a mimicking of Thomas; Springfield called it a "terrible skinning," and it was alluded to as "the skinning of Thomas." The crowd had "egged him on" with yells and cheers so that Lincoln gave Thomas a worse skinning than he intended; he went to Thomas's office and said he was sorry; he told friends he wasn't proud of the performance.

James Matheny joined Lincoln, Evan Butler, and Noah

Rickard, one evening, in dragging a man to the courthouse pump where they stripped him of his shirt, tied him to the pump, and gave the man's wife a switch and told her, "Light in." The man was a shoemaker who had been getting drunk regularly and always when drunk brutally beating his wife. Lincoln had warned him that if he beat his wife again he would have to take a beating himself. Matheny said the wife had to be encouraged to lay on with the switch—and after that night he and Lincoln didn't hear anything more about the shoemaker beating his wife.

When Colonel Dick Taylor, known also as "Ruffled Shirt" Taylor, on account of his wearing ruffled silk shirts, got sarcastic about the Whigs being elegant and wearing fine clothes while pleading for the plain people, Lincoln, who was debating with Taylor, listened coolly, but after a while slipped to the side of Taylor, and tore open a coat buttoned up close. A bulge of ruffled silk flew out, and there came to sight a colored velvet vest and a watch-chain with gold seals.

The audience roared, heard Taylor through, and then later heard Lincoln say, as Ninian Edwards recalled it: "While Colonel Taylor was making these charges against the Whigs over the country, riding in fine carriages, wearing ruffled shirts, kid gloves, massive gold chains with large gold seals, and flourishing a heavy gold-headed cane, I was a poor boy, hired on a flatboat at eight dollars a month, and had only one pair of breeches to my back, and they were buckskin. Now, if you know the nature of buckskin when wet and dried by the sun, it will shrink; and my breeches kept shrinking until they left several inches of my legs bare between the tops of my socks and the lower part of my breeches; and whilst I was growing taller they were becoming shorter, and so much tighter that they left a blue streak around my legs that can be seen to this day. If you call this aristocracy I plead guilty to the charge."

While Stuart was in Washington, Lincoln handled the law practice and kept track of politics. Out of the silences of the little law office, he sent letters to Stuart about the many errands he was running from day to day and the items of news, the twists of life he had his eyes and ears bent toward. Two of the letters to Stuart read:

SPRINGFIELD, November 14, 1839.

DEAR STUART:

I have been to the secretary's office within the last hour, and find things precisely as you left them. No new arrivals of returns on either side. Douglas has not been here since you left. A report is in circulation that he has abandoned the idea of going to Washington, though the report does not come in a very authentic form, so far as I can learn. Though, by the way, speaking of authenticity, you know that if we had heard Douglas say that he had abandoned the contest, it would not be very authentic. There is no news here. Noah, I still think, will be elected very easily. I am afraid of our race for representative. Dr. Knapp has become a candidate, and I fear the few votes he will get will be taken from us. Also some one has been tampering with old Esquire Wicoff, and induced him to send in his name to be announced as a candidate. Francis refused to announce him without seeing him, and now I suppose there is going to be a fuss about it. I have been so busy that I have not seen Mrs. Stuart since you left, though I understand she wrote you by today's mail, which will inform you more about her than I could. The very moment a Speaker is elected, write me who he is.

Your friend as ever,
A. LINCOLN.

SPRINGFIELD, December 23, 1839.

DEAR STUART:

Dr. Henry will write you all the political news. I write this about some little matters of business. You recollect you told me you had drawn the Chicago Masack money, and sent it to the claimants. A d—d hawk-billed Yankee is here besetting me at every turn I take, saying that Robert Kinzie never received the eighty dollars to which he was entitled. Can you tell me anything about the matter? Again, old Mr. Wright, who lives up South Fork somewhere, is teasing me continually about some deeds which he says he left with you, but which I can find nothing of. Can you tell me where they are? The legislature is in session and has suffered the bank to forfeit its charter without benefit of clergy. There seems to be little disposition to resuscitate it.

Whenever a letter comes from you to Mrs. S——, I carry it to her, and then I see Betty; she is a tolerable nice "fellow" now. Maybe I will write again when I get more time.

Your friend, as ever,
A. LINCOLN.

P.S. The Democratic giant is here, but he is not now worth talking about.

He closed one letter to Stuart with a reference to "Ruffled Shirt Taylor" delivering a speech which William May answered. "The way May let the wind out of him was a perfect wonder; neither you nor I ever saw a crowd in this country so near all on one side, and all feeling so good." To this letter was the postscript: "Japh Bell has come out for Harrison. Ain't that a caution?"

His first published speech in pamphlet form was coming off the printing-presses early in 1840 and he wrote Stuart: "Well, I made a big speech which is in progress of printing in pamphlet form. To enlighten you and the rest of the world, I shall send you a copy when it is finished." The speech was one of a series of discussions of issues of the day, each speaker taking an entire evening, the general public invited to attend, in the hall of the House of Representatives in Springfield.

The smallest audience of the season came to hear Lincoln, and he alluded to that fact and let it stand in the published pamphlet, which opened:

"Fellow citizens: It is peculiarly embarrassing for me to attempt a continuance of the discussion, on this evening, which has been conducted in this hall on several previous ones. It is so because on each of those evenings there was a much fuller attendance than now, without any reason for its being so, except the greater interest the community feel in the speakers who addressed them then than they do in him who is to do so now. I am, indeed, apprehensive that the few who have attended have done so more to spare me mortification than in the hope of being interested in anything I may be able to say. This circumstance casts a damp upon my spirits, which I am sure I shall be unable to overcome during the evening."

From this mournful beginning, the thirty-year-old orator swept out into a speech that ranged across many fierce issues of the hour. Not only was he the strong young man who could take an ax handle and go to the polls and alone open a way through a gang blocking passage to the voting-place; not only was he the athlete they had seen take two fighting men and throw them apart as though they were two kittens. He was impressionable, with soft spots, with tremulous pools of changing lights. Though he stood up loose-jointed and comic with appeals in street-corner slang, and dialect from the public square hitching-posts, yet at moments he was as strange and far-off as the last dark sands of a red sunset, solemn as naked facts of death or hunger.

He declared ten years of Democratic administration had cost more money than the first twenty-seven years of the country's government, including the cost of the War of 1812. "The large sums foolishly, not to say corruptly, thrown away, constitute one of the just causes of complaint against the Administration. The agents of the Government in connection with the Florida (Indian) war needed a certain steamboat; the owner proposed to sell it for $10,000.00; the agents refused to give that sum, but hired the boat at $100.00 per day, and kept it at that hire till it amounted to $92,000.00. The contract for carrying the mail upon a certain route had expired, and of course was to be let again. The old contractor offered to take it for $300.00 a year. One James Reeside bid $99.00, and received the contract. On examination, it was discovered that Reeside had received for the service on this route, which he had contracted to render for less than $100.00, the enormous sum of $1,999.00. This is but a single case. Many similar ones, covering some ten or twenty pages of a large volume, are given."

He took up discussion of the subtreasury plan proposed by the Democrats, declaring it "less safe" than the national bank plan of the Whigs. "By the subtreasury scheme the public money is to be kept between the times of its disbursement, by treasurers of the mint, custom-house officers, land officers, and some new officers to be appointed. Has a year passed since the organization of the Government, that numerous defalcations have not occurred among this class of officers? Look at Swartout with his $1,200,000, Price with his $75,000, Harris with his $109,000, Linn with his $55,000, together with some twenty-five hundred lesser lights."

With however much care selections of bank officers might be made, there would be some unfaithful and dishonest. "The experience of the whole world, in all bygone times, proves this true. The Saviour of the world chose twelve disciples, and even one of that small number, selected by superhuman wisdom, turned out to be a traitor and a devil. And it may not be improper here to add that Judas carried the bag—was the subtreasurer of the Saviour and his disciples."

He took the instance of a subtreasurer having in his hands $100,000 of public money. "His duty says, 'You ought to pay this money over,' but his interest says, 'You ought to run away with this sum and be a nabob the balance of your life.' And who that knows anything of human nature doubts that in many instances interest will prevail over duty, and that the subtreasurer will prefer opulent knavery in a foreign land to honest poverty at home?"

He inquired whether a penitentiary department annexed to the subtreasury was not itself an admission that they expected public money to be stolen. "Why build the cage if they expect to catch no birds? But as to the question how effectual the penitentiary will be in preventing defalcations, how effectual have penitentiaries heretofore been in preventing the crimes they were established to suppress? Has not confinement in them long been the legal penalty of larceny, forgery, robbery, and many other crimes, in almost all the states? And yet are not those crimes committed weekly, daily—nay, and even hourly—in every one of those states? Again, the gallows has long been the penalty of murder, and yet we scarcely open a newspaper that does not relate a new case of that crime. If, then, the penitentiary has ever heretofore failed to prevent larceny, forgery, and robbery, and the gallows and halter have likewise failed to prevent murder, by what process of reasoning, I ask, is it that we are to conclude the penitentiary will hereafter prevent the stealing of public money? But our opponents seem to think they answer the charge that the money will be stolen fully if they can show that they will bring offenders to punishment. Not so. Will the punishment of the thief bring back the stolen money? No more so than the hanging of a murderer restores his victim to life. What is the object desired? Certainly not the greatest number of thieves we can catch, but that the money may not be stolen. If, then, any plan can be devised for depositing the public treasure where it will never be stolen, never embezzled, is not that the plan to be adopted? Turn, then, to a national bank."

Toward the end of his speech, thirty-year-old Abraham Lincoln spoke like a man watching a crazy and cruel horizon. "Many free countries have lost their liberty; and ours may lose hers; but if she shall, be it my proudest plume, not that I was the last to desert, but that I never deserted her. I know that the great volcano in Washington, aroused and directed by the evil spirit that reigns there, is belching forth the lava of political corruption in a current broad and deep, which is sweeping with frightful velocity over the whole length and breadth of the land, bidding fair to leave unscathed no green spot nor living thing; while on its bosom are riding, like demons on the waves of hell, the imps of that evil spirit, and fiendishly taunting all those who dare to resist its destroying course with the hopelessness of their effort; and knowing this, I cannot deny that all may be swept away. Broken by it I, too, may be; bow to it I never will."

The allusions to imps, lava, waves of hell, and fiendish taunts, concerned a town seventy miles from Springfield, where a wild drama had been acted out two years before. A young man in the town of Alton told men he must speak what he believed ought to be spoken. And the men to whom he so spoke answered that if he did speak what he believed ought to be spoken, they would kill him. He had brought a printing-press up from St. Louis, intending through the columns of his weekly newspaper to speak what he believed ought to be spoken; they threw his printing-press into the Mississippi River. He brought another printing-press to Alton; they wrecked it. And a third time he brought a printing-press to Alton, and they circled by night with torches and guns around the warehouse where he had the printing-press, and they set the warehouse on fire, and they shot him and killed him. And over the Illinois prairies and from the frontier to the eastern coast of America there was discussion about whether this young man, Elijah P. Lovejoy, was right or wrong in saying, against repeated warnings, that he must speak what he believed ought to be spoken; discussion flared up, sank down, flared up again about gag rule and gag government.

In Springfield, as Abraham Lincoln read the newspapers, the picture of what happened at Alton shocked him. That was his own word for it; he was shocked. Feet on the office table, gazing across the public square, he sat huddled with his thoughts.

When a bill came up in the legislature to throw off to the territory of Wisconsin the fourteen northern counties of the State of Illinois, he fought to defeat it. He wanted Illinois to have Chicago, a port on one of the Great Lakes within its borders, connecting the West with the East. If the measure had won, it would have left Illinois depending on the Ohio and Mississippi rivers for water transportation, with its main economic outlets toward the South, with its future tied closer to the South. The bill was beaten by 70 votes to 11.

At Page Eaton's carpenter shop one afternoon he stopped and talked. Page Eaton allowed that everybody said Lincoln would never make a good lawyer because he was too honest. And as Eaton told it: "Lincoln said he had a notion to quit studying law and learn carpentering. He thought there was more need of carpenters out here than lawyers."

Chapter 50

AMONG the men with whom Lincoln was mixing in company day
by day in his Springfield life as he passed thirty years of age,
there were future congressmen, governors, senators, judges. He
was watching masters in the game of politics and law. He saw
the young Stephen A. Douglas move from job to job; Douglas
had been state's attorney, member of the Illinois legislature, had
become register of the land office at Springfield, and was always
mentioned for congressman.

Watching the operations of some of his fellow citizens, he
learned more ways and habits of politics than are told of in the,
books. After trying a case in the courthouse, gossiping on street
corners a few minutes and stopping in at two or three stores,
and then going to his office and reading the latest newspapers,
he could put his feet on the office table, tilt back his chair, and
look out over the moving shadows of the public square with
enough history and philosophy to supply him for hours of
thought, surmise, deduction, suspicion, mystery.

The spinning of weaves and webs was going on, schemers
winding back and forth trying to piece together their schemes.
In order to live and stand up and be one of the men among men
in that frontier town and state in the years around 1840, a man
had to know schemers, had to know how to spot a scheme when
he saw one coming, and how to meet scheme with scheme. It
was not only Abe Lincoln's honesty that had put him in the
front among leaders of the Whig party, nor only that he had
personality and was a vote-getter on the stump and at electioneering; it was also that he was a schemer: he had a long head
and could gun for game far off. He was peering at Stephen A.
Douglas, the register of the land office, just as he had peered at
unknown lights moving in shallows of the Mississippi River as
he drew near in a flatboat.

A young man lit up with wild human enthusiasms had begun

clerking in the Speed store, and sleeping upstairs in the big room with Speed and Lincoln. He was William H. Herndon, whose father had taken him out of Illinois College at Jacksonville when the killing of Lovejoy started Abolition bonfires among its professors and students. He had been with Lincoln on one or two stumping trips, and had first seen Lincoln as he was riding horseback along the Sangamon River at the time Lincoln piloted the *Talisman* over the broken dam at New Salem. Young Herndon was thinking of studying law. Between these two men, Lincoln nine years the older, there was a trust and understanding not common among men. They belonged with Speed to a club of young men who met and read their writings to each other; Lincoln once entertained them with rhymes about the mistakes of men and women toward each other, one reading:

> Whatever spiteful fools may say,
> Each jealous ranting yelper,
> No woman ever went astray,
> Without a man to help her.

Interest in politics, the science of government, and the destiny of the human race was so keen at this time that the young Democrats and Whigs had a debating tournament that ran eight days straight, Sunday excepted, four speakers to a side, each speaker taking an evening. Lincoln's night to speak came last, and, as the listeners to politics and the science of government had their ears full of discussions by that time, Lincoln had the smallest audience of all.

The future held the thoughts of the young men. What with railroads coming West, the border would move, the Great Plains fill up with settlers, the frontier would shift from the Mississippi River to the Rocky Mountains, and after that to the Pacific Coast.

Peoria ran stages daily to Springfield, three times a week to Galena, Ottawa, and Rushville, and twice a week to Oquawka. The name "O-quaw-ka" was mentioned by people as a place where white men had a town; it was not an Indian tribe nor a bird or rabbit. Seven steamers made trips between Peoria, St. Louis, and Pittsburgh; another ran between St. Louis and the Rock River. History and destiny were in the air; the name of Stone's Landing was changed to Napoleon; the name of Goose Run to Columbus River.

The land was now all surveyed; fences were coming; if timber for rail-fencing was not handy, there was the Osage orange hedge which with a few years' growth would keep cows in a pasture and out of a cornfield on the prairie farms. Land speculators now held the larger part of the land in Illinois. By 1837, there had been issued 17,075 patents for 2,831,840 acres of land; in 1839 were recorded 1,132,872 land sales. The wilderness was passing into the hands of landlords and speculators. Romulus Riggs, who lived in Philadelphia and gave his daughter the name of "Illinois," offered 226 quarter-sections of land for sale at prices from $5.00 to $40.00 an acre; of his total holdings he wished to sell 42,560 acres.

In state and national politics, the western public lands became an issue. Martin Van Buren, the New York Tammany Democrat who was picked by Andrew Jackson to follow him in the White House, was beaten in the wild campaign of 1840 partly because of his record of having voted against western internal improvements, against the Cumberland Road, the Illinois and Michigan Canal grant, and the reduction of the price of public lands. William Henry Harrison, the first Whig and the first northern man from west of the Allegheny Mountains, entered the White House. The campaign and the election filled the Illinois Whigs with enthusiasm and faith; some predicted their party had come to stay, that the Democratic party was hitting a slump that would mean its death. The Democrats had charged that Harrison was kept in a cage in a little Ohio town where a committee of Whigs spoke and thought for him; also they peddled a story that the women of Chillicothe, Ohio, had formally presented him with a petticoat.

The Whigs, however, set forth Harrison as another game fighter like Andrew Jackson, but without Jackson's faults.

Certain Democrats having scornfully referred to Harrison as a drinker of hard cider who lived in a log cabin, the slogans "hard cider" and "log cabin" were taken up by the Whigs. When Maine went heavy for Harrison at its early state election, the Whig songbooks came out with a rhyme: "Oh, have you heard how Maine went? She went, hell-bent, for Governor Kent, and Tippecanoe, and Tyler too."

One of Lincoln's early speeches in the campaign was in Alton, where it was announced by large handbills declaring:

ATTENTION! THE PEOPLE!!

A. Lincoln, Esq'r., of Sangamon County,
one of the Electoral Candidates, will Address
the People this Evening!! At Early Candlelighting,
at the ☞ Old Court Room ☞ (Riley's
Building). By request of Many Citizens.
Thursday April 9th, 1840.

In this campaign Lincoln did more stumping than in any previous campaign. He was matched against Douglas in many debates. He took up the nickname by which Whigs referred to all Democrats—"Locofocos" or "Locos." At a meeting of New York Democrats two factions were trying to control the meeting. One gang turned off the gas-lights, and in the darkness the other gang, who had come prepared, took the new friction matches, called "Locofoco," from their pockets, struck their matches and lighted the room and ran the meeting.

Lincoln spoke from a wagon at a big conclave of Whigs in Springfield in June, which was attended by 15,000 people, some from as far as Chicago. "They came in carriages and wagons, on horseback and on foot. They came with log cabins drawn on wheels by oxen, and with coons, coonskins, and hard cider. They came with music and banners, thousands from long distances." Among the Whig orators were Fletcher Webster, a son of Daniel Webster, E. D. Baker, John J. Hardin, the Rev. John Hogan, and Ben Bond, a son of Shadrach Bond.

One man who heard Lincoln make this wagon speech at the big Springfield powwow, wrote about it afterward:

"The questions involved were not such as enlisted and engaged Lincoln's best thoughts. At times he discussed the questions in a logical way, but much time was devoted to telling stories to illustrate some phase of his argument, though more often the telling of these stories was resorted to for the purpose of rendering his opponents ridiculous. In that kind of oratory he had no equal in the state. One story he told on that occasion was full of salient points, and well illustrated the argument he was making. It was not an impure story, yet it was not one it would be seemly to publish; but rendered, as it was, in his inimitable way, it contained nothing that was offensive to a refined taste."

In the audience that Lincoln spoke to were delegates from Chicago; they had been hauled by fourteen teams; it took them three weeks to make the trip. One log cabin on wheels had been hauled by thirty yoke of oxen; it had a hickory tree growing by a cabin, with live coons in the tree, and a barrel of hard cider on tap by the cabin door. The Chicago delegates were flying a petticoat, a Democratic symbol of Harrison as a warrior; they had torn it away from Democrats on the way from Chicago. There was singing:

> Without a why or a wherefore
> We'll go for Harrison therefore.

A large handbill got out by the Whigs, with Lincoln's name printed among other Whig electors, was headed "To the Friends of the National Road." The slogan "Freemen, Strike Home!" stood in large type. In smaller type were such accusations as, "The scows, pile-drivers, hammers, &c. &c. used in constructing the harbor at Chicago, and which is now unfinished, have been sold by order of government for $201—having cost more than $6,000." Van Buren and the Democrats were blamed for the failure to build the Cumberland road on through the West, while the pledge was offered, "Elect Harrison and the National Road is saved."

Banker, merchant, mechanic, and farmer toasted Harrison in mugs of hard cider. A Galena rally had 2,846 men and 340 women; at Carlinville were 3,000. Illinois voted for Harrison. A. Lincoln as one of the electoral college cast his vote for the first northern and western man to be sent to the White House. It was a famous campaign. The only one like it before was the one in which Andrew Jackson and his Democratic organization

National Road

TICKET.
FREEMEN,
Strike Home!

FOR PRESIDENT,
WM. HENRY HARRISON.
FOR VICE-PRESIDENT,
JOHN TYLER.

ELECTORS.
CYRUS WALKER, of McDonough,
BUCKNER S. MORRIS, of Cook,
SAMUEL D. MARSHALL, of Gallatin,
EDWIN B. WEBB, of White,
AB'M LINCOLN, of Sangamon.

From a Whig campaign sheet in 1841. In the Barrett Collection.

overwhelmingly defeated John Quincy Adams. In both campaigns the winner was a fighting man who could ride, shoot, and look danger in the eye. Also in both campaigns the winner was close to the people of the soil, a plain man among the toilers. Also the tactics of the Harrison men consisted chiefly of personal attacks on Martin Van Buren, the President, just as, in the case of Jackson in 1826, the tactics consisted chiefly of attacks on John Quincy Adams, the President; each retiring President was accused of living in too high-toned a fashion in the White House. And finally, with Harrison as with Jackson, on his entrance into the White House, there was a feeling in many quarters that some great change, perhaps a revolution, had been accomplished; but people couldn't tell just what it was about.

The significant big point in each campaign was the proof it gave that sometimes the American democracy goes on a rampage and shows that it has swift and terrific power, even though it is not sure what to do with that power.

As between Jackson and Harrison there was the tragic difference that while each of them was stormed by office-hunters, Jackson was strong and cool enough to live and satisfy thousands of them—while they killed Harrison. And the White House was left in control of the halfway Whig, John Tyler, who was far from the figure, voice, and hope the people had voted for.

Among Illinois Whigs there were regrets. They carried their national ticket, but lost the state to the Democrats. This put a new color on a case they were interested in. Months earlier they had charged the Democrats with fraud in voting; thousands of Irish workmen in the canal zone had started a test action before a circuit judge who ruled that foreign-born inhabitants must be naturalized before they could vote. The Democrats took the case to the Supreme Court, knowing that if they lost the case they would lose thousands of votes.

Then came the newly elected legislature into session, with a Democratic majority holding power through the ballots of the canal-zone workers. This was the hour Stephen Douglas, register of the land office, seized; he wrote a draft of a bill; he made a speech in the rotunda of the capitol asking the legislature to pass the bill; the bill passed and became law; it threw out of office four circuit-court judges, set up five new supreme court judgeships, and arranged for the legislature to appoint nine new judges, who would be the supreme court of the state besides doing the work of the circuit-court judges who were thrown out. The bill passed the senate by a vote of 22 to 17, and the house by a vote of 45 to 40. By this move the Democrats saved the canal-zone vote for their party, appointed Democrats as clerks in half the counties of the state as provided in the bill, and placed Stephen A. Douglas, who could no longer be register of the land office under a Whig national administration, on the bench as a supreme court judge. The reply of the Whig party to this reform of the judiciary was a calm address issued by a committee of which Lincoln was a member, entitled, "Appeal to the People of the State of Illinois," declaring "that the independence of the judiciary has been destroyed, that hereafter our courts will be independent of the people, and entirely dependent on the legislature; that our rights of property and liberty of conscience can no longer be regarded as safe from the encroachments of unconstitutional legislation."

During this session of the legislature there were bitter feelings between the Whigs and Democrats. The voting was often close. Once when the Democrats wanted a quorum and the Whigs didn't, the Democrats locked the door of the house so as to keep the quorum in. Lincoln, Joe Gillespie, and another Whig raised a window and jumped out and hid.

It was a time in which the Democrats had many sneering and furious ways of saying that the Whigs were too respectable, while the Whigs on the other hand had many proud, cool ways of saying that the Democrats were not respectable enough.

Chapter 51

In the early days of Illinois there was a man named Ninian Edwards who stood foremost among politicians, land speculators, and citizens of wealth and influence. He had been born in Maryland in the opening year of the American Revolution, and was taken as a child along the Wilderness Road through Cumberland Gap to Lexington, Kentucky, where he grew up and became a lawyer, a circuit judge, and a judge of the court of appeals. He left his bench as chief justice of the courts of

Kentucky to take a commission from President Madison and to journey west and north into Illinois, of which newly carved territory he was the newly appointed governor.

As Shadrach Bond took the office of governor of Illinois, just admitted to the Union of States, Ninian Edwards was sworn in as the first United States senator, chosen to speak for the new state in Congress at Washington in 1818. He resigned as senator and was starting for Mexico City to act as United States Ambassador to Mexico when charges were filed by William H. Crawford, Secretary of the Treasury at Washington, that Edwards had helped get moneys deposited in a defaulting bank at Shawneetown, Illinois. He resigned as Ambassador to Mexico, and for years, then, Illinois politics was torn with "war on Ninian Edwards." He fought through scandalous campaigns when personal and political enemies charged him with embezzlement. He was master of connecting webs between banking, land speculation, and politics.

Elected governor of the state in 1826, he lived as one of its powerful and substantial citizens, holding land in blocks of thousands of acres and snapping up many tracts of land delinquent in tax payments. He died in 1833, with reminiscences of years when his wife helped him tie their horses close to the house at night because so many horse thieves prowled the country, years when he was organizing companies of riflemen and building stockade forts from the Missouri to the Wabash River.

Ninian W. Edwards, the son of Ninian Edwards, lived in Springfield, was one of the "Long Nine," was of the same age as Abraham Lincoln, and the two had campaigned and electioneered together over Sangamon County. The Edwards house stood two stories high and was big enough to hold within its walls a dozen prairie-farmer cabins. Its walls and chimneys were of brick, with porches running the lengths of two sides of the house; a large one-story kitchen stretched flat to the rear of the house; its tall windows went higher than a tall man's arms would reach.

Green blinds opened out from the second-story windows.

Brocades of wooden scrollwork embellished the eaves; an orna‐
mented railing guarded the margins of the second-story portico.
Solid and aristocratic sash, door, and blind wooden-work per‐
formed offices of use and decoration. A roadway shaped in the
outline of a broad banjo permitted carriages to enter, deposit
guests on the front veranda, and half-circle out to the street with
convenience and facility. Along with the Forquer house which
had a lightning-rod, it was in a class with the handsome and
distinguished houses of Springfield. At its north end was a
parlor where parties, teas, dances, soirées were held.

Lincoln was a signer of one printed invitation to a cotillion
ball at the Edwards house. He joined three other Springfield
men in a written request sent to the wife of a Quincy member
of the legislature, Lincoln writing:

To the Honorable Mrs. Browning:
  We, the undersigned, respectfully represent to your honoress that
we are in great need of your society in the town of Springfield and there‐
fore humbly pray that your honoress will repair forthwith to the seat
of Government bringing in your train all ladies in general who may be
at your command and all Mrs. Browning's sisters in particular.

This was the same Mrs. Browning to whom he had written the
long letter about his love affair with Miss Mary Owens—and
Mrs. Browning, when she met Lincoln in Springfield, spoke to
him as though the letter was one of his jokes, just a prank of
his strange, whimsical mind, as though in a gay, story-telling
mood he had invented, made up out of his head, an adventure
to have a laugh over.

He had played "muggins," sitting opposite a young woman,
looking her in the eye, touching the plate in his lap when she
touched hers, and finally winning the game by not once taking
his eyes from hers, and by always repeating each motion she
made in touching her face with her fingers or thumbs. But
when they led him to a mirror he saw his face streaked black;
the plate put in his lap for the game had been sooted over a
candle flame.

It seemed as though Lincoln at this time was looking for a woman. And yet there were things operating against him in the getting of a woman from among those who had come his way and met his fancy. He was backward, perhaps bashful, about telling any one woman truly how he felt about all women, that they had a harder path in life than men, that he felt sacred and mysterious urges living in the bodies of women, which he didn't feel about men, that there were soft mystic confusions about the behavior of women that upset him; and without showing that he was upset he would talk politics or science or the latest news, whatever it might be, or drift into droll and dry humors that would puzzle women.

In the matter of compliments, for instance, he was not at home with women. Among men, he could find compliments to speak. Picking a man's point of pride or interest and then saying something that was true and that pleased the man in connection with that pride or interest, was an act of his every day. With women, however, he did not have this gift of finding a high pride or interest about which he could make a winning and honest compliment.

"Lincoln goes out when they take him but he isn't much for society," one Springfield woman noticed. "I don't think he can be called bashful. He is never embarrassed that I see, and he seems to enjoy the ladies' company. But he does not *go* much, as some of the young men do."

There was Miss Sarah Rickard, sixteen years old, staying at Bill Butler's house where Lincoln took his meals. He gave her presents, was her escort at parties, lectures, entertainments; they saw a home-talent dramatization of "The Babes in the Wood," and attended together the first theatre performance with regulation stage and curtain in Springfield. To her, he pointed out that, her name being Sarah, and the Sarah of Bible times having become the wife of Abraham, it was written that she, Sarah Rickard, was foreordained to marry him, Abraham Lincoln.

Then came an older sister, telling Sarah she was too young to think about marrying. And at the time Lincoln's interest in her was growing keener, she sent him away, remarking afterward, "I found I was beginning to like him; but you know his peculiar manner and general deportment would not be likely to fascinate a young lady entering the society world."

He was odd; he did have a "peculiar manner"; he was homely, ironical, kindly, simple, whimsical, adroit, with a lean and fierce physical strength kept under fine control. And yet it was never said of him by those close to him, as was said of his father before him, "He had a way with women."

It seemed as though Miss Mary Owens and Miss Sarah Rickard both spoke of him as rather a strange apparition, an aloof and removed creature who mounted barriers or slipped through fine meshes where they could neither see nor feel barriers or meshes, while on the other hand he might drawl a slow earthy mother-wit about cheap common things, of all doorsteps and kitchens, somewhat like a farmer or a carpenter, too common and familiar for the woman in quest of romance with roses, moonlight—and compliments.

He was a paradox, so easy to see through with his funny street-corner stories, and so baffling when his face settled into granitic calm and there came into the depths of his eyes the shadows of a burning he had been through, and he was a changed man keeping to himself the gray mystery of the change.

It was this Lincoln who was going to parties at the two-story brick house of the Edwards' across the street from the new state capitol. It was this Lincoln—who seemed to be looking for a woman. His name had been on the printed invitations to a cotillion ball at the Edwards mansion.

Chapter 52

AND now there came to the house of Ninian W. Edwards in 1840 a young woman from Lexington, Kentucky. This was her second visit. She had been there three years before on a short visit. Now she had come to stay. She was Miss Mary Todd, and was a younger sister of the wife of Ninian W. Edwards, Elizabeth.

They were the granddaughters of Todds who had fought with Washington through the American Revolution and with Daniel Boone in Kentucky at the time Boone was saying he was "an instrument ordained by God to settle the wilderness." Their father, Robert Smith Todd, had been a captain in the War of 1812, had served in both houses of the legislature in Kentucky, and was president of the Bank of Kentucky in Lexington.

Miss Mary Todd was twenty-two years old, plump, swift, beaming, with ready answers slipping from a sharp tongue, in the year that Springfield, and Abraham Lincoln, became acquainted with her. She had her gifts, a smooth soft skin, soft brown hair, and flashing clear blue eyes. With her somewhat short figure sheathed in a gown of white with black stripes, cut low at the neck and giving free play to her swift neck muscles, her skirt fluffed out in a slightly balloonish hoop, shod in modish ballroom slippers, she was a centre of likes and dislikes among those who came to the house where her sister was mistress.

Though her tongue and its sarcasm that came so quickly and so often, brought dislikes and hates, there was a shine and a bubbling, a foaming over of vitality, that won friends. For Lincoln, as he came to know her, she was lighted with sprays of magnets. If only as a decorative outline, she struck him as paramount and incomparable.

She was the first aggressively brilliant feminine creature his friends ever knew of who crossed his path and waylaid him with resources known to an accomplished and vital woman. She haunted him and held his attentions by the use of age-old fascinations, difficult of analysis by man because they move in a world of intuitive half-lights, swift gestures, and shaded intonations, lies, white lies, and lies shifting a medium course between lies and white lies. He could keep his head and outguess lights, shoals, and sand-bars of the Ohio and Mississippi rivers and take a flatboat through; with Mary Todd he lost his head. His experience was rich with rivers, starved with women; as one woman remarked, he didn't *go* as much as other young men for "ladies' company."

Besides the charm that attached to Mary Todd in her smooth soft skin, soft brown hair, swift movement of neck muscles, flying glimpses of slippers, she was a triumph of cultivation: she had what were known as accomplishments; she had gone to the schools where the accomplishments were taught, and she had all that the most aristocratic schools of Kentucky could implant. She spoke and read the French language, had partaken often of dinners in which only talk in French was permitted, had read French classics of literature in the original.

Conversation, manners, belles-lettres, the piano and approved classical music, were taught in the schools she attended. How to be polite and suave while not stiff nor garrulous, how to mingle the sprightly and the reserved, how to conform in the stiff points of etiquette while maintaining a superior ease in the precise and the punctilious, these were subjects of instruction in which she had been tempered and drilled, coaxed, reminded, and told, from the time she wore bibs till she first stepped into a low-cut ballroom gown. The one word "nice" and the two words "nice people" were words almost born to her with her tongue.

She had kept a native and bottom fibre of strength and will; she had left her home in Kentucky and taken up a new home in Illinois because of a dispute with her stepmother. She was impetuous, picked the ridiculous angle, the weak point of any one she disliked and spoke it with thrust of phrase. In her first Springfield days Bill Herndon danced a waltz with her, and finding her the most amazingly smooth and easy waltzer he had ever danced with, he told her she seemed to glide through the waltz with the ease of a serpent. She drew back, flashed her eyes, retorted, "Mr. Herndon, comparison to a serpent is rather severe irony, especially to a newcomer," bowed with accomplished dignity, and was gone. She could be hurt, just like that, when no one wanted to hurt her.

Far from ordinary was Miss Mary Todd; she was vivid,

perhaps too vivid, ebullient, combative, too quick to "fly off the handle." She was in her element, moving in a swirl, delirious and inevitable when hot, stinging words were flying off her tongue, out of her lips. It connected directly with the fear and trembling that took her when a thunderstorm with zigzags of lightning came over the sky. Her temper colored her; she could shine with radiance at a gift, a word, an arrival, a surprise, an achievement of a little cherished design, at winning a withheld consent. A shaft of wanted happiness could strike deep in her.

The modish woman at a "levee" in Springfield then often wore eight or twelve starched petticoats with an overskirt of "changeable silk." There might be several "illusion skirts" worn over white satin. Mary Todd was read, informed and versed in apparel and appearance. She hummed gay little ditties putting on a flowered bonnet and tying a double-bow knot under her chin. A satisfying rose or ostrich plume in her hair was a psalm.

She embodied a thousand cunning, contradictory proverbs men have spoken about woman as a wildcat and as a sweet angel. She was vivid, perhaps too vivid. From far back in her forerunners of proud, passionate people had come this drag and lift that mixed in her personality, this paradoxical burden and balloon of personality. Her mother had died when she was a child. Visiting at Walnut Hills near Lexington, she was with a party of girls in a room when an alarm came that Indians were near. The other girls scampered under beds, into closets, but Mary Todd, finding no place to hide, stood in the centre of the room crying, "Hide me, O my Saviour, hide."

Style was instinctive with her; fashion was of her desires; when she was a girl and hoop skirts were worn by women, she toiled by candlelight till late in the night basting a hoop skirt with weeping willow twigs, starting for Sunday school the next day with a girl chum, both wearing white dresses stretched tight over silly, homemade hoops; their aunt saw them and called: "What frights you are! Take those things off and then go to

Sunday school." While offhand observers spoke of her as having "bounce" and "spunk," it was an understanding among her friends that she had what they chose to call "ambition" and was "an ambitious woman." She was intense with the quality Kentuckians refer to in their horses as "high-strung."

Mary Todd was decisive. She and Mercy Levering once went out in muddy weather, taking along an armful of shingles. On Fifth Street they laid shingles ahead to step on while crossing. When they came back they saw the shingles wouldn't hold them up out of the mud. Hart, the drayman, came along with his two-wheeled sloping dray. Mary Todd called to him to give them a lift. He gee-hawed over next to the sidewalk and backed up. Mary Todd climbed on. But Mercy Levering didn't; she was afraid of how she would look and still more of what people would say. And as Mary Todd was driven to the Edwards' house, windows flew up and heads popped out to see, as Dr. E. H. Merryman put it in verses later, "this lady gay in silken coat and feathers white, a-riding on a dray."

There was "go" to her, an urge sending her toward place, power, station, "high degree." She cared deeply for all objects representative of class, the acclaim of prizes, blue ribbons, distinction. Again, like certain fast horses of the blue-grass country, she "chafed at the bit" if the restraints of life, the leashes put on the frail, mortal limbs and hours of woman, were too much and too many; or again she was full of the lust of being vividly and proudly alive for the gaze of others; her stride and attitude was that of the horse champing, the hoofs wanting to go, to be a winner known to grandstands, vast amphitheatres of spectators. She was a crucible of forces, of a blood with flame in its currents, a brain with far contrasts, with explosions sometimes that shook the entire physical framework, the entire retort that held the pathos of her fate; her tears could flow from sacs that had containers of the strength of salt tears; her laughter could dimple in wreaths running to the core of her; she was born to impulses that rode her before she could ride them. And yet after excesses of temper had worn her to a

babbling and moaning exhaustion, she could rise and stand up
to battle again for a purpose definitely formed.

The Todds traced back to Scottish Covenanters who fought
the king and the established church of England; among Covenanters sentenced to transportation to the American colonies
were two Todds; their vital and stubborn blood ran in Mary
Todd. She was of a Presbyterian line crossed with Episcopalian.
Her telling a Kentucky friend, before leaving for Illinois, that
she was going to be the wife of some future President of the
United States, may have been a piece of idle gossip or the evidence of a hope for distinction.

Society life, the social drama and its gleaming mirrors and
garnished promenades, called to her; life should be a series of
ceremonial occasions—interspersed with sleep, forethought, and
preparations for ceremonial occasions. In the phrasing of a
breakfast greeting, in the tuck of a napkin corner and the disposition of its folded triangles as related to knife, fork, plate, in
the employment of a spoon for the conveyance of hot soup or
the negotiation of a fork of green peas, in the buckling of a
slipper or the knotting of a satin sash, there was a correct style;
and superior persons were known by their use of the correct
style; beyond their portals was the human rabble shading off
into the incorrect, the common, the ignorant, the vulgar, the
dirty, the indecent, and the perfectly disgusting.

During her first year in Springfield both Abraham Lincoln and
Stephen A. Douglas took their turns at being entertained by
Mary Todd in the big parlor of the Edwards house, took their
turns at escorting her to parties and balls; she was asked which
of the two she intended to have for her husband, and answered,
"The one that has the best chance of being President."

In the Edwards circle they believed there were clues to her
character in a remark she passed at a party around a fireside
one evening. A young woman married to a rich man far along
in years was asked, "Why did you marry such a dried-up husband, such a withered-up old buck?" Her answer was, "He had
lots of horses and gold." And the quick-tongued Mary Todd

said in surprise: "Is that true? *I* would rather marry a good man, a man of mind, with bright prospects for fame and power, than to marry all the horses, gold, and bones in the world."

Chapter 53

ALONG in the year 1840 Lincoln and Mary Todd plighted their troth and were engaged to be married. Ninian W. Edwards and his wife had argued she was throwing herself away; it wasn't a match; she and Lincoln came from different classes in society. And her stubborn Covenanter blood rose; she knew her own mind and spoke it: Lincoln had a future; he was her man more than any other man she had met.

The months passed. Lincoln, the solitary, the melancholy, was busy, lost, abstracted; he couldn't go to all the parties, dances, concerts Mary Todd was going to; she flared with jealousy and went with other men. She accused him; tears; misunderstandings; they made up, fell out, made up again. The wedding was set for New Year's Day, 1841. In the kitchen of the Edwards house the wedding cakes were put in the oven.

And then something happened. The bride was ready. The groom didn't come. It was a phantom wedding, mentioned in hushes. There was gossip and dispute about whether the wedding had been set for that date at all.

On the day set for the wedding, Lincoln took his seat and answered roll-call in the legislature, and during two months was absent from his seat only seven days. He toiled with the Whigs on an "Appeal to the People of the State of Illinois," on circulars and protests trying to rouse public opinion against the Democrats. He wrote letters, tried law cases.

And yet, as he walked the streets of Springfield, he was a haunted man. He had torn himself away from a woman; she had stood ready and waiting; his word had been pledged; he had failed to meet her; he had sent word he didn't love her and there could only be pain and misery in a marriage where the

man knew he didn't love her. And was he sure he didn't love
her? If he did love her it was a terrible wrong to leave her with
arms open, waiting for him; and even if he could be sure he
didn't love her, the tears and the storms of her heart came because he had been blind and foolish and gone farther than he
should have in telling her he loved her.

Once he had written it all out in a letter, how he had made a
mistake in telling her he loved her, and Speed had read the
letter and thrown it into a fire, saying words may be forgotten
but letters are a permanent record. And Speed had told him:
"If you have the courage of manhood, go see Mary yourself;
tell her if you do not love her, tell her so, tell her you will not
marry her." And he had gone from the Speed store saying he
would be careful not to say much and would leave Mary as
soon as he had told her. And he was gone an hour, two hours.

It was past eleven o'clock that night when he came back and
said to Speed: "When I told Mary I did not love her, she burst
into tears and, almost springing from her chair and wringing
her hands as if in agony, said something about the deceiver being
himself deceived. It was too much for me. I found the tears
trickling down my own cheeks. I caught her in my arms and
kissed her."

Speed told him he was a fool; he had renewed the engagement; and he said: "Well, if I'm in again, so be it. It's done,
and I shall abide by it." Then the wedding date had been set,
the wedding cakes baked. And he couldn't go.

So now he walked the streets of Springfield; he brooded,
looking out of the windows of the second-story law office; he
went to Dr. Henry's office; he took Dr. Henry's advice and
wrote a long statement of his case for a doctor in Cincinnati.
And the doctor answered that in this kind of case he could do
nothing without first a personal interview. He wrote his partner
Stuart: "I am now the most miserable man living. If what I
feel were equally distributed to the whole human family, there
would not be one cheerful face on the earth."

He was seeing Dr. Henry often, and wrote Stuart, "Whether

I shall ever be better, I cannot tell; I awfully forebode I shall not. To remain as I am is impossible; I must die or be better, it appears to me. The matter you speak of on my account you may attend to as you say, unless you shall hear of my condition forbidding it. I say this because I fear I shall be unable to attend to any business here, and a change of scene might help me. If I could be myself, I would rather remain at home with Judge Logan. I can write no more." He wrote to the *Sangamo Journal* meditations entitled "Suicide."

He begged Stuart to go the limit in Washington toward the appointment of Dr. Henry as postmaster at Springfield. "You know I desired Dr. Henry to have that place when you left; I now desire it more than ever—I have within the last few days been making a most discreditable exhibition of myself in the way of hypochondriasm, and thereby got an impression that Dr. Henry is necessary to my existence—Unless he gets that place he leaves Springfield."

He further urged the merits of Dr. Henry, added that nearly all the Whig members of the Legislature besides other Whigs, favored the doctor for Postmaster. He declared, "My heart is very much set upon it," and ended the painful letter, "Pardon me for not writing more; I have not sufficient composure to write a long letter."

The legislature adjourned. Josh Speed was selling his store and going back to his folks in Kentucky. Lincoln went with him.

As the redbud, the honeysuckle and the clambering springtime roses of Kentucky came out, the lost Lincoln struggled to come back. He told Speed one day that he had done nothing to make any human being remember that he had lived, that what he wished to live for was to connect his name with the events of his day and generation and to link his name with something that would be to the interest of his fellow men.

Slowly, he came back. A sweet and serene old woman, Joshua Speed's mother, talked with him, gave him a mother's care, and made him a present of an Oxford Bible.

In June he was in Springfield handling the cases of two clients accused of murder; excitement ran high and hangings were expected; but the man supposed to have been killed turned up alive. And Lincoln ended a long letter to Speed with the remark, "Hart, the little drayman that hauled Molly [Mary Todd] home once, said it was too *damned* bad to have so much trouble, and no hanging after all."

Writing to Speed's sister three months later from Bloomington. on the court circuit, he informed her:

Do you remember my going to the city, while I was in Kentucky, to have a tooth extracted, and making a failure of it? Well, that same old tooth got to paining me so much that about a week since I had it torn out, bringing with it a bit of the jaw-bone, the consequence of which is that I can neither talk nor eat. I am literally subsisting on savory remembrances—that is, being unable to eat, I am living upon the remembrance of the delicious dishes of peaches and cream we used to have at your house. When we left, Miss Fanny Henning was owing you a visit, as I understand it. Has she paid it yet? If she has, are you not convinced that she is one of the sweetest girls in the world? There is but one thing about her, so far as I could perceive, that I would have otherwise than it is—that is, something of a tendency to melancholy. This is a misfortune, not a fault. Is little Siss Eliza Davis at your house yet? If she is, kiss her o'er and o'er again for me. Tell your mother that I have not got her "present," an Oxford Bible, with me, but I intend to read it regularly when I return home. I doubt not that it is really, as she says, the best cure for the blues, could one but take it according to the truth.

A child was a natural belonging in the big arms of Lincoln. He could be free and familiar, lavish with compliments, mockery and cajolery, when among children or with any child. The kiss of a snuggling child for him, and his kiss for a snuggling child, this was homelike. The likes of little Siss Eliza Davis did him good.

Anything walking on two legs or four could have a corner in his lonesome heart. In his letter to Miss Speed, he sketched a steamboat scene that met his eyes traveling from Louisville to St. Louis:

A fine example was presented on board the boat for contemplating the effect of condition upon human happiness. A gentleman had purchased twelve negroes in different parts of Kentucky, and was taking them to a farm in the South. They were chained six and six together. A small iron clevis was around the left wrist of each, and this fastened to the main chain by a shorter one, at a convenient distance from the others, so that the negroes were strung together precisely like so many fish upon a trot-line. In this condition they were being separated forever from the scenes of their childhood, their friends, their fathers and mothers, and brothers and sisters, and going into perpetual slavery, where the lash of the master is proverbially more ruthless and unrelenting than any other where; and yet amid all these distressing circumstances, as we would think them, they were the most cheerful and apparently happy creatures on board. One whose offense for which he had been sold was an over-fondness for his wife, played the fiddle almost continually, and the others danced, sang, cracked jokes, and played various games with cards from day to day. How true it is that God tempers the wind to the shorn lamb, or in other words, that he renders the worst of human conditions tolerable, while he permits the best to be nothing better than tolerable.

Chapter 54

JOSHUA SPEED was a deep-chested man of large sockets, with broad measurement between the ears. A streak of lavender ran through him; he had spots soft as May violets. And he and Abraham Lincoln told each other their secrets about women. Lincoln too had tough physical shanks and large sockets, also a streak of lavender, and spots soft as May violets.

"I do not feel my own sorrows more keenly than I do yours," Lincoln wrote Speed in one letter. And again: "You know my desire to befriend you is everlasting."

The wedding-day of Speed and Fanny Henning had been set; and he was afraid he didn't love her; it was wearing him down; the date of the wedding loomed ahead of him as the hour for a sickly affair; he wrote Lincoln he was sick.

And Lincoln wrote a letter analyzing Speed, telling him what was wrong with his physical and mental system. It was a letter as tender as loving hands swathing a feverish forehead, yet direct and logical in its facing of immediate, practical facts. It was a letter showing that the misery of Abraham Lincoln in the unlucky endings of his love affairs with Ann Rutledge and with Mary Todd, must have been a deep-rooted, tangled, and baffling misery.

"You are naturally of a nervous temperament," he told Speed. "And this I say from what I have seen of you personally, and what you have told me concerning your mother at various times, and concerning your brother William at the time his wife died." Besides this general cause, he gave three special reasons for Speed's condition. "The first special cause is your exposure to bad weather on your journey, which my experience clearly proves to be very severe on defective nerves. The second is the absence of all business and conversation of friends, which might divert your mind, give it occasional rest from the intensity of thought which will sometimes wear the sweetest idea threadbare and turn it to the bitterness of death. The third is the rapid and near approach of that crisis on which all your thoughts and feelings concentrate."

Lincoln's broodings over the mysteries of personality, and the connections of a man's behavior with the juices and currents of his body, his ideas about his own shattered physical system at the time he had wandered mumbling and friends had taken care of him, were indicated in his telling Speed: "If, as I expect, you will at some time be agonized and distressed, let me, who have reason to speak with judgment on such a subject, beseech you to ascribe it to the causes I have mentioned. and not to some false and ruinous suggestion of the Devil. The general cause— nervous debility, which is the key and conductor of all the particular ones, and without which they would be utterlv harmless, —though it does pertain to you, does not pertain to one in a thousand. It is out of this that the painful difference between you and the mass of the world springs." That is, Lincoln believed that he and his friend had exceptional and sensitive personalities. "Though it does pertain to you, it does not pertain to one in a thousand."

Their births, the loins and tissues of their fathers and mothers, accident, fate, providence, had given these two men streaks of lavender, spots soft as May violets. "It is out of this that the painful difference between you and the mass of the world springs." And Lincoln was writing in part a personal confession in telling Speed: "I know what the painful point with you is at all times when you are unhappy; it is an apprehension that you do not love her as you should. What nonsense! How came you to court her? Was it because you thought she deserved it, and that you had given her reason to expect it? If it was for that, why did not the same reason make you court at least twenty others of whom you can think, and to whom it would apply with greater force than to her? Did you court her for her wealth? Why, you know she had none. But you say you reasoned yourself into it. What do you mean by that? Was it not that you found yourself unable to reason yourself out of it? Did you not think and partly form the purpose of courting her the first time you ever saw her or heard of her?" Reason had little to do with it at that early stage. "There was nothing at that time for reason to work upon. Whether she was moral, amiable, sensible, or even of good character, you did not, nor could then know, except, perhaps, you might infer the last from the company you found her in. All you then did or could know of her was her personal appearance and deportment; and these, if they impress at all, impress the heart, and not the head.

"Say candidly, were not those heavenly black eyes the whole basis of all your early reasoning on the subject? Did you not go and take me all the way to Lexington and back, for no other purpose but to get to see her again? What earthly consideration would you take to find her scouting and despising you, and giving herself up to another? But of this you have no apprehension; and therefore you cannot bring it home to your feelings. I shall be so anxious about you that I shall want you to write by every mail."

Thus ended a letter which had begun, "My dear Speed: Feeling, as you know I do, the deepest solicitude for the success of the enterprise you are engaged in, I adopt this as the last method I can adopt to aid you, in case (which God forbid!) you shall need any aid."

A few days before Speed's wedding, Lincoln wrote a letter to the bridegroom. "I assure you I was not much hurt by what you wrote me of your excessively bad feeling at the time you wrote. Not that I am less capable of sympathizing with you now than ever, but because I hope and believe that your present anxiety and distress about her health and her life must and will forever banish those horrid doubts which I know you sometimes felt as to the truth of your affection for her. If they can once and forever be removed (and I almost feel a presentiment that the Almighty has sent your present affliction expressly for that object) surely nothing can come in their stead to fill their immeasurable measure of misery. The death scenes of those we love are surely painful enough; but these we are prepared for and expect to see; they happen to all and all know they must happen. Should she, as you fear, be destined to an early grave, it is indeed a great consolation to know that she is so well prepared to meet it. Her religion, which you once disliked so much, I will venture you now prize most highly."

Lincoln hoped Speed's melancholy forebodings as to Fanny's early death were not well founded. "I even hope that ere this reaches you she will have returned with improved and still improving health, and that you will have met her, and forgotten the sorrows of the past in the enjoyment of the present. I would say more if I could, but it seems to me that I have said enough. It really appears to me that you yourself ought to rejoice, and not sorrow, at this indubitable evidence of your undying affection for her. Why, Speed, if you did not love her, although you might not wish her death, you would most certainly be resigned to it. Perhaps this point is no longer a question with you, and my pertinacious dwelling on it is a rude intrusion upon your feelings.

"You know the hell I have suffered on that point, and how tender I am upon it. You know I do not mean wrong. I have been quite clear of 'hypo' [hypochondria] since you left; even better than I was along in the fall.

"I have seen Sarah [Rickard] but once. She seemed very cheerful, and so I said nothing to her about what we spoke of. Old Uncle Billy Herndon is dead, and it is said this evening that Uncle Ben Ferguson will not live. This, I believe, is all the news, and enough at that unless it were better. Write me immediately on the receipt of this."

Speed's wedding-day came; the knot was tied. And in a few days he read lines from Lincoln at Springfield: "When this shall reach you, you will have been Fanny's husband several days. You will hereafter be on ground that I have never occupied, and consequently, if advice were needed, I might advise wrong. I do fondly hope, however, that you will never again need any comfort from abroad. But should I be mistaken in this, should excessive pleasure still be accompanied with a painful counterpart at times, still let me urge you, as I have ever done, to remember, in the depth and even agony of despondency, that very shortly you are to feel well again. I am now fully convinced that you love her as ardently as you are capable of loving. Your ever being happy in her presence and your intense anxiety about her health, would place this beyond dispute in my mind.

"I incline to think it probable that your nerves will fail you occasionally for a while; but once you get them firmly guarded now, that trouble is over forever. I think, if I were you, in case my mind were not exactly right, I would avoid being idle. I would immediately engage in some business, or go to making preparations for it, which would be the same thing. If you went through the ceremony calmly, or even with sufficient composure not to excite alarm in any present, you are safe beyond question, and in two or three months, to say the most, will be the happiest of men."

Thus messages went back and forth. "If I were you, in case

my mind were not exactly right, I would avoid being idle," wrote Lincoln.

One had undertaken to marry a woman, and was smitten with such fear that he didn't love her, that on the fixed wedding day he wandered alone and there was no wedding. And he was writing from Illinois to a cherished friend down across the Wabash and Ohio rivers, how to take care of himself so that he would be on hand when the wedding-bells rang. "I know the painful point with you is an apprehension that you do not love her as you should. . . . You know the hell I have suffered on that point, and how tender I am upon it." A postscript to one letter read, "I have been quite a man since you left."

And when the single man received a letter from his just married friend, he wrote: "Yours of the 16th instant, announcing that Miss Fanny and you are 'no more twain, but one flesh,' reached me this morning. I have no way of telling you how much happiness I wish you both, though I believe you can conceive it. I feel somewhat jealous of both of you now; you will be so exclusively concerned for one another, that I shall be forgotten entirely. . . .

"I regret to learn that you have resolved not to return to Illinois. I shall be very lonesome without you. How miserable things seem to be arranged in this world! If we have no friends, we have no pleasure; and if we have them, we are sure to lose them, and be doubly pained by the loss. I did hope she and you would make your home here; but I own I have no right to insist. You owe obligations to her ten thousand times more sacred than you can owe to others, and in that light let them be respected and observed. It is natural that she should desire to remain with her relatives and friends. As to friends, however, she could not need them anywhere; she would have them in abundance here."

In closing he asked his friend to write often, and added the postscript: "Poor Easthouse is gone at last. He died awhile before day this morning. They say he was very loath to die." A few dots indicated an unfinished thought at the end of the sentence, "They say he was very loath to die."

Chapter 55

By wagon and river routes, breweries in St. Louis and Chicago were sending to towns in southern and central Illinois stocks of ale, pale ale, extra pale ale, lager beer, porter, and brown stout. Kentucky distilleries were shipping many grades of rye and corn whisky. Up the Mississippi River from New Orleans came cargoes of liquors and liqueurs, wet goods as varied as Scotch whisky, Holland gin, French brandy and rum, Madeira wine, port, Teneriffe, dry and sweet wines, Malaga, claret, and other light and heavy alcoholics.

A crusade against heavy drinking was carried on by the Washington Society, thus named in the belief that General George Washington was a drinking man but knew when to stop—in fact, was a temperance man. In districts of other states than Illinois, sensational campaigns had been carried on against strong drink. The Springfield *Journal* reported in 1841: "Whisky is quoted at Dayton, Ohio, at twelve cents a gallon. The Washingtonian cause is flourishing there. Eight thousand have signed the Temperance pledge in Cincinnati, a fact which has had some effect in lowering the price of whisky."

Among the leading advocates of temperance in Springfield was Abraham Lincoln. So far in the forefront was he, at this time, as an enemy of strong drink, that he was chosen as the orator of the day at a large important gathering of Washington societies. The Springfield *Journal* on February 14 announced the "celebration" to be held on the 22d of the month, as follows:

The Washington Society of Springfield, and other invited societies, will meet at the Methodist Church at 10 o'clock A.M. The procession will be formed by Col. B. S. Clement, chief marshal, between 11 and 12 o'clock, and will proceed through several of the principal streets of the city, to the Second Presbyterian Church, where an address will be delivered by A. Lincoln, Esq., and several appropriate airs, prepared for the occasion, will be sung by the choir—and such other services as are proper for the occasion. The order of the procession will be as follows: First, Chief Marshal; Second, Sangamon Guards; Third, Committee of Arrangements; Fourth, President and Orator; Fifth, Vice-President, Secretary and Treasurer; Sixth, Invited Societies; Seventh, Springfield Society. Seats will be reserved for the ladies at the Second Church. By order, etc., William Porter, Secretary, Committee of Arrangements.

Under such auspices, and after riding around the public square in a carriage as "the orator of the day," Lincoln faced his audience with an address on "Charity in Temperance Reform." He took notice of the "new and splendid" success of the temperance cause, and then went on to analyze some points in temperance reform that didn't quite satisfy him. "The warfare hitherto waged against the demon intemperance has somehow or other been erroneous. Either the champions engaged or the tactics they have adopted have not been the most proper. These champions for the most part have been preachers, lawyers, and hired agents. They are supposed to have no sympathy of feeling or interest with those very persons whom it is their object to convince and persuade."

Then he pictured the reformed drunkard as the best of all temperance crusaders. "When one who has long been known as a victim of intemperance appears before his neighbors 'clothed and in his right mind,' a redeemed specimen of long-lost humanity, and stands up, with tears of joy trembling in his eyes, to tell of the miseries once endured, now to be endured no more forever; of his once naked and starving children, now clad and fed comfortably; of a wife long weighted down with woe, weeping, and a broken heart, now restored to health; and how easily it is all done, once it is resolved to be done; how simple his language!—there is a logic and an eloquence in it that few with human feelings can resist. They cannot say he is vain of hearing himself speak, for his whole demeanor shows he would gladly avoid speaking at all; they cannot say he speaks for pay, for he received none and asked for none. In my judgment, it is to the battles of this new class of champions that our late success is greatly, perhaps chiefly, owing."

Men selling liquor, and men drinking it, were blamed too much. Denunciation of dram-sellers and dram-drinkers was "both impolitic and unjust." And why? "Because it is not much in the nature of man to be driven to anything; still less to be driven about that which is exclusively his own business; and least of all where such driving is to be submitted to at the expense of pecuniary interest or burning appetite."

"When the dram-seller and drinker were incessantly told—not in accents of entreaty and persuasion, diffidently addressed by erring man to an erring brother, but in the thundering tones of anathema and denunciation with which the lordly judge often groups together all the crimes of the felon's life, and thrusts them in his face just ere he passes sentence of death—that they were the authors of all the vice and misery and crime in the land; that they were the manufacturers and material of all the thieves and robbers and murderers that infest the earth, that their houses were the workshops of the devil; and that their persons should be shunned by all the good and virtuous, as moral pestilences—I say, when they were told all this, and in this way, it is not wonderful that they were slow, very slow, to acknowledge the truth of such denunciations."

He quoted the maxim, "A drop of honey catches more flies than a gallon of gall," and urged: "If you would win a man to your cause, first convince him that you are his sincere friend . . . Assume to dictate to his judgment, or to command his action, or to mark him as one to be shunned and despised, and he will retreat within himself, close all the avenues to his head and his heart; and though your cause be naked truth itself, transformed to the heaviest lance, harder than steel, you shall no more be able to pierce him than to penetrate the hard shell of a tortoise with a rye straw."

He sketched the history of liquor-making and liquor-drinking. "The practice of drinking is just as old as the world itself. When all of us of maturity first opened our eyes upon the stage of existence, we found intoxicating liquor recognized by everybody, used by everybody, repudiated by nobody. It commonly entered into the first draught of the infant and the last draught of the dying man."

The sideboard of the parson and the ragged pocket of the houseless loafer both held whisky. "Physicians prescribed it in this, that, and the other disease; government provided it for soldiers and sailors; and to have a rolling or raising, a husking or 'hoedown' anywhere about without it was positively insufferable."

Everywhere it was a respectable article of manufacture and merchandise. The making of it was regarded as honorable. "He who would make most was the most enterprising and respectable. Large and small manufactories of it were everywhere erected, in which all the earthly good of their owners were invested. Wagons drew it from town to town; boats bore it from clime to clime, and the winds wafted it from nation to nation; and merchants bought and sold it, by wholesale and retail, with precisely the same feelings on the part of the seller, buyer, and bystander as are felt at the selling and buying of plows, beef, bacon, or any other of the real necessaries of life."

"Even then it was known and acknowledged that many were greatly injured by it," Lincoln declared. "But none seemed to think the injury arose from the use of a bad thing, but from the abuse of a very good thing. The victims of it were to be pitied and compassionated, just as are the heirs of consumption and other hereditary diseases. Their failing was treated as a misfortune, and not as a crime, or even as a disgrace. If, then, what I have been saying is true, is it wonderful that some should think and act now as all thought and acted twenty years ago? and is it just to assail, condemn, or despise them for doing so? The universal sense of mankind on any subject is an argument, or at least an influence, not easily overcome."

It was as though he had been speaking with the voice of the Tom Lincoln who hauled four hundred gallons of whisky from the Knob Creek farm in Kentucky up to the Pigeon Creek farm in Indiana. He spoke next with the voice of the Abe Lincoln who on a freezing night near Gentryville had lugged on his shoulders the snoring drunkard picked from a ditch alongside the road.

"Another error, as it seems to me, into which the old reformers fell, was the position that all habitual drunkards were utterly incorrigible and therefore must be turned adrift and damned without remedy. . . . There is in this something so . . . uncharitable, so cold-blooded and feelingless, that it never did, nor ever can, enlist the enthusiasm of a popular cause. We could not love the man who taught it—we could not hear him with patience. The heart could not throw open its portals to it, the generous man could not adopt it—it could not mix with his blood. It looked . . . like throwing fathers and brothers overboard to lighten the boat for our security."

Were the benefits of temperance to be only for the next generation, for posterity? "Posterity has done nothing for us; we shall do very little for it unless we are made to think we are at the same time doing something for ourselves. There is something ludicrous in promises of good or threats of evil a great way off. 'Better lay down that spade you are stealing, Paddy; if you don't you'll pay for it at the day of judgment.' 'Be the powers, if ye'll credit me so long I'll take another jist.'"

Out in the audience Lincoln could see his law partner, Bill Herndon, a hard drinker when he drank, and Lincoln offered the opinion: "If we take habitual drunkards as a class, their heads and their hearts will bear an advantageous comparison with those of any other class. There seems ever to have been a proneness in the brilliant and warm-blooded to fall into this vice—the demon of intemperance ever seems to have delighted in sucking the blood of genius and of generosity."

At the close of the address, he showed he was not yet free from the influence of the famous orator Daniel Webster, and other famous orators who furnished the examples for the rising young orators. "Happy day when—all appetites controlled, all poisons subdued, all matter subjected—mind, all-conquering mind, shall live and move, the monarch of the world. Glorious consummation! Hail, fall of fury! Reign of reason, all hail!"

That he ranged far in his guesses and his hopes was seen in his declaration: "Whether or not the world would be vastly benefited by a total and final banishment from it of all intoxicating drinks seems to me not now an open question. Three-fourths of mankind confess the affirmative with their tongues, and, I believe, all the rest acknowledge it in their hearts . . . When there shall be neither a slave nor a drunkard on earth—how proud the title of that land which may truly claim to be the birthplace and the cradle of those revolutions that shall have ended in that victory. How nobly distinguished that people who shall have planted and nurtured to maturity both the political and moral freedom of their species."

In the audience to which Lincoln spoke there were many reformed drunkards, men who had been familiar figures in the doorways of the town's dramshops. The tone of Lincoln's address was keyed to these men; he didn't drink; but he did wish to say, "In my judgment such of us as have never fallen victims have been spared more from the absence of appetite than from any mental or moral superiority over those who have."

And young Bill Herndon standing at the door of the Presbyterian church, as the people passed out, said he heard remarks showing there were people not at all pleased with the address. Herndon said he caught one remark, "It's a shame that he should be permitted to abuse us so in the house of the Lord."

Writing to Speed about the address, Lincoln said: "You will see by the last *Sangamo Journal* that I made a temperance speech which I claim that you and Fanny shall read as an act of charity to me; for I cannot learn that anybody else has read it, or is likely to. Fortunately it is not very long, and I shall deem it a sufficient compliance with my request if one of you listens while the other reads it."

On the same Washington's birthday anniversary on which he made his speech, he gave advice to George E. Pickett, who was starting East to be a West Point cadet:

"Deceit and falsehood, especially if you have got a bad memory, is the *worst* enemy a fellow can have.

"Now, boy, on your march, don't you go and forget the old maxim that 'one drop of honey catches more flies than a half-gallon of gall.' Load your musket with this maxim, and smoke it in your pipe."

Chapter 56

A WEEK or so after Joshua Speed's wedding day, he wrote to Lincoln saying that "something indescribably horrible and alarming" haunted him. And Lincoln, in answering Speed's letter, said he was ready to swear it was not the fault of the woman Speed had married.

He went further and ventured the guess that both he and Speed had been dreaming dreams. "I now have no doubt that it is the peculiar misfortune of both you and me to dream dreams of Elysium far exceeding all that anything earthly can realize."

And Lincoln recalled an old saying of his father: "If you make a bad bargain, hug it all the tighter." The single man wrote to his married friend this letter:

SPRINGFIELD, February 25, 1842.

DEAR SPEED:

I received yours of the 12th written the day you went down to William's place, some days since, but delayed answering it till I should receive the promised one of the 16th, which came last night. I opened the letter with intense anxiety and trepidation; so much so, that, although it turned out better than I expected, I have hardly yet, at a distance of ten hours, become calm.

I tell you, Speed, our forebodings (for which you and I are peculiar) are all the worst sort of nonsense. I fancied, from the time I received your letter of Saturday, that the one of Wednesday was never to come; and yet it did come, and what is more, it is perfectly clear, both from its tone and handwriting, that you were much happier, or, if you think the term preferable, less miserable, when you wrote it than when you wrote the last one before. You had so obviously improved at the very time I so much fancied you would have grown worse.

You say that something indescribably horrible and alarming still haunts you. You will not say that three months from now, I will venture. When your nerves once get steady now, the whole trouble will be over forever. Nor should you become impatient at their being even very slow in becoming steady. Again you say, you much fear that that Elysium of which you have dreamed so much is never to be realized. Well, if it shall not, I dare swear it will not be the fault of her who is now your wife. I now have no doubt that it is the peculiar misfortune of both you and me to dream dreams of Elysium far exceeding all that anything earthly can realize.

Far short of your dreams as you may be, no woman could do more to realize them than that same black-eyed Fanny. If you could but contemplate her through my imagination, it would appear ridiculous to you that any one should for a moment think of being unhappy with her. My old father used to have a saying, "If you make a bad bargain, hug it all the tighter"; and it occurs to me that if the bargain you have just closed can possibly be called a bad one, it is certainly the most pleasant one for applying that maxim to which my fancy can by any effort picture.

I write another letter, inclosing this, which you can show her, if she desires it. I do this because she would think strangely, perhaps, should you tell her that you received no letters from me, or, telling her you do, refuse to let her see them. I close this, entertaining the confident hope that every successive letter I shall have from you (which I here pray may not be few, nor far between) may show you possessing a more steady hand and cheerful heart than the last preceding it.

As ever, your friend,
LINCOLN.

A month passed and Lincoln had news from Speed that the marriage bells rang merrily. Speed wrote that he was far happier than he ever expected to be. To which Lincoln replied: "I know you too well to suppose your expectations were not, at least sometimes, extravagant, and if the reality exceeds them all, I say, Enough, dear Lord. I am not going beyond the truth when I tell you that the short space it took me to read your last letter gave me more pleasure than the total sum of all I have enjoyed since the fatal 1st of January, 1841."

Then he referred to Mary Todd for the first time in his letters to Speed, explaining why a piece of gladness could not live long with him. "Since then [the fatal 1st of January, 1841] it seems to me I should have been entirely happy, but for the never-absent idea that there is one still unhappy whom I have contributed to make so. That still kills my soul. I cannot but reproach myself for even wishing to be happy while she is otherwise. She accompanied a large party on the railroad cars to Jacksonville last Monday, and on her return spoke, so that I heard of it, of having enjoyed the trip exceedingly. God be praised for that."

As far as seventeen-year-old Sarah Rickard was concerned, his mind was easy; from her came no reproaches nor news of unhappiness. He wrote Speed: "One thing I can tell you which I know you will be glad to hear, and that is that I have seen Sarah [Rickard] and scrutinized her feelings as well as I could, and am fully convinced she is far happier now than she has been for the past fifteen months."

A flower had come with the Speed letter. "The sweet violet you inclosed came safely to hand, but it was so dry, and mashed so flat, that it crumbled to dust at the first attempt to handle it. The juice that mashed out of it stained a place in the letter, which I mean to preserve and cherish for the sake of her who procured it to be sent. My renewed good wishes to her in particular, and generally to all such of your relations who know me."

Three months later there came to Lincoln thanks and thanks from Speed for what he had done to bring and to keep them together. He wrote to Speed: "You make a kind acknowledgment of your obligations to me for your present happiness. I am pleased with that acknowledgment. But a thousand times more am I pleased to know that you enjoy a degree of happiness worthy of an acknowledgment. The truth is, I am not sure there was any merit with me in the part I took in your difficulty; I was drawn into it by a fate. If I would I could not have done less than I did.

"I always was superstitious; I believe God made me one of the instruments of bringing your Fanny and you together, which union I have no doubt he had foreordained. Whatever he designs he will do for me yet. 'Stand still and see the salvation of the Lord,' is my text just now. If, as you say, you have told Fanny all, I should have no objection to her seeing this letter, but for its reference to our friend here; let her seeing it depend upon whether she has ever known anything of my affairs; and if she has not, do not let her."

His reference to "our friend here" meant Mary Todd. Lincoln was now sure he had made a mistake first of all in not taking Speed's advice to break off his engagement with Mary Todd; and his second mistake was in not going through and keeping his resolve to marry her. "As to my having been displeased with your advice, surely you know better than that. I know you do, and therefore will not labor to convince you. True, that subject is painful to me; but it is not your silence, or the silence of all the world, that can make me forget it. I acknowledged the correctness of your advice too; but before I resolve to do the one thing or the other, I must gain my confidence in my own ability to keep my resolves when they are made.

"In that ability you know I once prided myself as the only or chief gem of my character; that gem I lost—how and where you know too well. I have not yet regained it; and until I do, I cannot trust myself in any matter of much importance. I believe now that had you understood my case at the time as well as I understood yours afterward, by the aid you would have given me I should have sailed through clear, but that does not now afford me sufficient confidence to begin that or the like of that again."

Such was the frank and pitiless self-revelation he did not wish Fanny Henning Speed to see unless she knew everything else along with it. He closed his letter, "My respect and esteem to all your friends there, and, by your permission, my love to your Fanny."

And in one sentence he had sketched himself, "I am so poor and make so little headway in the world, that I drop back in a month of idleness as much as I gain in a year's sowing."

One June evening he ended a letter to Speed, "Nothing new here. . . . I have not seen Sarah since my last trip, and I am going out there as soon as I mail this letter."

Chapter 57

MRS. SIMEON FRANCIS, wife of the editor of the *Sangamo Journal,* often invited a list of guests and entertained them in the parlor of the Francis house. She believed with her husband that Abraham Lincoln had a famous career ahead of him. Also she believed her friend Mary Todd to be a rare, accomplished, brilliant woman. In her eyes Lincoln and Miss Todd were a match; she would play her part as a matchmaker.

She invited Lincoln to a party in her parlor, brought the two of them together and said, "Be friends again." It was said that she told neither of the couple beforehand about her plan to have them meet again; it was said the meeting came to each of them as a surprise, and that neither Lincoln nor Miss Todd had any suspicions or advance information of the plan to bring them together to be told, "Be friends again."

Whatever of fate or woman-wit was at work, it did happen that they were friends again. But they didn't tell the world so. They had done that before. For a while their quiet meetings in the parlor of the Francis house were known only to Mrs. Francis.

Not even Mrs. Ninian Edwards knew what was going on till weeks had passed. Mrs. Edwards said later: "I asked Mary why she was so secretive about it. She said evasively that after all that had occurred, it was best to keep the courtship from all eyes and ears. Men and women and the whole world were uncertain and slippery."

Julia Jayne, a friend of Mary Todd, joined the quiet little parties in the Francis house. One day they read together an article written to be printed in the *Sangamo Journal.* It was a Whig attack on the state auditor of accounts, James Shields, who had issued an order that certain paper money, of which the people had more than they had of silver or gold money, would not be taken by the state government for taxes. Besides being a political attack on Shields as an official, it was a personal lampoon hitting at Shields's manners and clothes and struts in Springfield society.

Miss Todd and Miss Jayne told Lincoln to go ahead and have the article printed. It was written in the talk of backwoods farmers, alluded to the state officials as "High Comb'd Cocks," asked whether Shields's $2,400 a year would be paid in paper money or silver, mentioned the penitentiary, and declared: "Shields is a fool as well as a liar. With him truth is out of the question; and as for getting a good, bright, passable lie out of him, you might as well try to strike fire from a cake of tallow." This, however, was only a beginning. There was this swift, marvelous cartoon:

If I was deaf and blind, I could tell him [Shields] by the smell. I seed him when I was down in Springfield last winter. They had a sort of gatherin' there one night among the grandees, they called a fair. All the gals about town was there, and all the handsome widows and married women, finickin' about trying to look like gals, tied as tight in the middle, and puffed out at both ends, like bundles of fodder that hadn't been stacked yet, but wanted stackin' pretty bad. And then they had tables all around the house kivered over with caps and pincushions and ten thousand such little knickknacks, tryin' to sell 'em to the fellows that were bowin' and scrapin' and kungeerin' about 'em. They wouldn't let no Democrats in for fear they'd disgust the ladies, or scare the little gals, or dirty the floor.

I looked in at the window, and there was this same fellow Shields floatin' about on the air, without heft or earthly substances, just like a lock of cat fur where cats had been fighting. He was paying his money to this one, and that one, and t'other one, and sufferin' great loss because it wasn't silver instead of State paper; and the sweet distress he seemed to be in,—his very features, in the ecstatic agony of his soul, spoke audibly and distinctly, "Dear girls, it is distressing, but I cannot marry you all. Too well I know how much you suffer; but do, do remember, it is not my fault that I am so handsome and so interesting." As this last was expressed by a most exquisite contortion of his face, he seized hold of one of their hands, and squeezed, and held on to it about a quarter of an hour. "Oh, my good fellow!" says I to myself, "if that was one of our Democratic gals in the Lost Townships, the way you'd get a brass pin let into you would be about up to the head."

The article ended with declaring that if some change for the better did not come in state government, the taxpayers would not have a cow left to milk, "or a calf's tail to wring."

The name "Rebecca" was signed. It was followed by a second article also signed "Rebecca," this written by Miss Todd and Miss Jayne. Parts of it read: "Now I want you to tell Mr. S—— that, rather than fight, I'll make any apology; and if he wants personal satisfaction, let him only come here, and he may squeeze my hand. Jeff tells me the way these fire-eaters do is to give the challenged party choice of weapons, etc., which bein' the case, I'll tell you in confidence that I never fights with anything but broomsticks or hot water or a shivelful of coals or some such things; the former of which, being somewhat like a shillalah, may not be very objectionable to him. I will give him choice, however, in one thing, and that is, whether, when we fight, I shall wear breeches or he petticoats, for, I presume that change is sufficient to place us on an equality."

Shields was a bachelor, thirty-two years old, had been a lawyer ten years, and was born in Dungannon, County of Tyrone, Ireland. As a boy of fifteen in Ireland, he had challenged a veteran of Napoleonic wars to a duel. But when it came to the shooting the pistols wouldn't go off, the deadly enemies shook hands, and the veteran had taught Shields the French language as Shields later taught it when a school-teacher in Kaskaskia, Illinois. He asked the *Sangamo Journal* editor who wrote the articles and was told Lincoln took all the responsibility for them. Then Shields wrote Lincoln: "Whilst abstaining from giving provocation, I have become the object of slander, vituperation, and personal abuse. I will take the liberty of requiring a full, positive, and absolute retraction of all offensive allusions used by you in these offensive communications, in relation to my private character and standing as a man, as an apology for the insults conveyed in them. This may prevent consequences which no one will regret more than myself. Your ob't servant."

Lincoln's seconds notified Shields' seconds that the duel would be fought with cavalry broadswords, across a plank ten feet long and nine to twelve inches broad, within three miles of Alton, on the Missouri side of the Mississippi River. By horse and buggy, and by an old horse-ferry, the two parties traveled on September 22 to a sand-bar in the Mississippi River, located in the state of Missouri and beyond the reach of the Illinois laws against dueling.

Riding in a rowboat to the sandbar, Lincoln said he was reminded of the time a Kentuckian enlisted for the War of 1812. The sweetheart of the soldier told him she was embroidering a bullet pouch and belt for him to wear in battle and she would stitch in the words, "Victory or Death." He asked her, "Ain't that rayther too strong? S'pose you put 'Victory or Be Crippled'!"

Lincoln took a seat on a log and practiced swings and swishes in the air with his cavalry broadsword, while friends, lawyers, seconds on both sides, held a long confab. After the main long confabs there were shorter confabs with Lincoln and with Shields. Then a statement was issued declaring that although Mr. Lincoln was the writer of the article signed "Rebecca" in the *Sangamo Journal* of September 2, "yet he had no intention of injuring the personal or private character or standing of Mr. Shields as a gentleman or a man, and that Mr. Lincoln did not think, nor does he now think, that said article could produce such an effect; and had Mr. Lincoln anticipated such an effect, he would have forborne to write it; said article was written solely for political effect, and not to gratify any personal pique against Mr. Shields, for he had none and knew of no cause for any."

A crowd waiting on the Alton levee saw the ferryboat come near the shore with what seemed to be a man in blood-soaked clothes in the bottom of the boat. As the boat tied up they saw it was a log covered with a red shirt. The duel had become a joke. Lincoln and Shields came off the boat together, in easy and pleasant chat.

The weapon with which Lincoln was to have fought Shields was a good deal like the ax he had handled so many years as boy and young man. He told Bill Herndon: "I did not intend to hurt Shields unless I did so clearly in self-defense. If it had been necessary I could have split him from the crown of his head to the end of his backbone."

One man who made the trip to the sand-bar was asked how Lincoln behaved. He said: "I watched Lincoln closely while he sat on his log waiting the signal to fight. His face was serious. I never knew him to go so long without making a joke. He reached over and picked up one of the swords, which he drew from its scabbard. Then he felt along the edge of the weapon with his thumb, like a barber feels of the edge of his razor, raised himself to his full height, stretched out his long arms and clipped off a twig from above his head with the sword. There wasn't another man of us who could have reached anywhere near that twig, and the absurdity of that long-reaching fellow fighting with cavalry sabers with Shields, who could walk under his arm, came pretty near making me howl with laughter. After Lincoln had cut off the twig he returned the sword to the scabbard with a sigh and sat down, but I detected the gleam in his eye, which was always the forerunner of one of his yarns, and fully expected him to tell a side-splitter there in the shadow of the grave— Shields's grave."

The *Alton Telegraph and Democratic Review*, in an editorial, said of the two chief figures:

Both of them are lawyers—both have been to the legislature of this state and aided in the construction of laws for the protection of society. Why, therefore, they should be permitted to escape punishment, we are at a loss to conjecture. We are astonished to hear that large numbers of our citizens crossed the river to witness a scene of cold-blooded assassination between two of their fellow-beings. It was no less disgraceful than the conduct of those who were to have been actors in the drama. Hereafter we hope the citizens of Springfield will select some other point than Alton.

Lincoln wrote to Josh Speed:

You have heard of my duel with Shields, and I have now to inform you that the dueling business still rages in this city. Day before yesterday Shields challenged Butler, who accepted, and proposed fighting next morning at sunrise in Bob Allen's meadow, one hundred yards' distance, with rifles. To this Whitesides, Shields's second, said "No," because of the law. Thus ended duel No. 2. Yesterday Whitesides chose to consider himself insulted by Dr. Merryman, so sent him a kind of quasi-challenge, inviting him to meet him at the Planter's House in St. Louis on the next Friday to settle their difficulty. Merryman made me his friend, and sent Whitesides a note, inquiring to know if he meant his note as a challenge, and if so, that he would, according to the law in such case made and provided, prescribe the terms of the meeting. Whitesides returned for answer that if Merryman would meet him at the Planter's House as desired, he would challenge him. Merryman replied in a note that he denied Whitesides's right to dictate time and place, but that he (Merryman) would waive the question of time, and meet him at Louisiana, Missouri. Upon my presenting this note to Whitesides and stating verbally its contents, he declined receiving it, saying he had business in St. Louis, and it was as near as Louisiana. Merryman then directed me to notify Whitesides that he should publish the correspondence between them, with such comments as he thought fit. This I did. Thus it stood at bedtime last night. This morning Whitesides, by his friend Shields, is praying for a new trial, on the ground that he was mistaken in Merryman's proposition to meet him at Louisiana, Missouri, thinking it was the State of Louisiana. This Merryman hoots at, and is preparing his publication; while the town is in a ferment, and a street fight somewhat anticipated.

And a story arose, and was told as true to fact by many friends of Lincoln, that a pompous and punctilious challenger had come to him from Shields and told him that honor would have to be satisfied by mortal and bloody combat in the medieval manner, saying, "As the challenged party you will have the choice of weapons—what will your weapons be?" Lincoln's reply was, "How about cow-dung at five paces?"

Chapter 58

THE year after Lincoln's broken engagement with Mary Todd and the months in which he was writing letters to nerve Speed up to get married in the year 1842, were times filled with a good deal of action for Lincoln. It was said of him in this time, "He went crazy as a loon."

Yet there were friends of his who knew that at this very time he was plunged deep in stretches of work that made him forget his troubles. The same medicine that he prescribed for the nervous debility of Joshua Speed and the melancholy of Fanny Henning, he was giving himself in big doses. Activity, occupation, were good for whatever ailed them, he had said, and he kept his grip on himself by doses of activity, occupation.

In the summer of 1841, he went into law partnership with Stephen T. Logan, and he learned law from Logan. Though Logan had frowsy hair, wore cotton shirts and heavy shoes, and never put on a necktie, he was one of the most neat, scrupulous, particular, and exact lawyers in Illinois when it came to preparing cases, writing letters, and filing documents. In law practice Logan knew how to be thorough, how to make results come from being thorough. From him Lincoln learned; the word "thorough" became important among his words.

He argued before the supreme court in the widely known case of Bailey *vs.* Cromwell. Cromwell had sold Bailey a negro girl, saying the girl was a slave. Bailey had given a note promising to pay cash for the slave. Lincoln argued, in part, that the girl was a free person until she was proven to be a slave, and, if she was not proven a slave, then she could not be sold nor bought and no cash could be exchanged between two men buying and selling her. The supreme court took practically the same view, and Lincoln won his case.

He did law work for a Rock Creek quarryman, Isaac Cogdal, and meeting Cogdal a few weeks afterward on the Statehouse steps, he saw the quarryman had one arm off. Besides losing his arm he was losing his business, Cogdal said. Lincoln took out his pocketbook and handed Cogdal the note Cogdal had signed promising to pay a fee for law work Lincoln had done. It didn't look just right for him to take the note, Cogdal was trying to say. "If you had the money, I wouldn't take it," blurted Lincoln, hurrying away.

Over in Tazewell County he met a crooked lawyer. An old farmer named Case sold a breaking plow and three yoke of oxen. Two boys named Snow signed notes promising to pay for the plow and oxen. But since signing the notes they had come of age. They admitted on the witness stand they were using the plow and oxen to break prairie, and that they had signed the notes. Their lawyer pleaded they were infants or minors when the notes were signed and therefore they could not be held to pay. Lincoln's speech to the jury stripped the other lawyer of his pretensions.

"Gentlemen," he said, "these boys never would have tried to cheat old farmer Case out of these oxen and that plow, but for the advice of counsel. It was bad advice, bad in morals and bad in law. The law never sanctions cheating, and a lawyer must be very smart to twist it so that it will seem to do so. The judge will tell you what your own sense of justice has already told you, that these Snow boys, if they were mean enough to plead the baby act, when they came to be men should have taken the oxen and plow back. They cannot go back on their contract, and also keep what the note was given for." The jury, without leaving their seats, gave a verdict for old farmer Case.

Between law cases he could think about newspaper items such as one in 1842, reading:

Mr. Adams presents to the Senate (Jan. 24) a petition signed by citizens of Haverhill, Mass., *for the adoption of measures peaceably to dissolve the Union*, and moves its reference to a select committee with instructions to report the reasons why the prayers should not be granted; Mr. Gilmer offers a resolution of censure upon Mr. Adams for presenting such a petition; Mr Marshall offers a substitute declaring Mr. Adams' action the deepest indignity to the House and the people; violent debate ensues ten days, the resolution is laid on the table, reception of the petition is refused.

When Martin Van Buren stopped overnight in the town of Rochester, Illinois, a Springfield party took along Lincoln to help in a night of entertainment for the former President. The two main tavern performers that evening were Lincoln and Van

Buren. Lincoln opened his big ragbag of memories of life in Illinois, Indiana, and Kentucky, while Van Buren told about New York ways and New York lawyers as far back as Hamilton and Burr. Lincoln, of course, had a thousand funny, pointed anecdotes such as the one of the farmer who moved so often that when he was going to move again, the chickens could tell it and walked up and lay down to have their feet tied; his father's story of the man who was asked for a warrantee bill of a horse he was selling and he guaranteed him "sound of skin and skeleton and free from faults and faculties"; and so on. Van Buren said his sides were sore from laughing.

Lincoln might have told of a judge who, trying to be kindly, asked a convicted murderer, politically allied to him, "When would you like to be hung?" Or of the lawyer jabbing at a hostile witness who had one large ear, with the remark, "If he bit off the other ear he would look more like a man than a jackass." Or of the old man with whiskers so long it was said of him when he traveled, "His whiskers arrive a day in advance." Or of Abraham Bale, the tall and powerful-voiced preacher from Kentucky, who was baptizing new converts in the Sangamon River just below Salem Hill; as Bale was leading a sister out into the water, her husband, watching the ceremony from the bank, called out: "Hold on, Bale! Hold on, Bale! Don't you dround her. I wouldn't take the best cow and calf in Menard County for her."

He could have told Van Buren how Bill Engle, the Campbellite preacher from Sugar Grove, and Fog Atchison of Petersburg, took to jolly bragging about which raised the fatter sheep; and Engle got the laugh on Atchison by saying: "I tell you, Mr. Atchison, I have the fattest sheep. An ox hooked one the other day and we rendered it up. It was all tallow and its tail made a tallow candle."

But one day there came news that hurt Lincoln. Bowling Green was dead. In the house over at New Salem, at the foot of the bluff with the timber of oak growth climbing up, lay the body of his friend, teacher, companion, with the life gone.

This was the place where Nancy and Bowling Green had nursed him back to health, coaxed his mind to come back and live and be strong. There Nancy had prepared for him hot biscuits smothered in honey. And he had lain on their cellar door in the sunshine of cool autumn days reading Blackstone's Commentaries.

He rode out to the Green home; he stayed till the day of the funeral. Though he was not a Freemason, word came to him that the Masons, who were to conduct the funeral, wished him to make some remarks on the character and life of Bowling Green.

On the day of the burial the Masons in white aprons gathered in the Green cabin, the chaplain carrying the open Bible, the tyler his drawn sword and other regalia of the Masonic brotherhood. The master of ceremonies finally called Lincoln to the head of the coffin.

For a few moments Lincoln stood looking down at the still, white, round face of Bowling Green. He began to tremble, and there were struggles the length of his long, bony frame. He slowly turned and looked around; the room was filled with faces; in the doorways and at the windows were living faces looking at him, the faces of old New Salem and Clary's Grove and Sand Ridge and Wolf Creek friends.

A few words came off his lips, broken and choked words. Tears filled his eyes and ran down his cheeks; he gripped his hat, slowly lifted a handkerchief to his face, and smothered his face in the handkerchief. Then he turned to Nancy Green, who stood up from her chair and took the arm he offered her.

He stood with the widow, and slowly the tears came to an end and the struggles in the length of his long, bony frame came to an end. He looked toward the pallbearers; his hands calmly motioned them to take charge.

The lid was screwed on to the coffin, and Lincoln, with Nancy Green on his right arm, and his left hand in the hand of her granddaughter, followed the burial party to a corner of the farm where Bowling Green was laid away near the cabin he had built.

Chapter 59

AT the meetings of Lincoln and Mary Todd in the Francis home, Miss Todd made it clear to him that if another date should be fixed for a wedding, it should not be set so far in the future as it was the time before. Lincoln agreed with her.

Early in October he wrote to his friend Speed, as a single man to a trusted married friend, asking for information:

You have now been the husband of a lovely woman nearly eight months. You are happier now than the day you married her. Returning elasticity of spirits is manifested in your letters. But I want to ask you a close question, "Are you in feeling as well as judgment glad that you are married as you are?" From anybody but me this would be an impudent question, not to be tolerated; but I know you will pardon it in me. Please answer it quickly as I am impatient to know.

A few weeks later, on the morning of November 4, 1842, Lincoln came to the room of his friend James Matheny, before Matheny was out of bed. And to Matheny under the quilts he said, "I am going to be married today."

On the street that day he met Ninian W. Edwards and told Edwards that he and Mary were going to be married that evening. And Edwards gave notice, "Mary is my ward, and she must be married at my house."

And when Edwards asked Mary Todd if what he had heard was true, and she told him it was true, they all started to make the big Edwards house ready—as best they could on such short notice—for a wedding of one of the Edwardses. Mrs. Edwards sent for her sister Frances, to bake a cake. The big house was swept and garnished—as well as possible on such short notice.

Lincoln watched carefully a plain gold ring he carried, on the inside band of which the jeweler Chatterton had engraved the words, "Love is eternal."

And he had a fleeting thought or two of his old honest, tried, rugged friend John Hanks of cornfield and flatboat days. He had written Hanks a week or so before:

DEAR JOHN:
  I am to be married on the 4th of next month to Miss Todd. I hope you will come over. Be sure to be on deck by early candlelight.
                                              Yours,
                                                   A. LINCOLN.

At the Edwards house that evening, the Reverend Charles Dresser in canonical robes performed the ring ceremony of the Episcopal Church for the groom, thirty-three years old, and the bride, twenty-three years old. Behind Lincoln stood a supreme court judge, Thomas C. Brown, fat, bluff, blunt, and an able lawyer not accustomed to weddings. As Lincoln placed the ring on the bride's finger and repeated the form, "With this ring I thee endow with all my goods, chattels, lands, and tenements," the supreme court judge blurted out in a suppressed tone that everybody heard, "God Almighty, Lincoln, the statute fixes all that." The minister kept a straight face, became serious, and then pronounced Abraham Lincoln and Mary Todd man and wife in the sight of God and man.

Afterward came talk about the wedding, the bride, the groom. Jim Matheny said Lincoln had "looked as if he was going to slaughter." It was told at the Butler house where Lincoln roomed that, as he was dressing, Bill Butler's boy came in and wanted to know, "Where are you going?" Lincoln's answer being, "To hell, I suppose."

Mrs. Edwards said: "I am sure there had been no 'time fixed' for any wedding; no preparations had ever been made until the day that Mr. Lincoln met Mr. Edwards on the street and told him that he and Mary were going to be married that evening. The wedding guests were few; it was not much more than a family gathering. The entertainment was simple but in beautiful taste; the bride had neither veil nor flowers in her hair. There had been no elaborate trousseau for the bride, nor even a handsome wedding-gown; nor was it a gay wedding."

The bride's sister, Mrs. Frances Wallace, said: "The same morning they told Mrs. Edwards they were going to be married that night, she was terribly disappointed, for she could not get up a dinner in that short time. They asked me if I would help. So I worked all day. I never worked harder in my life, and in the evening we had a very nice little supper, but not what we would have had if they had given Mrs. Edwards time. Mr. Lincoln and Mary may have had a lovers' quarrel, for all I know. But I saw him the night he was married and he was not distracted with grief or anything else. He was cheerful as he ever had been, for all we could see. He acted just as he always had in company. No, no one stood up for him. Just he and Mary stood up alone, and Mr. Dresser married them. Mr. Herndon says that Mrs. Lincoln wore a white silk dress, but I know she never had a white silk dress. After I was married I gave her my white satin dress and told her to wear it till it got soiled but then to give it back to me, for I wanted to keep all things like that—my wedding dress, you know. She was not married in the white satin. It was too soiled. She may have been married in a white Swiss muslin but I think it was not a white dress at all. I think it was delaine or something of that kind."

The Springfield *Journal*, in a corner of its third page on Nov. 11, 1842, had the item:

MARRIED—In this city on the 4th instant, at the residence of N. W. Edwards, Esq., by Rev. C. Dresser, ABRAHAM LINCOLN, Esq., to Miss MARY TODD, daughter of Robert Todd, Esq., of Lexington, Ky.

And Lincoln, in his law office five days after the wedding, sent a letter to Marshall at Shawneetown. He began the letter, "Dear Sam: Yours of the 10th Oct. enclosing five dollars was taken from the office in my absence by Judge Logan who neglected to hand it to me till about a week ago, and just an hour before I took a wife. Your other of the 3d Inst., is also received."

Then he discussed two law cases, and ended the letter: "Nothing new here, except my marrying, which, to me, is a matter of profound wonder."

In January the new husband wrote Speed: "Mary is very well and continues her old sentiments of friendship for you. How the marriage life goes with us I will tell you when I see you here." And in July: "We shall look with impatience for your visit this fall. Your Fanny cannot be more anxious to see my Molly (Mrs. Lincoln) than the latter is to see her, nor so much as I am—Don't fail to come—We are but two, as yet—"

Chapter 60

MORE than four years had gone by since William Trailor was in jail in Springfield, charged with murder, and men around the public square were growling about "the rope" for Trailor. Then Lincoln had helped turn up, alive and healthy, the man who was supposed to have been killed, having stood by his client during false accusations and threats of lynching. And the years passed and Trailor couldn't or wouldn't pay the fee of his lawyer and best friend in the hours a noose was knotted for his neck. And Trailor died a peaceable, homelike death—without having paid his lawyer, his valued counsel. And Lincoln sued the estate of William Trailor, and collected $100.00.

Cash of many kinds came into his hands. He wrote one client, "Walters has paid me $703.25 (in gold) for you." Or again, "We send you enclosed two one hundred dollar Missouri bills." Or, "He paid me $74 State Bank paper, $42 Shawneetown paper and $2.59 cents silver."

"We foreclosed on Walter's house and lots and sold them and bought them in your name," he wrote Joshua Speed.

Then among involved angles of the transaction for Speed, which included a secret contract, "It was sold for about $1,200, the amount of Van's debt, but although you are the ostensible purchaser, we have a secret contract with Van that he is the purchaser for so much of the purchase money as is over and above what will pay you."

Law practice, however, didn't have the charm for Lincoln in 1844 that he found in politics. He spent days studying the tariff issue, delivered hour-and-a-half speeches, and took such a leader-ship as a protective-tariff advocate in Springfield that the *State Register* referred to him as "the great Goliah of the Junto."

So earnestly did he consider himself the mouthpiece and exponent of the protective tariff that he kept up a running combat of argument against the opposition—took on all comers as he did in wrestling days. The *State Register*, a Democratic organ, told its readers on March 22 that a free-trade speech by Judge Cav-erly, a Democratic presidential elector, "so disturbed Mr. Lincoln that he promised to forfeit his 'ears' and his 'legs' if he did not demonstrate that protected articles have been cheaper since the 1842 tariff than before."

The ways of Lincoln as a "mixer" in politics were in a letter he wrote Alden Hall of Pekin:

Springfield, Feby. 14, 1843.
Friend Hall:

Your county and ours are almost sure to be placed in the same con-gressional district—I would like to be its Representative; still circum-stances may happen to prevent my even being a candidate— If, how-ever, there are any Whigs in Tazewell who would as soon I should represent them as any other person, I would be glad they would not cast me aside until they see and hear farther what turn things take.

Do not suppose, Esq., that in addressing this letter to you, I assume that you will be for or against all other Whigs; I only mean, that I know you to be my personal friend, a good Whig, and an Honorable man, to whom I may, without fear, communicate a fact which I wish my particular friend (if I have any) to know.

There is nothing new here now worth telling.

Your friend as ever,

A. Lincoln.

Sam Marshall wrote from Shawneetown complaining that Lin-coln was careless about the Shawneetown bank cases and others. Lincoln explained that he had misplaced the letter about the bank cases and forgotten all about it. "The truth is, when I received

Springfield, Feby 14. 1843.

Friend Hall:

Your county and ours are almost sure to be placed in the same Congressional district — I would like to be its Representative, still circumstances may happen to prevent my even being a candidate. If, however, there are any whigs in Tazewell who would as soon I should represent them as any other person, I would be glad they would not cast me aside until they see and hear further what turn things take —

Do not suppose, Esq: that in addressing this letter to you, I assume that you will be for me against all other whigs; I only mean, that I know you to be my personal friend, a good whig, and an honorable man, to whom I may, without fear communicate a fact which I wish I wish my particular friends (if I have any) to know —

There is nothing new here now worth telling.

Your friend as ever
A. Lincoln

Lincoln as a "mixer" in politics stands forth vividly in this letter to Alden Hall. Four months after his wedding he is actively hunting political support that might make him a congressman. He writes of his congressional district, "I would like to be its Representative," and indicates, "Circumstances may prevent my even being a candidate." And he assures the fellow party worker in a neighboring county, "I know you to be my personal friend, a good Whig, and an honorable man."

*From the Original in the
Possession of Mrs. W. Halsted Vander Poel*

your letter, I glanced it over, stuck it away, postponed consideration of the cases mentioned, and forgot them altogether."

In the case of Gatewood *vs.* Wood and Wood, he wrote to
Marshall: "We would have failed entirely to get into court but
for an agreement with Mr. Eddy, which saved us. By the agreement we altered the record so as to make it appear that it had
been sent to the circuit court, also agreeing that at the next term
of court, all the papers and orders are to be altered then accord-
ingly *nunc pro tunc.*"

To beat the opposition in a case that honestly interested him,
Lincoln would ambush the enemy with any trick or device within
the law. In the Dorman-Lane case, for instance, he believed
certain rascals were trying to take a piece of land away from a
hard-working couple of young people who were getting a start
at farming. He wrote Sam Marshall, his partner in that case,
in 1845: "I think we can plead limitations on them, so that it
will stick for good and all. Don't speak of this, lest they hear
it, and take the alarm."

When the first baby came to the clients in that case, it was
a boy whom they named Samuel Marshall. And they promised
that if the second baby was a boy they would name it Abraham
Lincoln.

Chapter 61

LINCOLN didn't forget the *State Register* warning about his
"assumed clownishness." Herndon cautioned him; he carried
jokes too far in public; it came too easy for him to slip out of
his usual dignity, do a swift monkeyshine, and be back in his
own face and character before men knew he was mimicking.
On the stump and in courtrooms or hotel loafing rooms, he could
be pointedly funny when feeling that way. He described weddings and funerals where the expected dignity of events was
upset, incidents dealing with fiddlers, teamsters, mules, coons,
skunks. One of his important proverbs was remembered from
his father, "Every man must skin his own skunk."

He used words natural to farmers shucking corn in a cold November wind or carpenters putting the adze to oak rafters. He spoke of parts and members of the body in the words of common, hard-handed men, and often seemed to have some definite philosophy of human meekness, the frailty of mortal clay, the pride that goeth before a fall, the dignity whose assumptions suffer and wither in the catching of a greased pig.

When he had finished a story, he may have shocked or annoyed men who called themselves polite and who desired to be known as men of good taste, but other thoughtful men said there was always a point or a lesson or some genius of whim or nonsense connecting with the final strands of the tale or anecdote.

In the repertoire of characters he mimicked were circuit-riding preachers who snorted hellfire, Quakers, Irishmen, Germans, men of struts, and a stutterer who whistled between stutters. He could do a sketch of the drug-store man Diller irritated by little Judge Logan sitting in the store and whittling the chairs; Diller ordered Judge Logan out of the store; and the leader of the Sangamon County bar walked out in a huff saying he would never come back—though later he did.

He might compare the squabbling of politics and the howling of hostile factions to cats wailing with pain and spitting at each other at night outside the hotel rooms. In the morning perhaps the alley would be full of dead cats—so the sounds indicated. But in the morning the cats were at peace, with assured futures.

One hot day in July Lincoln drove his horse and one-seated gig from Bloomington to Tremont with Swett, a 200-pound man on one side of him, and Judge Davis, a 300-pound man on the other side. At Tremont he threw the livery-stable man the reins, calling out, "Put up that horse and let me get out of here quick." And he added a remark often recalled in that livery-stable, and often told among cronies of Swett. He mocked coarsely in a swift comic exclamation at his misery in a long drive on a hot day sitting between two sweating, odorous, large men.

One day in a courthouse on the Eighth Circuit, Lincoln rattled off a lingo changing the letters of words so that "cotton patch" became "potten catch" and "jackass" became "jassack." A dozen other words were given tricky twists. Some were strictly barnyard and tavern words—to be found published perhaps only in unexpurgated prints of Shakespeare and Burns. The court clerk asked Lincoln to write out a copy of it. And for many years that court clerk took special care of the scrap of paper on which Lincoln had scribbled a piece of nonsense.

Usher Linder said he noticed that Abe Lincoln and Abe's uncle Mordecai were a good deal alike as story-tellers. "No one took offense at Uncle Mord's stories. I heard him tell a bevy of fashionable girls that he knew a very large woman who had a husband so small that in the night she often mistook him for the baby, and that one night she picked him up and was singing to him a soothing lullaby when he awoke and told her that the baby was on the other side of the bed." Once when Linder was telling about Mordecai, Lincoln remarked, "Linder, I have often said that Uncle Mord ran off with all the talents of the family."

It was a horsey country of horsey men. A thirty- or forty-mile drive was counted an easy day. They spoke of one-horse towns, one-horse lawyers and one-horse doctors—even of one-horse horse doctors. They tied their horses to hitching posts half-chewed away by horse teeth. They brushed off horse hair from their clothes after a drive. They carried feed bags of oats. They spliced broken tugs with rope to last till they reached a harness shop.

Chapter 62

THERE were in 1846 in Springfield old settlers who remembered the Van Noy hanging twenty years previous in a hollow just south of where the new Statehouse was built. Van Noy stood in a wagon under the gallows, while the noose was put around his neck; the wagon drove off from under him and left his feet walking on air. These old settlers could tell about Nathan Cromwell, who went with his good-looking wife to the home of a man who had said something to or about Mrs. Cromwell; and he pointed a pistol at the man's heart and made him get down on his knees and beg Mrs. Cromwell's pardon.

And there was a man whose name had been forgotten, though what happened to him was remembered. He had been drinking all day and on a cold winter night started to go home along the St. Louis road. A couple of rods south of the Masters cornfield, later the intersection of Grand Avenue and Second Street, he fell or was thrown from his horse, and in the morning was frozen stiff; Dr. Merryman was called and pronounced the man dead.

Only twenty years had passed since the first regular shoemaker, Jabez Capps, had located his shop and store on the north side of Jefferson Street between First and Second. The first harnessmaker, Thomas Strawbridge, had come twenty-two years before. On the south side of Jefferson Street, near Second, stood a building that the old settlers pointed out as the first two-story brick store in Springfield; P. C. Canedy had opened his stock of books and drugs there sixteen years before. What had become northwest Jefferson and Second streets, a busy central corner of Springfield, was twenty-four years previous a piece of John Kelley's cornfield; on that spot had stood a log-cabin courthouse, the first county seat of Sangamon County. Away from it had swept the rolling prairie, a mile east and west, a half-mile north and south, bordered on the north by heavy timber and on the south by growths of pin oak, elm, cherry, and hackberry, with fringes of plum, crab-apple, and haw trees, besides hazel-brush and blackberry bushes, festoons of grapevines and winding strawberry runners.

In the heavy timber that had once stood between First and Third streets, boys used to gather pawpaws and dig ginseng and turkey peas. One of those boys, Zimri Enos, could recollect how his father loved big oxen and drove them with only a hazel stick for a goad, and how in the winter of the deep snow, 1831, his two big yoke of oxen plowed through snow that horses couldn't travel and brought from the timbers loads of wood for people whose cabin fires had gone out.

So early the town of Springfield was beginning, as a town, to have a memory.

It was only twenty-five years since, in the log-cabin courthouse then at Jefferson and Second streets, John Kelley was allowed by the county commissioner the sum of $42.50 due him by contract for building the courthouse, and $5.00 for "extras." At the same time the county was divided into four districts, and overseers for the poor were appointed, two for each district, with three trustees appointed by the county court to supervise the overseers of the poor. Then Robert Hamilton was allowed $84.75 for building the county jail, which the sheriff, John Taylor, found be a "no-account jail" and so told the county commissioners.

Since that time there had come a new courthouse, built of brick, in the middle of the public square, with a hip roof and cupola; it had cost $6,841.00, and was knocked down and carried off to make way for the new capitol, costing $240,000.00, nearly twice as much as was first estimated. And it was one of the settled memories of Springfield that the lawyer and politician, Lincoln, had log-rolled through the legislature the bill that located the capitol in Springfield. Besides Hoffman's Row, where Lincoln's office with Herndon was located, there was Chicken Row, a string of one-story shops and stores on another side of the square. But Hoffman's Row and Chicken Row were new. They were not of Springfield's past, to which the memories of old settlers ran.

They could recall how a near-by town named Sangamo, on a bluff of the river where Lincoln had built the Offut flatboat, had nearly won a decision from the county commissioners for the location of the county seat; and the commissioners had also come near to selecting for the county seat a town laid out by William S. Hamilton, a young lawyer who was the son of the famous Alexander Hamilton, and who had vanished after his plans were rejected. It was then that Elisha and John Kelley from North Carolina had named the town Calhoun, after the South Carolina senator, and it was so called until named after Spring Creek.

Along with some of the early settlers had come their slaves. The Kirkpatricks brought their colored boy, Titus, Colonel Thomas Cox his two girls, Nance and Dice, Daniel Cutwright his boy, Major, George Forquer, his boy, Smith. And Colonel Cox, who had come twenty-three years before, as Register of the Land Office, appointed by President Monroe, had bought out the Kelleys, put up a mill and distillery, and a hewn-log house with a hall and a brick chimney. Then debt and drink broke him, the law turned him out of house and home and he and his wife and two children took shelter in a deserted log cabin a mile and a half from town. First they had sold Nance and Dice, and the circuit-court clerk entered on the records that, on July 12, 1827, John Taylor bought at public auction the person, Nance, for $151.00, and the person, Dice, for $150.00, and the court commission was $15.40.

It was a later time that Erastus Wright came from Fort Clark to live in Springfield, where he traded eighty acres of land for a tame elk that he rode and drove to harness like a horse.

There were remembered stanzas, sung to an old Irish tune:

> She's bounded by the Wabash,
> The Ohio and the Lakes,
> She's crawfish in the swampy lands,
> The Milk-sick and the Shakes;
> But these are slight diversions,
> And take not from the joy,
> Of living in this garden land,
> The state of E-la-noy.
>
> Then move your family westward,
> Bring all your girls and boys,
> And cross at Shawnee Ferry,
> To the state of E-la-nois.

Chapter 63

THE thirty-seven-year-old son of Thomas Lincoln and Nancy Hanks Lincoln had changed with a changing western world. His feet had worn deerskin moccasins as a boy; they were put into rawhide boots when he was full-grown; now he had them in dressed calf leather. His head-cover was a coonskin cap when he was a boy, and all men and boys wore the raccoon tail as a high headpiece; floating down the Mississippi to New Orleans he wore a black felt hat from an eastern factory and it held the post-office mail of New Salem; now he was a prominent politician and lawyer wearing a tall, stiff, silk hat known as a "stovepipe," also called a "plug hat."

In this "stovepipe" hat he carried letters, newspaper clippings, deeds, mortgages, checks, receipts. Once he apologized to a client for not replying to a letter; he had bought a new hat and in cleaning out the old hat he missed this particular letter. The silk stovepipe hat was nearly a foot high, with a brim only an inch or so in width; it was a high, lean, longish hat and it made Lincoln look higher, leaner, more longish.

As he had gone along farther in law practice and politics, he had taken more care of his looks. His first partner, John T. Stuart, was one of the handsomest figures and best-dressed men in Springfield; and Lincoln had to take Stuart's place once in a courthouse near Springfield, handling a case for a client; when Lincoln introduced himself as the man sent by Stuart to take Stuart's place, the client, an Englishman accustomed to wigs and gowns in a courtroom, refused to take Lincoln as his lawyer, snorted with disgust, and hired another lawyer.

And though Lincoln had begun wearing broadcloth and white shirts with a white collar and black silk cravat, and a suggestion of sideburns coming down three-fourths the length of his ears, he was still known as one of the carelessly dressed men of Springfield, along with Stephen Logan, who wore unbleached cotton shirts and had sat two years as a circuit-court judge wearing an unbleached cotton shirt with no cravat or stock.

The loose bones of Lincoln were hard to fit with neat clothes; and, once on, they were hard to keep neat; trousers go baggy at the knees of a story-teller who has the habit, at the end of a story, where the main laugh comes in, of putting his arms around his knees, raising his knees to his chin, and rocking to and fro. Those who spoke of his looks often mentioned his trousers creeping to the ankles and higher; his rumpled hair, his wrinkled vest. When he wasn't away making speeches, electioneering or practicing law on the circuit, he cut kindling wood, tended to the cordwood for the stoves in the house, milked the cow, gave her a few forks of hay and changed her straw bedding every day.

He analyzed the tariff, the national banks, the public lands, and the annexation of Texas, while pailing a cow. One evening he went to where his cow was pastured with other cows, and as he told it: "I found the calves all together and away from the cows, and I didn't know my calf well enough to distinguish her from the others. Still, I picked out one that I thought was mine. Presently that identical calf went and sucked my cow, and then I knew it was mine."

He looked like a farmer, it was often said; he seemed to have come from prairies and barns rather than city streets and barber shops; and in his own way he admitted and acknowledged it; he told voters from the stump that it was only a few years since he had worn buckskin breeches and they shrank in the rain and crept to his knees leaving the skin blue and bare. The very words that came off his lips in tangled important discussions among lawyers had a wilderness air and a log-cabin smack. The way he pronounced the word "idea" was more like "idee," the word "really" more like a drawled Kentucky "ra-a-ly."

As he strode or shambled into a gathering of men, he stood out as a special figure for men to look at; it was a little as though he had come farther on harder roads and therefore had longer legs for the traveling; and a little as though he had been where life is stripped to its naked facts and it would be useless for him to try to put on certain pretenses of civilization. He may have figured out for himself about how far he could go and find it easy and healthy and comfortable for him to be in speech and looks the Indiana cornhusker and the Mississippi River flatboat-man. The manners of a gentleman and a scholar dropped off him sometimes like a cloak, and his speech was that of a farmer who works his own farm, or a lawyer who pails a cow morning and evening and might refer to it incidentally in polite company or in a public address. He was not embarrassed, and nobody else was embarrassed, when at the Bowling Green funeral he had stood up and, instead of delivering a formal funeral address on the character of the deceased, had shaken with grief and put a handkerchief to his face and wept tears, and motioned to the body-bearers to take his dead friend away. There was a natural grace to it; funerals should be so conducted; a man who loves a dead man should stand up and try to speak and find himself overwhelmed with grief so that instead of speaking he smothers his face in a handkerchief and weeps. This was the eloquence of naked fact beyond which there is no eloquence.

At the death of a great friend he could weep without shame, lone and inevitable; at a petty campaign lie alluding to his aristocratic relatives visiting him, he could laugh and say that only one had made a visit and he was arrested for stealing a jew's-harp. He could be immensely solemn, tenderly grave, quiz-zically humorous, and flatly comic. As he strode or shambled into a gathering of men, he stood out as a special figure to look at; some of the range of his feeling, the gamut of the solemn and comic, was registered in the angles of his body, in the sweeping lengths of extra long arms and legs, in the panther slouch of running and throwing muscles, in the wiry, rawbone frame that seemed to have been at home once handling an ax in tall timber, with the silent silhouette of an eagle watching.

Standing, Lincoln loomed tall with his six feet, four inches of height; sitting in a chair he looked no taller than other men, except that his knees rose higher than the level of the seat of the chair. Seated on a low chair or bench he seemed to be

The forty-year-old congressman, A. Lincoln. He writes Joshua Speed, "Being elected to Congress . . . has not pleased me as much as I expected."

The Bronze Lincoln.

crouching. The shoulders were stooped and rounded, the head bent forward and turned downward; shirt-collars were a loose fit; an Adam's apple stood out on a scrawny neck; his voice was a tenor that carried song-tunes poorly but had clear and appealing modulations in his speeches; in rare moments of excitement it rose to a startling and unforgettable falsetto tone that carried every syllable with unmistakable meaning. In the stoop of his shoulders and the forward bend of his head there was a grace and familiarity so that it was easy for shorter people to look up into his face and talk with him.

The mouth and eyes, and the facial muscles running back from the mouth and eyes, masked a thousand shades of meaning. In hours of melancholy, when poisons of dejection dragged him, the underlip and its muscles drooped; his friends felt either that he then was a sick man with a disorder of bile and secretions or else that his thoughts roamed in farther and darker caverns than ordinary men ventured into. Ordinarily there was a fresh, gracious calm; it was a grave, sad calm, perhaps gloomy, but strong with foundations resting on substrata of granite; a mouth shaped with depths of hope that its fixed resolves would be kept and held. And between this solemn mouth of Lincoln and at the other end of the gamut, his comic mouth, there was the play of a thousand shades of meaning. Besides being tragedian, he was comedian. Across the mask of his dark gravity could come a light-ray of the quizzical, the puzzled. This could spread into the beginning of a smile and then spread farther into wrinkles and wreaths of laughter that lit the whole face into a glow; and it was of the quality of his highest laughter that it traveled through his whole frame, currents of it vitalizing his toes.

A fine chiseling of lines on the upper lip seemed to be some continuation of the bridge of the nose, forming a feature that ended in a dimple at the point of the chin. The nose was large; if it had been a trifle larger he would have been called big-nosed; it was a nose for breathing deep sustained breaths of air, a strong shapely nose, granitic with resolve and patience. Two deepening wrinkles started from the sides of the right and left nostrils and ran down the outer rims of the upper lip; farther out on the two cheeks were deepening wrinkles that had been long crude dimples when he was a boy; hours of toil, pain, and laughter were deepening these wrinkles. From the sides of the nose, angular cheek-bones branched right and left toward the large ears, forming a base for magnificently constructed eye-sockets. Bushy black eyebrows shaded the sockets where the eyeballs rested with gray transformers of action, thought, laughter. Shaded into the gray of his eyes was a tinting of hazel. In his eyes as nowhere else was registered the shifting light of his moods; their language ran from rapid twinkles of darting hazel that won the hearts of children on to a fixed baffling gray that the shrewdest lawyers and politicians could not read, to find there an intention he wanted to hide.

The thatch of coarse hair on the head was black when seen from a distance, but close up it had a brownish, rough, sandy tint. He had been known to comb it, parting it far on the right side, and slicking it down so that it looked groomed by a somewhat particular man; but most of the time it was loose and rumpled. The comb might have parted it either on the far right or on the far left side; he wasn't particular.

Throughout his life as a grown man he was holding to the hacked-out slants of body that his father had in mind in the younger days when his frame stretched upward in a rapid, uneven growth, and his father said he looked like he needed a carpenter's plane put to him. In those days they had called him "Long Shanks"; and as a grown man his long shanks were a dominant feature of his physical presence. Yet it was true that men and women as varied as Stephen T. Logan and Hannah Armstrong felt about him something elusive, glancing, elfin, off and beyond all that was told by the gaunt, rambling lines of his physical structure. The eyes, the laughter, the play of words, a scrutinizing, drawling poise, curves that came and went with the tricks of sun-showers and rainbows—he gave out echoes and values. A cherishing of true testimonies ran out from his face and form. All he could do for Bowling Green was to weep; the words had not been made that could tell what he wanted to say in that hour. As the day came near for his marriage to the brilliant, fashionable daughter of a Kentucky bank president, he held odds even by writing an old friend—also of hacked-out and slanted structure—the plain, old, dependable, silent, truth-telling John Hanks who could not write his own name: "I hope you will come over; be sure to be on deck by early candlelight." The lizard story might be a rehearsal of a comic pantomime with two players having a line each to speak; and still further it might be a portentous allegory in democratic and religious behavior and words.

When he had bought his house at Eighth and Jackson streets from Rev. Charles Dresser there was a mortgage of $900 on it. And in the deed of title from Dresser to Lincoln this $900 mortgage wasn't mentioned. He trusted Dresser, took a chance on losing $900, just the personal assurance of the preacher who had married him. And the money was later paid in full.

It was natural that Abraham Lincoln was many things to many people; some believed him a cunning, designing lawyer and politician who coldly figured all his moves in advance; some believed him a sad, odd, awkward man trying to find a niche in life where his hacked-out frame could have peace and comfort; some believed him a superb human struggler with solemn and comic echoes and values far off and beyond the leashes and bones that held him to earth and law and politics.

In his own mind he did not divide people into good people and bad people. As he walked from his own home close to the cornfields near the city limits of Springfield and met people on his way to the courthouse and the post office, and as he watched the two-legged figures on their many errands or, forgetting their errands, moving around the public square, he saw good mixed in the bad and bad mixed in the good.

In his own mind he made the note: "The true rule in determining to embrace or reject anything, is not whether it have any evil in it, but whether it have more of evil than of good. There are few things wholly evil or wholly good. Almost everything is an inseparable compound of the two; so that our best judgment of the preponderance between them is continually demanded."

Chapter 64

THERE are certain old poems, old stories, old books, clocks, and jackknives, old rose and lavender keepsakes with musk and dusk in them, with a sunset smoke loitering in the faded shine of their walnut and mahogany stain and embellishment.

And we learn them by heart; we memorize their lines and outlines, and put them away in the chests and the attics of our memories, keeping them as keepsakes, taking them out and handling them, reciting their feel and rhythm, scanning their lines, and then putting them back till the next time they will be wanted, for they will always be wanted again.

Abraham Lincoln had such an old keepsake, a rhymed poem with stanzas having for him the sweet pathos of a slow, quaint tune hummed by a young woman to the auburn western sky of a late winter twilight. It spun out and carried further the hymn line, "Vain man, thy fond pursuits forbear."

It came from an old country across the sea and was written like an air from an old-fashioned spinet with its rosewood touched with a yellow tarnish. It was put together like some old melodrama that measures out life so that we want to cry as we look at it.

In the year he ran for Congress Lincoln sent William Johnston a copy of the poem, and later wrote him, "You ask me who is the author of the piece I sent you, and you do so ask me as to indicate a slight suspicion that I myself am the author. Beyond all question, I am not the author. I would give all I am worth, and go in debt, to be able to write so fine a piece as I think that is. Neither do I know who is the author." The poem read:

> Oh, why should the spirit of mortal be proud?
> Like a swift-fleeting meteor, a fast-flying cloud,
> A flash of the lightning, a break of the wave,
> He passes from life to his rest in the grave.

The leaves of the oak and the willow shall fade,
Be scattered around, and together be laid;
And the young and the old, the low and the high,
Shall molder to dust, and together shall lie.

The infant a mother attended and loved;
The mother that infant's affection who proved;
The husband, that mother and infant who blessed:
Each, all. are away to their dwelling of rest.

The maid on whose cheek, on whose brow, in whose eye,
Shone beauty and pleasure—her triumphs are by;
And the memory of those who loved her and praised,
Are alike from the minds of the living erased.

The hand of the king that the sceptre hath borne,
The brow of the priest that the mitre hath worn,
The eye of the sage, and the heart of the brave,
Are hidden and lost in the depths of the grave.

The peasant, whose lot was to sow and to reap,
The herdsman, who climbed with his goats up the steep,
The beggar, who wandered in search of his bread,
Have faded away like the grass that we tread.

The saint, who enjoyed the communion of Heaven,
The sinner, who dared to remain unforgiven,
The wise and the foolish, the guilty and just,
Have quietly mingled their bones in the dust.

So the multitude goes—like the flower or the weed
That withers away to let others succeed;
So the multitude comes—even those we behold,
To repeat every tale that has often been told.

For we are the same that our fathers have been;
We see the same sights that our fathers have seen;
We drink the same stream, we feel the same sun,
And run the same course that our fathers have run.

The thoughts we are thinking, our fathers would think;
From the death we are shrinking, our fathers would shrink;
To the life we are clinging, they also would cling—
But it speeds from us all like a bird on the wing.

They loved—but the story we cannot unfold;
They scorned—but the heart of the haughty is cold;
They grieved—but no wail from their slumber will come;
They joyed—but the tongue of their gladness is dumb.

They died—aye, they died—we things that are now,
That walk on the turf that lies over their brow,
And make in their dwellings a transient abode,
Meet the things that they met on their pilgrimage road.

Yea, hope and despondency, pleasure and pain,
Are mingled together in sunshine and rain;
And the smile and the tear, the song and the dirge,
Still follow each other, like surge upon surge.

'Tis the wink of an eye—'tis the draught of a breath—
From the blossom of health to the paleness of death,
From the gilded saloon to the bier and the shroud
Oh, why should the spirit of mortal be proud?

Such was one of the keepsakes of his heart. For him it spun out and carried further the hymn line, "Vain man, thy fond pursuits forbear." It was written by a young Scotchman, William Knox, who died when he was thirty-six years old in Edinburgh in 1836. And a young Scotchman, Jason Duncan, had first shown it to Lincoln in New Salem days.

In the letter to Johnston, explaining that beyond all question he was not the author of the poem, he also wrote: "In the fall of 1844, thinking I might aid some to carry the State of Indiana for Mr. Clay, I went into the neighborhood in that State in which I was raised, where my mother and only sister were buried, and from which I had been absent about fifteen years. That part of the country is, within itself, as unpoetical as any spot of the earth; but still, seeing it and its objects and inhabitants aroused feelings in me which were certainly poetry; though whether my expression of those feelings is poetry is quite another question. When I got to writing, the change of subject divided the thing into four little divisions or cantos, the first only of which I send you now, and may send the others hereafter." The enclosure read:

My childhood's home I see again,
  And sadden with the view;
And still, as memory crowds my brain,
  There's pleasure in it too.

O Memory! thou midway world
  'Twixt earth and paradise,
Where things decayed and loved ones lost
  In dreamy shadows rise,

And, freed from all that's earthly vile,
  Seen hallowed, pure, and bright,
Like scenes in some enchanted isle
  All bathed in liquid light.

As dusky mountains please the eye
  When twilight chases day;
As bugle-notes, that, passing by,
  In distance die away;

As leaving some grand waterfall,
  We, lingering, list its roar—
So memory will hallow all
  We've known, but know no more.

Near twenty years have passed away
  Since here I bid farewell
To woods and fields, and scenes of play,
  And playmates loved so well.

Where many were, but few remain
  Of old familiar things;
But seeing them, to mind again
  The lost and absent brings.

The friends I left that parting day,
  How changed, as time has sped!
Young childhood grown, strong manhood gray,
  And half of all are dead.

I hear the loved survivors tell,
  How naught from death could save,
Till every sound appears a knell,
  And every spot a grave.

I range the fields with pensive tread,
    And pace the hollow rooms,
And feel (companion of the dead)
    I'm living in the tombs.

Five months later he again wrote Johnston, the letter reading:

FRIEND JOHNSTON: You remember when I wrote you from Tremont last spring, sending you a little canto of what I called poetry, I promised to bore you with another sometime. I now fulfill the promise. The subject of the present one is an insane man; his name is Matthew Gentry. He is three years older than I, and when we were boys we went to school together. He was rather a bright lad, and the son of the rich man of a very poor neighborhood. At the age of nineteen he unaccountably became furiously mad, from which condition he gradually settled down into harmless insanity. When, as I told you in my other letter, I visited my old home in the fall of 1844, I found him still lingering in this wretched condition. In my poetizing mood, I could not forget the impression his case made upon me. Here is the result:

But here's an object more of dread
    Than aught the grave contains—
A human form with reason fled,
    While wretched life remains.

When terror spread, and neighbors ran
    Your dangerous strength to bind,
And soon, a howling, crazy man,
    Your limbs were fast confined:

How then you strove and shrieked aloud,
    Your bones and sinews bared;
And fiendish on the gazing crowd
    With burning eyeballs glared;

And begged and swore, and wept and prayed,
    With maniac laughter joined!
How fearful were these signs displayed
    By pangs that killed the mind!

And when at length the drear and long
   Time soothe thy fiercer woes,
How plaintively thy mournful song
   Upon the still night rose!

I've heard it oft as if I dreamed,
   Far distant, sweet and lone,
The funeral dirge it ever seemed
   Of reason dead and gone.

To drink its strains I've stole away,
   All stealthily and still,
Ere yet the rising god of day
   Had streaked the eastern hill.

Air held her breath; trees with the spell
   Seemed sorrowing angels round,
Whose swelling tears in dewdrops fell
   Upon the listening ground.

But this is past, and naught remains
   That raised thee o'er the brute;
Thy piercing shrieks and soothing strain
   Are like, forever mute.

Now fare thee well! More thou the cause
   Than subject now of woe.
All mental pangs by time's kind laws
   Hast lost the power to know.

O death! thou awe-inspiring prince
   That keepst the world in fear,
Why dost thou tear more blest ones hence,
   And leave him lingering here?

If I should ever send another, the subject will be a "Bear Hunt."
                   Yours as ever,
                     A. LINCOLN.

Yet a short time later he did send Johnston twenty-two verses of a piece he called "The Bear Hunt," mixing the backwoodsman's slang with picked pet words from stylish English poets.

Three verses get the bear running, nine verses have the bear chased, four have him fighting and dying, then six verses draw a moral and lesson. The piece read:

A wild bear chase didst never see?
　　Then hast thou lived in vain—
Thy richest bump of glorious glee
　　Lies desert in thy brain.

When first my father settled here,
　　'Twas then the frontier line;
The panther's scream filled night with fear
　　And bears preyed on the swine.

But woe for bruin's short-lived fun
　　When rose the squealing cry;
Now man and horse, with dog and gun
　　For vengeance at him fly.

A sound of danger strikes his ear;
　　He gives the breeze a snuff;
Away he bounds, with little fear,
　　And seeks the tangled *rough*.

On press his foes, and reach the ground
　　Where's left his half-munched meal;
The dogs, in circles, scent around
　　And find his fresh made trail.

With instant cry, away they dash,
　　And men as fast pursue;
O'er logs they leap, through water splash
　　And shout the brisk halloo.

Now to elude the eager pack
　　Bear shuns the open ground,
Through matted vines he shapes his track,
　　And runs it, round and round.

The tall, fleet cur, with deep-mouthed voice
　　Now speeds him, as the wind;
While half-grown pup, and short-legged fice
　　Are yelping far behind.

And fresh recruits are dropping in
  To join the merry corps;
With yelp and yell, a mingled din—
  The woods are in a roar—

And round, and round the chase now goes,
  The world's alive with fun;
Nick Carter's horse his rider throws,
  And Mose Hills drops his gun.

Now, sorely pressed, bear glances back,
  And lolls his tired tongue,
When as, to force him from his track
  An ambush on him sprung.

Across the glade he sweeps for flight,
  And fully is in view—
The dogs, new fired by the sight
  Their cry and speed renew.

The foremost ones now reach his rear;
  He turns, they dash away,
And circling now the wrathful bear
  They have him full at bay.

At top of speed the horsemen come,
  All screaming in a row—
'Whoop!' 'Take him, Tiger!' 'Seize him, Drum!'
  Bang—bang! the rifles go!

And furious now, the dogs he tears,
  And crushes in his ire—
Wheels right and left, and upward rears,
  With eyes of burning fire.

But leaden death is at his heart—
  Vain all the strength he plies,
And, spouting blood from every part,
  He reels, and sinks, and dies!

And now a dinsome clamor rose,—
  'But who should have his skin?'
Who first draws blood, each hunter knows
  This prize must always win.

But, who did this, and how to trace
　　What's true from what's a lie,—
Like lawyers in a murder case
　　They stoutly *argufy*.

Aforesaid fice, of blustering mood,
　　Behind, and quite forgot,
Just now emerging from the wood
　　Arrives upon the spot,

With grinning teeth, and up-turned hair
　　Brim full of spunk and wrath,
He growls, and seizes on dead bear
　　And shakes for life and death—

And swells, as if his skin would tear,
　　And growls, and shakes again,
And swears, as plain as dog can swear
　　That he has won the skin!

Conceited whelp! we laugh at thee,
　　Nor mind that not a few
Of pompous, two-legged dogs there be
　　Conceited quite as you.

And from then on there seemed to be no more exercises of
this kind. Lincoln quit his doggerel habit, writing to Johnston:
"I am not at all displeased with your proposal to publish the
poetry, or doggerel, or whatever else it may be called, which I
sent you. I consent that it may be done. Whether the prefatory
remarks in my letter shall be published with the verses, I leave
entirely to your discretion; but let names be suppressed by all
means. I have not sufficient hope of the verses attracting any
favorable notice to tempt me to risk being ridiculed for having
written them."

The mood of melancholy running through his verses could
drop off him like a cloak, while he lighted with a quizzical look
on his face. When his children were born, he chuckled. Even
before the first one was born, in the months when the stork was
promising to come, he joked Speed about the glad event coming.

A wild-bear chase, didst never see?
    Then hast thou lived in vain—
Thy richest bump of glorious glee,
    Lies desert in thy brain—

And furious now, the dogs he tears,
    And crushes in his ire—
Wheels right and left, and upward rears,
    With eyes of flaming fire—

But leaden death is at his heart,
    Vain all the strength he plies.
And, spouting blood from every part,
    He reels, and sinks, and dies—

And now a dinsome clamor rose,
    'Bout who should have his skin,
Who first draws blood, each hunter knows,
    This prize must always win—

But who did this, and how to trace
    What's true from what's a lie.
Like lawyers, in a murder case
    They stoutly argufy—

Lincoln writes doggerel, "The Bear Hunt."

From the original manuscript.

Speed first heard of the coming event from Bill Butler and so wrote Lincoln, who replied: "In relation to the 'coming events' about which Butler wrote you, I had not heard one word before I got your letter; but I have so much confidence in the judgment of a Butler on such a subject that I incline to think there may be some reality in it. What day does Butler appoint?"

And he countered: "By the way, how do 'events' of the same sort come on in your family? Are you possessing houses and lands, and oxen and asses, and menservants and maidservants, and begetting sons and daughters?" And he closed with, "Mary joins in sending love to your Fanny and you."

When the second boy came, he sketched the two of them and the family life for Speed. "We have another boy. He is very much such a child as Bob was at his age, rather of a longer order. Bob is 'short and low,' and I expect always will be. He talks very plainly,—almost as plainly as anybody. He is quite smart enough. I sometimes fear that he is one of the little rare-ripe sort that are smarter at about five years than ever after. He has a great deal of that sort of mischief that is the offspring of such animal spirits. Since I began this letter, a messenger came to tell me Bob was lost; but by the time I reached the house his mother had found him, and had whipped him, and by now, very likely, he is run away again. Mary has read your letter, and wishes to be remembered to Mrs. Speed and you, in which I most sincerely join her."

Chapter 65

LINCOLN and his law-partner, Stephen T. Logan, both had hopes of going to Congress; they didn't get along smoothly. Lincoln had left the partnership with regrets, for Logan was one of the foremost lawyers of the state and well started on a paying business. Logan had come to Illinois from Kentucky, a short sliver of a man, with a wrinkled, pinched face and tight lips. His head carried a thicket of frowsy hair, his voice rasped—yet he com-

manded attention when he spoke. He had been a circuit judge
two years. That he should have picked Lincoln for a junior
partner testified that Lincoln had unusual ability or character
of some sort. And that Lincoln should tell Usher F. Linder
that he had an ambition to become as good a lawyer as Stephen
T. Logan testified that Logan was far out of the ordinary as
lawyers go.

During the two years they met so often and worked together
in the same law office on the same cases, Lincoln had chances
to dig through and get at that magic or whatever it was that
made some people believe Logan could take apart and put
together again that colossal box of devices called government.
Logan knew how to be a lawyer so that people had fear and
respect for lawyers; Lincoln had his chance to watch Logan
every day, close up, to see how Logan did it. He was sorry to
break with Logan. But one day something happened between
him and Logan, so that he went to young William H. Herndon,
who had read the law books in the office of Logan & Lincoln on
the invitation of Lincoln, and had been admitted to the bar.

He asked Herndon to be his partner; Herndon didn't believe
his ears; he said, "Mr. Lincoln, don't laugh at me." "Billy, I
can trust you if you can trust me." They shook hands, opened
an office, and hung out the shingle "Lincoln & Herndon." Lincoln was nine years the older; for ten years he had been seeing
Herndon, off and on, watching the boy grow up to a young man.
He knew that when a mob killed Lovejoy at Alton, the president
of Illinois College at Jacksonville was with Lovejoy, and the
college, faculty and students were blazing with Abolitionist ideas.
Archer Herndon, the father of William, heard about it and said
he wasn't going to have his boy grow up "a damned Abolitionist
pup," and ordered him home to Springfield where he had clerked
in Josh Speed's store; he and Speed and Lincoln slept in the
same big room over the store and some nights talked each other
to sleep.

Once Lincoln had asked Herndon as to slavery, "What tells
you the thing must be rooted out?" The answer, "I feel it in

my *bones.*" And Lincoln sometimes mentioned issues, public questions, that had stood the test of "Bill Herndon's bone philosophy." They had an upstairs back-room office. There came the Abolitionist newspapers week by week stirring up Herndon, with the news of what the American Anti-slavery Society was doing, and the latest actions of the Liberty party. Though slight as a political organization, it had savagely swept Henry Clay out of the political reckoning in 1844, when Polk defeated Clay with the narrow popular majority of 38,801 and the Liberty party candidate got 62,270 votes which could have made Clay President.

For young Herndon there was far, passionate magic in words such as liberty, equality, brotherhood, justice, humanity. For him there was reality, driving and terrific, back of the phrase, "the cause of humanity." Sometimes the whole world of human struggle divided itself for him into two causes, the "high and noble cause," and the "low and degraded cause." Enthusiasms lighted torches in him and flung banners; a human cause must have bonfires of elation and faith. His father, Archer Herndon, was born in Virginia from Herndons who were in the Old Dominion as early as 1654, grew up in Kentucky, married, and moved to Illinois, arriving in 1821 in Sangamon County driving a one-mule cart, with the mother holding the two-year-old baby Billy. They stayed four years on a prairie farm five miles from Springfield and then moved to Springfield.

Herndon pictured the moving: "The whole way was clear bog; father made a small board cart, into which he threw the chickens, the little pigs, and the young children. He and I and mother walked beside the cart, which had two wheels. We skipped from hill to hill; and when the wheels of the cart stuck or floundered, we lifted them out of the mud and balanced them somehow on one of the hummocks. We reached Springfield at last. We had to build our log cabin on the edge of a ridge, while we labored to subdue the muck. The marks of bears' claws were deep in the trees right round us. Ten years later I killed a hundred snakes in three-quarters of a mile, so you may guess what it was then. There they all were: rattlesnakes, vipers, adders, and copperheads." "And what sort of a snake is the copper-head?" was asked. His answer was: "A mean thing. A rattle-snake rattles, a viper hisses, an adder spits, a black snake whistles, a water snake blows, but a copperhead just sneaks."

And he could go on with memories. "At nightfall we laid green logs in parallel rows, set them on fire, and drove the cattle between them. Then whichever way the wind blew, we could keep off the gallinippers, mosquitoes with stings three-quarters of an inch long. The dumb beasts knew what it meant and we never had to drive them again. They went in of themselves. Words cannot tell this life. The prairies of Illinois are watered with the tears, and enriched by the graves, of her women. The first generation lived on mush and pork. Fencing was too costly. No gardens could stand the herds of cattle, a thousand strong, which might come swooping over any minute. Just as our corn was ripe, the bears would strip the ears; just as the pumpkins grew golden, herds of deer would hollow out the gourds. As we got more land there was no transportation to carry away the crops."

A woman listening to Herndon remarked: "Standing in a log cabin in the edge of the prairie the other day, and looking over the half-drained surface, I said, almost unconsciously, 'I am sure this land was settled before the Lord was willing.' "

"To understand the pioneers," said Herndon, "you must know, first, how civilization had wronged them as poor whites; next, how nature gradually restored what civilization took. To do the work an enormous vitality was required. Such a vitality could not exhaust itself on the soil. No social excitement, no lecture, theater, book, or friendly talk offered itself to the tired laborer when he came home at night. To drink, to indulge in his passions, was the only change life offered him. For the women—God forgive the men who brought them here—if they sought stimulants or anodynes, how could they be to blame? Wild, hardy, genial, these men were a mixture of the rowdy and the roisterer. It was impossible to outwit or outwhip them."

Herndon was intense, sensitive, varied as his father and grand-father. His grandfather in Virginia had given slaves their free-dom; his father in Illinois had stood fast with those who fought to make Illinois a slave state; a brother of his grandfather had married the youngest sister of Patrick Henry; his father had kept a store, had fought politically with those who tried to call a convention to change Illinois from a free to a slave state, and had put up the first regular tavern in Springfield. The son grew up in a tavern, had a tavern eye for judging people, and took pride in the way he could size up men by looking in their eyes. He was of medium height, rather rawboned, with particularly high cheek-bones, dark eyes set far back in the sockets, and the careless shock of hair on his head was a peculiar black, a sort of blue-black. He had picked up tavern learning, the names of drinks men called for, the talk of men who talk about cards, horse races, chicken fights, women. Yet he was full of torches, banners, bonfires, lighted for what he called the cause of free-dom, justice, humanity.

As he and his senior law partner looked from the office window to the state capitol with its massive enigmatic walls, they had a good deal to talk about when there was time. And in their talk, one was always "Mr. Lincoln" and the other plain "Billy."

Chapter 66

ONCE in late summer, after showers had soaked the earth and sent the corn higher, Lincoln passed a cornfield a block from his home, meeting young Alexander Black, who noticed Lincoln had his head bowed forward, his chin at his breast, wrapped in thought. "He will pass by me without speaking," said young Alexander to himself. But as they met Lincoln's face lighted, he nodded his head, beckoned with a hand toward the field, and said, "This rain makes the corn laugh."

Toward the courthouse and the public square there were city lots where corn was growing; off toward the country were cornfields. The panorama of the ways of growing corn was before their eyes from the front yard and the back yard of the Eighth Street home.

Always, as the seasons passed from year to year, that panorama of corn was one of the immense facts. In the spring they saw the sweet, black loam turned over and laid in furrows, with a shine and a gleam on the strips of stiff dirt curved with a steel plow curve as they lay waiting for the seed kernels. And the teeth of the harrow tore the stiff dirt loose and the frame of the harrow leveled it, and the yellow kernels of maize were dropped in and covered over. The regular, never-failing Illinois rain came; the black loam soaked in the rain; the kernels of corn sent out white strands of feelers, spreading webs of roots taking their nourishment, their requisites, from the loam. In June the young corn-leaves came up to look at the sun and tell the sun, "Here we are."

Then slow work of the sun, the air, and the loam lifted the leaves higher; the stalks thickened; and as the weeks passed it came time for the little ears of corn to push out their cobs, with little soft white kernels in rows, all laid in close-wrapped husks, with silk threads running soft and green forming pads parallel to the rows of kernels on the cobs. As the weeks passed, the silk of this corn ran out of the opening where the ends of the husk wrappers met; and the sun tanned the cornsilk with darkening copper and maroon. The weeks came when the green corn was full-grown; the stand of the corn would hide a tall man if it was a good corn year. At the top of the stalks, highest of all, were tassels, plumes, announcements. Being full-grown, the corn changed under the sunshine of early autumn; the green leaves, tassels, blades, husks, all turning to tan and brown and gray, while the full-grown kernels on the cobs stiffened and hardened till each was rooted in its niche and corner. The ripened ears, the corn crop of the season, were ready for the shucking.

Then men came and tore off the ears, stripped the husks, and threw the red, white, and gold ears into wagons. It was harvest time. The stalks were cut close to the roots, piled, tied shaped into patient, mysterious dummies that waited by dawn and noon till they were hauled away. The stumps of the stalks stood bare, marking the rows where the corn crop had grown.

The corn kernels had been shelled off cobs and saved as meal for men, and fodder for cattle, hogs, horses, chickens; they were the year's guarantee against hunger; they stood off famine and gave man a permit to live another year. Harvest time had come and gone. Afterward came the months when snow blew across the fields, and covered the stumps, and the fields were white and lonely.

Chapter 67

Two farmers, Samuel Wycoff and Dennis Forrest, came to see Lincoln one day. Each owned a quarter-section of land in Township Fourteen North of Range Six, West, in Sangamon County. They had a dispute concerning a small strip of land, each claiming it. And they agreed in writing to submit their dispute "to the arbitrament of Abraham Lincoln, who is to hear the evidence and thereupon decide which is the owner of the disputed land, and what line is hereafter to be the dividing line." Furthermore, "We hereby mutually bind ourselves in the penal sum of five hundred dollars, as liquidated damages, to abide by the decision he shall make, and each to give and allow the other peaceable possession and enjoyment of his own side of the line so to be designated."

Two weeks later Lincoln handed the two farmers, who had come to him instead of a court, his decision, reading: "In pursuance of agreement, having fully heard the evidence, I decide that the land in dispute between Wycoff and Forrest belongs to said Wycoff, and that the old United States Surveyor's line, beginning at the West end thereof, and running thence Easterly as marked through the timber by said U. S. Surveyor, so far as the timber extends, and continuing the same course as so marked, the proper distance to reach the East side of the lands of said Wycoff and Forrest above described, shall hereafter be the dividing line between the said lands of the parties."

Once a jury picked by the Menard County sheriff got filled up with men of whom Lincoln said: "I would like to throw the whole panel out, for I know every single one of them; but I can't object to a man among them." It was a murder case, with Lincoln called in as a prosecutor. Two brothers named Denton had got into a dispute with a brother-in-law named Brown. They fought with axes; Brown was killed; the Dentons were the only witnesses.

During the trial, which lasted a week, Lincoln felt sure the jury wouldn't convict; he left the questioning of witnesses and the final plea to the jury with another prosecutor. And, as it happened, the jury freed the Dentons. Lincoln had sensed from the first that it would be uphill work to convict with that particular jury—and Lincoln never made much of a record when called in as a prosecutor.

Fine points in justice came before him. He pressed a claim of John Warner against John Calhoun, who had been his chief when he was a surveyor; he questioned Calhoun as to transfers and assignments of property. Then there was the case of Nancy Green, who had loaned $200.00 and got a note for it, but couldn't collect. She put it in Lincoln's hands. He had to collect it from Mentor Graham, the New Salem schoolmaster who had helped Lincoln learn the science of surveying and had loaned Lincoln books. Lincoln sued Graham, won the suit, but didn't force immediate payment. What he asked was that the schoolmaster should do his best to pay the woman. This was the second suit Lincoln won for Nancy Green, the first being a dissolution of her marriage-bond with Aaron Green.

He took a case to the supreme court, and wrote Marshall, his Shawneetown friend: "At the request of Mr. Eddy, I got the judgment reversed. This was no business of yours, and I now only ask, as a favor of you, that if Mr. Eddy is well, you say to him I would like to have the little fee in the case, if convenient."

In the divorce case of Samuel Rogers *vs.* Polly Rogers, Lincoln represented the husband and advised that no charge of adultery be made. In the development of the case he filed an affidavit: "A. Lincoln being first duly sworn says that he was employed as counsel in the case of Samuel Rogers *vs.* Polly Rogers for a Divorce; that he, the affiant, drew up the complainant's bill; that said complainant at that time told this affiant that he could prove that the said defendant had been guilty of adultery with one William Short while she was living with said complainant; but that affiant advised said complainant not to make the charge in his bill as there was other sufficient grounds upon which to obtain a divorce, to-wit, absence of more than two years." In effect, Lincoln was ready to help his client get a divorce, but was not willing to make an unnecessary public record against the woman in the case.

In the same year Thomas McKibben came to Lincoln down in Coles County. Jonathan Hart had called McKibben a horse thief. Lincoln brought court action against Hart for slander, demanding $2,000.00 damages. The case was tried; McKibben was awarded $200.00; Lincoln was paid a fee of $35.00. And old Thomas Lincoln, the father of Abraham Lincoln, living in his log cabin out from Charleston, came in to town and was handed the $35.00, as required by Abraham Lincoln, who had left instructions with the clerk of the court thus to deliver the money to his father and get a receipt.

In Lincoln's Springfield office was an account book marked "Day Book of Lincoln & Herndon," in one place, and in another "Lincoln & Herndon's Fee Book." The fees in 180 cases for the year 1846 were entered, mostly by Lincoln; one fee was $2.50; two were $3.00; in 64 cases the charge was $5.00; in five, $7.00; in 63, $10.00; in five, $50.00; in one, $100.00; and in the remainder from $15.00 to $25.00. One entry read, "Scott *vs.* Busher (for Def't). To attending case in Menard Cir. Court if it ends where it is. Paid $20." Another case, tried before a justice of the peace, was recorded, "Negro *vs.* Robert Smith (for Deft.) To attending case of Negro Bob. J. P. $5.00."

His reputation was spreading as a man and lawyer of whom people said, "He'll be fair and square." He couldn't talk just to be talking. At a political meeting, where an orator was speechifying splendiferously with arms uplifted, and with a voice bawling and ranting neither fact nor argument, Lincoln turned to friends and said in an undertone, "Cut his galluses and let him go up!"

Lincoln couldn't talk against time if there was nothing to talk about. His quitting-time, for speaking, came earlier than for other lawyers. With nothing to say, he was dumb. In a criminal case he tried with Usher F. Linder, the two of them agreed that in the strategy of the case each should make the longest speech possible, and go on talking till he was used up. And, as Linder told it afterward, Lincoln's performance ran out of wind at the end of an hour, while he, Linder, rambled on in a three-hour speech to the jury.

A doctor at Matamora, Robert C. Lamson, said that he had learned from Lincoln, who had stayed overnight at his house several times, that it was a healthy habit to tell other people all he positively knew about one thing or a few things, and to say nothing at all about things he wasn't sure of. Of a patient doomed to pass away, Lamson used to remark, "He's got the can't-help-its," a phrase he said he had picked up from hearing Lincoln use it.

Homely phrasings of Lincoln often lingered and were repeated. The lawyer Bagby at Pekin told Lincoln of a lawsuit with a highly educated minister as the important witness. And the minister had an extra-fine sense of the distinctions and definitions of words. Bagby found the witness would not testify positively to things which Bagby knew that the witness knew. "I think so" and "I believe so" were the answers. Finally Bagby asked, "What do you mean by the expression 'I think'?" The witness answered at once, "That, sir, is the knowledge I have of my recollection of things of which I am not positively certain." He was then asked, "What do you mean by the expression, 'I believe'?" To which he just as smoothly answered, "That is the faith I have in the existence of objects of which I have a distinct recollection." Which made Lincoln chuckle, "He came out of the same hole he went in at."

Chapter 68

PASSIONS, deaths, reputations, the incessant and shifting forces of life, the stuff of the plays of Shakespeare and the books of Boccaccio and Rabelais, plain tales of life's surprises, put the stain of their designs on the parchments of Lincoln's law practice. Among his clients were descendants of Cain and Abel, of David and Bathsheba, of prodigal sons, of virgins who brought oil or came empty-handed.

Lincoln petitioned the supreme court for a rehearing in the case of Patterson *vs.* Edwards, which was a suit between two women in which one charged the other was the mother of a negro child. In a closely reasoned brief, the argument of Lincoln dwelt on allegations. "The words alleged are: 'Mrs. Edwards has raised a family of children by a negro, and I can prove it.' If we change the language from the second person, past tense, as detailed by the witnesses, to the first person, present tense, as spoken by Mrs. Patterson, the words proved by Mrs. Seymour to have been spoken by Mrs. Patterson are: 'I did tell Julius Scoville that Mrs. Edwards has had children by a negro, and all her children are negroes.'" He discussed whether in law it is sufficient to prove words equivalent to those identically charged. "While we understand words amounting to the *identical* charge alleged, as being, in the sense of the law, not *merely equivalent* words, but *the* words alleged, notwithstanding a slight literal or verbal variance—we insist that a variance to be material in the law must be a variance in *sense*. If we are right in this, we ask, 'Is there any difference *in sense* between saying a woman has *raised* children by a negro, and saying she *had* children by a negro?'"

In as simple a manner as though he were addressing a jury

of farmers, he presented certain points to the supreme court.
"On the question of arrest of judgment this court declared that
the words, 'Mrs. Edwards has raised a family of children by a
negro' do not, 'in their plain and popular sense, or in common
acceptation, *necessarily* amount to a charge of adultery.'
Wherein these words vary from, or fall short of such a charge,
the opinion does not state. Whether the court believe that these
words do not mean that Mrs. Edwards had raised a family of
children, of whom she was the *mother*, and a negro was the
father; or whether, admitting this, the court believe she may
have been the wife of the negro, and therefore, may have borne
children by him without adultery, the opinion shows nothing
from which we can judge. Until the decision of this court, we
had never supposed there could be a rational doubt that these
words would be construed by all who might hear them, as the
declaration construes them. We have thought, and still do
think, that if twelve plain men should enter this room and each,
out of the hearing of the others, should be told these words, not
one of them would fail to attach to them the very meaning that
the declaration attaches to them." Then, saying, "But we may
be mistaken," he branched out into old and new rules in courts,
and a train of judicial decisions bearing on the construction of
words of doubtful meaning.

In the July term, A.D. 1845, in the Sangamon circuit court,
Lincoln and Herndon represented Jonathan and Susan Miller,
who were defendants against charges of slander brought by
William and Martha Ann Beaty. In Lincoln's handwriting, the
plea opened: "And the said defendants come and defend the
wrong and injury, when, where, etc., and say the said Susan is
not guilty in manner and form as the said plaintiffs, in their said
declaration have alleged, and of this, they, the said defendants,
put themselves upon the county, etc. And for further plea in
this behalf the said defendants (now disclaiming all intention of
affirming the truth of the supposed slanderous words in the said
declaration mentioned) say plaintiffs *actio non*, because they say
that at time of the supposed speaking of the supposed slanderous

words in the said declaration mentioned, by the said Susan, she, the said Susan did speak the said words, in the connection following, and not otherwise, that is to say: 'I' (the said Susan, meaning) 'have understood that Mrs. Beaty' (the said Martha Ann meaning) 'and Dr. Sullivan were seen together in Beaty's' (the said William's, meaning) 'stable, one morning, very early, in the very act'—'It certainly is a fact'—'Jo Shepherd can prove it by two respectable witnesses'—'Mrs. Beaty' (the said Martha Ann, meaning) 'and Dr. Sullivan were seen in the very act'— 'They' (the said Martha Ann and the said Dr. Sullivan, meaning) 'were caught in the very act'—'Old Mr. Vandergrift' (one Thomas Vandergrift, meaning) and the said Thomas (by the hearers, then and there being understood to be meant) 'told Mr. Miller' (the said Jonathan, meaning) 'so at the tanyard.' And the said defendants aver, that before the speaking of the words aforesaid, to wit on the (blank) day of May, A.D. 1845, at the county aforesaid, the said Thomas Vandergrift did speak and tell said words as aforesaid to the said Jonathan—and so the said defendants say that she, the said Susan, did speak the said words in the said declaration mentioned, as lawfully she might, for the cause aforesaid. And the said defendants are ready to verify; wherefore they pray judgment, etc." In the document written by Lincoln and Herndon in the case, two replications follow, each of about the same length, one written by Herndon, the final one by Lincoln.

Chapter 69

IN the year 1843 a man named Robert Matson came from his home in Bourbon County, Kentucky, and bought a large tract of land in Coles County, Illinois, not many miles from the cabin of Thomas Lincoln in that county. Matson started farming his land, naming it Black Grove farm, bringing with him his slaves from Kentucky to plant and gather the crops. When the harvests were over he took the negroes back to Kentucky, working his Illinois land with a different gang of slaves each year.

One free negro, Anthony Bryant, stayed in Illinois from year to year, acting as foreman or overseer for Matson, studying the Bible at odd times, learning to spell his way slowly through some of the chapters. In the year 1847 Bryant's slave wife and four children were brought from Kentucky, and put to work on the Matson farm.

Matson's housekeeper, Mary Corbin, who was more than a housekeeper to him, one day exploded with anger and spoke terrible words to Jane Bryant, the wife of Anthony. "You're going back to Kentucky," shrieked Mary Corbin, "and you're going to be sold way down South in the cotton fields."

Anthony Bryant heard what seemed to be a death sentence on his wife, and drove as fast as horseflesh would let him to the village of Oakland, two miles away. There he talked to Hiram Rutherford, a young doctor from Pennsylvania, and Gideon M. Ashmore, from the Duck River country of Tennessee. And in the middle of that night Anthony Bryant, his wife and one child, on horseback, and three children on foot, arrived at the Ashmore home in Oakland. They stayed at the Ashmore home several days while Robert Matson and his friend, Joseph Dean, argued and threatened. Then Matson went before William Gilman, justice of the peace, swore that the negro woman and her children were his property, and they were arrested and locked up in the county jail at Charleston.

Squire Gilman heard the arguments of Orlando B. Ficklin for the negroes, and of Usher F. Linder for Matson. The squire decided he didn't have authority on the question of freedom or slavery for the negroes, and turned the prisoners back into the hands of the sheriff. After the Bryant woman and her children had spent forty-eight days in jail, the sheriff, A. G. Mitchell, put into the hands of lawyers a bill to be collected from Matson. The main item read, "To keeping and dieting five negroes forty-eight days at 37 cents each per day, $107.30."

Next, Matson was arrested and convicted, the charge being that he had lived unlawfully with Mary Corbin, a woman not his wife. After that Matson brought an action against Rutherford and Ashmore, claiming damages for the unlawful seizure and holding of his property, negro slaves.

The main action came when Matson went into circuit court, demanding the release of his property on grounds of habeas corpus and calling for $2,500.00 damages from Rutherford, valuing the slaves at $500.00 apiece. When the summons in the case was served on Rutherford, he rode to Charleston, found Abraham Lincoln sitting tilted in a chair on the tavern veranda, interrupted as Lincoln had finished telling one story and was going to start on another, and they went to one side for a talk.

As Rutherford told his troubles, he noticed Lincoln growing sober, sad, looking far off, shaking his head in a sorry way. "At length, and with apparent reluctance, Lincoln answered that he could not defend me, because he had already been counselled with in Matson's interest," said Rutherford, later. "This was a grievous disappointment and irritated me into expressions more or less bitter in tone. He seemed to feel this, and endeavored in his plausible way to reconcile me to the proposition that, as a lawyer, he must represent and be faithful to those who counsel with and employ him. I appeared not to be convinced, retorting that 'my money was as good as any one's else.' Although thoroughly in earnest I presume I was a little hasty."

A few hours later Lincoln sent a message to Rutherford, and followed the first message quickly with a second. "The interview and my quick temper," said Rutherford, "made a deep impression on Mr. Lincoln, I am sure, because he dispatched a messenger to me with the information that he had sent for the man who had approached him in Matson's behalf, and if they came to no more decisive terms than at first he would probably be able to represent me. In a very brief time this was followed by another message, that he could now easily and consistently free himself from Matson and was, therefore, in a position if I employed him to conduct my defense. But it was too late; my pride was up, and I plainly indicated a disinclination to avail myself of his offer. Instead, I employed Charles H. Constable, a lawyer who had emigrated to Illinois from Maryland, a classical scholar, fluent and ready in debate, and of commanding physical presence. Ashmore made terms with Orlando B. Ficklin, a Kentuckian, who had won renown as a lawyer."

The case came to trial before Judges Willson and Treat, of the supreme court of the state, with Lincoln and Usher F. Linder as counsel for Matson. Farm hands went on the witness stand for Matson and swore he had told them at the time he brought the slaves to his Illinois land that he didn't intend to keep them there permanently.

It seemed as though Matson's lawyers expected to win by showing that Matson had no plans for permanently locating slaves in Illinois. And yet, when Lincoln presented his statements for Matson, they sounded like a searching inquiry into the cold facts and the elemental justice of the case, rather than an argument for a plaintiff. A Coles County lawyer, D. F. McIntyre, got the impression that Lincoln was clumsy at handling the case in favor of his client. He made no attack on the defense, no attempt to batter down the points of the opposition, and practically gave his case away by the outright admission that if the Kentucky slave owner had brought his slaves to Illinois for the purpose of working them and using them as slaves on the Coles County farm, the negroes were thereby entitled to freedom. McIntyre noted that Lincoln said the whole case turned on one point. "Were these negroes passing over and crossing the State, and thus, as the law contemplates, *in transitu,* or were they actually located by consent of their master? If only crossing the State, that act did not free them, but if located, even indefinitely, by the consent of their owner and master, their emancipation logically followed. It is, therefore, of the highest importance to ascertain the true purpose and intent of Matson in placing these negroes on the Black Grove farm."

McIntyre noted further: "When Mr. Lincoln arose to make

the closing argument, all eyes were fixed upon him. Every person in the court room was curious to hear what reasons he could or would assign, in behalf of this slave holder, to induce the court to send this mother and her four children back into lives of slavery. But strange to say Lincoln did not once touch upon the question of the right of Matson to take the negroes back to Kentucky. His main contention was that the question of the right of the negroes to their freedom could only be determined by a regular habeas corpus proceeding."

Judge Willson leaned forward over the bar and asked: "Mr. Lincoln, your objection is simply to the form of the action by which, or in which this question should be tried, is it not?" "Yes, sir."

Then came the high point of the day for Lincoln. Judge Willson asked: "Now, if this case was being tried on issue joined in a habeas corpus, and it appeared there, as it does here, that this slave owner had brought this mother and her children, voluntarily, from the State of Kentucky, and had settled them down on his farm in this State, do you think, as a matter of law, that they did not thereby become free?" And Lincoln answered, "No, sir, I am not prepared to deny that they did."

Linder then argued, for Matson, that slaves were chattel property, the Federal Constitution protected such property, and it could not lawfully be taken from him. But the court decree on October 17, 1847, declared Jane Bryant and her four children "are discharged from the custody as well of the Sheriff as of Robert Matson and all persons claiming them as slaves, and they shall be and remain free from all servitude whatever to any person or persons from henceforward and forever."

And Matson quietly slipped away toward the Wabash River, quit the county, and without paying Lincoln his fee. Rutherford saw Lincoln leave Charleston for the next county on the circuit. "As he threw across the animal's back his saddlebags, filled with soiled linen and crumpled court papers, and struck out across the prairie, he gave no sign of any regret because, as a lawyer, he had upheld the cause of the strong against the

weak." Thus spoke Rutherford, who had put up the barriers
after Lincoln had gone the limit trying to break into the case
on the side he preferred.

As Lincoln straddled his gray mare and rode in the October
prairie haze, he might have recalled the remark he once made
to a lawyer who had asked him to go in on a case he didn't
believe in, and he had said: "You'll have to get some other fellow
to win this case for you. I couldn't do it. All the while I'd be
talking to that jury I'd be thinking, 'Lincoln, you're a liar,' and
I believe I should forget myself and say it out loud."

Chapter 70

FOUR years after his marriage to Mary Todd, Lincoln was
thirty-seven years old, and getting ready to leave Springfield to
go to Washington, D.C., to sit, vote, and speak as the one and
only Whig congressman elected from the state of Illinois. He
had become what was called a public man.

Mary Todd had borne him two children, the first in 1843
named Robert Todd, the second in 1846 named Edward Baker.
She, the daughter of a Kentucky bank president, had married
him with all his debts; they had started their married life as
two boarders and roomers at four dollars a week in the Globe
Tavern. Though he was still not out of debt, and still paying
installments on the old debts from New Salem days when his
grocery store winked out into bankruptcy, they had bought a
house and lot on Eighth and Jackson streets, a few blocks from
the public square, with a story-and-a-half frame house on it;
from the front windows they could watch the corn grow on fields
between their parlor and the public square.

His run for congressman was against Peter Cartwright, an
old-fashioned circuit rider, famous as an evangelist and exhorter
and a Jackson Democrat. Years before little Abe Lincoln had
helped his father at chopping logs for their cabin near Little
Pigeon Creek in Indiana, Cartwright had rode the Salt River

circuit with Bible and rifle; if a sinner came in drunk and inter-rupted the sermon Cartwright jumped from the pulpit and per-sonally threw him out; a deacon spoke a cold, precise, correct prayer and Cartwright had to say, "Brother, three prayers like that would freeze hell over"; he had a contempt for Yankees and snorted that they were "imps who eat oysters." When a presiding elder at a church meeting in Tennessee whispered to Cartwright, pointing out a visitor, "That's Andrew Jackson," the reply was: "And who's Andrew Jackson? If he's a sinner God'll damn him the same as he would a Guinea nigger."

Cartwright was twenty-four years older than Lincoln, and, besides his own children and grandchildren, he could count on political support from a big personal acquaintance including not only church members who believed in his religious faith but also sinners who admired the swift, clean way he could throw dis-turbers out of church. The people farther east with their man-sions, elegance, and fashions, New York with its dancers from Paris, roused sarcasm from him; he was proud of the human stuff of Kentucky and Illinois; the Democrats picked him as the one man who had the best chance of taking the Springfield district away from the Whigs.

Cartwright's men spread reports during the campaign that Lincoln's wife was a high-toned Episcopalian, that Lincoln in a temperance speech in Springfield had said that drunkards are as good as Christians and church members, that Lincoln was a "deist" who believed in God but did not accept Christ and the doctrines of atonement and punishment, that Lincoln said, "Christ was a bastard." Lincoln made speeches and election-eered personally over the district, wrote many letters, and near the end of the campaign was sure he would win. Months earlier a Democratic friend said he did not like to vote against his party but he would vote for Lincoln if Lincoln told him the vote was needed. A few days before election Lincoln told him, "I have got the preacher, and I don't want your vote."

In spite of warnings he went anyhow to a religious meeting where Cartwright was to preach. In due time Cartwright said,

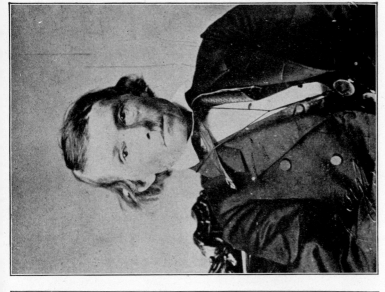

Abraham Lincoln of Illinois (left) and Alexander Stephens of Georgia (right). They were Whig congressmen together, and Lincoln once wrote Stephens, "This is the longest letter I ever wrote in my life." One weighed 180 pounds, the other 90 pounds. Jefferson Davis called Stephens "the little pale star from Georgia." *See* pages 377, 378.

The lawyer Abraham Lincoln (lower) and the Matamora Courthouse (upper left) and the Petersburg Courthouse (upper right).

"All who desire to lead a new life, to give their hearts to God, and go to heaven, will stand," and a sprinkling of men, women, and children stood up. Then the preacher exhorted, "All who do not wish to go to hell will stand." All stood up—except Lincoln. Then said Cartwright in his gravest voice, "I observe that many responded to the first invitation to give their hearts to God and go to heaven. And I further observe that all of you save one indicated that you did not desire to go to hell. The sole exception is Mr. Lincoln, who did not respond to either invitation. May I inquire of you, Mr. Lincoln, where you are going?"

And Lincoln slowly rose and slowly spoke. "I came here as a respectful listener. I did not know that I was to be singled out by Brother Cartwright. I believe in treating religious matters with due solemnity. I admit that the questions propounded by Brother Cartwright are of great importance. I did not feel called upon to answer as the rest did. Brother Cartwright asks me directly where I am going. I desire to reply with equal directness: I am going to Congress." The meeting broke up.

Two years before this campaign Lincoln had met charges somewhat like those of Cartwright's supporters. At that time he was seeking nomination for Congress and the friends of Edward D. Baker brought several points against him. He wrote to a friend: "It would astonish if not amuse the older citizens to learn that I (a strange, friendless, uneducated, penniless boy, working on a flatboat at ten dollars a month) have been put down here as the candidate of pride, wealth, and aristocratic family distinction. Yet so, chiefly, it was. Baker is a Campbellite, and therefore, as I suppose, got all that church. My wife has some relations in the Presbyterian churches and some with the Episcopalian churches, and therefore, wherever it would tell, I was set down as either one or the other, while it was everywhere contended that no Christian ought to go for me, because I belonged to no church, was suspected of being a deist, and had talked about fighting a duel." He and Baker were good personal friends and he made it clear that Baker had nothing to do with the politics of personal misrepresentation.

One day the campaign tale again was told to him in a store in Springfield that he belonged to a proud family and his aristocratic relatives came to visit him. And A. Y. Ellis said he heard Lincoln explain: "That sounds strange to me because I do not remember of but one who ever came to see me, and while he was in town he was accused of stealing a jew's-harp."

He wrote letters; he sat at a desk, dipped a quill pen into an ink bottle and wrote to editors, politicians, voters, precinct workers. And there was a deadly accuracy to his letters; he put things in an exact way so that what he meant could be clearly understood; if it was a promise he made it as specific as possible, telling just what he could do and what he couldn't do in filling the promise; if it was a compliment what there was to it was all there, entirely sincere, standing up under the test of repeated reading.

As he would finish a sentence or a paragraph he read it out loud usually to see how it would sound; the sound of words helped him see more clearly just what he was saying. Often he wrote in a pinched, crabbed, labored style, bringing in details of fact, and citing arrays of facts, but when the letter was finished all the crabbed details massed together into a smooth, compact surface that made a truthful letter, a letter that he could stand by afterward.

Ink bottles were emptied and filled again as he wrote piles of letters, with his eye on a seat in Congress. "I have written to three or four of the most active Whigs in each precinct of the county," he wrote a friend in Marshall County.

The man he had had to beat for the nomination was Hardin. And he had only compliments for Hardin in a letter to B. F. James: "Hardin is a man of desperate energy and perseverance, and one that never backs out; and, I fear, to think otherwise is to be deceived in the character of our adversary." He reckoned the counties for and against his nomination: "I can possibly get Cass, but I do not think I will. Morgan and Scott are beyond my reach; Menard is safe to me; Mason neck and neck; Logan is mine. I suppose Tazewell is safe. Keep your eyes continually

on Woodford and Marshall. Let no opportunity of making a
mark escape. When they shall be safe, all will be safe, I think."
A newspaper said he should be nominated for governor; he let
it be understood he wished to be mentioned for governor if the
mention would help him go to Congress; the goal was Congress.

A movement against Lincoln was on foot in a town; he wrote
the editor of the paper there, "I want you to let nothing prevent your getting an article in your paper of this week." He
could appeal frankly, "If your feelings toward me are the same
as when I saw you (which I have no reason to doubt), I wish
you would let nothing appear in your paper which may operate
against me. You understand. Matters stand just as they did
when I saw you."

The blunt little sentence crept in often, "You understand."
Some letters ended, "Confidential, of course," or "Don't speak
of this, lest they hear of it," or "For your eye only." There
were times to travel in soft shoes. "It is my intention to take
a quiet trip through the towns and neighborhoods of Logan
County, Delevan, Tremont, and on to and through the upper
counties. Don't speak of this, or let it relax any of your vigi-
lance. When I shall reach Tremont, we will talk everything over
at large."

A direct personal appeal was phrased, "I now wish to say to
you that if it be consistent with your feelings, you would set a
few stakes for me." No personal feelings against Hardin must
be permitted. "I do not certainly know, but I strongly suspect
that General Hardin wishes to run again. I know of no argument to give me a preference over him, unless it be 'Turn about
is fair play.' " And again, to another: "It is my intention to
give him [Hardin] the trial, unless clouds should rise, which are
not yet discernible. This determination you need not, however,
as yet, announce in your paper, at least as not coming from me.
In doing this, let nothing be said against Hardin. Nothing de-
serves to be said against him. Let the pith of the whole argument be, 'Turn about is fair play.' "

Chatter came to his ears that his friend Edward D. Baker would go for the nomination. He wrote Henry Dummer, "Before Baker left, he said to me, in accordance with what had long been an understanding between him and me, that the track for the next congressional race was clear to me so far as he was concerned; and that he would say so publicly in any manner and at any time I might desire."

At no time would he be shaken in his belief in Baker's friendship; to Martin Morris at Petersburg went the message: "I have heard it intimated that Baker had been attempting to get you or Miles, or both of you, to violate the instructions of the meeting that appointed you, and to go for him. I have insisted, and still insist, that this cannot be true. Surely Baker would not do the like. If any one should get the nomination by such extraordinary means, all harmony in the district would inevitably be lost. Honest Whigs (and very nearly all of them are honest) would not quietly abide such enormities. I repeat, such an attempt on Baker's part cannot be true. Write me at Springfield how the matter is. Don't show or speak of this letter." . . . And later when the second baby came to the Lincoln home it was named Edward Baker.

Friends of old days long gone arose as ghosts. There was James Short, the farmer who bought at auction Lincoln's horse and surveying instruments and gave them back to Lincoln after they were seized for debt in New Salem. At the end of a letter, Martin Morris at Petersburg was told: "You should be sure to have men appointed delegates that you know you can safely confide in. If yourself and James Short were appointed from your county, all would be safe; but whether Jim's woman affair a year ago might not be in the way of his appointment is a question. I don't know whether you know it, but I know him to be as honorable a man as there is in the world. You have my permission, and even request, to show this letter to Short; but to no one else, unless it be a very particular friend, who you know will not speak of it." It was Short who said that when Lincoln worked on his farm, "He husked two loads of corn to my one."

If a man had promised not to take sides in a fight, he wanted that man to stay put. "Now tell me, is Morris going it openly? You remember you wrote me that he would be neutral." And in fixing up political fences it would be worth while to know who was trying to tear the fences down. "Nathan said that some man, who he could not remember, had said lately that Menard County was going to decide the contest and that that made the contest very doubtful. Do you know who that was? Don't fail to write me instantly on receiving, telling me all—particularly the names of those who are going strong against me."

There must be harmony, joint purpose; a regiment of political workers facing an enemy must not fight among themselves. "Previous to General Hardin's withdrawal some of his friends and some of mine had become a little warm; and I felt, and meant to say, that for them now to meet face to face and converse together was the best way to efface any remnant of unpleasant feeling, if any such existed. I did not suppose that General Hardin's friends were in any greater need of having their feelings corrected than mine were. Since I saw you at Jacksonville, I have had no more suspicion of the Whigs of Morgan than of those of any other part of the District. I write this only to try to remove any impression that I distrust you and the other Whigs of your county." In politics there are insinuations published in newspapers not worth answering. "So far as this communication may relate to the convention, I prefer that your paper let it 'stink and die' unnoticed." He took on debaters as carelessly as in the Black Hawk War he took on wrestlers. "If alive and well I am sure to be with you on the 22d. I will meet the trio of mighty adversaries you mention, in the best manner I can."

Out of the ink bottle on the law-office desk in Springfield came not only schemes, plans, arrangements, compliments, inquiries. There were human issues asked about by people not so interested in votes, delegates, and party victories. Two men at Hennepin wanted to know from Lincoln where he stood on Texas. In the year 1844 the big question was Texas. Should it be let

into the Union of states, along with its slaves, or not? Henry
Clay, the Whig candidate for President, had said two weeks before he was nominated that annexation of Texas would bring war
with Mexico and was not called for, changing this later to saying
that if Texas did come into the Union it might not do much
harm because the slaves were to die off and the slavery question
too, only to say again before Election Day that he had no particular change to make from what he first said about annexation.

Lincoln, however, took a stand from which he made no change.
He wrote to the men at Hennepin:

I perhaps ought to say that individually I never was much interested
in the Texas question. I never could see much good to come of
annexation, inasmuch as they were already a free republican people
on our own model. On the other hand, I never could very clearly see
how the annexation would augment the evil of slavery. It always
seemed to me that slaves would be taken there in about equal numbers,
with or without annexation. And if more slaves *were* taken because
of annexation, still there would be just so many the fewer left where
they were taken from. It is possibly true, to some extent, that with
annexation some slaves may be sent to Texas and continued in slavery
that otherwise might have been liberated. To whatever extent this
may be true, I think annexation is an evil. I hold it to be the paramount duty of us in the free States, due to the Union of the States,
and perhaps to liberty itself (paradox though it may seem) to let the
slavery of the other States alone; while, on the other hand, I hold it
to be equally clear that we should never knowingly lend ourselves,
directly or indirectly, to prevent that slavery from dying a natural
death—to find new places for it to live in, when it can no longer exist
in the old.

Besides keeping track of neighborhood politics, the hundreds
of names of men for and against him, he was following national
drifts with an eye for the big facts. In a Whig circular of which
he was the chief writer, he discussed the tariff and national banking and public lands, and, arguing against low prices for state
and Government lands, said: "By the time one of the original
new States (Ohio, for example) becomes populous and gets
weight in Congress, the public lands in her limits are so nearly

sold out that in every point material to this question she becomes
an old State. She does not wish the price reduced, because there
is none left for her citizens to buy."

The circular argued for the Whigs to stand together. "That
'union is strength' is a truth that has been known, illustrated,
and declared in various ways and forms in all ages of the world.
That great fabulist and philosopher Æsop illustrated it by his
fable of the bundle of sticks; and he whose wisdom surpasses
that of all philosophers has declared that 'a house divided
against itself cannot stand.' " And there were moments when
he was working so fast and toiling with so many details that he
didn't have time or take time to use simple words and make his
points clear to common people. He used long words such as
"independent" and "predestination" that had kept him awake
at night as a boy trying to figure out the meaning of the meaning. In the Whig circular it was written, "The resolution declares the expediency of Mr. Clay's Land Bill. Much incom-
prehensible jargon is often used against the constitutionality of
this measure."

Chairmen at political meetings introduced him as an Illinois
man known from Galena at the north to Cairo in the south, from
the Mississippi River on the west to the Wabash on the east.

He had campaigned in Indiana for Henry Clay for President,
and when he made his speech in Gentryville, his old employer,
Josiah Crawford, was in a front seat, proud of the boy that had
husked corn in his fields. Crawford noticed Lincoln didn't use
books nor read statistics in his speech; he wanted to know,
"Where's your books, Abe?" And Abe laughed, "It's my stuck-
out lip." They smiled, remembering the days and nights when
the boy pushed out his underlip while tussling with a book to
get at its meanings.

He had gone to Kentucky and talked with Henry Clay, and
grasped Henry Clay's hand, and he had found Henry Clay a
little different from what he had expected, colder, stiffer, more
precise, farther from the people than he had imagined.

He had seen the word "roorback" come into the American lan-

guage. The Whigs used a story that James K. Polk, the Democratic nominee for President in 1844, had marched a gang of
slaves South to be sold, each slave branded "J.K.P.," saying
the story came from a travel book written by Baron von
Roorback.

Lincoln was going to Washington to sit, to speak, and to vote
under the big white dome, the only Whig congressman from a
state in a rough triangle between Lake Michigan, the Mississippi
River, and the Wabash. His letters, appeals, speeches, conversations, and explanations had gone to the eyes and ears of thousands of people; he had poured himself out tirelessly to be a
congressman. He had written to Richard Thomas of the town
of Virginia, "If you should hear any one say that Lincoln don't
want to go to Congress, I wish you, as a personal friend of mine,
would tell him that you have reason to believe him mistaken.
The truth is, I would like to go very much."

He was now what was called a public man; he was trying to
read the mind and the feelings of the public, to look under surface currents and find the deep important drifts, and to connect
public opinion and feeling with politics. He was reading faces,
voices, and whispers; he listened for insinuations, pretensions,
truths, in the little changes to be seen and heard in the faces,
voices, whispers, he met. He was trying to learn how to tell
what men want to live for and what they are willing to die for,
by what was spoken in faces, voices, whispers.

While his campaign for Congress was on, some Whig friends
clubbed together and raised $200.00 and handed it to him for
personal campaign expenses. After the election he handed them
back $199.25, saying he had spent only 75 cents in the cam-
paign. "I did not need the money. I made the canvas on my
own horse; my entertainment, being at the houses of friends,
cost me nothing; and my only outlay was 75 cents for a barrel
of cider, which some farmhands insisted I should treat to." The
count of ballots had given Lincoln 6,340 votes, Cartwright 4,829,
and Walcott (Abolitionist) 249.

He had been elected to Congress and was to go to the halls

where Clay, Webster, Calhoun had spoken and reached the ears of the nation; after hundreds of speeches and letters, after thousands of handshakes, after scheming and waiting and struggling, he had become a congressman; and he wrote Josh Speed, "Being elected to Congress, though I am very grateful to our friends for having done it, has not pleased me as much as I expected."

Chapter 71

NEARLY a year had passed between the time of Lincoln's election to Congress and his going to Washington. He watched and waited. War began with Mexico. Rifle companies of young men who had drilled regularly, and marched in processions on the Fourth of July, were offering themselves for service; of 8,370 volunteers in Illinois only 3,720 could be taken; they went down the Mississippi, across the Gulf to Texas, and on into Mexico; they were writing letters back home about occasional deer-meat and wild grapes as a change from rations of pork and beans; they were writing about plantations, sugar cane, cypress trees, Spanish moss, prickly pear and cholla, tarantulas and Texans.

Edward D. Baker had raised a regiment, received a commission as colonel, and gone to Mexico. John J. Hardin, whose seat in Congress Lincoln was to take, was killed while leading his regiment in a charge at the battle of Buena Vista. The third and fourth regiments of Illinois volunteers distinguished themselves in the campaign against the City of Mexico and in the Battle of Cerro Gordo. James Shields, challenger of Lincoln to a duel, received wounds at Cerro Gordo. Two of the three Illinois colonels at Buena Vista were killed.

In Washington the young congressman, Stephen A. Douglas, spoke for aggressive war against Mexico. John Quincy Adams wrote of Douglas in his diary, "In the midst of his roaring, to save himself from choking, he stript off and cast away his cravat, unbuttoned his waistcoat, and had the air and aspect of a half-naked pugilist." Douglas quoted from General Andrew Jackson, "The wanton character of some of the outrages upon the persons and property of our citizens, upon the officers and flag of the United States, independent of recent insults to this Government, would justify, in the eyes of nations, immediate war." For himself Douglas said: "Aside from the insults to our flag, the indignity to the nation, and the injury to our commerce, it is estimated that not less than ten millions of dollars are due our citizens for these and many other outrages which Mexico has committed within the last fifteen years. When pressed by our Government for adjustment and remuneration, she has resorted to all manner of expedients to procrastinate and delay. She has made treaties acknowledging the justice of our claims, and then refused to ratify them on the most frivolous pretexts. Gentlemen have the hardihood to tell us that the President has unwisely and unnecessarily precipitated the country into an unjust and unholy war. They express great sympathy for Mexico, profess to regard her as an injured and persecuted nation—the victim of American injustice and aggression. They have no sympathy for the widows and orphans whose husbands and fathers have been robbed and murdered by the Mexican authorities; no sympathy with our own countrymen who have dragged out miserable lives within the walls of her dungeons, without crime and without trial; no indignation at the outrages upon our commerce and shipping, and the insults to our national flag; no resentment at the violation of treaties and the invasion of our territory. I despair of ever seeing my country again in the right, if they are to be the oracles."

Douglas quoted Frederick the Great, "Take possession first and negotiate afterward," and declared: "That is precisely what President Polk has done. He has taken possession and proposed to negotiate."

And while the Whigs politically had stood against the declaration of war, calling it a fight for a land grab, they took the position that the war having been started and the nation committed to it, the thing to do was to fight it through with no stint of sacrifice. This was the position of General Zachary Taylor, a Whig in politics, who commanded the American army in its expedition across the Rio Grande and into northern Mexico to the Battle of Buena Vista. It was also the position of such Whigs as Colonel Baker and Colonel Hardin, who was killed. Sons of the famous Whigs, Daniel Webster and Henry Clay, died in field service on Mexican soil.

Lincoln watched events, collected facts and data, worked on the policies he would stand for in Congress. He noticed that dinners, barbecues, brass bands, fireworks, cannon salutes, speeches of welcome met the returning soldiers; five thousand people gathered in Springfield for the home greeting. Returning officers received high appointments; in Menard County five returned volunteers were elected to the offices of judge of probate, clerk of the county commissioner's court, assessor, treasurer, and recorder.

Lincoln wrote to O. H. Browning of Quincy about law and politics in which they were interested. "Don't fret yourself about trouble you give me; when I get tired I'll tell you. I am glad you sent this letter, because it reminds me to write the result of your two cases of Moore *vs.* Brown and God knows who all."

After reporting the news of lawsuits, he told Browning what he expected the then assembling constitutional convention might do. "Indeed, indeed, I do not know what they are doing in the convention. Some things I have fears for. I am not easy about the Courts. I am satisfied with them as they are, but shall not care much if the judges are made elective by the People, and their term of office limited. I fear, however, something more, and as I think, much worse than all this, to wit, 'A Puppy Court,' that is, a Judge in each county, with civil jurisdiction in all cases up to a thousand dollars, and criminal in all cases not capital. 'A Migratory Supreme Court' and salaries so low as to exclude all respectable talent. From these—may God preserve us. As to what I and everybody else are doing, I am preparing to go to the Chicago River & Harbor Convention, and everybody is doing pretty much what everybody is always doing."

In Chicago he stood on the shore of Lake Michigan and looked across its stretch of blue water rising to meet the sky. It was the largest mass of fresh water he had ever looked on; he had known large rivers; a vast inland fresh-water sea was new to him. He learned that Chicago had installed a slaughterhouse where they killed 130 cattle a day and exported to the English market. A fast-settling north country was hauling its produce to Chicago; in one year when other points were paying 40 and 50 cents a bushel for wheat, the Chicago market was paying 87 cents and $1.00 a bushel; farmers and wheat-buyers were hauling wheat to Chicago from as far as 250 miles away; lines of 10 and 20 wagons headed for Chicago were common; one line of 80 wagons loaded with wheat had been counted; in Ottawa one year a firm advertised for 50 teams to haul wheat to Chicago. The city was attacking the problem of quicker movement of crops that farmers were holding for higher prices. Governor Ford of Illinois had remarked: "I have known whole stacks of wheat and whole fields of corn to rot, or to be dribbled out and wasted to no purpose; and whole droves of hogs to run wild in the woods so as never to be reclaimed, whilst the owner was saving them for a higher price."

Delegates came to the River and Harbor Convention from all the northern states; seven from Connecticut; 28 from Massachusetts; 27 from Pennsylvania. From Missouri came 45, from South Carolina one. Daniel Webster, Henry Clay, and other famous national leaders sent letters of hope that the convention would bring internal improvements.

Here Lincoln met Horace Greeley, editor of the *New York Tribune,* and Thurlow Weed, boss of the Whig party in New York. Greeley wrote for his paper: "In the afternoon Hon. Abraham Lincoln, a tall specimen of an Illinoisan, just elected to Congress from the only Whig district in the state, was called out, and spoke briefly and happily." The *Chicago Journal* told its readers: "Abraham Lincoln, the only Whig representative to

Congress from this State, we are happy to see in attendance
upon the Convention. This is his first visit to the commercial
emporium of the State, and we have no doubt his first visit
will impress him more deeply, if possible, and inspire a higher
zeal for the great interest of river-and-harbor improvements.
We expect much from him as a representative in Congress, and
we have no doubt our expectations will be more than realized,
for never was reliance placed in a nobler heart and a sounder
judgment. We know the banner he bears will never be soiled."
The convention, run by Whigs, went on record in favor of more
river and harbor improvement, and against the Democratic
President James K. Polk, for his failure to help lake harbors
with Government money.

The question of the tariff would be sure to come up in Congress, and Lincoln was putting down on paper his thoughts as
they came to him about the protective tariff which the Whig
party favored. "Iron, and everything made of iron, can be produced in sufficient abundance, and with as little labor, in the
United States as anywhere else in the world; therefore all labor
done in bringing iron and its fabrics from a foreign country to
the United States is useless labor. The same precisely may be
said of cotton, wool, and of their fabrics, as well as many other
articles." He made note of certain naked first principles which
were the starting-points for a system of economics:

"If at any time all labor should cease, and all existing provisions be equally divided among the people, at the end of a single
year there could scarcely be one human being left alive; all
would have perished by want of subsistence. So, again, if upon
such division all that sort of labor which produces provisions
should cease, and each individual should take up so much of
his share as he could, and carry it continually around his habitation, although in this carrying the amount of labor going on
might be as great as ever so long as it could last, at the end of
the year the result would be precisely the same—that is, none
would be left living. The first of these propositions shows that
universal idleness would speedily result in universal ruin; and

the second shows that useless labor is, in this respect, the same as idleness. I submit, then, whether it does not follow that partial idleness and partial useless labor would, in the proportion of their extent, in like manner result in partial ruin; whether, if all should subsist upon the labor that one-half should perform, it would not result in very scanty allowance to the whole.

"In the early days of our race the Almighty said to the first of our race, 'In the sweat of thy face shalt thou eat bread'; and since then, if we except the light and the air of heaven, no good thing has been or can be enjoyed by us without having first cost labor. And inasmuch as most good things are produced by labor, it follows that all such things of right belong to those whose labor has produced them. But it has so happened, in all ages of the world, that some have labored, and others have without labor enjoyed a large proportion of the fruits. This is wrong and should not continue. To secure to each laborer the whole product of his labor, or as nearly as possible, is a worthy object of any good government.

"The habits of our whole species fall into three great classes— useful labor, useless labor, and idleness. Of these the first only is meritorious, and to it all the products of labor rightfully belong; but the two latter, while they exist, are heavy pensioners upon the first, robbing it of a large portion of its just rights. The only remedy for this is to, so far as possible, drive useless labor and idleness out of existence."

Chapter 72

By stage and by steamboat Lincoln traveled East, crossed the Allegheny mountain range, rested his eyes on the Potomac River, on the slopes where George Washington had lived most of his years, and gazed up the broad pathway of Pennsylvania Avenue connecting the White House where President James K. Polk lived and the Capitol with its mystic white curves under which the Congress of the United States was to sit in deliberation on laws, measures, and events, and the name of Abraham Lincoln was to be called in the roll-calls.

Here he stood for the first time at the hub of the wheel of government, the central point from which the armies and navies of the United States, the post offices and postmasters, the public lands, the rivers and harbors, the seacoasts and the lighthouses, the customs officials, ambassadors, consuls, expeditions, and commanders, were controlled, advised, dismissed, appointed, pensioned, paid in currency.

Here came ambassadors from Europe, Asia, South America, Mexico, with their wives, servants, uniforms, appropriate apparel, trunks, portfolios, diplomatic missions, phrases, conventions, precedents. Republics, kings, queens, czars, ameers, pashas, and shahs had told these representatives what to look for and what to say in Washington.

Before the time of the birth of Abraham Lincoln there never was on any one spot of the earth such a collection of representatives, from such far-flung areas of the earth's surface, as the aggregation of ambassadors in Washington when he first came to that city. In no previous century was such an aggregation possible; the sailing vessels, steamships, and new spheres of contact and influence set up by the factory system and world trade had made it possible. It was a shrinking earth on which humanity was doing business; the curves of travel around it were growing smaller. Had not General Jackson said that Texas must be annexed because if she were not annexed she would form an alliance with Great Britain and that alliance would make war for control of western America?

So this was Washington, where only a few years before General Harrison had keeled over and died under the tumult of the office hunters who came asking jobs, where John Tyler had kept a bowl of juleps in the summer and of egg-nog in the winter for whosoever called at the White House; where John Howard Payne, the author of the song "Home, Sweet Home," had come in his poverty and been appointed consul at Tunis to go and die in Africa far from his own sweet home; where Samuel F. B.

Morse had set up his magnetic telegraph for congressmen to examine and criticize, where, by the narrow vote of 89 to 83, they had handed him $25,000.00 to experiment with, though Representative Cave Johnson said half the money should be used for experiments in mesmerism, while Representative Houghton said half should go to the Millerites who were announcing the end of the world to come shortly, as New York merchants put signs in their windows, "white muslin for ascension robes."

This was Washington; where Senator William Allen of Ohio was saying of the boomers booming themselves for the Presidency, "Sir! they are going about the country like dry-goods drummers, exhibiting samples of their wares"; where Pennsylvania Avenue was a mudhole after a heavy rain, and on Polk's inauguration day parading soldiers slipped and sprawled in the mud; where there were two inauguration balls, one at $10.00 a ticket in Carusi's saloon, and one at $2.00 a ticket in the National Theatre where there was a scramble for supper victuals, the best hats, cloaks, and canes were stolen early in the evening, and Commodore Elliot had his pocket picked and lost not only his money but a lock of hair from the head of General Jackson and a lock of hair from the head of James Madison; where Mrs. Polk was told, "Madame, you have a very genteel assemblage tonight," and replied, "Sir, I have never seen it otherwise"; where General Felix Grundy McConnell of Alabama had come to the congressional assembly wearing a blue swallow-tailed coat, light cassimere pantaloons, and a scarlet vest, accompanied by two sparkling French milliner girls dressed in Parisian dancing costumes; where the Secretary of State, William Learned Marcy, worked at home after breakfast on writing notes to foreign governments, seated in a loose dressing-gown with an old red handkerchief on the table before him, and a snuffbox from which he had used so many pinches that his voice and breath had changed for the worse; where there were congressmen for and against the carrying of mails on the Sabbath; where congressmen sat, spoke, voted according to what they considered the logic, the common sense, or the justice of a passionate human cause as presented in a bill before the house; where congressmen sat, spoke, voted according to the tobacco, rice, cotton, or slave-labor interest of their section and district, or according to the iron, steel, canal, railroad, milling and manufacturing interest, or according to the corn, pork, river and harbor, or internal improvement interest of their district and section; where there were fixers always fixing human causes that would not stay fixed, that always broke out in a new place that needed fixing, so that the fixers would again go to work saying that this time they expected it would stay fixed.

Here were the stage and footlights where Jackson, Clay, Calhoun, Webster, and John Quincy Adams had spoken their lines so many years. Jackson, the most passionate and forthright of all, Calhoun offering merciless logic, Webster polished oratorical periods, Clay many sentences varying the styles of all, and John Quincy Adams offering the queries of the perplexed, honest philosopher. Jackson had gone; the footlights were out for him; soon another and another was to go; in a few years the stage would be dark for a little row of players who had put their impress on every large issue and event in the Government for thirty years and more. After them were to come other players; they would have lines to speak on a fiercely lighted stage.

On the halfway line between the states of the North and of the South they had placed and laid out this city; it was built on something resembling an oath that the states North and South belonged together and should meet at a halfway point; and since the year it was platted into streets the human streams had coursed over the crest of the Allegheny Mountains, beyond to the Mississippi River, out to the Rocky Mountains, and now were threshing out the news of the Mexican War and of gold in California and of the Frémont exploring expeditions; so that soon, it was seen, the little city with the big white dome on the Potomac River would be the gathering place of men from states at distances staggeringly beyond anything in the dreams and plans of those who placed and laid out the city.

This was the one planned city in America, with its spaces and outlooks measured by design rather than accident; with an architecture and a layout of streets deliberate and free-handed; in the mystic float of the Capitol dome rested some mystery of the republic, something that people a thousand miles from the Potomac River believed in and were ready to die and make sacrifices for.

Here were libraries, museums, documents, gardens. Here were dialects from Louisiana to Maine, from the Carolinas to Minnesota; the soft southern drawl, the Yankee nasal twang, the slow western slang. Here were more boarders and roomers, ready to pack and go on short notice, than in any other city in the world. Here Abraham Lincoln and his family were to board and room for two years beginning in December of 1847.

Chapter 73

THE Lincoln family, with the two boys, Bob and Ed, one four years old, the other eighteen months old, rented lodgings on Capitol Hill, to live in a city ten times the size of Springfield, Illinois. By the banks of the Potomac, and not the Sangamon, Abraham Lincoln was to spend his thirty-ninth birthday anniversary and round out his fortieth year. He had become a legislative member of the Washington government, which spent sixty million dollars a year; he and two hundred other men were to decide on what the sixty million would be spent for; he was a lawmaker of the American republic.

Into his hands came a 509-page book, embroidered with gilt scrolls, gilt edges, the gilt title "The Constitution" on the back, and on the front cover in gilt letters:

HON. ABRAHAM LINCOLN
REP^E. U.S. ILL.

The printer of the book, W. Hickey of Philadelphia, took the first eight pages of the book and filled them with testimonials in ornamental scroll type telling what an excellent book he had assembled and printed. The language throughout the book was splendiferous, and in the style Eighth Circuit lawyers in Illinois called "orgmathorial." Of the Constitution it declared, "Esto Perpetua!!!" three exclamation points being necessary to carry the enthusiasm.

As in Springfield, Illinois, so it was in the national capital: nearly all the lawmakers were lawyers. Already acquainted with many through newspapers and published speeches, Lincoln studied them further as they sat at their desks or rambled through the lobbies, the House post office, the Capitol grounds. He found men, such as Alexander Stephens of Georgia, Andrew Johnson of Tennessee, Joshua Giddings of Ohio, who like himself had come up from cabins of poverty. He took the measure of such aristocrats as Robert C. Winthrop of Boston, Speaker of the House; he searched the gentle, thoughtful face of Horace Mann, full of hope for a universal free school system; he joked the six Democrats from Illinois, who were keeping their eyes on the record of the one Whig from their state.

He sat at breakfasts in the home of Daniel Webster where William, a negro he had freed, and Daphne, a slave negro woman not yet freed, were servants, though the fact of Daniel Webster of Massachusetts having neglected to free the negro woman, Daphne, whom he owned, was a carefully kept secret; he scrutinized the cherubic, bland face of Horace Greeley, with pink skin fresh as that of a farm hand just come from milking, and a little round forehead contemplative of public abuses to be corrected by righteous citizens.

Horace Greeley often would point to an "abuse" and announce, "We propose to attack this abuse." He spread on the front page of the *New York Tribune* one morning the mileage charges of congressmen, "showing the amount of miles charged and mileage pocketed by each member at the last Session." In the case of Abraham Lincoln, for instance, the official distance from

Washington by the shortest mail-route to Springfield was 780 miles but Lincoln had charged the government for travel by a route of 1,626 miles, and collected $1,300.80, which the *Tribune* figured was $676.80 in "excess of mileage over what it would have been if the distance had been computed by the most direct mail-route." The Lincoln mileage account, like that of nearly all members of Congress from the West, assumed that the way to travel from the West was to go to Chicago and take a steam-boat and ride on the Great Lakes to Buffalo. The law provided payment for mileage by "the usually traveled road," and the *Tribune* declared: "The usually traveled road for a great many Members of the last Congress was an exceedingly crooked one, even for politicians. The wrong, as respects their cases, is not in them but in the *law*." Greeley urged: "If the People will only give a little thought to this subject, they will do themselves a service, for I am confident the Mileage abuse is the parent of many others. Let every man do a little, and soon 'the crooked shall be made straight.'"

Lincoln had his money bothers. He accepted from Senator Stephen A. Douglas on December 21, 1847, a note to Messrs. Corcoran and Riggs, reading, "Pay to A. Lincoln or order one hundred and sixty-seven dollars and charge same to my account."

At the mess table in Mrs. Spriggs's boarding-house, where Lincoln took his meals, he ate with four Pennsylvania congress-men, Patrick Thompson of Mississippi, Elisha Embree of In-diana, Joshua Giddings, and others. As the Mississippi and Ohio members between helpings of victuals clashed over the slavery issue, Lincoln sometimes interrupted and steered the discussion into a good-natured channel. At Caspari's bowling alley, near Mrs. Spriggs's place, he tried for ten-strikes with his long right arm and told yarns between plays and games; men dropped in just to hear him loosen up with his stories. One listener com-mented later: "He indulged with great freedom in the sport of narratives, some of which were very broad. His witticisms seemed for the most part to be impromptu, but he always told the anecdotes and jokes as if he wished to convey the impression that he had heard them from someone; but they appeared very many times as if they had been made for the occasion."

In the House of Representatives post office Lincoln was at home in a corner where story-tellers met. After listening to others during the Christmas holidays he had let go a few reminiscences of the Black Hawk War. "By New Year's he was recognized as the champion story-teller of the Capitol," wrote a newspaper man. "His favorite seat was at the left of the open fireplace, tilted back in his chair, with his long legs reaching over to the chimney jamb. He never told a story twice, but appeared to have an endless repertoire always ready, like the successive charges of a magazine gun."

He might have told stories like an old Illinois favorite of his, one that he told in the legislature when a good law was proposed and a member spoke against it; it was unconstitutional. The member had shaggy, overhanging eyebrows, wore spectacles, and wanted his fellow members to understand he had keen eyes for any points not constitutional. Lincoln said the debate reminded him of an old fellow on the Wabash River who had shaggy, overhanging eyebrows and wore spectacles. One morning this old fellow was looking up a tree near his cabin and thought he saw a squirrel sitting on a high branch. Getting his rifle, he fired one load, reloaded, fired again, but couldn't hit the squirrel. He asked a boy, "Don't you see that squirrel, humped up about halfway up the tree?" "No, I don't," said the boy, and, looking keenly into his father's face, he broke out: "I see your squirrel! You've been shooting at a louse on your eyebrow!"

Lincoln had anecdotes such as one about John T. Stuart, the Whig, and Stephen A. Douglas, the Democrat, stumping Sangamon County and arriving late one night at a tavern. The landlord showed them two beds, each with a man sleeping in it. Douglas asked the landlord their politics. One was a Whig and the other a Democrat, the landlord told them. And Douglas said, "Stuart, you sleep with the Whig and I'll sleep with the Democrat." Or he could tell of the Kentucky magistrate who was tired of hearing two lawyers wrangling after he had given his decision. He admonished them, "If the court is right—and she think she air—why, then, you air wrong, and she knows you is—shut up."

In the House post office there were members who could tell such stories as the one of General Jackson going to Harvard to take a degree of Doctor of Laws so that he could, if he chose, write LL.D. after his name. The old general knew plenty of Smoky Mountain dialect and plenty of Choctaw and Cherokee and Creek Indian lingo, but no Latin, and he had got up from a sick bed to go to the exercises where the sheepskin degree was to be handed him. President Quincy of Harvard made the presentation speech in Latin, and as Jackson accepted he made a little response, in a voice so low and mumbling that few in the audience understood him. Some said that he spoke a few modest, simple words in English. Others said that he replied, "Caveat emptor; corpus delicti; ex post facto; e pluribus unum; Ursa Major; sic semper tyrannis; quid pro quo; requiescat in pace."

There were anecdotes such as the one concerning Robert Owen, the Indiana congressman from the Ohio and Wabash River district. After a campaign debate with an opponent, Owen heard two farmers talking, "Did you hear Owen talk?" asked one. "Yes," said the other, "I hearn him." "Now, ain't he a hoss?" was next asked. And the answer was, "Well, yes; they're both blooded nags. They make a very pretty race." It was Owen who told a farmer in Posey County that he hesitated about running for the legislature because, having been born in England, he was an adopted American citizen and his foreign birth would be brought up against him. The Posey County farmer replied: "Well, it oughtn't to. A man isn't a horse, if he was born in a stable."

It was a time when pigs roamed the streets of Washington sniffing for food. In saloons and taverns were lithographs showing President Tyler at a steamboat dock. His secretary was calling: "Captain, hold on there, Ex-President Tyler is coming. Hold on!" And the captain, a Henry Clay Whig, pulled the engine bell, looked scornfully at the Tyler party, and yelled: "Ex-President Tyler be dashed! Let him stay!" And there was the grog ration in the navy to talk about. It was said two congressmen voted to cut down the ration, and then said to each other, "Now we can go out and have a drink."

Chapter 74

AT the time Lincoln swore his oath and took his seat as congressman the war with Mexico was nearly over. American armies in Mexico were clinching their hold on that country. The Government in Washington spent $27,000,000 and the lives of 27,000 soldiers. Mexico was beaten. The question of the day was: "What next? What price shall we force from Mexico to pay us for what the war has cost us?"

One answer to this question came from a man who stood up on crutches in the Senate; he was six feet high, lean of build, with wide gray-blue eyes, a thin shrewd nose, bushy eyebrows, proud, independent, positive. He had been shot in the foot at the Battle of Buena Vista and stayed in the saddle with his bleeding foot till the battle was won; his father and uncles had served in Revolutionary War armies from 1776 to Yorktown; three of his older brothers had fought in the War of 1812, two of them being officially commended for gallantry at the Battle of New Orleans; he himself had graduated from the West Point military academy and served twelve years in the regular army of the United States; he had been in Illinois and Wisconsin through the Black Hawk War.

His name was Jefferson Davis; he had been colonel of the Mississippi Rifles, a crack regiment of young aristocrats from Mississippi; he was a cotton planter with several thousand acres at Biloxi, Mississippi; the governor of Mississippi had appointed him United States senator to fill a vacancy. Now he was asking Congress to vote money to send ten regiments of soldiers to garrison the cities and provinces of Mexico and to hold that territory till the Washington government decided what to do with it.

In a speech on March 17, 1848, Senator Davis told the Senate: "I hold that in a just war we conquered the larger portion of Mexico and that to it we have a title which has been regarded as valid ever since man existed in a social condition—the title of conquest. It seems to me that that question is now, how much shall we keep, how much shall we give up, and that Mexico cedes nothing."

Yucatan should be annexed, or England would take it, Davis believed. Furthermore, if the American advance to the isthmus was resisted by Britain, he would make war on Britain; also, if Britain set foot in Cuba, America should interfere. He was a fighting man, sensitive, proud, independent, positive.

The Ten Regiments bill passed the Senate by a vote of 29 to 19; it went to the House; there it never came to a vote; it was pigeonholed by the Committee on Military Affairs; Whigs controlled the House.

South and North the politicians hesitated, straddled. There was confusion. Congressman Lincoln stood up and pointed at James K. Polk, the head of the government, calling him "a bewildered, confounded, and miserably perplexed man." Only five southern states had voted solidly for the Ten Regiments bill. In the other southern states there was opposition to the taking of all Mexico and the annexation of it to the United States. John C. Calhoun, the Senator from South Carolina, along with senators from Tennessee and Georgia, voted against ten regiments of regulars to garrison Mexico; they saw danger in the scheme. In the North, however, Senator Benton of Missouri was for it; so was Senator Lewis Cass of Michigan. In short, the South was not solid in favor of the dream of the "fire eater" for national expansion southward; yet there were northern politicians who spoke and voted the wish of the big cotton planters on every important bill. The Senate, controlled by the planters through the Democratic party, voted for the Ten Regiments; the House, controlled by Whigs less under the thumb of the planters, pigeon-

holed the Ten Regiments. The two leading members of the
House committee on military affairs, which did the pigeonholing,
were Robert Toombs and Howell Cobb of Georgia. Yet though
Toombs and Calhoun, both from cotton states, opposed the Ten
Regiments bill, they were bitter political enemies; when Calhoun
had started a movement for the organization of a separate southern party, with an eye toward secession from the Union, Toombs
and other Whigs had got inside of the movement and broken
it up.

On all bills and measures hitting at slavery, the South voted
solid. On the matter of secession from the Union as an advantage
to the South and the slavery institution, southern congressmen
were not solid. There were members such as Robert Toombs and
Alexander Stephens of Georgia, who believed that slavery would
have a better chance with the southern states in the Union than
out. They called the extremists "fire eaters," and "ultras."

What seemed to be architectural statesmanship sometimes
traced into spitework or the backwashes of cunning politics.
Congressman Brinkerhoff wanted offices for friends back home,
and, not getting what he wanted from President Polk, set out
to knife the Administration. He wrote a proviso to ride with
the appropriations bill, and took it to Judge David Wilmot, a
quiet member from Pennsylvania. Wilmot looked it over, inquired about the meaning of it, and said he guessed he would
introduce it, since he was asked. Thus came into Congress a
little piece of writing that called up storms of debate. It provided that any new territory that came into the United States
from the Mexican War treaty should be free and not slave territory. Onto one bill after another it was put as an amendment.
Voted down, it came back. Lincoln spoke "Aye" for the Wilmot
Proviso so many times he couldn't exactly remember how many;
he guessed it was "about forty times," at least.

Tom Corwin of Ohio had killed himself politically when he
broke out in the Senate one day with the declaration: "Were I
a Mexican, as I am an American, I would say to the invader:
'We will welcome you with bloody hands to hospitable graves.'"

Stephen A. Douglas had held to his original stand that President
Polk had properly done what Frederick the Great had done in
Silesia, by the rule, "Take possession first and negotiate after-
ward."

There seemed to be in the air the beginnings of a realization
of an ocean-bound republic, with the territory from the Atlantic
to the Pacific coasts in the hands of the United States. It was
a carrying further of the thought of General Jackson years before that Texas must be annexed; more and more western territory must be taken into the Union, or there would be alliances
formed that would make war for the control of western America.

In England, the *United Service Magazine* had commented editorially:

It is rather extraordinary that although France and ourselves are
always on the alert and alarm if any European power shows the slightest
intention of making a grab at a few miles of territory to which it may
have taken a fancy, yet the wholesale seizure by Brother Jonathan, of
vast territories, rich and fertile, and belonging to other and weaker
powers, is regarded with the most perfect apathy, and is scarcely considered worth the attention of European governments. It is impossible
but to admire the tremendous results of the cunning and diplomacy
of this republic, which, creeping on insidiously and by degrees, and
treating with perfect contempt what we in Europe may say or think
of their doings, are slowly but surely adding to its already enormous
extent of territory; swallowing in its capacious maw tracts of land large
enough for empires. One good point about him is, that he does not
make the least pretence to abstemiousness, and openly avows that sooner
or later *all* North America, and no little share between the tropics,
with all the West Indian islands, must in the natural course of events
fall into his ready jaws.

For many of the free-riding and free-shooting men of the
Southwest, who lived in the saddle, the Mexican War was a
grand adventure across a grand piece of country. They felt
in their way something of the size of the adventure as told by a
British officer writing in the *Montreal Gazette:*

From the 42d degree of latitude, and Santa Fe to Vera Cruz, a line,
say of 2,500 miles, is now covered by American troops or ships of

war, and though so immensely long, all perfectly safe in its rear, and resting upon supplies. The American government has, in a short time, established a grander base of operations (in extent) than has ever been seen in modern warfare.

While the war was in its beginning, the *Spectator* in London had given this long-range picture:

The present petty warfare they are waging on the frontier is but an episode in the great plot. General Taylor's force is but the precursor of the real army of invasion—the squatter and the backwoodsman, men in whom it is a hereditary and invincible instinct always to depart from before the approach of civilization, to avoid every spot where law has been established, and never to feel themselves at home except on debatable ground. By men like these, coming by twos and threes, then by scores and hundreds, and finally in multitudes, like carrion birds to the quarry, the northern provinces of the republic (of Mexico) will be overrun; and thence, the process will be continued until the whole territory is filled and mastered by these unprincipled and desperately energetic immigrants.

And the *Spectator* coupled with this picture another one:

The fate of Mexico has an immediate practical importance for all classes of men in this country, being separably identified with that of a vast amount of British capital. Expunge Mexico from the list of nations, and with the same blow you put out the fires on thousands of English hearths. Already we have suffered enough by the waste and decay of the wealth we have invested in that country; the annihilation of what remains would scatter bankruptcy among our merchants, paralyse our industry, disorder all the functions of our national life, and spread starvation among our working classes.

And again the *Spectator:*

The Isthmus of Tehuantepec, that majestic region, teeming with boundless wealth, washed by two oceans, traversed through half its breadth by a navigable river, which offers at its mouth the finest harbor in the Gulf of Mexico, may now be secured by Englishmen. Will they refuse to accept a region which was selected by the sagacious mind of the great conqueror Cortes to constitute his own private domain? If so, the French will be delighted to grasp the prize we disdain.

The *Morning Chronicle* in London told its readers that an offer of England to step in as umpire between the United States and Mexico had met with a refusal at Washington, and commented: "We shall apply to the transatlantic statesmen the remarks of the Athenians to the Melians, 'We wonder at their simplicity more than we admire their magnanimity.'" The simplicity referred to found voice in a paper far out in Missouri, in the *St. Louis Union:*

> The barbarism of the Mexican nation, and the unsettled condition of its government, have conspired to keep hidden one of the first agricultural and manufacturing nations on earth. . . . The war will facilitate the march of improvement in many respects. The day is not very distant when a race of civilized men must people the shores of the Pacific lying in comparative neighborship with China. A trade so valuable as one which might readily be established between the Atlantic coast and China, across this continent, cannot for many years be neglected.

To Lincoln his own way was clear; there were no zigzags in the course of his thinking about the war. His public speeches and his confidential letters to Herndon back home fitted together in all parts, pieces, corners, and dovetails.

Behind the war he saw politics. He believed one motive back of the war was that Polk and the Democratic party wanted to take away public attention from the backdown of the Democratic party on the Oregon boundary; they had said they would take all land up to the "fifty-four-forty" or they would fight Great Britain; the slogan had been "fifty-four-forty, or fight"; they had backed down; and in order to cover up they started a war where they were sure they could win, and the winnings looked good. That was the big reason. Next to that was another reason; the Democrats knew that the war would win more territory into which the southern planters could spread out with cotton, slave labor, and the politics of cotton and slavery.

He saw at a desk in the Senate chamber the spare figure of John C. Calhoun, with a face carved by merciless events, a time-worn forehead with the relentless thoughts back of it: "People do not understand liberty or majorities. The will of the majority is the will of a rabble. Progressive democracy is incompatible with liberty. Those who study after this fashion are yet in the horn-book, the A B C of governments. Democracy is leveling —this is inconsistent with true liberty. Anarchy is more to be dreaded than despotic power. It is the worst tyranny. The best government is that which draws least from the people, and is scarcely felt, except to execute justice, and to protect the people from animal violation of law."

With his power slipping from him, the eye of Calhoun was on Jefferson Davis as the one to follow in his own independent paths of southern leadership. When President Polk had sent Colonel Davis a commission as brigadier general of volunteers, Davis had sent back the commission with the message to the President that states only had the power to grant such a commission. In the summer of 1848, Davis had told the Senate: "If folly and fanaticism and pride and hate and corruption of the day are to destroy the peace and prosperity of the Union, let the sections part like the patriarchs of old, and let peace and good will subsist among their descendants. Let no wounds be inflicted which time may not heal. Let the flag of our Union be folded up entire, the thirteen stripes recording the original size of our family, untorn by the unholy struggle of civil war."

Davis was offering the counsel to the people of Mississippi: "The generation which avoids its responsibility sows the wind and leaves the whirlwind as the harvest to its children; let us get together and build manufactories, enter upon industrial pursuits, and prepare for our own self-sustenance." Of slavery he told his people: "If slavery be a sin, it is not yours. It is a common-law right and property in the service of man; its origin was divine decree—the curse upon the graceless son of Noah."

Yet Davis was not sure but that the states North might develop a cheaper labor that would push labor out of the states South. "Leave the country to the south and west open," he urged, "and speculation may see in the distant future slavery pressed by a cheaper labor to the tropical regions." Yet he also believed the development might take still another course; he noted that laws of the states of Ohio, Indiana, and Illinois forbade free negroes from entering those states; the next development might be the extension of slavery into those states.

Chapter 75

LINCOLN sat as a member of the congressional committee on post offices, and, in bringing in a report on post-office matters, he started to tell the House that all the Whigs in committee voted for the report, and all the Democrats, except one. He was interrupted; didn't he know it was out of order to tell on the floor what happened in the committee-room?

"He then observed," said the House minutes, "that if he had been out of order in what he said, he took it all back as far as he could. He had no desire, he could assure gentlemen, ever to be out of order—though he never could keep long in order."

Up over the speaker's desk was a clock with a yellow face, telling time for the congressmen. Over the clock stood a marble woman, busy writing in a book; she was supposed to be the figure of History, watching the congressmen.

A bill to raise the salary of a judge in western Virginia from $1,800.00 to $2,500.00 a year, came up; the House minutes recorded, "Mr. Lincoln said it came, then, to this: that the people in the western district of Virginia had got eleven courts to be held among them in one year, for their own accommodation; and being thus better accommodated than their neighbors elsewhere, they wanted their judge to be a little better paid. In Illinois there had been, until the present season, but one district court held in the year. There were now to be two. Could it be that the western district of Virginia furnished more business for a judge than the whole state of Illinois?"

As to making speeches on the floor of the house, Lincoln wrote back to Herndon at the Springfield law office: "By way of getting the hang of the House, I made a little speech two or three days ago on a post-office question of no general interest. I find speaking here and elsewhere about the same thing. I was about as badly scared, and no worse, as I am when I speak in the court." This was a try-out; a more thorough effort was to come. "As you are all so anxious for me to distinguish myself I have concluded to do so before long."

Getting the floor of the House on January 12, 1848, he defended the vote of his party given a few days previous "declaring that the war with Mexico was unnecessarily and unconstitutionally commenced by the President." He spoke of his impression of how he and others believed they ought to behave while their country was engaged in a war they considered unjustly commenced. "When the war began, it was my opinion that all those who because of knowing too little, or because of knowing too much, could not conscientiously oppose the conduct of the President in the beginning of it should nevertheless, as good citizens and patriots, remain silent on that point, at least till the war should be ended."

Now he was forced to break silence; the President was telling the country, continually, that votes of the Whigs for supplies to the soldiers in the field were an indorsement of the President's conduct of the war. Then too, the President was holding back documents and information to which the public was entitled.

Lincoln had earlier introduced resolutions and demands that the President should locate the exact "spot" where the war began. He now accused the President of marching an American army out of proven American territory into land not established as American soil, and there shedding the first blood of the war. The President was attempting "to prove by telling the truth what he could not prove by telling the whole truth."

Back in Illinois were political enemies murmuring that Lincoln was revealed as a Benedict Arnold in his "spot" resolutions. He now wanted the folks back home to see him pressing the President for the documents of the war, all of them. "Let the President answer the interrogatories I proposed. Let him answer fully, fairly, and candidly. Let him answer with facts and not with arguments. Let him remember he sits where Washington sat, and so remembering, let him answer as Washington would answer. As a nation should not, and the Almighty will not, be evaded, so let him attempt no evasion—no equivocation. And if, so answering, he can show that the soil was ours where the first blood of the war was shed—then I am with him."

And if the President refused to answer or set up pretenses that there was nothing to answer? "Then I shall be fully convinced of what I more than suspect already—that he is deeply conscious of being in the wrong; that he feels the blood of this war, like the blood of Abel crying to Heaven against him."

He dramatized James K. Polk. "Originally having some strong motive to involve the two countries in a war, and trusting to escape scrutiny by fixing the public gaze upon the exceeding brightness of military glory—that attractive rainbow that rises in showers of blood—that serpent's eye that charms to destroy— he plunged into it, and has swept on and on till, disappointed in his calculations of the ease with which Mexico might be sub-dued, he now finds himself he knows not where.

"How like the half-insane mumbling of a fever-dream is the whole war part of his late message! At one time telling us that Mexico has nothing whatever that we can get but territory; at another showing us how we can support the war by levying con-tributions on Mexico.

"The President is in no wise satisfied with his own positions. First he takes up one, and in attempting to argue us into it he argues himself out of it, then seizes another and goes through the same process, and then, confused at being able to think of nothing new, he snatches up the old one again. His mind, taxed beyond its power, is running hither and thither, like some tortured creature on a burning surface, finding no position on which it can settle down and be at ease. . . .

"He knows not where he is. He is a bewildered, confounded, and miserably perplexed man. God grant he may be able to show there is not something about his conscience more painful than all his mental perplexity."

If Lincoln could have known what had happened in the White House, he would have known that, behind its closed doors, two men saw President Polk every day and did their best to push him into taking all of Mexico. The two men were James Buchanan of Pennsylvania, Secretary of State, and Robert J. Walker of Mississippi, Secretary of the Treasury.

For months the President hesitated; he was precisely what Lincoln had characterized him, a bewildered, confounded, and miserably perplexed man. Of Walker the President noted in his diary, "He was for taking all of Mexico"; of Buchanan the notation was similar. Finally, he wrote in his diary, after endless advice to seize the whole territory of the Mexican nation: "I replied that I was not prepared to go to that extent, and furthermore, that I did not desire that anything I said should be so obscure as to give rise to doubt or discussion as to what my true meaning was; that I had in my last message declared that I did not contemplate the conquest of Mexico."

In rehearsing the start of the Mexican War, Lincoln for the first time told in public his views about revolutions and the rights of peoples to revolutionize. His declarations had a breath of the smoky days of Washington, Jefferson, and the American Revolution. "Any people anywhere being inclined and having the power have the right to rise up and shake off the existing government, and form a new one that suits them better. This is a most valuable, a most sacred right—a right which we hope and believe is to liberate the world. Nor is this right confined to cases in which the whole people of an existing government may choose to exercise it.

"Any portion of such people that can may revolutionize and make their own of so much of the territory as they inhabit. More than this, a majority of any portion of such people may revolutionize, putting down a minority, intermingled with or near about them, who may oppose this movement. Such minority was precisely the case of the Tories of our own revolution. It is a quality of revolutions not to go by old lines or old laws; but to break up both, and make new ones."

All of Mexico, including Texas, he pointed out, had revolution- ized against Spain, after which Texas revolutionized against Mex- ico, raising the question of just how far the boundary-line ran that was fixed by the Texas revolution. So far as Lincoln could learn, the "spot" where the first blood of the war was shed was outside the Texas line and over in Mexican territory. It, the spot, was located between two rivers on a strip of land over which the United States government did—or did not—exercise jurisdic- tion. And Lincoln was trying to get President Polk to tell just how far the jurisdiction of the United States was exercised over that strip of land—if at all.

He used his own house and lot in Springfield, his ownership of it, to illustrate his point. "It is possible that jurisdiction may be exercised between two rivers without covering all the country between them. I know a man, not very unlike myself, who ex- ercises jurisdiction over a piece of land between the Wabash and the Mississippi; and yet so far is this from being all there is between those two rivers that it is just one hundred and fifty- two feet long by fifty feet wide, and no part of it much within a hundred miles of either (river). He has a neighbor between him and the Mississippi—that is, just across the street, in that direc- tion—whom I am sure he could neither persuade nor force to give up his habitation; but which nevertheless he could certainly annex, if it were to be done by merely standing on his own side of the street and claiming it, or even sitting down and writing a deed for it."

He voted for all supplies for soldiers, for every help to the fighting men in the field, yet also for every possible measure that would lay blame on President Polk and the administration. He hoped the folks back home would understand from his speeches how he looked at the war. But the folks back home refused to understand.

Even Bill Herndon couldn't see it. He wrote Herndon:

You fear that you and I disagree about the war. I regret this . . . because if you misunderstand I fear other good friends may also. I will stake my life that if you had been in my place you would have voted just as I did. Would you have voted what you felt and knew to be a lie? I know you would not. Would you have gone out of the House—skulked the vote? I expect not. If you had skulked one vote you would have had to skulk many more before the end of the session. No man can be silent if he would. You are compelled to speak; and your only alternative is to tell the truth or a lie. I cannot doubt which you would do.

He named Whig congressmen, who had been officers through some of the fiercest fighting in Mexico; they were voting to condemn the war, the administration and the conduct of the President. He closed the letter to Herndon:

I do not mean this letter for the public, but for you. Before it reaches you, you will have seen and read my pamphlet speech, and perhaps been scared anew by it. After you get over your scare, read it over again, sentence by sentence, and tell me honestly what you think of it.

What bothered Herndon and others back home was a resolution maneuvered through Congress by the Whigs, voicing thanks to the officers of the Mexican War—with a stinger for the Polk administration. It added to the thanks the words, "in a war unnecessarily and unconstitutionally begun by the President of the United States." The vote was 82 to 81.

In a second letter to Herndon, Lincoln explained that the President of the United States is the same as a king, in power, if he can do what President Polk had done in commencing the Mexican War:

Allow the President to invade a neighboring nation whenever he shall deem it necessary to repel an invasion, and you allow him to do so whenever he may choose to say he deems it necessary for such purpose, and you allow him to make war at pleasure. Study to see if you can fix any limit to his power in this respect. If today he should choose to say he thinks it necessary to invade Canada to prevent the British from invading us, how could you stop him? You may say to him, "I see no probability of the British invading us"; but he will say to you, "Be silent: I see it, if you don't."

The Constitution gave the war-making powers to Congress, as Lincoln understood it, by this reasoning:

Kings had always been involving and impoverishing their people in wars, pretending generally, if not always, that the good of the people was the object. This our convention understood to be the most oppressive of all kingly oppressions, and they resolved to so frame the Constitution that no one man should hold the power of bringing this oppression upon us. But your view destroys the whole matter, and places our President where kings have always stood.

His guess was correct that if Herndon was misunderstanding there would be others misunderstanding. The *Belleville Advocate* for March 2 came along with a report of a meeting in Clark County of patriotic Whigs and Democrats who adopted this declaration: "Resolved, That Abe Lincoln, the author of the 'spotty' resolutions in Congress, against his own country, may they long be remembered by his constituents, but may they cease to remember him, except to rebuke him—they have done much for him, but he has done nothing for them, save in the part they have taken in their country's cause." The *Illinois State Register* was telling its readers of newspapers and public meetings that declared Lincoln to be "a second Benedict Arnold."

To Rev. J. M. Peck, Lincoln wrote a letter. The minister had spoken at a Belleville celebration of the battle of Buena Vista, saying, after an exhibit of facts, "In view of all the facts, the conviction to my mind is irresistible that the Government of the United States committed no aggression on Mexico." To him Lincoln wrote: "Not in view of all the facts. There are facts which you have kept out of view." And he went on:

It is a fact that the United States army in marching to the Rio Grande marched into a peaceful Mexican settlement, and frightened the inhabitants away from their homes and their growing crops. It is a fact that Fort Brown, opposite Matamoras, was built by that army within a Mexican cotton-field, on which at the time the army reached it a young cotton crop was growing, and which crop was wholly destroyed and the field itself greatly and permanently injured by ditches, embankments, and the like. It is a fact that when the Mexicans captured Captain Thornton and his command, they found and captured them within another Mexican field.

Now I wish to bring these facts to your notice, and to ascertain what is the result of your reflections on them. If you deny that they are facts, I think I can furnish proof which shall convince you that you are mistaken. If you admit that they are facts, then I shall be obliged for a reference to any law of language, law of States, law of nations, law of morals, law of religions, any law, human or divine, in which an authority can be found for saying those facts constitute "no aggression." Possibly you consider those acts too small for notice. Would you venture to so consider them had they been committed by any nation on earth against the humblest of our people? I know you would not. Then I ask, is the precept, "Whatsoever ye would that men should do to you, do ye even so to them" obsolete? of no force? of no application? I shall be pleased if you can find leisure to write me.

Lincoln went to the State Department, sleuthing for facts, trying to satisfy himself that the treaty signed between Mexico and the Republic of Texas had been copied correctly from the original for its publication in the newspaper *Niles Register*. And what he learned at the State Department indicated that President Polk had never sent to that department for its official copy of the treaty, and that the President had based his statements about the document from reading the copy of it published in *Niles Register*.

So Lincoln told Congress, with a shade of a quizzical tone, "If any one should suppose that *Niles Register* is a curious repository of so mighty a document as a solemn treaty between nations, I can only say that I learned to a tolerable degree of certainty, by inquiry at the State Department, that the President himself never saw it anywhere else."

One evening at the library of the Supreme Court, after digging in many books and documents, he drew out volumes to read in his room at Mrs. Spriggs's boarding-house. The library was going to close for the night. And he took his books, piled them on a table, pulled a large bandanna out of his hip pocket, tied it around the books, ran a stick through the knots, slung the stick over his shoulder, and walked out of the library of the Supreme Court in the way natural to him, in the way he carried his earthly belongings from his canoe on the Sangamon River up into the town of New Salem when he was going to clerk in Offut's store. Over his shoulder was a short circular blue cloak he had bought since he came to Washington.

Thus he walked to his Capitol Hill lodging, where he untied the knots of his handkerchief bundle, read his books, took a brass key from his vest pocket and wound his watch, read his books, put his boot-heels into a bootjack and pulled off his boots, blew out the candlelights and crept into a warm yellow flannel night-shirt that came down halfway between his knees and ankles. Then he slept the sleep of a man who had been searching Washington dissatisfied with mere claims, looking for the foundations of claims.

He may have dreamed of old Tom Lincoln writing for money and pleading, "I haven't a thing I could sell."

And there was a sweetness in Tom writing, "The Old Woman is well."

Chapter 76

ONE morning in February of 1848 a man sat at his desk in the House of Representatives writing a piece of poetry. He was an old man; he had been born in 1767, or seven years before the Revolutionary War commenced with the firing of shots at Lexington; and he was a very practical man, even though on this morning, as the House was called to order for business, he was writing a piece of poetry.

A resolution was introduced expressing thanks to the generals of the Mexican War for their brave conduct and skilled strategy; the clerk had read, "Resolved by the House, That"—when there was a cry and a stir and the members of the House looked toward the old man; he had stood up as if he might speak once more from the floor where he had spoken hundreds of times; he clutched his desk with groping, convulsive fingers, then he sank back into his chair with a slump; a friend and two doctors carried him to a sofa and he was taken first into the rotunda and then into the Speaker's room. Mustard poultices were placed on his chest and back; he was rubbed and given a friction treatment.

About an hour afterward he spoke a few words. "This is the last of earth, but I am content." His wife, relatives, and friends stood by his side; one was Henry Clay of Kentucky, who held the old man's hand and looked into the old man's face, while tears came into his eyes. At the funeral services in Washington one Representative from each state was in attendance; they escorted the body to Faneuil Hall in Boston; the body was laid in a grave in Quincy, Massachusetts.

This was the end of John Quincy Adams, his life, career, and works. For seventeen years he had been a member of Congress; during eight of those years he had fought against the "gag rule" by which Congress voted against any petitions relating to slavery being received; each year the majority against him was less until the gag rule was beaten; he had been President of the United States from 1825 to 1829, and before that was Secretary of State under President Monroe and had more of a hand in writing the Monroe Doctrine than did Monroe; earlier yet he had been in London and Paris at work with Henry Clay and Albert Gallatin on the treaty that ended the War of 1812.

This same John Quincy Adams saw Napoleon come back to Paris from Elba; he was in Russia representing President Madison at the time the armies of Napoleon were burned out of Moscow and sent reeling and harried back toward France; before that he had been a professor of rhetoric and oratory at Harvard University; he had come to Harvard after serving as United States Senator from Massachusetts and helping President Jefferson make the Louisiana Purchase; Washington had appointed him Minister to Portugal, after which his father, President John Adams, sent him to Berlin; before his graduation from Harvard he had served as a secretary to the American commissioners who negotiated the treaty of peace that ended the Revolutionary War in 1782; the year before that he was with the American envoy to Russia, following university studies at Paris and Leipzig.

A sweet, lovable man who had led a clean life full of hard work, steady habits, many dangers, furious enemies, such was John Quincy Adams. Most of the days of his life he got out of bed and put on his clothes before half-past four in the morning, and then read one or two chapters in the Bible. When in Washington he took a swim every morning, summer and winter, in the Potomac River. He was a little undersized, wore delicate sideburns, had a mouth with the peace of God on it, and spoke often as though his body was a rented house and John Quincy Adams would step out of the tenement and live on. His last words there in February of 1848 fitted him. "This is the last of earth, but I am content."

One day four years before he died, John Quincy Adams of Massachusetts wrote four little verses to another congressman, Alexander Stephens of Georgia, the wizened, wry, dry member, weighing less than a hundred pounds, known to Jefferson Davis as "the little pale star from Georgia." The verses were titled "To Alexander H. Stephens, Esq., of Georgia," and two of them read:

> We meet as strangers in this hall,
>   But when our task of duty's done,
> We blend the common good of all
>   And melt the multitude in one.

> As strangers in this hall we met;
>   But now with one united heart,
> Whate'er of life awaits us yet,
>   In cordial friendship let us part.

He drew men to him, this Alexander Stephens; in his black eyes, set deep in a large-boned, homely head, there was a smolder by which men knew he would play politics only so far, after which a personal sincerity must be considered. He stood up one day to speak on the Mexican War and declared: "All wars, to be just, must have some distinct and legitimate objects to be accomplished. . . . One of the strangest . . . circumstances attending this war is, that though it has lasted upwards of eight

Washington, Feb. 2. 1848

Dear William

    I just take up my pen to say, that Mr. Stephens of Georgia, a little slim, pale-faced, consumptive man, with a voice like Logan's, has just concluded, the very best speech, of an hours length, I ever heard. My old, withered, dry eyes, are full of tears yet. If he writes it out any thing like he delivered it, our people shall see a good many copies of it—

             Yours truly

             A. Lincoln

To W. H. Herndon

Lincoln of Illinois and Stephens of Georgia were Whig Allies and personal friends. Stephens said, "I was as intimate with Mr. Lincoln as with any other man, except perhaps Mr. Toombs." The letter above is a slightly reduced facsimile from the original in the Barrett collection.

months, at a cost of many millions of dollars, and the sacrifice of many valuable lives, both in battle and by the diseases of the camp, no man can tell for what object it is prosecuted. And it is to be doubted whether any man, save the President and his Cabinet, knows the real and secret designs that provoked its existence. To suppress inquiry, and silence all opposition to conduct so monstrous, an executive ukase has been sent forth, strongly intimating, if not clearly threatening, the charge of treason, against all who may dare to call in question the wisdom or propriety of his measures.

"It is to be seen," said Stephens, "whether the free people of this country have so soon forgotten the principles of their ancestors as to be so easily awed by the arrogance of power. For a very little further interference with the freedom of discussion, Charles X, of France, lost his throne; and for a very little greater stretch of royal prerogative, Charles I, of England, lost his head. There are some things more to be dreaded than the loss of a throne, or even the loss of a head—amongst which may be named the anathema of a nation's curse, and the infamy that usually follows it."

And it happened that on February 2, 1848, while sitting at his desk in the House of Representatives, Abraham Lincoln wrote a note to his law partner, Herndon, saying: "I just take up my pen to say that Mr. Stephens, of Georgia, a little slim, pale-faced, consumptive man, with a voice like Logan's, has just concluded the best speech, of an hour's length, I ever heard. My old, withered, dry eyes are full of tears yet. If he writes it out anything like he delivered it, our people shall see a good many copies of it."

Chapter 77

LINCOLN got "the hang of the House," as he called it, and made speeches on internal improvements, public roads, rivers, harbors, canals, saying in one speech that so far as he could see there was the same wrangling in state legislatures and in counties and towns as there was in the national Congress, over improvements. "One man is offended because a road passes over his land, and another is offended because it does not pass over his; one is dissatisfied because the bridge for which he is taxed crosses the river on a different road from that which leads from his house to the town; another cannot bear that the county should be got in debt for these same roads and bridges; while not a few struggle hard to have roads located over their lands, and then stoutly refuse to let them be opened until they are first paid the damages."

As a first step toward fair dealing out of the nation's money for needed improvements among the states, Lincoln suggested statistical information to guide congressmen, saying he did not see much force in one member's objection "to counting all the pigs and chickens in the land." Though the speech was mainly constructive and practical, it was lighted with the observation: "An honest laborer digs coal at about seventy cents a day, while the President digs abstractions at about seventy dollars a day. The coal is clearly worth more than the abstractions."

Mainly, the speech was coaxing, advisory, conciliatory, hoping to get practical work done. "Difficulty though there be, let us meet and encounter it. Determine that the thing can and shall be done, and then we shall find the way. Let each contribute his mite in the way of suggestion." He was voicing the wishes of the Chicago river and harbor convention. To pay for canals with canal tolls and tonnage duties, before canals were dug, was like the Irishman and his new boots. "I shall niver git 'em on till I wear 'em a day or two, and stretch 'em a little."

Often during the first half of the year 1848, Lincoln was rushed with work. He wrote Archibald Williams a letter about politics, closing: "Excuse this short letter. I have so many to write that I cannot devote much time to any one. Yours, as ever." And to Richard Thomas: "Excuse the shortness of this letter; I am really very much hurried. Yours, as ever." And again to Thomas, "In great haste, yours as ever."

Tacked on to some of his letters were the abrupt, odd postscripts of a quizzical man of affairs. To one: "Taylorism seems to be going right, for which I am glad. Keep the ball rolling." To Andrew McCallen: "Don't pay postage on letters to me. I am entitled to them free." To Samuel Marshall, at Shawnee-town, Illinois, after short news about a law case, "As to the matter of your lost horse, I will look into it, & do something if I can."

And to his old friend Richard Thomas he had to explain he had no influence with President Polk. "As to Mr. Graham's application for a Lieutenancy, I have already submitted it to the President in the best way I could think of it to give it success. I wrote him about it; and do not know anything more that I can do for him. You know I can have no intimacy with the President, which might give me personal influence over him."

In replying to Rev. Henry Slicer, who had written to ask why he was excluded from the funeral services of John Quincy Adams, Lincoln wrote that he had not been consulted, knew nothing about it, and, "So entirely ignorant was I, in relation to your having been excluded from the funeral services of Mr. Adams, that, until I received your letter, I should have given it as my recollection, that you actually did participate in those services." He advised E. B. Washburne on a political campaign matter, "Make Baker help about it. He is a good man to raise a breeze."

Lincoln turned out dozens of letters a day, "fixing his political fences." He ordered *The Battery*, a Whig campaign paper, sent to S. A. Hurlbut at Belvidere, Illinois, and wrote: "If it strikes you as giving promise of being a good campaign paper, please get as many subscribers as you can and send them on—I have put you down for one copy, the subscription for which I will pay myself if you are not satisfied with it."

Back in Sangamon and other counties of his district were Whigs who wanted to be officers in the army. They wrote Lincoln to get them commissions from the Democratic Administration. He wrote to the Springfield postmaster: "The thing that perplexes me more than most anything else, are the cases of Whigs calling on me to get them appointments to places in the army, from the

President. There are two great obstacles in the way which they do not understand—first, the President has no such appointments to give—and secondly, if he had, he could hardly be expected to give them to Whigs, at the solicitation of a Whig member of Congress."

One February day in 1848, a scandal arose from an affair at Mrs. Spriggs's boarding-house. The negro servant in the house had been buying his freedom at a price of $300.00; he had paid all but $60.00 when, one day, two white men came to the house, knocked him down, tied and gagged him, took him to a slave jail, and had him sent to New Orleans for sale. Joshua Giddings of Ohio asked for a hearing by Congress to get at the facts; he was voted down by 98 to 88.

Giddings and Lincoln enjoyed each other's company. Lincoln was not radical in Giddings's way. But both the men had streaks of stubborn and personal quality. Each was meek about picking a fight. Giddings had made a speech in Congress a few years previously, taking a violent stand against slavery. A southern member had lurched against Giddings, shoved Giddings out of an aisle, and thrust a right hand into a vest pocket as if he might have a bowie knife there. Giddings inquired, "Did you push me?" "I did." "Intentionally?" "Yes." "For the purpose of insult?" "Yes." "Well, sir, we are in the habit of leaving men who wantonly insult others to the contempt of public opinion." At that point, friends from North and South interfered.

Chapter 78

ALEXANDER STEPHENS in telling about friendships in the Thirtieth Congress said, "I was as intimate with Mr. Lincoln as with any other man except perhaps Mr. Toombs." They had comradeship; scrawls of personal tragedy, pinches of hunger and fate, were on their two faces; yet they had depths of clean laughter together.

Whereas men looked up toward Lincoln's head and asked,

"How's the weather up there?" Stephens said, "Men address me familiarly as 'my son'; such often happens to me." Each felt it uphill work to act the part of a Great Man. Stephens once wrote in a diary: "I believe I shall never be worth anything, and the thought is death to my soul. I am too boyish, unmanful, trifling, simple in my manners and address."

Both were uneasy amid women, Stephens once writing in his diary after examining drawings of ancient statues: "With the Gladiator and Venus I am delighted. Pity but some of our fashionable belles would take a lesson from this form of true grace, the Venus; they would change their present disgusting waspish shape."

Both had stories mocking at their dignity as lawyers. Stephens used to pass a shoe-shop in Crawfordsville, Georgia, and heard a voice, "Who is that little fellow that walks so fast by here every day?" and a replying sarcastic voice, "Why, *that's* a *lawyer!*" And he had visited a farmer uncle in Pennsylvania who asked at family dinner, "What business do you follow, Alex?" "I am a lawyer, Uncle." Then silence, broken by the uncle's husky voice, "Alex, don't you have to tell lies?"

Stephens, Lincoln and five other Whigs, in the winter of 1847-48, organized the Taylor Club, with members nicknamed the Young Indians. They saw that the Whig war hero, who had protested against leading his troops onto Mexican soil and starting a war of invasion, and then had obeyed orders and gone in and fought as a wildcat from hell, would make a candidate the Democrats couldn't keep from getting into the White House.

How to get Taylor nominated was the high point with the Young Indians. Lincoln sent many letters west urging Taylor as the candidate who would take the Democrats "on the blind side." Stephens worked with connections South and North. He noticed that Taylor speakers in New York were howled down and Taylor meetings broken up by the Dead Rabbits and Bowery Boys whose fists were at the service of Whig politicians who didn't consider Zach Taylor in their plans.

And Stephens got Toombs, the affable, persuasive, companionable Toombs, to go to New York and pay two hundred dollars to "Isaiah Rhynders, captain among roughs and shoulder-hitters," for "a fair and uninterrupted hearing from a New York audience in behalf of Taylor."

Rhynders met Toombs at the Astor House, and, as Stephens told it, "entered cheerfully into the engagement, and said it would cost two hundred dollars: it would require that to secure the necessary force. Toombs closed with him. At a certain noted saloon Toombs went and met the captain and his subal-terns, Bill Ford, Sullivan, and other noted boxers. Nothing passed but such agreeable chat as Toombs knew how to give in his peculiar style, and the glass to his company."

A large audience came to the meeting on the following night; leading Taylor politicians were on hand; one introduced Toombs, who as the orator of the evening began, "Fellow Citizens of New York," when yells shot out: "Slaveholder! Slaveholder!" Toombs was quiet a moment, took a fresh start, and then yells came: "Hurrah for Clay! Hurrah for Clay!" Cool and un-ruffled, Toombs stood at ease, commenced once more, and then, as Stephens told the events: "There was the greatest row you ever saw. 'Put him out!' rang from one side of the hall to the other, and everywhere a stalwart arm was seen pitching some fellow out. Rhynders' men were at work. Some who were being pitched out exclaimed: 'I made no noise,' and the reply was, 'You have chalk on your back and you've got to go.' In two minutes the hall was cleared of some forty 'chalk-backs.' " Rhynders had scattered his men through the audience, marked the backs of all who yelled interruptions, and on the cry "Put them out!" all chalk-backs were hustled to the doors and thrown into the street.

"The audience was quiet and orderly while Toombs gave them one of his masterly harangues," said Stephens. "The wildest enthusiasm prevailed, loud shouts of applause went up, and then came 'Three cheers for old Zach!' given with a vim as Toombs took his seat. Our victory was complete; we had a foothold in New York; our battery in that stronghold of the enemy did effective work. Great events often turn on small ones."

In their philosophy of direct political action both Stephens and Lincoln took into reckoning that element Lincoln indicated in writing Herndon that year to be sure to line up "the wild shrewd boys."

Chapter 79

LINCOLN went to Philadelphia in June as a delegate to the national convention of the Whig party and helped nominate General Zachary Taylor, the hero of the Mexican War, for president. He wrote to Illinois: "Taylor's nomination takes the Locos (Democrats) on the blind side. It turns the war thunder against them. The war is now to them the gallows of Haman, which they built for us, and on which they are doomed to be hanged themselves." And he analyzed: "One unmistakable sign [of victory] is that all the odds and ends are with us—Barnburners, Native Americans, Tyler men, disappointed office-seeking Locofocos, and the Lord knows what." The nickname "Barnburners" had been given discontented Democrats who had drawn out and formed a new organization they called the Free Soil party; they were named after the farmer who burned his barn to drive the rats out.

The Whig nomination of General Zachary Taylor had peculiar angles; he was nicknamed "Old Rough and Ready"; and he had spoken positively, before the war commenced, his view that a war was not called for; it was only when direct orders to move reached him that he took his troops to where the first blood was shed. He kept quiet on the slavery issue, and it was said that a letter to him from a southern planter read:

SIR:

I have worked hard and been frugal all my life, and the results of my industry have mainly taken the form of slaves, of whom I own about a hundred. Before I vote for President, I want to be sure that the candidate I support will not so act as to divest me of my property.

To which General Taylor, who had a plantation in Louisiana, replied:

Sir:

I have the honor to inform you that I too have been all my life industrious and frugal, and that the fruits thereof are mainly invested in slaves, of whom I own *three* hundred.

Yours,

One day in July, Lincoln stood up on the floor and began remarks that carried him striding back and forth up the aisle of the house. It was a stump speech that had the champing of a campaign war-horse in it, with a sniffing of defiance and contempt for the enemy, and a snorting of challenge for the opposition to come on and do battle. It was the kind of horse-play that veteran stump speakers use to send the farmers home refreshed and perhaps convinced. He lammed and lambasted General Lewis Cass, of Michigan, the Democratic nominee for President. It was rough-and-tumble, meant to "raise a breeze."

Lincoln pictured the Democrats' use of General Jackson's nickname, "Old Hickory." "Hickory poles and hickory brooms your never-ending emblems, even now your campaign paper here is proclaiming that Cass and Butler are of 'Hickory stripe.' Like a horde of hungry ticks you have stuck to the tail of the Hermitage lion to the end of his life; and you are still sticking to it, and drawing a loathsome sustenance from it, after he is dead.

"A fellow once advertised that he had made a discovery by which he could make a new man out of an old one, and have enough of the stuff left to make a yellow dog. Just such a discovery has General Jackson's popularity been to you. You not only twice made President of him out of it, but you have had enough of the stuff left to make Presidents out of several comparatively small men since; and it is your chief reliance now to make still another."

Then came pointed mockery and the bubbling jokes that across southern Illinois had given the name of Abe Lincoln a special tang. The Democrats were trying to make a heroic military figure out of their presidential candidate, General Cass, who had been a volunteer aid to General Harrison at the battle of the Thames, and had held a command during an Indian war. So Lincoln pitched in: "Mr. Speaker, old horses and military coat-tails, or tails of any sort, are not figures of speech such as I would be the first to introduce into discussions here; but as the gentleman from Georgia has thought fit to introduce them, he and you are welcome to all you have made or can make by them. If you have any more old horses, trot them out; any more tails, just cock them and come at us. I repeat, I would not introduce this mode of discussion here; but I wish gentlemen on the other side to understand that the use of degrading figures is a game at which they may not find themselves able to take all the winnings. ('We give it up!') Aye, you give it up, and well you may. The point—the power to hurt—of all figures consists in the truthfulness of their application. They are weapons which hit you, but miss us.

"But in my hurry I was very near closing this subject of military tails before I was done with it. There is one entire article of the sort I have not discussed yet—I mean the military tail you Democrats are now engaged in dovetailing into the great Michigander [General Cass]. Yes, sir; all his biographies have him in hand, tying him to a military tail like so many mischievous boys tying a dog to a bladder of beans. True, the material they have is very limited, but they drive at it with might and main. He *in*vaded Canada without resistance, and he *out*vaded it without pursuit. As he did both under orders, I suppose there was to him neither credit nor discredit in them; but they constitute a large part of the tail He was volunteer aid to General Harrison on the day of the battle of the Thames; and as you said in 1840 Harrison was picking huckleberries two miles off while the battle was fought, I suppose it is a just conclusion with you to say Cass was aiding Harrison to pick huckleberries.

"By the way, Mr. Speaker, did you know I am a military hero? Yes, sir; in the days of the Black Hawk War I fought.

bled, and came away. If General Cass went ahead of me in picking huckleberries, I guess I surpassed him in charges upon the wild onions. If he saw any live, fighting Indians it was more than I did; but I had a good many bloody struggles with the mosquitoes, and although I never fainted from the loss of blood, I can truly say I was often very hungry. Mr. Speaker, if ever I should conclude to doff whatever our Democratic friends may suppose there is of black-cockade federalism about me, and therefore they shall take me up as their candidate for the Presidency, I protest they shall not make fun of me, as they have of General Cass, by attempting to write me into a military hero."

Next he took up General Cass's record while governor of the Territory of Michigan, to show that the governor drew $1,500.00 a year for office rent and clerk hire as Superintendent of Indian Affairs without really having a separate office or hired clerk. Then he passed to the matter of General Cass during nine years drawing ten rations a day from the Government at $730.00 a year. And further: "At eating, his capacities are shown to be wonderful. From October, 1821, to May, 1822, he ate ten rations a day in Michigan, ten rations a day here in Washington, and near five dollars' worth a day on the road between the two places! There is an important discovery in his example—the art of being paid for what one eats, instead of having to pay for it. Hereafter, if any nice young man should owe a bill which he cannot pay in any other way, he can just board it out.

"Mr. Speaker, we have all heard of the animal standing in doubt between two stacks of hay and starving to death. The like of that would never happen to General Cass. Place the stacks a thousand miles apart, he would stand stock-still midway between them, and eat them both at once, and the green grass along the line would be apt to suffer some, too, at the same time. By all means, make him President, gentlemen. He will feed you bounteously—if—if there is any left after he shall have helped himself."

The moment came when he had only three minutes left and had to close. He spoke of splits and breaks in the Democratic party ranks, and wound up: "I have heard some things from New York; and if they are true, one might well say of your party there, as a drunken fellow once said when he heard the reading of an indictment for hog-stealing. The clerk read on till he got to and through the words, 'did steal, take, and carry away ten boars, ten sows, ten shoats, and ten pigs,' at which he exclaimed, 'Well, by golly, that is the most equally divided gang of hogs I ever did hear of!' If there is any other gang of hogs more equally divided than the Democrats of New York are about this time, I have not heard of it."

The *Baltimore American* said the speaker kept the House roaring. "He would commence a point in his speech far up one of the aisles, and keep on talking, gesticulating, and walking until he would find himself, at the end of a paragraph, down in the center of the area in front of the clerk's desk. He would then go back and take another *head*, and *work down* again. And so on." The paper hit off Lincoln as "a very able, acute, uncouth, honest, upright man, and a tremendous wag withal."

Lincoln had his personal ways, his own methods of playing politics. A first element to line up, in his plans, was the young men, especially the shrewd, wild boys such as those who were his never-failing guards in Sangamon County, at Clary's Grove, Sand Ridge, and Wolf Creek.

He wrote to Herndon: "As to the young men, you must not wait to be brought forward by the older men. For instance, do you suppose that I should ever have got into notice if I had waited to be hunted up and pushed forward by older men? You young men get together and form a 'Rough and Ready Club' and have regular meetings and speeches. Take in everybody you can get. As you go along gather up all the shrewd, wild boys about town, whether just of age or a little under age,— Chris Logan, Reddick Ridgely, Lewis Zwizler, and hundreds such. Let every one play the part he can play best,—some speak, some sing, and all 'holler.' Your meetings will be of evenings; the older men, and the women, will go to hear you; so that it will not only contribute to the election of 'Old Zach,' but will

be an interesting pastime, and improving to the intellectual fac‑
ulties of all engaged. Don't fail to do this."

Then he went on to write a line and speak in a tone he didn't
use often. "This makes me a little impatient," he told Herndon.
The last letter from Herndon had asked for all the speeches
made in Congress about General Taylor, the Mexican War, and
campaign issues. He explained: "I have regularly sent you the
'Congressional Globe' and 'Appendix,' and you cannot have ex‑
amined them, or you would have discovered that they contain
every speech made by every man in both houses of Congress,
on every subject during the session. Can I send any more?
Can I send speeches that nobody has made?"

Lincoln was trying to figure out what had happened back home.
The Whig newspapers were not publishing the speeches of Whig
congressmen as they should. "With the exception of my own
little speech which was published in two of the then five, now
four, Whig papers, I do not remember having seen a single
speech or even extract from one, in any single one of those
papers."

And he was trying to figure where Herndon had been keeping
himself; he knew Herndon was a widely read scholar and lost
himself in books sometimes, and, too, that Herndon was a hard
drinker when he drank and lost himself at the taverns some‑
times. He wrote: "You ask how Congress came to declare that
war had existed by the act of Mexico. Is it possible you don't
understand that yet? You have at least twenty speeches in
your possession that fully explain it."

And he wrote wearily, "I will, however, try it once more," and
launched off into a complete statement unraveling in a simple
way what went on in Congress, how the Whigs were forced to
vote that war existed by act of Mexico or else vote against
money and supplies for the soldiers in the field. "They did not
want to vote against sending help to General Taylor, and there‑
fore they voted for both together. Is there any difficulty in
understanding this? Even my little speech shows how this
was."

Then from the young partner and friend at Springfield came a bitter letter. And the older man at Washington wrote that he was young once—but now he was no longer young. "Your letter is exceedingly painful to me; and I cannot but think there is some mistake in your impression of the motives of the old men. I suppose I am now one of the old men; and I declare, on my veracity, which I think is good with you, that nothing could afford me more satisfaction than to learn that you and others of my young friends are doing battle in the contest, and endearing themselves to the people, and taking a stand far above any I have ever been able to reach in their admiration. I cannot conceive that other old men feel differently. Of course I cannot demonstrate what I say; but I was young once, and I am sure I was never ungenerously thrust back. I hardly know what to say. The way for a young man to rise is to improve himself every way he can, never suspecting that anybody wishes to hinder him.

"Allow me to assure you that suspicion and jealousy never did help any man in any situation. There may sometimes be ungenerous attempts to keep a young man down; and they will succeed, too, if he allows his mind to be diverted from its true channel to brood over the attempted injury. Cast about, and see if this feeling has not injured every person you have ever known to fall into it."

They were two fine friends. The older man tried to reach across the Alleghenies and the plains and tell it. "In what I have said, I am sure you will suspect nothing but sincere friendship. I would save you from a fatal error. You have been a laborious, studious young man. You are far better informed on almost all subjects than I have ever been. You cannot fail in any laudable object, unless you allow your mind to be improperly directed. I have somewhat the advantage of you in the world's experience, merely by being older; and it is this that induces me to advise."

Yes, Lincoln was growing older. He wrote notes, memoranda, on what he thought General Taylor ought to say as presidential candidate. "Were I President, I" should do so and so, on the tariff, the national debt, a national bank. And, "In the final treaty of peace [with Mexico], we shall probably be under the necessity of taking some territory; but it is my desire that we shall not acquire any extending so far south as to enlarge and aggravate the distracting question of slavery."

Back pay was due Joseph Ferguson, who had died in Mexican War service. The father of the soldier was writing from Springfield to Lincoln, "I am very much in want of the money and would be glad to have you call and obtain it immediately and forward the same to me without delay." And Lincoln made calls at the War Department in Washington until the matter was adjusted.

Sometimes his past, of the days before he was born, interested him. A Shenandoah Valley congressman mentioned the Lincolns of Rockingham County, Virginia. It was there his grandfather, Abraham Lincoln, had lived. He wrote to one David Lincoln, at Sparta, Virginia, and was told that the Lincolns of Virginia had come from Berks County, Pennsylvania. Several letters passed between the congressman and David Lincoln about their kinfolk. But later, in writing to a Jesse Lincoln in Tennessee, Abraham referred to David of Virginia, saying, "I forget, if he informed me, which of my grandfather's brothers was his father." He was interested in his genealogy, but not enthusiastic. On Christmas Eve of 1848, he sent his father twenty dollars, as asked for, and wrote a letter with kindly, sly digs at the poor excuses offered by Tom Lincoln in asking for the money.

Chapter 80

LINCOLN delivered a speech in Congress on July 27 of 1848 in which he outlined a portrait or sketched a cartoon of another politician. Yet in his very caricature of another man there was a report of himself, a revelation of what he would rather quit politics than to be and do. In fact, he knew he was slipping in popularity and influence at home because of his refusal to be obedient to public opinion on the Mexican War issue.

He analyzed the wiggling weasel course of General Lewis Cass, the Democratic presidential candidate, on the Wilmot Proviso. In 1846 General Cass was for the Proviso at once; in March, 1847, he was still for it, but not just then; in December, 1847, he was against it altogether. "This is a true index to the whole man," declared Lincoln. "When the question was raised in 1846, he was in a blustering hurry to take ground for it. He sought to be in advance, to avoid the uninteresting position of a mere follower; but soon he began to see glimpses of the great Democratic ox-gad waving in his face, and to hear indistinctly a voice saying: 'Back! Back, sir, back a little!' He shakes his head and bats his eyes and blunders back to his position of March, 1847; but still the gad waves, and the voice grows more distinct and sharper still, 'Back, sir! Back, I say!'—and back he goes to the position of December, 1847, at which the gad is still, and the voice soothingly says: 'So! Stand at that.'"

The style of the speech was "scathing and withering," a newspaper commented. Lincoln wasn't always humble. He could be cutting and scornful.

Chapter 81

LINCOLN had decided after a short stay of his wife in Washington that it would be best for her to return to Springfield, which she did. When again she wished to go East she wrote to him asking him about it as though in such a case it was for her to ask and for him to advise or decide.

He signs his letters to her, "Affectionately" or "Most Affectionately," and the name "A. Lincoln." She signs her letters, "Truly yours," and initials and dash, "M. L——." His salutation is "My Dear Wife" or "Dear Mary," and hers "My Dear Husband."

He wrote her he hated to sit down and direct documents back

to Illinois voters, and he hated to be in an old boarding-house room by himself. While she was there he had thought she hindered him in attending business, but since then, having nothing but business, no variety, the daily routine had grown tasteless

All of the boarders with whom she was on decided good terms, he wrote, sent their love to her, while the others of the house were saying nothing. He has been shopping in the stores of Washington, as she asked, but cannot find a pair of plaid stockings of any sort to fit "Eddy's dear little feet."

He wished her to enjoy herself in every possible way, he wrote, but as to her open intimacy with a certain Wickliffe family he asked if there were not danger of her wounding the feelings of her own good father.

One letter Lincoln wrote to his wife that year, read, in full, as follows:

Washington, July 2, 1848.

My dear wife:
Your letter of last sunday came last night— On that day (sunday) I wrote the principal part of a letter to you, but did not finish it, or send it till tuesday, when I had provided a draft for $100 which I sent in it— It is now probable that on that day (tuesday) you started to Shelbyville; so that when the money reaches Lexington, you will not be there— Before leaving, did you make any provision about letters that might come to Lexington for you? Write me whether you got the draft, if you shall not have already done so, when this reaches you— Give my kindest regards to your uncle John, and all the family— Thinking of them reminds me that I saw your acquaintance, Newton, of Arkansas, at the Philadelphia Convention— We had but a single interview, and that was so brief, and in so great a multitude of strange faces, that I am quite sure I should not recognize him, if I were to meet him again— He was a sort of Trinity, three in one, having the right, in his own person, to cast the three votes of Arkansas— Two or three days ago I sent your uncle John, and a few of our other friends each a copy of the speech I mentioned in my last letter; but I did not send any to you, thinking you would be on the road here, before it would reach you— I send you one now— Last wednesday, P. H. Hood & Co. dunned me for a little bill of $5—38 cents, and Walter Harper & Co. another for $8—50 cents, for goods which they say you bought— I hesitated to pay them, because my recollection is

Washington, July 2. 1848.

My dear wife:

Your letter of last Sunday came last night. On that day (Sunday) I wrote the envelope had of a letter to you, but did not finish it, or send it till today, when I had provided a draft for $100 while I sent in it. It is now probable that on that day (Tuesday) you wrote to Shelbyville, so that when this now you reaches Lexington, you will not be there. Before leaving, did you make any provision about letters that might come to Lexington for you? — was not whether you got the draft, if you please not have already done so, when this reaches you. Give my kindest regards to your uncle John, and all the family.

I believe he was incensed that every body who knew who it was, that have caught him.

I have had no letter from home, since I wrote you before, except a short business letter, which have no interest for you—

By the way, you are not interested to me without a girl; however, then now you have has left you? Get another as soon as you can to take charge of the old cabin—

Father expected to see you before, some come, but let it now; say to you Harry, some come when you please—

Kiss and love the dear Nances—

Affectionately
A. Lincoln.

that you told me when you went away, there was nothing left unpaid—
Mention in your next letter whether they are right—

Mrs. Richardson is still here; and what is more, has a baby—so
Richardson says, and he ought to know— I believe Mary Hewett has
left here and gone to Boston— I met her on the street about fifteen
or twenty days ago, and she told me she was going soon— I have
seen nothing of her since—

The music in the Capitol grounds on saturdays, or, rather, the interest in it, is dwindling down to nothing— Yesterday evening the
attendance was rather thin— Our two girls, whom you remember
seeing first at Canisis, at the exhibition of the Ethiopian Serenaders,
and whose peculiarities were the wearing of black fur bonnets, and
never being seen in close company with other ladies, were at the music
yesterday— One of them was attended by their brother, and the
other had a member of Congress in tow— He went home with her;
and if I were to guess, I would say, he went away a somewhat altered
man—most likely in his pockets, and in some other particular— The
fellow looked conscious of guilt, although I believe he was unconscious
that everybody around knew who it was that had caught him—

I have had no letter from home, since I wrote you before, except
short business letters, which have no interest for you—

By the way, you do not intend to do without a girl, because the one
you had has left you? Get another as soon as you can to take charge
of the dear codgers— Father expected to see you all sooner; but let
it pass; stay as long as you please, and come when you please— Kiss
and love the dear rascals—

Affectionately

A. LINCOLN.

A letter dated "Lexington, May —, 48," arrives one day from
Mrs. Lincoln; he may think old age has set its seal upon her:
"in few or none of my letters, I can remember the day of the
month. I must confess it is one of my peculiarities; I feel
wearied and tired enough to know, that this Saturday night,
our babies are asleep, and as Aunt Maria B. is coming in for
me to-morrow morning, I think the chances will be rather dull
that I should answer your last letter to-morrow."

She gives news from her sister Frances at Springfield. Willie
is recovering from another spell of sickness. As to Springfield,
she reports it "as dull as usual."

Then the family Kentucky news, "Eddie has recovered from his spell of sickness." Bobby came across a kitten, brought it to the house, Eddie spied it, fed it with bread, was delighted over it. "In the midst of his happiness Ma came in, she you must know dislikes the whole cat race, I thought in a very unfeeling manner, she ordered the servant near, to throw it out, which of course, was done, Ed—screaming and protesting loudly against the proceeding, she never appeared to mind his screams, which were long & loud, I assure you."

She sketches her mother. " 'Tis unusual for her nowadays, to do anything quite so striking, she is very obliging & accommodating, but if she thought any of us were on her hands again, I believe she would be worse than ever—In the next moment she appeared again in a good humor, I know she did not intend to offend me—By the way she has just sent up a glass of ice cream, for which this warm evening, I am duly grateful."

Then the wife in Kentucky writes to her husband in Washington wishing he and she were together. She wants to go East, join him, and visit eastern cities "sightseeing." Her uncle, James Parker of Mississippi, is to travel East to put his eldest daughter in school in Philadelphia. Why shouldn't she travel with her uncle and meet her husband in Washington?

"I believe it would be a good chance to pack up and accompany them," she writes. "You know I am so fond of sightseeing, & I did not get to New York or Boston, or travel the lake route—But perhaps dear husband cannot do without his wife next winter, and must needs take her with him again—I expect you would cry aloud against it."

She darts from topic to topic. "How much, I wish instead of writing, we were together this evening, I feel very sad away from you—Ma and myself rode out to Mr. Bell's splendid place this afternoon, to return a call, the house and grounds are magnificent, Frances would have died of their rare exotics—It is growing late, these summer eves are short, I expect my long scrawls, for truly such they are, weary you greatly."

Then came more news or chat, and, "I must bid you good

night—Do not fear the children have forgotten you, I was only jesting—Even E— eyes brighten at the mention of your name —My love to all."

Just before writing the sentence "I must bid you good night," she had written the two words "with love" and crossed them out.

Chapter 82

EARLY in September of 1848 Lincoln stumped New England for the national Whig ticket. He rode into new territory, and saw the factories, mills, shops, foundries, that made the middle Atlantic states and New England rich and powerful; regions that were almost nations by themselves; the white faces of thousands of wage-workers. He was a man immensely and intensely impressed by facts that spread before his eyesight; he could analyze, deduce, synthesize facts that came within earshot; he would pick up facts and play with them, turn them over in his mind, and make them pay out with results beyond facts.

As committees of Whigs escorted him, they felt, often, here was a sober, sad man from far west, with a strangeness they could not solve. As he loosened and lightened, they felt they knew him; he was so warmly and simply human; then he would lapse to the sober, sad face again, the slouching, angular shoulders that drooped. In Boston he saw Faneuil Hall and looked up some of its avenues and its rows of mansions past which Boston mobs, carrying ropes, had dragged agitators of the public peace. At Cambridge, near the walls of Harvard University, he delivered a speech. At Lowell, he spoke, and saw there the incessant movement of its thousands of power looms and spindles translating raw cotton fabrics to be moved on the new steam cars and the new steamships into far home and world markets.

At Worcester, he was introduced by an ex-governor of the State, Levi Lincoln; the two of them traced back to a Samuel Lincoln who had come two hundred years before to Hingham, Massachusetts; Abraham said to Levi, "I *hope* we both belong,

as the Scotch say, to the same clan; but I *know* one thing, and
that is, that we are both good Whigs." He told the state Whig
convention at Worcester that in speaking "this side of the mountains" he felt modest and referred to his home people looking
on his auditors as "instructed and wise."

The new Free Soil party reminded him of the Yankee peddler
who offered for sale a pair of pantaloons "large enough for any
man, and small enough for any boy." As to slavery, he believed
the people of Illinois agreed with the people of Massachusetts,
except perhaps that they did not keep so constantly thinking
about it.

The *Boston Advertiser* noted: "Mr. Lincoln has a very tall and
thin figure, with an intellectual face, showing a searching mind,
and a cool judgment. He spoke in a clear, cool, and very eloquent manner, for an hour and a half, carrying the audience
with him, only interrupted by warm and frequent applause."
At Cambridge a reporter sized him up as "a capital specimen
of a Sucker Whig, six feet at least in his stockings." There
were halls where his head almost scraped the ceiling. "They
were struck with his height, as he arose in the low-studded
hall."

A young Whig, George H. Monroe, and others, called at the
Tremont House in Boston to take Lincoln to Dedham for a day
speech. "He was as sober a man in point of expression as I
ever saw," said Monroe, telling about it later. "In the cars he
scarcely said a word to one of us. He seemed uneasy. . . . I
should say the atmosphere of Boston was not congenial to him.
We took him to one of the most elegant houses in the town of
Dedham, and here he seemed still less . . . at home. The thing
began to look rather blue for us. When we went over to the
hall it was not much better. It was a small hall and only about
half full; for Mr. Lincoln had not spoken in Boston yet, and
there was nothing in his name particularly to attract. But at last
he arose to speak, and almost instantly there was a change.

"His indifferent manner vanished as soon as he opened his
mouth. He went right to work. He wore a black alpaca sack,

and he turned up the sleeves of this, and then the cuffs of his shirt. Next he loosened his necktie, and soon after he took it off altogether. All the time he was gaining upon his audience. He soon had it as by a spell. I never saw men more delighted. His style was the most familiar and offhand possible. His eye had lighted up and changed the whole expression of his countenance. He began to bubble out with humor. But the chief charm of his address lay in the homely way he made his points. There was no attempt at eloquence or finish of style. But, for plain pungency of humor, it would have been difficult to surpass his speech. The speech . . . ended in a half-hour. The bell that called to the steam cars sounded. Mr. Lincoln instantly stopped. 'I am engaged to speak at Cambridge tonight and I must leave.' The whole audience seemed to rise in protest. 'Go on! Finish it!' was heard on every hand. One gentleman arose and pledged to take his horse and carry him across country. But Mr. Lincoln was inexorable."

That evening Lincoln spoke at Tremont Temple, following the speech of William H. Seward, Governor of New York, and in a few weeks to be elected United States senator. The Whig newspaper, *The Atlas,* the next morning printed a column of Seward's speech and itemized Lincoln's as "powerful and convincing, and cheered to the echo."

Governor Seward was telling his audiences that year: "The party of slavery leaves the mountain ravine and shoal to present all their natural obstacles to internal trade and free locomotion, because railroads, rivers, and canals are highways for the escape of bondsmen. The party of liberty would cover the country with railroads and canals, to promote the happiness of the people, and bind them together with the indissoluble bonds of interest and affection."

Lincoln told Seward at their hotel that night that he had been thinking about what Seward said in his speech. "I reckon you are right. We have got to deal with this slavery question, and got to give much more attention to it."

He left Boston on the steam cars one Saturday morning, and

from the windows as he traveled he saw the walls of the cotton mills, with their power-driven looms, their miles of spindles, with their bobbin boys and girls.

At Albany he stopped off and talked with Thurlow Weed, the Whig boss of New York; they went out and visited Millard Fillmore, the Whig candidate for Vice President. He rode on the Erie Canal to Buffalo, visited Niagara Falls, went down Lake Erie, and overland to Chicago and Springfield.

After visiting his family, his law partner, and friends, he turned his law-office corner into a shop where he whittled on a wooden model of a steamboat with "expansible buoyant chambers," "sliding spars," and ropes and pulleys. It was an invention, he told Herndon, and was going to work a revolution in steamboat navigation. On the way from Niagara Falls, the steamboat he was on got stuck on a sand-bar; the captain ordered barrels, boxes, and empty casks forced under the vessel; they lifted the vessel off the sand-bar with their "expansible buoyant chambers." So Lincoln finished off a model, and wrote a description of its workings, all to be patented.

Between times, he and Herndon talked about Niagara Falls. "What made the deepest impression on you?" asked Herndon. The answer: "The thing that struck me most forcibly when I saw the Falls was, where in the world did all the water come from." And he wrote notes for a lecture: how the geologist can prove by the wearing back of the Niagara plunge that the world is at least fourteen thousand years old; how Niagara calls up the past. "When Columbus first sought this continent—when Christ suffered on the Cross—when Moses led Israel through the Red Sea—nay, even when Adam first came from the hand of his Maker; then, as now, Niagara was roaring here. The eyes of that species of extinct giants whose bones fill the mounds of America have gazed on Niagara, as ours do now. Contemporary with the first race of men, and older than the first man, Niagara is strong and fresh today as ten thousand years ago. The Mammoth and the Mastodon, so long dead that fragments of their monstrous bone alone testify that they ever lived, have gazed on Niagara—in that long, long time never still for a single moment, never dried, never froze, never slept, never rested."

In the autumn weeks before Election Day, Lincoln stumped Illinois for the national and state Whig ticket, helping to make General Taylor President. His stand on the Mexican War he sometimes tried to make clear by saying the United States was like the farmer who said, as to wanting more land: "I ain't greedy; I only want what jines mine." Stephen T. Logan, running for Lincoln's seat in Congress, lost the race to a Democrat who was a Mexican War veteran.

Chapter 83

BACK home in Springfield, Lincoln had to help decide which Whigs should have plums. The Springfield postmaster, J. R. Diller, had done his best to defeat Lincoln's plans, and Lincoln recalled how five years previously he had got the postmastership for Diller. He had written a letter on December 16, 1844, to Congressman Hardin, reading:

DEAR JOHN J.:
    You perhaps know of the great scramble going on here about our Post Office. Upon general principles, you know this would be no concern of the Whigs, but in this particular case, if it be in your power to do anything, you may thereby do a favor to some of your friends here, without disobliging any of them, so far as I believe—The man we wish appointed is J. R. Diller—The reason is that Major Spotwood's family, now comparatively destitute, will be *favoured* by it—I write this by an understanding with Diller himself who has seen its contents.

And having thus helped put Diller into office, Lincoln later found it necessary to ask politely that Diller be put out. This he did in a letter to the Postmaster General, recommending Abner Y. Ellis for the office, and declaring: "J. R. Diller, the present incumbent, I cannot say has failed in the proper discharge of any of the duties of the office. He, however, has been an active partisan in opposition to us."

Lincoln went to Washington, sat as a congressman who had failed of reëlection, introduced resolutions to abolish the slave trade in the District of Columbia, watched the hungry office-hunters come swarming in on President Taylor, tried and failed to land a high diplomatic appointment for Ned Baker, delivered a few remarks on the public lands, looked on the riotous whirl of the President's inauguration ball, had his hat stolen and walked Washington streets bareheaded at three o'clock in the morning, said good-by here and there—and came home to Springfield, through as a congressman.

Then during four or five months he carried on a campaign of letter-writing and conferences aimed at getting for himself or for some other Illinois man the appointment of Commissioner of the General Land Office at Washington, salary $3,000 a year. Finally the politics of the affair seemed to narrow down to where Lincoln personally would have to go after the office or it would be lost to the Whigs of southern Illinois.

Early in June he was writing friends: "Would you as soon I should have the General Land Office as any other Illinoisan? If you would, write me to that effect at Washington, where I shall be soon. No time to lose."

Later in June he was in Washington wearing a linen duster, carrying a carpetbag, offering President Taylor eleven reasons why he should be named for the land-office job.

The appointment went to Justin Butterfield, who had marshaled northern Illinois and Chicago influence, besides that of Daniel Webster. And from then on, for months and years, Cyrus W. Edwards of Illinois refused to speak to Lincoln because he believed he himself should have had the land office, and Lincoln's handling of the affair had lost it to him. "To lose the friendship of Mr. Edwards by the effort for him," wrote Lincoln, "would oppress me very much, were I not sustained by the utmost consciousness of rectitude."

Lincoln's decision then was to stay in Springfield and practice law. During the spring he had been busy, as a leading Whig, in recommending Whigs to be appointed by the Taylor Administration to various offices. Toward the end of July he wrote to John M. Clayton, the Secretary of State, that President Taylor's policy of throwing all responsibility for appointments on departments was having a bad effect.

It is fixing for the President the unjust and ruinous character of being a mere man of straw. This must be arrested, or it will damn us all inevitably. It is said Gen. Taylor and his officers held a council of war, at Palo Alto (I believe); and that he then fought the battle against unanimous opinion of those officers. This fact (no matter whether rightfully or wrongfully) gives him more popularity than ten thousand submissions, however really wise and magnanimous those submissions may be. The appointments need be no better than they have been, but the public must be brought to understand, that they are the *President's* appointments. He must occasionally say, or seem to say, "by the Eternal," "I take the responsibility." Those phrases were the "Samson's locks" of Gen. Jackson, and we dare not disregard the lessons of experience.

Your Ob't Sev't.

The months passed by and 3,400 Democratic office-holders were turned out and 3,400 Whigs put in their places. Shady claims of former years were brought up; the Secretary of War, Crawford, was paid, as his share of one claim, the sum of $115,000.00. President Taylor, sixty-four years old, walked the streets of Washington alone enjoying the weather; or he rode on "Old Whitey," the horse that went through the Mexican War with him; his wife, who didn't like leaving the Louisiana plantation to go to Washington, spent most of her time knitting in the White House; gas was installed to light the White House; new furniture and carpets were put in; when the President was introduced to a dozen young women in white dresses at a party one evening, he smiled slowly. "I have been so long among Indians and Mexicans that I hardly know how to behave myself, surrounded by so many lovely women."

Sam Houston came on from Texas as senator, wearing a vest made from a panther skin, and during Senate sessions sat whittling sticks of soft pine-wood supplied by the sergeant-at-arms.

The months passed and General Taylor sat in the hot sun near the Washington Monument and listened to two Fourth of July orations for nearly three hours; he drank ice-water, he went home to the White House and ate from a basket of cherries; he drank goblets of iced milk; he disobeyed his doctor and ate more cherries and iced milk; he had stood against all the ravages of Mexico and wild life in the Southwest; but he could not stand civilization. He said, "In two days I shall be a dead man." His mind was clear to the last and he murmured, "I have endeavored to do my duty."

Henry Clay had come back as senator from Kentucky, seventy-three years old; he had wept over his loss of the Presidency; he had seen two Whigs, who had beaten him for the nomination, die in office. He went to balls and parties, kissed the pretty girls as he chose, and played cards in his room at the National Hotel, always with a glass of toddy standing by, made from Kentucky Bourbon County whisky.

And out in Illinois Abraham Lincoln was settling down and straightening out his desk and papers in the law office with Bill Herndon. He was asking no nominations.

Chapter 84

ON the same front page of the *Illinois State Journal,* where Abraham Lincoln and W. H. Herndon announced, in 1849, they were "attornies and counselors-at-law," was the statement of J. H. Adams, at the Sign of the Big Hat, "He is determined to sell hats at the lowest prices." Adams enumerated fresh arrivals of hats, viz., beaver, fine brush, Angola drab, nutria, smooth cassimere, fashionable pearl, otter, moleskin, plush, Spanish shape, muskrat of French style, and round-crown Russia, also wool hats of all colors. Adams, however, was not alone in meeting the hat needs of Sangamon County. The New Hat Store was opening with hats "which will favorably compare with those made in St. Louis or any other city, fine moleskin hats, silk hats, fine Rusia, and Rough and Ready Hats, warranted to stand hard service."

Adams lived by and for hats, and sometimes looked like a hat of a man, while John G. Ives led a quiet tick-tock, tick-tock existence, and looked like a clock of a man. Ives informed Springfield that "having been engaged in this city over eight years, in the repairing of clocks and watches, I feel confident I can give satisfaction to all who may favor me with their custom." Those having any disorder of the body were told that Birchall & Owen's drug-store kept Dr. Keeler's Panace which would cure all ills, including "constitutional debility, mercurial and hereditary predispositions, etc."

The saddle-maker, Amos Camp, said his motto was "Live and let live." Lowery, Lamb & Co. were selling a plow they said was "the best plough in the country for breaking up stubble and foul ground, as it is almost impossible to choke it." R. F. Ruth, the harness-maker, had put in a stock of saddles, saddlebags, carpetbags, carriage whips, and silver- and brass-mounted carriage and buggy harness, besides an assortment of horse collars, blind bridles, backbands, bellybands, long and short tugs.

Arrivals were announced of steel pens, Havana cigars, feather beds, india-rubber shoes, coal stoves, Russia parlor-stoves with self-regulators, silk fans, music boxes, eight-day brass clocks, silver candlesticks, ladies' buskins, bootees, slippers, chameleon silks, satin de chine, ladies' work-boxes, earrings, card cases, bracelets, Boston butter-crackers, new-style side and hanging lard-lamps, silk-fringed Thibet shawls, French merinoes, plaid lustres, drab modes. And at Hickox Brothers were 100 muffs for ladies, misses and children at fifty cents to fifteen dollars.

Rev. N. H. Hall, D.D., of Lexington, Kentucky, published a notice as to the day and hours he would preach in the First Presbyterian church, "God willing." Watson's saloon announced, "Oysters, sardines and other 'fixens' can be had at all hours except Sundays and Sunday nights." D. Barnes advertised, "Wanted, 10,000 deer skins—The highest price paid in cash for deer skins."

During the agitation for laying plank pavements around the public square of Springfield, and on the streets leading from the main hotels to the railroad depots, it was told that a traveling man one muddy week during spring rains, was saluted by another traveling man, "Didn't I see you yesterday morning sitting on a box in the middle of the street?" "No," was the reply, "I was sitting on top of the Chenery House bus."

Civilization was creeping in. Year by year, with no violence, but with slow, steady accretions, as an organic growth, civilization was rooting itself. Lincoln strolled hither and yon, on his shoulders the scrawny blue military cape he had bought in Washington when he was a member of the Congress of the United States. He saw cow pastures his feet had worn paths on, filled with lumber frame cottages; fences hedged the old paths. He saw city lots where a log cabin had stood and the dishes inside were pewter; in their stead had come a brick house with a pantry and little fan-shaped ice-cream dishes tinted with gold and blue violets.

"Who is bound for California?" queried a want ad, saying, "All persons who feel interested in the California Expedition will meet in the courthouse Saturday evening at early candlelight."

Lincoln was a spectator and a philosopher as he rambled and saw his fellow townsmen making out as well as they could with life. It interested him when a man such as John Hutchinson, the undertaker, opened a line of cabinet furniture, and announced: "He also continues the undertaking, as heretofore, and is proprietor of the new burying ground, which is laid off in small lots, suitable for families. Also half lots and graves for one person. Coffins of every size and quality ready made, and as cheap as can be had in the city of the same quality; and hearse-gentle horse and careful driver furnished as heretofore."

Yet Lincoln's life was not held down to the humdrum of Springfield. He had law cases in towns out on the Eighth Circuit. On the day before Christmas of 1849, he was in Cincinnati, Ohio, writing a letter to Peter Hitchcock, chief justice of the supreme court of Ohio, at Columbus. Either that day or the next Lincoln expected to get the brief of the other side in the case, and then go on to Columbus, for the hearing. He was associated with T. D. Lincoln of Cincinnati. Their client was Linus Logan, whose steamboat, *Mail,* was rammed by the steamboat, *Clipper,* on the Ohio River. Lincoln's client had won a verdict of $3,760.00 in a lower court. In the hearing before the supreme court at Columbus, this verdict was sustained.

Chapter 85

THE little frame house which was the Lincoln home on the corner of Eighth and Jackson streets in Springfield was painted white, with green blinds, and white chimneys. Under the care of Mary Todd Lincoln, who was spick and span about such things, it was a clean, snug-looking place. There the ex-congressman, back from Washington, settled down to law practice, shoveled snow from the front door to the street, from the back door to the barn and the outhouses.

As he put the currycomb to the horse and slicked axle grease on his buggy wheels, he could think about little Stephen A. Douglas, the short, thick-chested, blue-eyed man who had been a common struggler with the rest of them in Springfield a few years back, now sitting in conferences with Clay, Calhoun, and Webster at Washington, a defender of the memory of Andrew Jackson, and fast taking place as a national leader of the Democratic party.

It seemed only yesterday that Simeon Francis caught Douglas by the hair and jammed him against a hayrack on the public square. And James Shields, whom he had met on a sand-bar in the Mississippi River and was ready to cleave in two with a cavalry broadsword, was Douglas's colleague from Illinois in the Senate. The mayor of Springfield was John Calhoun, his old friend who had started him as a surveyor. They were all Democrats. Among Whigs luck was the other way; his old law partners were practicing law; Stuart had been in Congress and never got back; Stephen T. Logan, the little thin-lipped, sharp-voiced, bushy-haired man who had tried hard to be elected, had not reached Congress but had stayed at home and become known as one of the ablest lawyers in Illinois.

Quaint statistical facts stood in plain garb in the newspaper-columns; puppets with prophetic fingers. Eighty thousand cords of wood were burned yearly in the railroad locomotives of the country; but coal had been tried out and coal mines were opening up. In April of 1848, when the telegraph lines from New York had reached as far as Niles, Michigan, the *Tribune* of Chicago notified its readers that perhaps in two weeks Chicago would have telegraphic connection with New York, Boston, and Washington. "When that takes place, look to the *Tribune* for late news."

The slavery question seemed to be settled by the Omnibus Bill. Five negroes were in jail down on the public square; they were fugitive slaves, and, according to the law, would go back to their owners. And yet, though the slavery question did seem settled, there were more quiet men here and there who were helping to pass on runaway negroes, up from Jacksonville, Springfield, Bloomington, on up to Galesburg, Princeton, Chicago, and so to Canada, where the British law prohibiting slave ownership made them safe.

The northern part of Illinois had been filling up with settlers. Towns such as Princeton and Galesburg were like little pieces of New England, more Yankee than some towns in New England which had filled their factories with newcomers from Europe. Irish and Germans were swarming into Chicago by thousands. At Bishop Hill was a settlement where the women wove rag-carpets and wore black kerchiefs around their heads, knotted under the chins; it was a spot as humanly Swedish as Sweden. Yes, Illinois was changing. What was ahead in politics, no man could tell. The one sure thing was that the people from Kentucky, Tennessee, and Virginia and the Carolinas, who had controlled Illinois, were to be outnumbered and outvoted at some time in the near future.

Up in Bureau County was Owen Lovejoy, brother of Elijah; over in Ohio was Joshua Giddings; Edward D. Baker had gone to California and was lighting the Sacramento Valley with his oratorical torch.

New men, new issues, were coming. The writing of the history of the country would have to be with new names.

Over the breakfast and supper table at the Lincoln home, the woman of the house told him her hopes that he would move onward and upward to a high place where his name would shine. He knew that fame, name, and high place would please her more than anything else. When he made a move in politics he usually knew her view of it; she told him her views, and plainly. She read, she talked with people of influence, she gave him her judgment. She told him when she was pleased, when she wasn't.

He believed in dreams and tried to read his dreams for their connections with his future. She believed in signs; she told him about signs, portents. Both were superstitious. Both had hopes.

As the ex-congressman and prominent Whig leader shoveled snow, he had thoughts and hopes.

News came one day as he was trying a case over in Bloomington. The Whig administration at Washington had a message for the leading Whig in Illinois. Was he willing to take an appointment as governor of the Territory of Oregon? Lincoln made a quick answer. Whether he would go depended on what he heard from his wife. Her decision was "No." She was willing to live in Washington as the wife of the general landcommissioner, but she did not care to live in a pioneer country separated by weeks of wagon travel from the settled regions of the country.

Illinois itself then had enough silent places. The plumes of smoke from the breakfast and supper fires of the cabins along the Sangamon were lonely enough. The corn-fed population of the Midwest frontier was only beginning to learn how to raise corn, and fatten and market cattle and hogs. The corn belt was young. It had yet to learn how to fill the food bunkers of cities and armies.

It was the time Ralph Waldo Emerson of Concord, Massachusetts, sent his friend Tammas Carlyle over in Scotland a bag of Indian corn, or maize, as a sample of a great American product. The Scotchman replied:

I have already drawn up a fit proclamation of the excellencies of this invaluable corn, and admonitions as to the benighted state of English eaters in regard to it;—to appear in *Fraser's Magazine* soon. It is really a small contribution towards World-History, this small act of yours and ours; there is no doubt to me, now that I taste the real grain, but all Europe will henceforth have to rely more and more upon your Western Valleys and this article.

How beautiful to think of lean tough Yankee settlers, tough as gutta-percha, with most occult unsubduable fire in their belly, steering over the Western Mountains, to annihilate the jungle, and bring bacon and corn out of it for the Posterity of Adam! The Pigs in about a year eat up all the rattlesnakes for miles round: a most judicious function on the part of the Pigs. Behind the Pigs comes Jonathan with his all-conquering ploughshare,—glory to him too! Oh, if we were not a set of Cant-ridden blockheads, there is no myth of Athene or Herakles equal to this fact;—which I suppose will find its real "Poets" some day or other; when once the Greek, Semitic, and multifarious other cobwebs are swept away a little! Well, we must wait. Adieu, dear Emerson; I had much more to say. Forgive me, forgive me all trespasses,—and love me what you can.

The Scotchman was trying to picture what was going on across America. He wrote again:

Only a hundred years ago, and the Mississippi has changed as never valley did: in 1751 older and stranger, looked at from its present date, than Balbec or Nineveh! Say what we will, Jonathan is doing miracles (of a sort) under the sun in these times now passing.

And that year, after a trip West in which he stopped in Springfield, Illinois, two days and lectured, Emerson wrote to Carlyle:

I went down the Ohio River to its mouth; walked nine miles into, and nine miles out of the Mammoth Cave, in Kentucky,—walked or

sailed, for we crossed small underground streams,—and lost one day's
light; then steamed up the Mississippi five days, to Galena. In the
Upper Mississippi, you are always in a lake with many islands. "The
Far West" is the right name for these verdant deserts. On all the
shores, interminable silent forest. If you land, there is prairie behind
prairie, forest behind forest, sites of nations, no nations. The raw
bullion of nature; what we call "Moral" value not yet stamped on it.
But in a thousand miles the immense material values will show twenty
or fifty Californias.

Thus at Pittsburg, on the Ohio, the Iron City, whither, from want
of railroads, few Yankees have penetrated, every acre of land has three
or four bottoms; first of rich soil; then nine feet of bituminous coal;
a little lower, fourteen feet of coal; then iron, or salt; salt springs,
with a valuable oil called petroleum floating on their surface. Yet this
acre sells for the price of any tillage acre in Massachusetts; and, in a
year, the railroads will reach it, east and west.

And two years later Emerson wrote Carlyle:

I went lately to St. Louis and saw the Mississippi again. The powers
of the River, the insatiate craving for nations of men to reap and cure
its harvests, the conditions it imposes,—for it yields to no engineering,
—are interesting enough. The Prairie exists to yield the greatest
possible quantity of adipocere. For corn makes Pig, pig is the export
of all the land, and you shall see the instant dependence of aristocracy
and civility on the fat four-legs. Workingmen, ability to do the work
of the River, abounded. Nothing higher was to be thought of. Room
for us all, since it has not ended, nor given sign of ending, in bard
or hero.

'Tis a wild democracy, the riot of mediocrities, and none of your
selfish Italies and Englands, where an age sublimates into a genius, and
the whole population is made into Paddies to feed his porcelain veins,
by transfusion from their brick arteries. Our few fine persons are apt
to die. "The beautiful is never plentiful!"

Chapter 86

LINCOLN studied and worked on law cases as never before in
his life. For five years politics was a side issue. He said he
was out of politics. He traveled on the Eighth Judicial Circuit

with a court that moved across fourteen counties, staying two days to two weeks in each county seat among "a very litigious people."

From September till Christmas and from February till June, he was away from his Springfield home, handling all kinds of law cases, driving a buggy across the prairie of fourteen counties in all kinds of weather. It was his way of earning a living, keeping bread and butter in the home pantry at Springfield. He dropped into a way of life that kept him in close touch with people, their homes, kitchens, barns, fields, their churches, schools, hotels, saloons, their places for working and worshiping and loafing.

For the first time he held in his arms the white still body of a child of his own; he could call the name of Eddie to his boy and the boy had no ears to hear nor breath to answer.

This was his own kith and kin, who had come out of silence and gone back to silence, back where Nancy Hanks had gone the year he helped his father peg together a plank coffin.

He tried to pierce through into the regions of that silence and find replies to questions that surged in him.

On the day Eddie was buried, a funeral sermon was pronounced by Rev. James Smith of the First Presbyterian Church, and a friendship developed between the Lincoln family and the Reverend Mr. Smith. The minister had been a wild boy in his young days in Scotland, had been a scoffer at religion, and had been a preacher in Kentucky; he could tell a story—he and Lincoln were good company.

The Lincolns rented a pew in the church. Mrs. Lincoln took the sacrament, and joined in membership. Reverend Mr. Smith presented Lincoln with a copy of his book, "The Christian's Defence," a reply to infidels and atheists; it argued that the creation of the world, as told in the Book of Genesis, the fall of man in the Garden of Eden, the flood which ended with Noah's Ark on Mount Ararat were true events, that the books of the Old Testament are not forgeries, that a number of profane authors testify to the truth of the New Testament evangels, that only an atheist can deny divine inspiration; the divine authority of the Scriptures is proved from prophecy and its fulfilment.

Lincoln read "The Christian's Defence," said he was interested, later attended revival meetings held in the First Presbyterian Church, and said he was interested. But when asked to join the church he said he "couldn't quite see it."

To his law partner he remarked: "There are no accidents in my philosophy. Every effect must have its cause. The past is the cause of the present, and the present will be the cause of the future. All these are links in the endless chain stretching from the Infinite to the finite." The *Edinburgh Review* was on their office table periodically, and in Herndon's library Lincoln read as he chose, from volumes by Locke, Kant, Fichte, Herbert Spencer; the sermons and essays of Theodore Parker and Ralph Waldo Emerson; Thomas Paine's "The Age of Reason" and "Common Sense"; Gregg's "Creed of Christendom"; Volney's "The Ruins of Empires"; Feuerbach's "Essence of Christianity"; McNaught on "Inspiration."

Lincoln read some of these, and read carefully a second time "Vestiges of the Natural History of Creation," by Robert Chambers, a Scotchman who said his book was "the first attempt to connect the natural sciences with the history of creation." The rock layers over the earth hold the bones of animals and plants showing that the world was millions of years in the making, that God practiced at making many other animals before at last he made man, according to Chambers's book. It interested Lincoln; six or eight years before, he had read a copy borrowed of James W. Keys; now he read again carefully the sixth and revised edition in Herndon's library. Many ministers were telling their congregations the book was a bad book, was against the teachings of the Bible; other ministers were saying it was a book worth reading.

Close friends of Lincoln, such as his law partner Herndon, and Matheny, who stood as best man at his wedding, had a notion Lincoln was a sort of infidel. They said Lincoln told them he did not believe the Bible was the revelation of God, and in a little book he wrote in New Salem he tried to prove Jesus was not the Son of God. "Lincoln did tell me that he did write a little book on infidelity—I got it from Lincoln's mouth," said Matheny. "An infidel, a theist, a fatalist," was Herndon's notion.

And yet Lincoln read the Bible closely, knew it from cover to cover, was familiar with its stories and its poetry, quoted from it in his talks to juries, in political campaigns, in his speeches, and in his letters. There were evangelical Christian church members who felt he was a solemn, earnest, religious man.

Still others, like Jesse W. Fell at Bloomington, felt that he held a good deal the same views as the famous heterodox New England preachers, Theodore Parker and William Ellery Channing. When Fell talked with enthusiasm about Channing's sermons, Lincoln showed such a keen interest that Fell asked Lincoln if he would like to have a complete collection of the sermons. So Fell bought a special edition for Lincoln, who put it in his little library where it kept company with "Exercises in the Syntax of the Greek Language," by Rev. William Nielson, D.D.

On page 34 was a sentence reading in Greek, "Ye have loved me, and have believed that I came forth from God," with the words "from God" crossed with a pen and the words "from nature" scribbled in Lincoln's handwriting.

When word came that his father down on the Coles County farm was dying, Lincoln wrote a letter to John D. Johnston, the stepson at the farm.

I feel sure you have not failed to use my name, if necessary, to procure a doctor, or anything else for father in his sickness. My business is such that I could hardly leave home now, if it was not as it is, that my own wife is sick-a-bed (It is a case of baby-sickness, and I suppose is not dangerous.) I sincerely hope father may recover his health, but at all events, tell him to remember to call upon and confide in our great and good merciful Maker, who will not turn away from him in any extremity. He notes the fall of a sparrow, and numbers the hairs of our heads, and He will not forget the dying man who puts his trust in Him. Say to him that if we could meet now it is doubtful whether it would not be more painful than pleasant, but that if it be his lot to go now, he will soon have a joyous meeting with many loved ones gone before, and where the rest of us, through the help of God, hope ere long to join them.

When death was close by, and there was a murmur out of deep rivers, and the moan of a long wind out of a cavern of dark stars, Lincoln often used Bible language.

The young printer, Gilbert J. Greene, drove out with him from Springfield one time to a farmhouse where a woman was dying. Lincoln was to draw up her last will and testament. After the paper was signed and witnessed, as the young printer remembered what happened, the woman asked, "Mr. Lincoln, won't you read a few verses out of the Bible for me?"

A Bible was brought; but, instead of taking it, the lawyer began reciting from memory the psalm, "Though I walk through the valley of the shadow of death I will fear no evil, for thou art with me; thy rod and thy staff they comfort me." And again, without taking the Bible, he repeated such verses as, "Let not your heart be troubled; ye believe in God, believe also in me," and "In my Father's house are many mansions; if it were not so I would have told you. I go to prepare a place for you."

He had told Mrs. Rankin, over near New Salem, that before he learned to read as a boy he had heard his mother saying over certain Bible verses day by day as she worked. He had learned these verses by heart; the tones of his mother's voice were in them; and sometimes, as he read these verses, he seemed to hear the voice of Nancy Hanks speaking them. This he told Mrs. Rankin one day when a Sunday-school convention was being held at Petersburg and the question was discussed as to the age at which children were morally responsible and prepared to be taught the Bible.

Mrs. Rankin was a friend of the preacher, Peter Cartwright, who ran for Congress against Lincoln; in her house Cartwright was called "Uncle Peter." And she had heard that Cartwright claimed Lincoln was no Christian and that Lincoln had said, "Christ was a bastard." Yet Lincoln was also a friend of the family. At her house he had borrowed books; there they had reached out kindly hands when he was groping and trying to pierce the silence into which Ann Rutledge had faded. So one evening Mrs. Rankin told him she knew the Cartwright charges against him were false; and yet—there was the question of what his religion really was.

The raising of the question made Lincoln restless; he stood up, crossed the room, rested an elbow on the fireplace mantel, and ran his hand through his hair. He said slowly that he could not discuss the character and religion of Jesus Christ in stump speeches. "That is no place for it."

He mentioned "shadows and questionings" that came to him at New Salem. "There came into my life sad events and a loss that you were close to; and you knew a great deal about how hard they were for me, for you were, at the time, a mutual friend. Those days of trouble found me tossed amid a sea of questionings. They piled big around me. Through all I groped my way until I found a stronger and higher grasp of thought, one that reached beyond this life with a clearness and satisfaction I had never known before. The Scriptures unfolded before me with a deeper and more logical appeal, through these new experiences, than anything else I could find to turn to, or ever before had found in them. I do not claim that all my doubts were removed then, or since that time have been swept away. They are not.

"Probably it is to be my lot to go on in a twilight, feeling and reasoning my way through life, as questioning, doubting Thomas did. But in my poor, maimed, withered way, I bear with me as I go on a seeking spirit of desire for a faith that was with him of the olden time, who, in his need, as I in mine, exclaimed, 'Help thou my unbelief.' "

He had by now slowed down from his first restless feeling; he left the fireplace and took his chair again. "I do not see that I am more astray—though perhaps in a different direction— than many others whose points of view differ widely from each other in the sectarian denominations. They all claim to be

Christians, and interpret their several creeds as infallible ones. I doubt the possibility, or propriety, of settling the religion of Jesus Christ in the models of man-made creeds and dogmas.

"It was a spirit in the life that He laid stress on and taught, if I read aright. I know I see it to be so with me. The fundamental truths reported in the four gospels as from the lips of Jesus Christ, and that I first heard from the lips of my mother, are settled and fixed moral precepts with me. I have concluded to dismiss from my mind the debatable wrangles that once perplexed me with distractions that stirred up, but never absolutely settled anything. I have tossed them aside with the doubtful differences which divide denominations. I have ceased to follow such discussions or be interested in them. I cannot without mental reservations assent to long and complicated creeds and catechisms.

"If the church would ask simply for assent to the Savior's statement of the substance of the law: 'Thou shalt love the Lord thy God with all thy heart, and with all thy soul, and with all thy mind, and thy neighbor as thyself,'—that church would I gladly unite with."

That was the way Mrs. Rankin remembered Lincoln talking about his religion that evening. She was sure that if she didn't remember all his words exactly as he spoke them she did get his thought clear, because he spoke his words in a slow manner and meant his words to be so clear that his thoughts would be remembered afterward.

Some who knew him in his home town said he was careless about church, never went inside of a church. Others, such as his friend, James C. Conkling, had other views. Of Lincoln's taking the pulpit and giving an address before the Springfield Bible Society, Conkling said: "When he had finished, he came down and slid into the seat with me. He was somewhat puzzled to understand why he had been selected to talk about the Bible. He whispered to me, 'I don't know why on earth they got me to make this kind of a speech unless it was to milk the Gentiles.'"

For the Kickapoo Indian, Johnny Kongapod, Lincoln used an epitaph that had the breath of his religion in it:

> Here lies poor Johnny Kongapod;
> Have mercy on him, gracious God.
> As he would do if he was God
> And you were Johnny Kongapod.

He was troubled about man, about God, about his country. Driving to Petersburg one day with Herndon, the year after he came back from Washington, he broke out: "How hard, oh, how hard it is to die and leave one's country no better than if one had never lived for it! The world is dead to hope, deaf to its own death struggle, made known by a universal cry, What is to be done? Is anything to be done? Who can do anything? And how is it to be done? Do you ever think of these things?"

And he was trying to live up to the pieces of advice which he boxed in with a lead pencil in his book of exercises in Greek syntax:

> Deliberate slowly, but ex-
> ecute promptly, the things which
> have appeared unto thee proper
> to be done.
> Love, not the immoderate
> acquisition, but the moderate en-
> joyment, of present good.

Chapter 87

"THE great Calhoun is dead," mourned South Carolina and her neighbors in 1850. "The great Henry Clay is dead," cried other mourners in 1852; and in that same year was heard the cry, "The great Daniel Webster is dead."

All three had been congressman, senator, Secretary of State; all three had missed the Presidency by narrow margins of whimsical ballots. They had spoken yes and no on the War of 1812, on the Mexican War, and they were dying as the country was blundering along with grave problems they had failed to solve.

In their places were rising new young leaders to play with public opinion. Moving toward a chief place in the Democratic party was young Stephen A. Douglas. The names of Seward of New York, Sumner of Massachusetts, Chase of Ohio, Greeley of the *Tribune*, were beginning to count.

Among the Abolitionists rose young Wendell Phillips, aristocratic, handsome, ironical, scathing, bitter not only with the bitterness of a man in anguish over slaves chained, flogged, bought and sold, but bitter with some added tincture of a man gnashing and jeering at a whole humanity of chattels and puppets. He invented a form of oratory staccato with sneers and javelins. There were hours when he seemed to be a personally foiled creature who was able to make people think his own frustrations were the frustrations of the dreams of democracy. Eggs kept overlong in storage crossed the air and broke on his face as he was speaking from a platform; he wiped the smear from his face and smiled, "They are fresh." He embodied proud yearnings and gifts of contempt.

Far to the south lived Jefferson Davis, the choice of Calhoun for southern leadership; six feet high, loose-jointed, a West Pointer who walked militarily erect, with a springy step, his war-wounded foot healed. He had for his body servant the black man called Pemberton, who had been with him in the Black Hawk War and again was with him through the Mexican War when the southerners of the Mississippi Rifles had their own slave servants along. From his cotton plantation and slave quarters at Biloxi, Mississippi, he could look out on the Gulf of Mexico. His home soil was swept by tropic breezes from a salt gulf whose warm waters touched Mexico, Yucatan, Cuba, Haiti; the breath of his home outlook in winter was different from that of bleak and frozen New England and that of the

Northwest where blizzards piled their snowdrifts up to the latches
of the cabin doors of the settlers.

Often Davis could vision the so-called Union of states as two
sections or confederacies with two cultures, fated to separate.
When it seemed that California was going to be let into the Union
as a free state there were mass meetings in all parts of Mississippi;
as Davis left for Washington he believed the state of Mississippi
would draw out of the Union and be joined by other states.

In Illinois was the potential Abraham Lincoln trying a law
case in Chicago, and called on to deliver the address at memorial
exercises for General Zachary Taylor. He spoke mournfully and
quoted seven stanzas from the star poem of the album of his
memory, "Oh, Why Should the Spirit of Mortal Be Proud?" In
Taylor's character he noted two traits, "absence of excitement
and absence of fear."

When Henry Clay, foremost of Whigs, died in 1852, Lincoln
was named to deliver a fifty-minute speech of eulogy at a
memorial meeting in the statehouse in Springfield. As he searched
among papers, speeches, and books, he found less material than
he expected. He tried to put his hand on a model eulogy that
Henry Clay had spoken about some other great man. But except for a few lines on the death of John Calhoun, it seemed
that Clay never had eulogized anybody.

Lincoln had a feeling that Henry Clay had been rather cold,
hard, selfish, with personal ambitions that had helped wreck
the Whig party. But this, of course, couldn't be put into a speech.
Neither could he put into a speech his own picture of Henry
Clay's manipulation of the famous compromise measures in Congress. Lincoln mentally noted, but not for the eulogy: "When
Clay wanted to carry an important measure, he drew it up in
such a way as to embody his own idea as nearly as he could,
and at the same time not be offensive to those whose aid was
indispensable—he then presented it to the strong men whose help
he must have or whose opposition he must stifle, and who were
of strong wills, and either argued them into its support, or made
such concessions and modifications as they insisted on, or added

palatable features to suit them, and thus got a powerful force enlisted in behalf of his measure:—then he visited the members of feeble wills and simply bullied them into its support without yielding one iota to them." This, too, could not be put into a speech of eulogy.

In the address, as given, he noted that Clay was born in 1777 and grew up with the country; when Clay got his start in politics the Union of states was holding together; when he quit, the Union was holding together; Clay must have had something to do with it. "Mr. Clay's predominant sentiment, from first to last, was a deep devotion to the cause of human liberty." And, "Our country is prosperous and powerful; but could it have been quite all it has been, and is, and is to be, without Henry Clay?"

He referred to "Mr. Clay's eloquence," saying: "All his efforts were for practical effect. He never spoke merely to be heard. He never delivered a Fourth of July oration, or a eulogy on an occasion like this."

One little chapter in the life of Clay fascinated Lincoln. That had to do with an hour when Clay forgot himself and tore loose a speech that was so wild, bold, and free that the reporters dropped their pencils and the language of it was never written down. This lost speech lived in the memories of men as the best speech Clay ever made.

A speech that Lincoln's best friends were sorry about was delivered this year. It was a reply to remarks of Stephen A. Douglas in Richmond, Virginia. Douglas was four years younger than Lincoln, had come as a Vermont Yankee to Illinois about the same time as Lincoln, and had fought his way to high Democratic leadership.

A streak of jealousy ran through Lincoln's opening remarks to the Scott Club of Springfield. "This speech [that of Douglas at Richmond] has been published with high commendations in at least one of the Democratic papers in this state, and I suppose it has been and will be in most of the others. When I first saw it and read it I was reminded of old times, when Judge Douglas was not so much greater a man than all the rest of us, as he is now—of the Harrison campaign twelve years ago, when I used to hear and try to answer many of his speeches; and believing that the Richmond speech, though marked with the same species of 'shirks and quirks' as the old ones, was not marked with any greater ability, I was seized with a strange inclination to attempt an answer to it; and this inclination it was that prompted me to seek the privilege of addressing you on this occasion."

He took up Douglas's statement that Providence had saved the country from one military administration by the timely removal of General Taylor, and closed his speech: "Let us stand by our candidate [General Scott] as faithfully as he has always stood by our country, and I much doubt if we do not perceive a slight abatement in Judge Douglas's confidence in Providence, as well as in the people. I suspect that confidence is not more firmly fixed with the judge than it was with the old woman whose horse ran away with her in a buggy. She said she 'trusted in Providence till the britchin' broke,' and then she didn't know 'what on airth to do.' The chance is, the judge will see the 'britchin' broke'; and then he can at his leisure bewail the fate of Locofocoism as the victim of misplaced confidence."

Election Day came in that year of 1852. The Whig party went to pieces. General Winfield Scott, the hero of Vera Cruz, was snowed under, carried only four states, and the Democrats sent to the White House the young Colonel Franklin Pierce, handsome, well educated, conciliatory, the hero of a campaign book written by Nathaniel Hawthorne, author of "The Scarlet Letter," a great writer of books who earned his living as a custom-house official.

Chapter 88

WHEN Robert Todd, the bank president and cotton-yarn manufacturer, died at his home in Lexington, Kentucky, in 1849, Abraham Lincoln had spent some days in Lexington attending to the division of the estate in behalf of his wife, Mary Todd Lincoln, the second eldest daughter of Robert Todd. Four years later a suit was filed against Lincoln charging that he had collected money in Illinois for Robert Todd.

"I find it difficult to suppress my indignation towards those who have got up this claim against me," Lincoln wrote his lawyer at Lexington. He pushed for action to show when he had collected money, from whom, where they lived, and when. He wrote long letters to his lawyer with particular instructions, and traced the cause of the suit back to the bad feeling held by Levi O. Todd against his three sisters who lived in Springfield. Levi Todd asserted that his father had let the sisters have money freely—and there was money owing the estate.

"This matter harasses my feelings a good deal," Lincoln again wrote his lawyer, again with special instructions. At the trial it was proven that another lawyer in Illinois had made the collections referred to in the suit.

The record cleared Lincoln completely, and he wrote his lawyer, "I expect and desire you to be paid a separate fee for your attention to that suit; and to authorize you to retain what you shall deem reasonable on that account, out of any money of mine which is or may come into your hands. If nothing further for me is, or is likely to be in your hands, write me and I will forward you the amount."

Another money matter to look after was down on the Coles County farm where Sally Bush Lincoln, his stepmother, was living. Her son, John D. Johnston, wrote asking for eighty dollars. Lincoln replied: "Your request for eighty dollars I do not think it best to comply with now." He had husked corn in Indiana with John D. Johnston and knew Johnston's ways. He wrote advice: "You are not lazy, and still you are an idler. I doubt whether, since I saw you, you have done a good whole day's work in any one day. This habit of uselessly wasting time is the whole difficulty; it is vastly important to you, and still more so to your children that you should break the habit."

He promised he would give Johnston one other dollar for every dollar Johnston went to work and earned. "If you hire yourself at ten dollars a month, from me you will get ten more, making

twenty dollars a month for your work. In this I do not mean
you shall go off to St. Louis, or the lead mines, or the gold mines
of California, but I mean for you to go at it for the best wages
you can get in Coles County. You say you would almost give
your place in heaven for seventy or eighty dollars. Then you
value your place in heaven very cheap, for I am sure you can,
with the offer I make, get the seventy or eighty dollars for four
or five months' work."

On a trip to Coles County, Lincoln found out that Johnston
was anxious to sell the land he lived on and move to Missouri.
He wrote to Johnston:

Such a notion is utterly foolish. What can you do in Missouri
better than here? Is the land any richer? Can you there, any more
than here, raise corn and wheat and oats without work? Will anybody
there, any more than here, do your work for you? If you intend to
go to work, there is no better place than right where you are; if you
do not intend to go to work, you cannot get along anywhere.

Squirming and crawling about from place to place can do no good.
You have raised no crop this year; and what you really want is to
sell the land, get the money, and spend it. Part with the land you
have, and my life upon it, you will never after own a spot big enough
to bury you in. Half you will get for the land you will spend in
moving to Missouri, and the other half you will eat, drink, and wear
out, and no foot of land will be bought. Now, I feel it my duty to
have no hand in such a piece of foolery. I feel that it is so even on
your own account, and particularly on mother's account.

The eastern forty acres I intend to keep for mother while she lives;
if you will not cultivate it, it will rent for enough to support her—
at least it will rent for something. Her dower in the other two forties
she can let you have, and no thanks to me. I do not write in any
unkindness. Your thousand pretenses for not getting along are all
nonsense; they deceive nobody but yourself. Go to work is the only
cure for your case.

Thus a stepson to the son of his stepmother. In all the letters
of Lincoln to John D. Johnston there shines far back the feeling
of love and care for Sally Bush Lincoln. It was she who tried
to tell what there was between her and young Abe in saying,
"His mind and mine, what little I had, seemed to run together."

Chapter 89

In the little white house with the green blinds and the white chimneys at Eighth and Jackson streets, Mary Todd Lincoln had in ten years' time borne four children. In the winter of 1850 came William Wallace; in the spring of 1853 came Thomas, nicknamed Tad.

At the cradles of these babies, at the grave of one who had died, the mother and father had stood together. For these little ones who came, pink, soft, and helpless, lying on their backs and kicking their heels toward the ceiling, Lincoln was thankful.

To handle them, tickle them, and talk their goo-goo talk, and watch them grow, had an appeal for his sense both of the solemn and of the ridiculous. Kittens he had always liked; where other men enjoyed hunting and fishing, he found sport in petting kittens. And babies, particularly his own babies, were sacred keepsakes loaned out of a silence.

As the years had passed, the two who had so suddenly and independently married came to understand that each was strong and each was weak. Habits held him that it was useless for her to try to break. If he chose to lie on the front-room carpet, on the small of his back, reading, she knew that was his way. Likewise if he came to the table in his shirt-sleeves and ate his meat and potatoes absently, with his eyes and his thoughts far off, that too was his way.

She tried to stop him from answering the ring of the front-door bell; the servant should answer the bell. But he would go to the front door and ask the callers what was wanted. Once two fine ladies wanted Mrs. Lincoln; he looked the house over and came back to ask the callers in, drawling pleasantly, "She'll be down soon as she gets her trotting harness on."

And when his wife wrangled with the iceman claiming an over-charge or when she screamed at John Mendonsa that she would pay only ten cents a quart for berries, that they were not worth fifteen cents, he spoke quietly to her as "Mary," and did his best to straighten things with the iceman or the berry-picker. Mary had sewed her own clothes, had sewed clothes for the children; he let her manage the house.

Young Chevalier Henry Haynie came to the law office asking money for a new hose cart for the volunteer fire company. And he told Haynie and a committee: "Boys, when I go home to supper—Mrs. Lincoln is always in a fine, good humor then—I'll say to her, over the toast: 'My dear, there is a subscription paper being handed round to raise money to buy a new hose cart. The committee called on me this afternoon, and I told them to wait until I consulted my home partner. Don't you think I had better subscribe fifty dollars?' Then she will look up quickly and exclaim: 'Will you never learn, never learn? You are always too liberal, too generous. Fifty dollars! No, indeed; we can't afford it. Twenty-five's quite reasonable enough.' "

And he chuckled: "Bless her dear soul, she'll never find out how I got the better of her; and if she does, she'll forgive me. Come around to-morrow, boys, and get your twenty-five dollars."

A workman caring for the Lincoln yard went to Lincoln's office to ask about cutting down a tree. "What did Mrs. Lincoln say?" was Lincoln's question. "She said yes." "Then, in God's name, cut it down to the roots."

There were friends and relatives of Mrs. Lincoln who felt sorry for her. One said: "Mrs. Lincoln comes of the best stock, and was raised like a lady. Her husband was the opposite, in origin, in education, in breeding, in everything; and it is therefore quite natural that she should complain if he answers the doorbell himself instead of sending the servant to do so. Neither is she to be condemned if she raises 'merry war' because he persists in using his own knife in the butter, instead of the silver-handled one intended for that purpose."

Among servant girls in Springfield Mrs. Lincoln had a reputation of being hard to get along with. A girl named Maria came; she would stay a few days, maybe a month, said the other girls

But she stayed two years. Lincoln had arranged to pay her a dollar a week extra, Mrs. Lincoln knowing nothing about the extra dollar.

"The madame and I began to understand each other," said Maria. "More than once, when she happened to be out of the room, Mr. Lincoln, with a merry twinkle in his eye, patted me on the shoulder, urging, 'Stay with her, Maria, stay with her.' "

When John Bradford bought a new carriage and invited Mrs. Lincoln to join him and his family for a drive in the country, he said she came out of the house nervous and wrought up and he had a suspicion she had been in a wrangle with a new servant girl, for just as she settled back in her seat she exclaimed with a sigh: "Well, one thing is certain: if Mr. Lincoln should happen to die, his spirit will never find me living outside the boundaries of a slave state."

A law student, Gibson W. Harris, in the office of Lincoln and Herndon, often ran errands out to the Lincoln home. Twice, when Lincoln was away on the circuit, he was Mrs. Lincoln's escort at a ball. He remarked: "I found her to be a good dancer; she was bright, witty, and accomplished. The sportive nickname she gave me was Mr. Mister. Mr. Lincoln showed great consideration for his wife. She was unusually timid and nervous during a storm. If the clouds gathered and the thunder rolled, he knew its effect on his wife and would at once hasten home to remain there with her till the skies cleared and the storm was safely over."

In many important matters Lincoln trusted her judgment. Herndon noted: "She was an excellent judge of human nature, a better reader of men's motives than her husband and quick to detect those who had designs upon and sought to use him. She was, in a good sense, a stimulant. . . . She kept him from lagging, was constantly prodding him to keep up the struggle. She . . . wanted to be a leader in society. . . . Realizing that Lincoln's rise in the world would elevate and strengthen her, she strove in every way to promote his fortunes, to keep him moving, and thereby win the world's applause."

She wrote to him one spring when he was in Washington that her headaches were gone; he wrote back the news was good considering it was the first spring since they were acquainted that she had been free from headaches.

He asked her to get weighed and report to him how many pounds she had put on. And he could joke her, "I am afraid you will get so well and fat and young as to be wanting to marry again."

Having bought a set of shirt-bosom studs, he wrote her they were set in gold—modest, pretty, little ones—only costing fifty cents apiece or $1.50 for the set of three.

On leaving home he would beg her not to let the children forget father. Once when away he had a dream about bad luck happening to Bobby, and called it a foolish dream, but couldn't rid himself of its impression till a letter from home said Bobby was safe and well.

Living next door to the Lincolns, and watching their ups and downs, was a shoemaker, James Gourley. When the Lincoln cow went dry, Lincoln stepped over to Gourley's for milk.

"He used to come to our house with his feet in a pair of loose slippers, wearing an old, faded pair of trousers fastened with one suspender," was Gourley's impression. "Our rooms were low, and one day he said, 'Jim, you'll have to lift your loft a little higher; I can't straighten out under it very well.' To my wife, who was short, he used to say that little people had advantages; they required 'less wood and wool to make them comfortable.' I think the Lincolns agreed moderately well. As a rule Mr. Lincoln yielded to his wife—in fact, almost any other man, had he known the woman as I did, would have done the same thing. She was gifted with an unusually high temper and that invariably got the better of her. She was very excitable and when wrought up had hallucinations.

"I remember once when her husband was away from home she conceived the notion that some rough characters had designs on her and the hired girl. She had worked herself up to a furious pitch, weeping and wailing loud enough to be heard by the neighbors, and even asked me to spend the night at her house guarding the premises and thus protect her and her girl. Of course I expressed a willingness to do whatever she asked, although I knew the whole thing was imaginary. This was not the only time her demonstrations were loud enough to be heard by some of her neighbors.

"If she became excited or troublesome, as she sometimes did when Mr. Lincoln was at home, it was interesting to know what he would do. At first, he would apparently pay no attention to her. Frequently he would laugh at her, which is a risky thing to do in the face of an infuriated wife; but generally, if her impatience continued, he would pick up one of the children and deliberately leave home as if to take a walk. After he had gone, the storm usually subsided, but sometimes it would break out again when he returned.

"Notwithstanding her unfortunate temper and her peculiarities generally, I never thought Mrs. Lincoln was as bad as some people here in Springfield represented her. The truth is, she had more than one redeeming trait. She and I rarely differed—in fact, we were good friends. Although I do not believe she could plead justification for many of the things she did, yet, when I hear her criticized by some people, I cannot but recall what she once said to me about her husband, which was that, if he had been at home as much as he ought, she could have been happier and loved him more."

Harriet Hanks, a daughter of Dennis, stayed at the Lincoln house a year and a half, going to school in Springfield, and leaving because she couldn't get along with Mrs. Lincoln. "I often heard Mr. Lincoln say he could eat corn cakes as fast as two women could make them," said Harriet. "He seldom ever wore his coat in the house, and went to the table in his shirt-sleeves, which annoyed his wife, who loved to put on style. One day he undertook to correct his child and his wife was determined that he should not, and attempted to take it from him; but in this she failed. She tried tongue-lashing, but met with the same fate, for Mr. Lincoln corrected the child, as a father ought to, in the face of his wife's anger, and that too without changing his countenance or making any reply to her."

So there was talk about Mrs. Lincoln over Springfield. She economized in the kitchen in order to have fine clothes; she had a terrible temper and tongue; so the talk ran. That her husband had married her a thousand dollars in debt, that he charged low fees as a lawyer and was careless about money, and that she had managed the household so well that her husband trusted her and let her have her own way in all the household economy, didn't get into the gossip. That she was often sorry, full of regret, after a bad burst of temper, didn't get into the gossip.

She had borne four children for the man she had chosen for a husband at a time when she had a wide range of choices, when an elegant marriage in her own class was planned for her. She had chosen one of the loneliest, strangest men in the world—for a husband. She had chosen him deliberately, calling him back when over and again he tried to slip away. She sewed clothes for herself and her children. She read and spoke French, keeping on with her studies.

While he was away six months of the year, she kept up connections socially that were of value politically. There were others saying, as young Gibson Harris said, "I found her to be a good dancer; bright, witty, accomplished." She had soft brown hair, clear blue eyes that swept with laughter or scorn. She liked fixing herself up, making herself pretty.

As Lincoln sat across from her at the breakfast table, he could see on her hand the plain gold ring he had once placed there—on the inside of it the words Chatterton, the jeweler, had engraved, "Love is eternal."

He had bought that ring only a little while after he had written his Kentucky chum, Joshua Speed, that his father used to say, "If you make a bad bargain, hug it all the tighter."

Chapter 90

As Lincoln walked the streets of Springfield and as he rode the circuit of twelve counties, living in hotels and courthouses, he met people shaken and stirred by slavery; they had read a book; the book had set their hearts on fire with hate; they hated the South, the people of the South; it was a hate that made them hate their own country, its laws, its flag; they believed their own country guilty of a crime worse than the crimes of any other country in any other time.

They had read a book; men couldn't pitch hay or fix a wagon, women couldn't wash dishes or knit baby-shirts, without thinking of the book, its terrible pages, and the terrible story. They moaned the word "Terrible!" to each other; a few could only be silent and pray to God. The book was a personal book with a personal story for its origin.

In the year 1849 there was living at Walnut Hills, just a little outside of Cincinnati, a woman who was thirty-eight years old and the mother of six children, all living. She worked hard, and for thirteen years had done most of the sewing and washing for the family; she had put together the house furniture and varnished it, made her own pillows, pillowcases, bedspreads, quilts, and mattresses. When a neighbor found her laying cloth on the floor and cutting a dress for herself, the neighbor asked if she had a pattern to go by, getting the answer, "I guess I know my own shape."

She cut and sewed her husband's coats; and besides was a cobbler cutting leather soles and nailing leather heels onto uppers she had cut and sewed so as to lace the shoes up behind. Her husband read the Greek, Hebrew, Latin, and Arabic languages, and was Bible professor in the Lane Theological Seminary at Walnut Hills. Only that year he had told her: "There is no woman like you in this wide world. Who else has so much

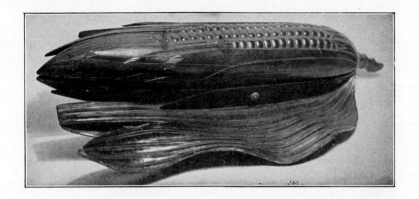

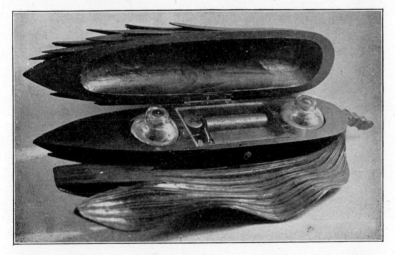

Mrs. Lincoln's ink stand and music box—corn-belt craftsmanship.

From the Barrett Collection. Photograph by Jun Fujita

China gravy bowl, plate, pitcher, metal candlestick, majolica pitcher, given by Mrs. Lincoln to Usher F. Linder for his wife (upper); Lincoln's watch chain and key (side); Lincoln's watch (center); Lincoln's pocketknife (bottom).

Originals in Barrett Collection

enterprise with so little extravagance; so much tongue with so little scold; so much sweetness with so little softness?" And she had answered, "If you were not already my dearly loved husband, I should certainly fall in love with you."

As to growing old and taking care of six children, she wrote to a school-days friend:

I like to grow old and have six children and cares endless. I wish you could see me with my flock all around me. They sum up my cares, and were they gone I should ask myself, What now remains to be done? They are my work, over which I fear and tremble.

She was born and raised in Connecticut, reading in the "New England Primer":

Young pious Ruth
Left all for truth.

And such rhymes as:

Young Obadias,
David, Josias,
All were pious.

Her father was a Congregational minister and read aloud to his children from Milton's poem, "Paradise Lost." Sometimes she cried and sometimes her father cried when he read about how Beelzebub was thrown out of heaven and then began gathering together the lost angels thrown out with him, and how Beelzebub broke into tears as he tried to rally them. "Thrice he essay'd, and thrice, in spite of scorn, Tears, such as angels weep, burst forth." On Sunday nights after services, when the children begged him, the father took down his violin and played, "Go to the Devil and Shake Yourself."

She read Sir Walter Scott's novel, "Ivanhoe," seven times as a girl, and learned by heart and recited many scenes from that book. At thirteen she was translating the Latin poet, Ovid, into English, and the next year was teaching the Latin classic, Virgil.

in the Hartford Female Seminary, also studying French and Italian and drawing and painting.

Life was grave, serious, as she heard her father preach a sermon on the text, "I call you not servants, but friends," and plead, "Come, then, and trust your soul to this faithful Friend." Into her eyes came tears, and she answered, "I will," and sat through sacramental service. On the same day she had gone to her father's study corner in the attic of their house and crept into his arms, whispering, "Father, I have given myself to Jesus and He has taken me." And the father held her, and his tears fell on her hair. And he said: "Is it so? Then a new flower has blossomed in the Kingdom this day."

Then had come the moving to Cincinnati, a stopover in New York, which city she said would "kill her dead" if she stayed; it was "an agreeable delirium." And in the years of bearing her children and taking care of her husband, whose health was delicate, and doing many kinds of housework she found time to write articles that magazines printed and paid for. One book of her sketches had been published. She broke down, and went to a water cure in Vermont for six months, and came home with aches in her eyes so that for six months she could not stand daylight, and lived in darkened rooms. It was then she wrote a school-days' friend, "I like to grow old and have six children and cares endless."

There was a tracery of curves in her face, lines of pansy edging. She was a little trim woman, with blue-gray eyes full of changes, often dreamy, with ringlets of dark-brown hair clinging to the temples of her forehead, and quick little hands that illustrated her words or spoke for her without words.

As a seventeen-year-old girl teaching in her sister's female seminary in Hartford, she had said, "Where persons are determined to be anything, they will be!" The word "determination" had specific value for her. It was determination that set her father's face toward locating in the West in the Ohio River country. He said he had thought seriously of "consecrating all my children to God in that region who are willing to go." He had a vision of schools, churches, libraries, colleges, culture, and religion working a development of national spirit in the West. "If we gain the West, all is safe; if we lose it, all is lost. This is not with me a transient flash of feeling, but a feeling as if the great battle is to be fought out in the valley of the Mississippi, and as if it may be the will of God that I shall be employed to arouse and help marshal the host for the conflict. These are only my thoughts, but they are deep, and yet withal, my ways are committed to God."

The father and the daughter had solemn depths. When the books of the British poet, Byron, were published, the father had preached a sermon about the wasted life of the poet, and the daughter had read and been astonished by "The Corsair." She was only eleven years old when she asked what the line meant, "One I never loved enough to hate," and was told, "Oh, child, it's one of Byron's expressions."

When her father told her one day, "My dear, Byron is dead —gone!" the daughter was silent. So was the father a minute or two; then he added: "Oh, I am sorry that Byron is dead. I did hope that he would live to do something for Christ. What a harp he might have swept!"

And the girl went up a slope called Chestnut Hill where there was a strawberry field. She had a basket and meant to pick the red ripe berries. Instead she lay on her back among daisies, looked up into a blue sky, and wondered where Byron had gone and how it was with his soul.

Yes, there was a tracery of curves in her face, lines of pansy edges. In the Hartford school, when girls had asked if they could just once be allowed to do this or that, she answered them: "Allow you? I have not the power; you can do so if you think best." And she wrote her sister, "The force of moral influence seems equal to that of authority, and even stronger." One girl liked animals, bugs, things that creep, weave, fly, swim, and had under her desk cover a little menagerie of spiders, tumble-bugs, frogs; it was against the rules; the teacher made a new rule, that she and this girl should share the fun and the learning to be had from the little zoölogical garden hidden under the desk cover.

And so the year 1849 had come and she saw with it a pestilence of cholera come to Cincinnati; on a single day there were 120 deaths. She buried one of her own children. She got along as best she could with her curly-headed twins and the three other little ones, while her husband was off at Brattleboro, Vermont, seeking health.

Then her husband came back and again took up biblical exegesis in the Lane Theological Seminary, and the old threads of life were taken up. Standing at the front door of her Walnut Hills home, she could see a flaring in the sky over Cincinnati sometimes where a house was burning. And she knew again that a mob was at work. At the foot of the hills ran the Ohio River, the border line on one side of which negroes were property and the other side not.

Back and forth across this line she had seen the anger and the hate of men flame and spit and with the years going by it was getting worse. Down in the big town had been James G. Birney, who had given freedom papers to his slaves on an Alabama plantation and had published a weekly journal, *The Philanthropist*, in a fireproof building. Her brother, an editor on the *Cincinnati Journal*, was keeping loaded revolvers handy. Another brother had been a collector for a New Orleans commission house and told her about life in that city and in the Red River district. He told of seeing a slave mother leap from the deck of a Mississippi River steamboat, with a girl child who was to be sold. She had driven on a stormy night along Mill Creek to the farmhouse of the Quaker, John Vanzandt, with a negro girl who didn't have freedom papers, and whose lawful owner was hunting his property. She had crossed the Ohio River, visited with friends at a Kentucky plantation, and seen the slave system under the kindlier and more intelligent masters and overseers.

A call came for her husband at Bowdoin College, Maine. The family moved. The mother stayed ten days in Boston at the home of a brother; there the Abolitionist organization and propaganda was shaping into a sort of religious crusade; it had leaped into a fiercer stride with the passage at Washington of a law requiring all people North to help slave hunters from the South in the capture of runaway property.

All the smoldering fire in the woman, which had been softened and kept down when she lived on the Ohio River, shot up into blazing desires for sacrifice, even martyrdom. "I feel as if I should be willing to sink with it, were all this sin and misery to sink in the sea." A brother, a brother's wife, told her to use her pen. It roused her determination—one of her keywords was "determination." "I will write something—I will if I live."

She went to Bowdoin, wrote her brother's wife that a new-come baby was holding her back. "As long as the baby sleeps with me nights I cannot do anything, but I will do it at last. I will do that thing if I live."

One Sabbath at church a chapter of a book started to write itself as she sat listening to the sermon. She wrote it and read it to her children and the tears ran down their faces; the father came in; he cried too.

Then, while caring for her six children, and with a feeling that she was in her way helping to ransom countless unborn children, writing furiously out of her mother-heart, she wrote the chapters and they were sent with the ink hardly dry to *The National Era* for publication under the title, "Uncle Tom's Cabin, or Life Among the Lowly."

They were published as a book in 1852; eight power presses were soon printing copies of it; the sales reached more than 300,000; letters and poems came to her from Whittier, Holmes, Longfellow, and many others; from England came letters of praise from Dickens, Macaulay, Kingsley, Lord Carlisle, the Earl of Shaftesbury; in Great Britain were sold 150,000 copies in a year; in Paris a dramatization of the book was produced in eight acts to an overflow audience that sat till half-past one in the morning for the final curtain-drop; translations came out in France, Germany, Denmark, Sweden; in Italy editions of "Il Zio Tom" were sold in all cities; in Wales appeared "Caban F'

Ewythr Twm." Another year saw translations into Armenian, Russian, Bengalese, Persian, Japanese, and Chinese.

A check for $10,000.00 arrived four months after the publication of the book. The author and her husband went on their first sea voyage; she wrote to her children that the ocean was a "restless, babbling giant." She returned from Europe to write "A Key to Uncle Tom's Cabin; presenting the Original Facts and Documents upon which the Story is Founded, together with Corroborative Statements, verifying the Truth of the Work."

A lone little woman, with a houseful of children to take care of, with the grass not yet grown over one baby's grave, with her breasts hardly dry from the nursing of a new baby, had written a book timed with the same hours that the antislavery movement was gathering an ever fiercer stride and voice, becoming a terrible, irreconcilable crusade, chanting of eyes that saw the glory of the coming of the Lord, of a just God to come and trample out the vintage where the grapes of wrath were stored.

In the flow of her story of slavery, she had seldom paused to deal with some of its peculiar growths. It would have interfered with the swift movement of her drama to notice that in certain southern states the laws permitted free negroes to own slaves; and by inheritance, gift, and purchase 4,500 free negroes were in 1830 recorded as owning slaves, and in a number of cases free negroes controlled large plantations. Slaves of negroes were in some cases the children of a free father who had purchased his wife; if the free negro husband of the slave woman did not buy her freedom, as many husbands failed to do, the children of the marriage were born slaves and were the lawful property of the father. Some husbands held off from buying freedom for their wives; an unsatisfactory wife could be sold; a negro shoemaker in Charleston, South Carolina, bought his wife for $700.00, and, finding her hard to please, sold her a few months later for $750.00. A negro Baptist minister in St. Louis was recorded in 1836 as the owner of twenty slaves. Samuel Gibson, a Mississippi free negro, in 1844 took six slaves he owned to Cincinnati, and gave them freedom papers.

Little Harriet Beecher Stowe had set out to register in the bosoms of millions of other Christians her own shame of Christian civilization in America, and her own cry for martyrdom. A picture of a slave society was what she tried to make in a large panoramic structure, and it had become mixed with a great personal ideal of the Christ Man. Her hero, Uncle Tom, was a black Christ. He embodied all the implications of the saying, "The meek shall inherit the earth." He did what he was told to do; his word was trusted by his master; he could suffer grimly and humbly in his belief that Heaven, a world after this one, would take him in and put right all wrongs. He did what he was told to do until he was told to tell which way runaway slaves had run; then, bleeding from whip thongs, his skin and flesh welted and pounded, he died moaning forgiveness to the master who had ordered another obedient negro to beat him to death. It was the story of Judea located south of the Ohio River, with a whipping-post for a Cross, slave owners for Pharisees, ministers and politicians for hypocrites and Pilates, and a cotton plantation for the scene of a Passion Play.

By the device of dramatizing a black Christ, she led millions of people to believe there were two countries with two cultures in the United States; in one humanity was desecrated; in the other it was held sacred. She became the prophetess of a passionately emotional point of view that south of the Ohio River was a widespread and terrible wrong, while north of the Ohio River nothing so much was wrong; only in the South was there a vicious and brutal control by exploiters over producers; in the North was no comparable cruelty, mismanagement of the common welfare, and ignorant wastage of the lives of a lower class existing chiefly for the ease and profit of an upper class.

Yet while Mrs. Stowe read the first manuscript sheets of her book to her weeping husband and children, a committee of the legislature of Massachusetts was circulating a report prepared the year before on conditions in that New England state. The report was dry, factual, painstakingly accurate, crabbedly truthful, as even in tone as the accents of a surgeon reporting a pulse-beat or a definite condition of a particular anatomical area; that is, the report was in method the opposite of "Uncle Tom's Cabin." In the industrial belt of the northern states were some 4,000,000 wage laborers, most of them held in a control analyzed in the Massachusetts committee report; it declared:

The Legislature, with the intention of promoting the manufacturing interest, has by its action interfered with and destroyed the natural relations as existing between the class of employers and the class of employees. That natural equality of condition, which ought to exist between the two classes, does not practically exist between the corporations and the great mass of laborers in their employment.

These immense artificial persons, with far larger powers than are possessed by individuals, are not chastened and restrained in their dealings with the laborers, by human sympathy and direct personal responsibility to conscience and to the bar of public opinion.

The transactions between the corporations and the laborers are conducted by agents, who are hired to so manage, as to make the most profits for the stockholders; and the stockholders, throwing all responsibility upon the corporations, receive their dividends with a high opinion of the fidelity and efficiency of these several agents, high and low, who have managed profitably, but they know nothing of the hardships endured by the laborers, whose work has produced all they thus receive. The larger corporations employing large numbers of laborers, all act substantially in concert, in dealing with laborers, and avoid all competition in overbidding for labor.

They are thus enabled to fix inexorably, without consultation with the laboring class, all the terms and conditions of labor. The will of the corporations thus becomes law, and declares how many hours the laborers shall work, and how much shall be their compensation. From the decision of these powerful employers, large masses of the laboring people have practically no escape. Circumstances practically compel them to submit to the offered terms. Many of them must do so, or have no work at all; and to some, this is equivalent to having no honest means of support.

The power of the corporations, thus exercised in determining the conditions of labor of large numbers of the laboring classes, not only oppresses those whom they employ, but also exerts a powerful influence to depress the condition and prolong the hours of labor of every branch of industrial pursuit.

The report suggested as a first step a shorter workday.

Thousands of women and girls, 8,000 in one city, were tending
the looms and bobbins of New England mills, working twelve to
fourteen hours a day, and the report noted:

Instead of the female operatives being nearly all New England girls,
as was formerly the case, large numbers of them are now foreigners.
The infusion of foreigners has been rapid, and is going on at a constantly increasing rate. In a few years, an entire modification and
depression of the state of society in and about manufacturing places
will be wrought by this cause.

By the present system of working, no sufficient time is allowed between working and sleeping, for the improvement of the mental faculties. Their working twelve hours or more, per day, in the noxious
air of the factories, tends to deaden mental vigor, although it may not
quench the intellectual fire once lighted.

Far different results must be anticipated for the future when there
is taken into consideration the rapid influx of foreigners, which is fast
changing the character of the factory population. If this change continues to go on, there will be gathered into the manufacturing places
a strictly manufacturing population permanently bound by circumstances to factory employments, similar in character to the factory
population of England. Then, the evils of excessive hours of labor
will become manifest in the depressed tone of the moral and intellectual character of the mass of operatives, and also in their deteriorated
physical condition.

One evil result of devoting so much time to labor is the increased
competition of labor. Prolonging the hours of labor decreases, in some
degree, its wages. In Massachusetts, there is always a surplus of labor
unemployed. Those, therefore, who are out of employment through
the effects of the excess of the hours of labor, go into the labor market
and underbid those who are at work, and thus the general rate of
wages is reduced.

And far out among the farmers near the frontier, Lincoln was
writing in a notebook some of the points that stood out big for
him as he looked at the relations of Man and Master, the upper
and lower classes of America.

He could see two sorts of inequality, "the British aristocratic
sort" and "the domestic slavery sort." Neither was as good as
"a society of equals" where every man had a chance.

He had heard southern men declare slaves were better off in the South than hired laborers in the North. Yet he would argue, "There is no permanent class of hired laborers amongst us. Twenty-five years ago I was a hired laborer. The hired laborer of today labors on his own account today, and will hire others to labor for him tomorrow."

He set up the indictment, "Although volume upon volume is written to prove slavery a good thing, we never hear of the man who wishes to take the good of it by being a slave himself."

And he writhed as a man under the weight of some heavy conundrum of history in writing, "As labor is the common burden of our race, so the effort of some to shift the burden onto the shoulders of others is the great durable curse of the race."

Chapter 91

THE Northwest and the South were paying their large debts in New York. While the centre of politics was Washington, the money centre of the country was New York. Canals, railroads, steamboats, crop transfers were handled through the nation's financial capital at the lower end of Manhattan Island. Affairs of size in cash outlay waited on word from New York. The streams of cash from the Mississippi and Gulf regions led to New York and the East. Nearly two-thirds of the banking capital of the country was in the East; per capita circulation in the East was $16.50 as against $6.60 for the country as a whole.

In a small eastern area of 200,000 square miles were factories, mills, stores, shipping-lines, railways, and banks that earned yearly returns equal usually to the total of capital invested. The bulk of the banking profits of the country was in the control of eastern banks. The list of bank presidents in New York City showed an interesting percentage of them as having accumulated $100,000 to $500,000 in New England or the middle eastern states, and then moving to New York, the American vortex of cash and credit. A new bank was started for every month in the year in New York City in 1851. And in the two years following fifteen more banks opened their doors.

Among large fortunes were some out of the "African trade." A book published for bankers and merchants, "Wealth and Biography of the Wealthy Citizens of New York," rated Peter Harmony as worth $1,500,000. "The ship, *Warsaw*, sold in 1844, made him $90,000 in one voyage round Cape Horn. Some of his ships to Africa brought out cargoes, it is said, that paid a profit equal to the difference in price between negroes in Africa and Cuba."

Whisky, cotton, and real estate had brought Stephen Whitney ten million dollars. "He was born in Connecticut, and began life as a poor boy by retailing liquor, and finally dealt in the article by the wholesale. The great impetus to his fortune, however, was given by several heavy but fortunate speculations in cotton. His investments in real estate doubled his fortune."

William P. Furniss, a millionaire, "made all his money in the South, and is now a broker in Wall Street." John Suydam's estate of $700,000 came from cotton speculation. "Mercantile business south, at Mobile" was the source of Jonathan Hunt's million. Samuel Packard, $500,000, was plainly "a rich cotton planter, resident in New York," while Isaac Packard got his $250,000 from "negro plantations in Cuba," and Mauran Oroondates came by his $500,000 "in the southern trade, and by the steam-ferry at Havana."

Little pieces of land on Manhattan Island had doubled, and kept doubling, in price. Henry Brevoort's father left him an eleven-acre farm, and when Ninth and Tenth streets cut across Fifth Avenue where the cows were once pastured, Brevoort had become a millionaire. Peter G. Stuyvesant, of the ancient Knickerbockers, was rated at $4,000,000, mostly real estate. The estate of Stephen Van Rensselaer also came to $4,000,000, and was divided between two sons, "one of whom owns Albany County, and the other Van Rensselaer County."

Iron, coal, hardware, drugs were the sources of fortunes invested mainly in real estate. Anson G. Phelps, worth $1,000,000, owned Pennsylvania iron mines, a part of Missouri mountain, "altogether perhaps a half-million acres," and had "contracts to supply the Federal Government with nearly all the copper used for the national vessels."

Sometimes the little book published for the information of bankers and merchants came close to impertinence. It rated Morgan Lewis at $700,000 and declared, "He acquired his estate by marrying a Livingston of wealth." And there was the odd item about Thatcher T. Payne, brother of John Howard Payne, author of the song, "Home, Sweet Home." He was "of a family part Jew from the east end of Long Island, not far from Montauk," and his $100,000 came "through marriage with a wealthy widow." Benjamin L. Swan had $500,000. "His firm was peculiarly lucky in commercial arrangements during the late Mexican War."

The name of Vanderbilt was looming. Cornelius, rated at $1,200,000, had only begun on transportation and finance that would bring him tens of millions. In Daniel Drew, president of the Erie Railroad, was an example of a financier performing a vital and important public service and charging for the service a price unknown to the public. He had millions; just how many he did not tell, if he knew. He had organized and reorganized the Erie and was one of the first adepts in railroad accounting. The estimated construction cost of connecting New York and Lake Erie was $2,000,000. But when built it had cost $15,000,-000. And the total capital obligations were $26,000,000. Thus at last a rail line ran between the seaboard and the Great Lakes.

The railroad and the telegraph speeded up trade, sent the volume of business higher, and initiated the piling up of such personal fortunes as the New World had not seen before. Millionaires were getting common. "With princely fortunes accumulating on the one hand, and the stream of black poverty [from Europe] pouring in on the other," said the *New York Tribune,* "contrasts of conditions are springing up as hideous as those of the old world."

John Jacob Astor was rated as high as $50,000,000 and as low as $25,000,000. "He has, by the sole aid of his own industry, accumulated a fortune scarcely second to that of any individual on the globe, and has executed projects that will perpetuate his name to the latest age." At eighteen years of age he had left his home in Baden, Germany, "resolved to be honest and industrious, and never to gamble." He clerked in a fur store, went into the fur business for himself, and built trade till he was able to send sixty men to locate a fort and trading-post, Astoria, on the Columbia River.

Next he had a chain of forts and posts in the northern Pacific Coast wilderness, trading hardware, knickknacks and rum to Indians and white trappers for furs later shipped to China and traded for teas, silks, nankeens. "His ships now ploughed every sea."

Two-thirds of his profits year by year went into real estate and first mortgages. "In case of foreclosure, which has often happened, he has bought the property in at much less than its real value. . . . Mr. Astor has vast tracts of land in Missouri, Wisconsin, Iowa, and other parts of the West. . . . His income must be $2,000,000 a year, or $4 a minute. . . . It has been remarked of him that Mr. Astor was capable of commanding an army of 500,000 men. . . . During active life he resided in a large house in the lower part of Broadway, and lived in a style of princely magnificence, attended by servants from some of the various nations with which he traded, among them some from the Empire of the Celestials. His house was furnished with the richest plate, and his apartments adorned with works of art, among which was a Cupid by Mignard."

Thus was America growing. Thus life was arranging itself at the financial capital of America. New York had a nickname. It was known among Americans as the Front Door.

Emerson, the Concord preacher, saw war, revolution, violence, breeding in the antagonisms of bold, powerful men. "Vast property, gigantic interests, family connections, webs of party, cover the land with a network that immensely multiplies the dangers of war."

Chapter 92

As Lincoln traveled over the fourteen counties of the Eighth Judicial Circuit six months of the year, making his home in Springfield, with occasional trips north and south in the state, there was a feel of change in the air. He had seen the frontier pass from Illinois and move west of the Mississippi. He had floated past St. Louis, a town of 5,000 people, and had seen it grow to 74,000 in twenty years. He had watched Springfield with less than a thousand people grow to 4,500; its citizens had voted for no license to saloons. He had seen cholera arrive in Springfield and the mayor ordering a day of prayers against the plague.

The public square that Lincoln saw just before turning up the stairway to his law office was sketched by the *Journal* when it urged: "Our streets and alleys should be cleaned everywhere, especially in and around the neighborhood of the square. The brickbats, trash, old hats, old boots, and shoes, rags, bones, manure and many other things which grace our streets, should be hauled off, and hog holes filled up."

The town council had passed an ordinance to stop the running at large of hogs in the streets; the council had repealed the ordinance, and finally settled the matter by a law providing that no hogs should run at large in the streets of the capital city of Illinois unless the said hogs had rings in their noses.

The hog-raisers of the state in 1850 counted 1,915,907 hogs. Travelers from Chicago said cows ambled along the sidewalks of that city as freely as the people, while residents of Quincy had their saying that geese filled the streets and as scavengers were superior to hogs.

Besides Springfield, the cities of Quincy and Rockford had voted no license to saloons. The slogan, "The saloon must go," was heard. A petition with 26,000 signers asked the legislature in 1853 for a state-wide vote on liquor-selling in Illinois; the legislature refused. Nearly all the Whig newspapers were for temperance, and had nicknamed the Democratic party the "Whisky party"; at the far southern point of Egypt, the Cairo *Weekly Times and Delta* declared, "The use of intoxicating drinks seems more natural than the use of water."

In 1855, the question went to a vote; the proposed prohibition law, modeled on the one in force in Maine, was beaten by a majority of 14,447 votes. In Chicago and in the canal and railroad zones, with the largest number of foreign-born voters, the balloting was heaviest against the proposed law.

Lincoln was asked if he were a temperance man. He replied: "I am not a temperance man, but I am temperate to this extent: I don't drink."

The temperance movement had its main strength among the New Englanders who had filled up northern counties of the state. Raiding squads with axes knocked holes in whisky barrels and destroyed liquor stocks in the smaller towns; such raids were not attempted in Chicago, where 800 saloons were licensed.

In the air, strung on poles, were "lightning wires"; a telegraph operator in Pekin told Lincoln all he could tell about electric currents and the Morse alphabet; the telegraph connected Chicago, Springfield, and St. Louis. Within two years a network of wires joined all parts of Illinois in a system controlled by Judge John D. Caton, called "the telegraph king of the West." The *Journal* and the *Register* at Springfield announced they would have telegraphic news; if the President at Washington issued a message they would publish it as it came over the lightning wires; likewise with steamboat explosions, train robberies, murders. Eight newspapers were published daily in Illinois in 1850; they increased in four years to twenty; also in the state were 118 weekly publications. Chicago had seven daily newspapers, fifteen weeklies, and six monthly and other periodicals. In the southern part of the state the publications were fewer; the *Southern Illinois Advocate* of Shawneetown was the only newspaper in ten counties; its principles and aims were unlimited—"universal liberty abroad, and an ocean-bound republic at home."

The West was beginning to feel its oats and lift its voice. The *Gem of the Prairie,* the weekly magazine of the *Chicago Tribune,* declared: "The West must have a literature peculiarly its own. It is here that the great problem of human destiny will be worked out on a grander scale than was ever before attempted or conceived."

When southern representatives in Congress spoke threats of leaving the Union, at the time California was admitted as a free-soil state and the South felt itself losing ground politically, Texas was reported to be making ready to defy the Federal Government by force of arms. The *Alton Telegraph* voiced the opinion, "The great and patriotic West has become strong enough to strangle the monster of disunion the moment it shall venture to raise its head."

This, while Senator Douglas was telling the country from the floor of the Senate: "There is a power in this nation greater than either the North or the South—a growing, increasing, swelling power, that will be able to speak the law to this nation, and to execute the law as spoken. That power is the country known as the great West—the Valley of the Mississippi, one and indivisible from the Gulf to the Great Lakes, and stretching on the one side and the other, to the extreme sources of the Ohio and the Missouri—from the Alleghenies to the Rocky Mountains. There, sir, is the hope of this nation—the resting-place of the power that is not only to control, but to save the Union. This is the mission of the great Mississippi Valley, the heart and soul of the nation and continent."

And while Douglas was openly telling the country this sentiment, his right-hand man in the House of Representatives was secretly writing Governor French of Illinois that if Texas defied the Federal Government, it would be the signal for the whole South to draw out of the Union; and therefore he advised strengthening the state militia, warning the governor: "I would prepare for this storm—I would provide against portentous violence. This, as a citizen of Illinois and a lover of the Union, I call upon you to do."

The human inflow from Europe came before Lincoln's eyes. He saw Germans, Irish, and English by tens of thousands come into the state. Fourteen steamboats, ice-locked in the Mississippi River near Cairo in the winter of 1854, were loaded with 2,000 German and Irish immigrants. Up at Nauvoo, where the Mormon colony had moved out and crossed the Great Plains and the Rocky Mountains, to settle at the Great Salt Lake in the midst of the Great American Desert, had come a group of French Communists. Near Athens in Sangamon County was a settlement of Norwegians; north of Springfield was a huddle of Portuguese.

The Germans outnumbered all others; Lincoln carried a German grammar and studied the language in a night class. He wrote "nix com raus" in letters. A Turnverein was organized in Springfield in 1851.

In Bureau and Sangamon counties were Fourier phalanxes, experiments aimed at making perfect model human corners on earth, planned somewhat after Brook Farm, the famous phalanx in New England started by Albert Brisbane and having Horace Greeley, Charles A. Dana, and Nathaniel Hawthorne among its members.

Many new organizations were started; societies, unions, lodges, churches. Some were ancient, tested, filling deep human wants; others were new, fantastic, untried. And it seemed that Lincoln didn't belong to any organization, new or old, secret or open, except the Whig party, the state bar, and the American Colonization Society.

Chapter 93

LATE in the afternoon of an autumn day in 1850 Abraham Lincoln is riding in the rattletrap buggy which he drives from one courthouse to another across the fourteen counties of the Eighth Judicial Circuit. He has spoken only occasionally to "Old Buck," his horse; the head and the haunches, the hair and the ribs of "Old Buck," are familiar to him; he has curried and cleaned this horse; the ears of "Old Buck" have a language for him; he knows the places where the tugs and collar have worn the hair off and left the horsehide.

On this drive, however, he has spoken hardly at all to "Old Buck"; he is lost in one of the dark moods that come to him; the rattle of the buggy, the jog of the horse, the flutter and flip of the blackbirds picking up corn and wheat in the fields, the rumble of wagons, axles and wheels, the far sounds of cow bells and grunting hogs and sudden zigzags of scared grouse in the pasture grass—to these he is lost.

The smell of the moist loam is in the air; one or two frosts of a passing week have whitened the ground, gone into mist under the morning sunshine; and there is in the air a faint memory of these frosts, as well as a ghostly recollection of the marching, majestic panoramas of the laughing corn, their stalks and tassels, their ears with a shine of yellow and of red gold.

The time is the coming of evening when all the revealed shapes of daylight take on the rags or the silks of mist and dark and form themselves into fine or comic apparitions not seen in daylight; it is the time when men of dreams or mathematics, or both, have to be keener and more elusive with the outlines of their reveries or the statements of their theorems. Circling the horizon levels is gray haze, the first hint of Indian summer.

The red ball of the sun performs the final arc of its day and drops below the prairie line. While the lamplighters of the cities of men are doing their daily work, the sprinklers of the stars are doing their daily stint up in the spans of the evening sky. Up the sky has come a little silver sliver of an early moon, a basket-shaped baby moon; as mist wraps around it in moments it might be a shining papoose cover.

To these little moving fire-spots on the sky, the life of a man or a nation of men is put down in two easy almanac dates, telling of a coming and of a going away. "Mortal man with feet of clay, Gone tomorrow, here today." Ten years slip into a man's life and slip out, each year "a swift-fleeting meteor, a fast-flying cloud," each year "a flash of the lightning, a break of the wave."

In the ten years now just ahead in the life of Abraham Lincoln, the human procession marches, toils, fights, laughs, sings, scrambles, dances, prays, its supreme wonder the simple fact of birth, speech, song, its supreme majesty the plain fact of death, silence, night. Behind that filmy tissue called The Future, events are operating, facts toiling to their ends, shaping destiny, history.

In the ten years between 1850 and 1860, the country grows; its 23,000,000 people become 31,000,000. The United States has 2,000,000 more people than Great Britain. The United States becomes one of the Powers of the World. And it is only beginning to grow. A secretary in Washington figures that in forty years more the country will have a hundred million people.

A legend spreads. Henry Clay on his last ride from Washington to Kentucky steps out of a stage, goes back a few paces, leans over and puts his ear to the ground as if listening. "What are you listening for, Mr. Clay?" the driver asks. "I was listening to the tread of unnumbered thousands of feet that are to come this way westward."

In ten years the ships at the ports of the country unload 2,600,000 people from overseas. In one year come 400,000. The East grows 21 per cent, the South 28 per cent, the Northwest 77 per cent, in population. Little towns peep up on the prairies where there used to be only gophers and jack rabbits. Cities swell from little towns. The country grows.

The peopling of America with labor supplies, for the operation of her factories and mills, for the breaking of her prairies and the raising of crops and building of towns on these prairies, goes on directly connected with events in Europe. Into America come men, women, and children who saw the dark year of 1848 in Europe, when the barricades and battalions of revolution arose from London to Moscow, from Prussia on the north to Sicily on the south.

In England the speeches, pamphlets, and street meetings of the

Chartist movement scare the government into passing a law making seditious speeches an act of felony. The habeas corpus act is suspended in Ireland.

No less than 17,000 constables are sworn in to keep the peace in London when a crowd of a half-million persons is to gather on Kensington Common. One agitator cries: "If a few hundreds do fall on each side, they will only be the casualties in a mighty movement."

Police and troops with guns are mounted on public buildings; military arrangements are put into the hands of none less than the conqueror of Napoleon, the Duke of Wellington. Street traffic is ordered suspended out of fear that wagons may be used for street barricades as in Paris revolts. A proclamation is issued, warning the people against assembling for disorderly purposes.

The mammoth mass action assembly planned for Kensington Common collapses. Feargus O'Connor, the chief organizer of the movement, broken with grief, loses his mind and spends years in the quiet of an asylum.

The British government employs its guns not only to keep order among its home-born people; in far Afghanistan 30,000 Sikhs with sixty guns, screened by a thick jungle, slaughter 2,500 British officers and men in the opening of a campaign that ends with British batteries, bayonets, and cavalry in control of the disputed region. In South Africa, a fourth war with the wild Kafir tribes ends with the British flag flying over the Orange River territory; Boer settlers in near-by territory are declared to be under a British protectorate.

And though the white men of the north are thus bringing civilization to the jungles of Africa and Asia, that civilization has not yet learned how to guard itself from the filth of cholera; in London a thousand persons a day die from the plague and a total of 50,000 die in England and Wales.

The search goes on for markets, more people and territory where the products of the British power looms can be sold; a British steamship meeting a fleet of Chinese pirates shoots to pieces thirteen of the junks. The ports of Burma are blockaded;

up the terraces of the Great Pagoda at Rangoon go the British
bayonets hoisting their banner over the golden dome of the final
sacred Pagoda. A fifth war is fought with the wild Kafir tribes,
and martial law proclaimed throughout Cape Colony in South
Africa.

When the Czar of Russia tries to get footholds on the Black
Sea and control of Constantinople, the British army and navy
join with allied European forces and fight a war in the Crimea.
The famous Light Brigade charges. "All in the valley of Death
rode the six hundred." They are of England's strong arm keeping the routes clear and the connections open for the trading
vessels carrying the cargoes from the power looms of Manchester
and Lancaster and West Riding.

And these wide-flung actions are little chapters in the new
development of world trade in world markets, wider and fresher
markets being wanted because of the immense output from the
new machines, the power-driven looms taking more and more
millions of pounds of cotton from the southern American states
and more and more millions of bushels of corn from far western
America to feed the growing populations. As at times the mills
slow down and men are out of jobs, and as land becomes scarcer
in proportion to the population, there is an added attraction in
the call of America and its prairies where land is cheap, and the
black soil sometimes six feet deep.

Europe has grim memories of 1848; civilization was shaken
into wild pieces of hunger and hate. The French February
revolution spread to every corner of Europe. King, emperor,
czar, and sultan loaned each other money, guns, armies. Thousands of barricaded workmen took power and possession over the
cities of Paris and Vienna, held those cities for weeks and were
shot down and their revolutions blown off the map by superior
guns and fighting forces.

So far did the revolutions go in the old feudal governments of
Prussia and Austria that Prince William left Berlin for London,
leaving placards saying that his palace was the property of the
nation; the Austrian Prince Metternich, chased out of Vienna,

told a friend in London, "I have sometimes ruled Europe, but Austria never."

As the news of the barricades in Paris reached Czar Nicholas in Russia, he had mobilized his armies and ordered a manifesto written, closing with the words from Isaiah, "Listen, ye heathen, and submit, for with us is God." In Italy and Hungary governments changed hands like chess pieces; Garibaldi, Mazzini, Kossuth became famous names.

And republics set up for a few days or weeks by the revolutionists were tumbled over. In France, Louis Napoleon, a whiskered nephew of Napoleon the First, took a crown as Emperor.

Such events set the faces of hundreds of thousands of homeless, landless, propertyless peasants and city workmen toward America. In England, Ireland, Germany, France, and Italy, they sell their pigs and chickens, they scrape and save, they borrow money from relatives and friends in Europe or America, pack their belongings in sacks, bundles, and handkerchiefs, and cross the "big pond," wondering how much of what they hear they will find to be true in America, the wonder country, where across thousand-mile prairies the plow and harrow had not yet put teeth into the rich black soil. It can hardly be true. They will see.

By war and by treaty there has come on the map of the United States, Texas, and the open spaces to be shaped into the states of California, New Mexico, Arizona, Utah, Nevada, Oregon, Washington, Montana, and parts of Colorado, Wyoming, and Kansas.

A homestead bill comes before Congress; the bill says any free white citizen who settles on 160 acres and farms it five years shall have it free of cost; the bill is changed; he must pay for the land; a sliding scale of prices is fixed.

For ten years argument goes on about what shall be done with millions of acres of public lands. The Government owns the land; the Government says who shall next own it. In the twenty years between 1840 and 1860, the Government lets go of 269,406,415 acres; it sells 68,752,889; it gives away the rest: it gives a single railroad 2,500,000 acres, and the railroad in seven years sells half this land for $14,000,000.

In Washington, congressmen, senators and Cabinet officials squabble about what shall be done with the public lands, millions of acres Northwest and Southwest. There are land speculators, business interests, powerful in Washington, who for reasons of their own do not want free land for actual settlers. A few senators such as Stephen A. Douglas, and congressmen such as John Wentworth and William Richardson of Illinois, Andrew Johnson of Tennessee, try to get a free homestead law. They fail.

Philosophers, farmers, and mechanics, calling themselves an Industrial Congress, meet in Chicago, and declare "the free land proviso would everywhere, on the cotton plantations of the South, and in the cotton factories of the North, unite all lovers of freedom and humanity, against all haters of freedom and humanity, and would strip the question of all prejudices resulting from sectional and partial agitation." They put the blame for bad feeling between the North and the South not only on the planters and landlords of the South, but also on forces in the North, which they name as "Factory Lords, Landlords, Bankers, Speculators, and Usurers." For a simple, honest homestead law, the country waits. A movement with the slogan, "Vote yourself a farm," rises and disappears.

Free-land bills keep coming up in Congress; it is argued by Andrew Johnson of Tennessee that the poor whites trying to farm stony corners on the slopes of the Allegheny Mountains ought to have a chance to break west and settle on free land; a Virginia congressman pooh-poohs the idea that every man has a right to land; a radical from Pennsylvania says the eastern manufacturers are afraid of western free land because it would take men from the factories and send wages higher; another congressman says it is the big landholders North and South who are stopping the passage of a free-land bill.

An embryo—a tugging, unborn baby—of a giant industrial and transportation civilization takes form and grows. The organism of society breaks the cords and bonds tying it to handicraft pro-

duction and the organic structure resting on feudal land-ownership; the society functioning its production and distribution of
the means of life through capital and capitalists, issues definitely
from its birth folds. It is the end of feudal society: the knickerbockers, silk stockings, and silver snuffboxes are gone, in America
and Europe; the pantaloons, the Prince Albert coat, the stovepipe
hat, the Havana cigar have arrived.

The transcontinental railroad, the iron-built, ocean-going
steamship, the power-driven factory—the financiers and rulers
of these are to be the rulers of an earth ruled by the white race.
Europe connects coal and steel areas with factory cities by railways. Russia runs a rail line from St. Petersburg to Moscow.
Into northern Africa, into fringes of Asia, the rail paths go;
among tombs of the Pharaohs and amid walled altars of China,
the whistle of the locomotive is heard. The society resting on
land-ownership gives way to the new civilization operating through
control of finance, industry, and transportation.

Of railroads men had said, "They begin anywhere and end
anywhere." Between cities, rivers, and lakes and canals there
were connecting short lines, stub roads for local service. Then
the Erie Railroad puts a line through from a station near New
York City across Pennsylvania to Dunkirk on Lake Erie; the
Atlantic Ocean and the Great Lakes are connected now by rail
to the north. The Baltimore & Ohio line pushes on through to
St. Louis; the seaboard and the Mississippi Valley are joined by
steel rails. Twenty-one thousand miles of rails are laid. Total
railroad mileage grows from nine to thirty thousand.

Gradually between the seaboard and the Mississippi River there
comes a net of lines with cars hauling the pork and grain of the
West to the factory towns of the East, to the holds of vessels
sailing to the factory cities of Europe; the cars come back loaded
with sewing machines, churns, scissors, saws, steel tools.

The American threshing machine, which Cyrus H. McCormick
has been perfecting for twenty years, goes into a competition
with the threshing machines of other nations. The London *Times*
pokes fun at the McCormick machine—before the test. In the

race the American machine cleans 740 litres of wheat while the English machine cleans 410, and while six threshers with the flails of Bible times clean 60 litres. The official report of the Fair says, "The triumph of the American reapers worked a new era in agriculture."

Man toils, thinks, sweats for new tools, so that one farmer will be able to do the work of ten. New reaping and threshing machinery comes on the farms. Fewer wheat and oat harvests rot in the fields. Single-handed, a farmer can gather the crop on a quarter-section of land. Grain drills, corn planters, wagons and buggies with springs under the boxes and seats are bought by the farmers. The new churns, the new sewing machines, help the farmer's wife.

Over in England a man works on improving artillery; he is trying to make guns stronger and cheaper; his name is Bessemer; he invents a way to force a blast of air through molten cast iron, resulting in a hard steel that he can sell $100 a ton cheaper than other steel of the same quality. The Bessemer process comes to America, where a man named Kelly is experimenting with that same process. Everything made of steel becomes cheaper. Steam fire-engines, gas-lighting systems, the Hoe revolving cylinder-press, vulcanized rubber, photography, the use of anesthesia, these arrive.

In London they build a big palace of iron and glass and hold an international exhibition of the products of inventive, dextrous Man. In New York, too, they hold an exhibition in the Crystal Palace. More and more is heard of discoveries, inventions, products, improvements, conveniences.

The white man has spread his ships around the earth. Once the earth was wilderness. Now it is to be civilization. White men say so. England begins building all her ocean-going ships of iron.

In the Middle West, there is keen interest in Stephen A. Douglas's plan for a railroad the length of the state of Illinois. He is asking the Federal Government to make land grants along the railroad route. Congress refuses.

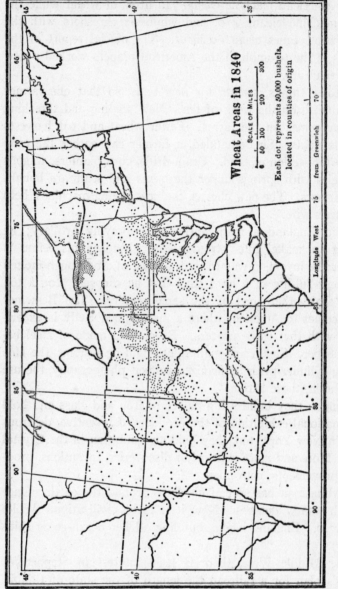

Wheat Areas in 1840

SCALE OF MILES

0 50 100 200 300

Each dot represents 50,000 bushels,
located in counties of origin

Longitude West   75   from Greenwich   70°

*This map and the one on opposite page were drawn by William E.
Dodd for his book "Expansion and Conflict." (Houghton Mifflin Co.).*

As the wheat areas thicken in the west and thin out in the east, the political balance of power in Washington shifts to the northwest.

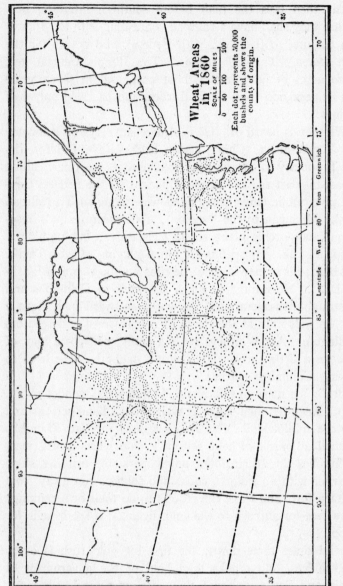

Wheat Areas
in 1860
SCALE OF MILES
0   50   100   200
Each dot represents 50,000
bushels and shows the
county of origin.

The epic of wheat is immensely involved in the epic of America. It made Chicago important to London. It was a factor in splitting old political formations. Compare, particularly, the midwest and northwest states in this map and the one on the opposite page.

Douglas then lays the plan before southern interests, proposing that they shall have a railroad connecting with the Illinois Central, running to the Gulf, with Federal land grants for the southern states. This bill passes. The Illinois Central gets 2,500,000 acres of land free without cost, and in seven years receives $14,000,000 from its land sales, and has sold only half its holdings.

Asa Whitney is heard of. He is a merchant, lays up a fortune in New York, sails to China, comes back with a feel for distances. From city to city he goes holding mass meetings, calling for a coast-to-coast railway across America: let the Federal Government give public lands thirty miles wide along such a railroad from Lake Michigan to the Pacific. Public meetings pass resolutions in favor of his plan; so do legislatures; but nothing is done; it is all talk. He spends his fortune trying to get a Pacific railroad built; his money is gone; he runs a milk-wagon in Washington, D. C. He wanted to finish the work of Columbus and have a straight passage around the world westward from Europe to Asia; he sells milk at the doors of congressmen and senators in Washington. Asa Whitney: he is a crank, perhaps a man of vision, born a little early. His epitaph might be "He tried to finish what Columbus started."

California is a place to talk about, to guess and wonder about. There in a week ten men shake gravel through hand screens and shake out a million dollars of gold nuggets; the San Francisco city council adjourns without setting a date when it will meet again, churches close their doors, newspapers stop printing, ships lie in harbor with no sailors; cooks and soldiers run away from the military forts and leave the officers to do their own cooking; there is a free-for-all rush to the gold diggings; a spade sells for $1,000.00.

The wild times tame down; the first big gold rush is over; gunmen, thieves, and crooks take hold of the government of California and San Francisco; they own or control governors, mayors, judges; 2,500 private citizens organize a committee, hold military drill, set up courts; and, defying the regular, legal government, they hang and deport murderers, firebugs, thieves, and make property and life safer. The Committee of Vigilantes, they call themselves. It is a little revolution in the name of safety for property and life.

Across the Great Plains stretching east from the foothills of the Rocky Mountains toward the Mississippi River, move wagon trains; a traveler counts 459 wagons in ten miles along the Platte River. They are moving across vast empty prairies. Between the Arkansas River on the south and the Canadian border far to the north is the land not settled, not really opened for settlement, not peaceably organized and humanly made ready for settlement.

A territory of Kansas is organized, but there is civil war in this territory; riders from Missouri, a slave state, get on their horses with rifles and ride over into Kansas and battle with Abolitionists from New England. It is a taunt hurled from the antislavery platforms of New England that shipments of boxes marked "Books" are sent to Kansas, the boxes incasing rifles. In the settlement at Osawatomie is a quiet, stubborn man with his family; morning and night they have Bible reading and prayers. The enemy kill two of his sons; he steals horses from the enemy and kills sons of theirs; it is war. The man's name is John Brown.

Over in Clay County, Missouri, are two boys growing up, Frank and Jesse James; they are learning to ride and shoot, to be reckless about life; the enemy burn their house, shoot their mother in the arm so the arm has to be cut off; it is war.

Into Kansas come men from many parts of the country: John Calhoun, who used to be county surveyor of Sangamon County in Illinois, becomes Governor of Kansas. There comes Robert J. Walker; he controlled politics in the Democratic party in the state of Mississippi twenty years back; he was the first to put Jefferson Davis into politics; he was Secretary of the Treasury under President Polk; he came within an inch of getting President Polk to annex all Mexico to the United States; he is Governor of Kansas when the slavery men let the people vote on a state

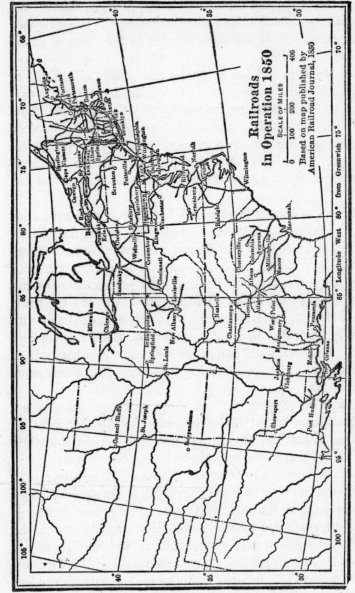

Railroads
in Operation 1850

SCALE OF MILES

0   100   200   400

Based on map published by
American Railroad Journal, 1850

Rail lines in 1850 are mostly stubs connecting cities or waterways in short haul traffic.
*This map and the one on opposite page were drawn by William E.
Dodd for his book "Expansion and Conflict" (Houghton Mifflin Co.).*

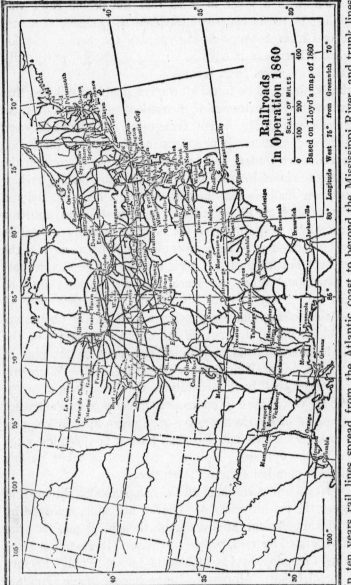

Railroads
in Operation 1860

SCALE OF MILES

0   100   200   400

Based on Lloyd's map of 1860

In ten years rail lines spread from the Atlantic coast to beyond the Mississippi River, and trunk lines carry a long haul traffic. The iron horse is a strange and powerful factor in economic and political development.

constitution, with a joker in it so that the people can't vote slavery out; he meets his friend, Stephen A. Douglas, at a conference in Chicago; they tell the country the Kansas election is crooked. There are months in which the whole country talks about the latest news from Kansas.

In the South are to be found all the imaginable conditions that lie between the two extremes of plantations managed by owners who are efficient, kindly, decent, thoughtful, and plantations and jail yards and auctions managed by hard, hopeless plantation owners and slave traders and breeders. On one plantation the owner issues printed instructions, going into full details on how "The overseer shall see that the negroes are properly clothed and well fed; he shall lay off a garden of at least six acres, cultivate it as part of his crop, and give the negroes as many vegetables as may be necessary. The negroes shall not be worked in the rain, or kept out after night. Sick negroes are to receive particular attention. When the negro shall die, an hour shall be set apart by the overseer for his burial; and at that hour all business shall cease, and every negro who is on the plantation, who is able to do so, shall attend the burial. Humanity on the part of the overseer, and unqualified obedience on the part of the negro, are, under all circumstances, indispensable. Whipping, when necessary, shall be in moderation, and never done in a passion; and the driver shall in no instance inflict punishment except in the presence of the overseer, and each negro man will be permitted to keep his own axe, and shall have it forthcoming when required by the overseer. No other tool shall be taken by any negro without permission from the overseer."

In the North are to be found all the imaginable conditions that lie between the two extremes of factories and mills managed by owners who are efficient, kindly, decent, thoughtful, and factories and mills operated by hard, hopeless owners. The Hamilton Manufacturing Company in Massachusetts issues "Public Factory Rules," proclaiming: "All persons in the employ of the Hamilton Manufacturing Company are to observe the regulations of the room where they are employed. They are not to be absent from

Joshua Giddings

John Quincy Adams

Harriet Beecher Stowe

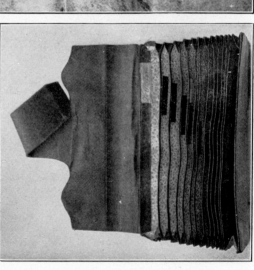

Lincoln's shawl.

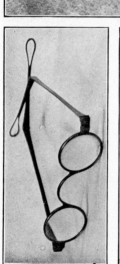

Lincoln's spectacles (upper). Lincoln's wallet, with compartment marked "Herndon" (lower).

work without the consent of the overseer, except in cases of sickness, and then they are to send word as to the cause of their absence. They are to board in one of the houses of the company and give information at the counting-room where they board, when they begin, or, whenever they change their boarding-place; and are to observe the regulations of their boarding-house. Those intending to leave the employ of the company are to give at least two weeks' notice thereof to their overseer. All persons entering into the employment of the company are considered as engaged for twelve months, and those who leave sooner, or do not comply with all the regulations, will not be entitled to a regular discharge. The company will not employ anyone who is habitually absent from public worship on the Sabbath or known to be guilty of immorality."

Peace societies organize; they aim to stop war; they circulate Charles Sumner's oration on "The True Grandeur of Nations"; he says, "There is no war which is honorable, no peace which is dishonorable." However, the National Convention of Reformers, headed by Parke Godwin, raises a point and asks a question: "The Peace Societies are built upon a noble foundation of justice and philanthropy, but must not expect success in establishing permanent peace, or its parent, justice, in the intercourse of nations, established upon the right of conquest. Why shall not the laws, which create motives in all men to obtain from all their fellow citizens, by cunning, or any force not expressly forbidden in the law, all their lands, houses, goods, wares and merchandise, also stimulate nations to foreign conquest and warlike aggression?"

The first undersea telegraph messages are sent; Washington and London exchange words. And the breech-loading rifle arrives; man shoots bullets quicker and oftener.

Wendell Phillips, the aristocratic young lawyer who dropped law practice to become an Abolitionist agitator, says the churches are slow in their duty, hurling the taunt: "The theatres in many of our large cities bring out, night after night, all the radical doctrines and all the startling scenes of 'Uncle Tom.' They preach immediate emancipation, and slaves shoot their hunters with applause. The theatre, bowing to its audience, has preached immediate emancipation, and given us the whole of 'Uncle Tom'; while the pulpit is either silent or hostile." Yet in hundreds of communities, it is the church people who carry on the antislavery organizations, hide runaway negroes in barns, cellars, wagons, and man the stations of the Underground Railroad; in a little church built of walnut wood in Galesburg, Illinois, they hide negroes in the steeple.

Frederick Douglass, the escaped mulatto slave, edits a paper, the *North Star;* always the runaway slaves, sleeping by day, heading north by night, try to follow the north star. Says Frederick Douglass, "Prejudice against free colored people has shown itself nowhere so invincible as among mechanics of the north." In Virginia, white mechanics go on a strike because negroes have been put to work alongside of them to learn skilled mechanical labor. The *Charleston Mercury* editorially hopes the white strikers will be crushed; interference and rebellion from white workmen has the same spirit as that of a black slave insurrection.

Civil war in Kansas comes near to spreading out over the whole country in 1856. Fifteen hundred miles from Kansas people make sacrifices in order that Kansas shall not be a slave territory. Emerson, in far-off Massachusetts, says, "We must learn to do with less, live in a smaller tenement, sell our apple-trees, our acres, our pleasant houses."

The faith of Emerson in the Government is gone. "I think the towns should hold town meetings, and resolve themselves into Committees of Safety, go into permanent sessions, adjourning from week to week, from month to month. I wish we could send the Sergeant-at-arms to stop every American who is about to leave the country. Send home every one who is abroad, lest they should find no country to return to. Come home and stay at home, while there is a country to save." As his eyes sweep the years ahead of the nation, he cries, "The hour is coming when the strongest will not be strong enough."

On a late afternoon of an autumn day in the year 1850 Abraham Lincoln, sitting in his rattletrap buggy, might have been lost still deeper in his thoughts if he could have snatched the film of tissue off the Future and read events to operate in the ten years to come. The babblings, confusions, and mixed paths of those events, as well as the human majesty of some of their outstanding performances, might have had for him the same mystery as the coming of evening in autumn haze, when all the revealed shapes of daylight take on the rags or the silks of mist and dark, and form themselves into fine or comic apparitions not seen in broad daylight. Hours come when men of dreams or mathematics, or both, have to be keener and more elusive with the outlines of their reveries or the statements of their theorems.

Chapter 94

Young Bill Green, who had clerked in the Berry & Lincoln store, slept in the same bed with Lincoln and held Kirkham's Grammar while Lincoln recited, was in northern Illinois in 1852, and met some families of movers at Princeton. One was the Carr family, who had come from the Mohawk Valley to Chicago by boat, and were going by wagon to the little log city of Galesburg in Knox County, where the Rev. George Gale and a company from Whitesboro, New York, had plans for churches, schools, colleges, religion, culture, and freedom, in the new prairie region.

Clark E. Carr, the boy of the family, listened with sharp ears to the talk of Bill Green. He was the same Bill Green who was on a witness stand one time when John T. Stuart asked him who were the principal citizens of New Salem, Green answering: "There are no principal citizens; every man in New Salem neighborhood is a principal citizen."

He had a Tennessee skill in telling stories, and the Carrs told him he was the best at spinning yarns that they had ever heard. He replied: "I ain't a primin' to a curi's young feller who used

to keep a grocery down whar I live. He kin make a cat laugh.
I've seen the whole neighborhood turn out to hear him tell stories.
They ain't all jest the kind fer women to listen to, but they's
always a pint to 'em. He's a great big feller, with a big mouth,
and he kinder acts it all out, smilin' and laffin'. I never seed a
real clown, but he'd make one. But I've seen him when he was
the solumest man in ten states. When he kem back from runnin'
a flatboat to New Orleans, ef anybody said anything about niggers
he would git so solum, an' tell about a nigger auction he seed in
New Orleans—how they sold a fambly, the man to one planter
and his wife to another an' passeled the childern out among the
highes' bidders, an' he thought it was awful. I've seen him turn
pale," Green went on, "when talkin' about this auction, and seem
to take sick to his stomick, and then begin to cuss and take on;
an' I've heard him say he'd ruther tend sawmill all his life than
to sell niggers, an' he'd ruther do all the work on a plantation
hisself than to buy a nigger boy or girl from its mammy. I
never once heerd him swar excep' when talkin' o' that nigger
auction."

Mr. Carr interrupted. "He must be an Abolitionist." "Ab'litionist! Ab'litionist!" cried Green. "You bet he ain't. He's a
true loyal man, who loves his country. No, he's no Ab'litionist."

And what had become of this young man? "Wal," Green
went on, "he went an' larned law, made speeches, run fer the
legislatur, set up in Springfield, an' got to Congriss. But he's
only a kind of a jackleg lawyer—an' as fer Congriss, he couldn't
git 'lected ag'in, an' now he's kind o' played out."

And his name? Green went on: "He's as good a feller as ever
lived; but he's kinder common—sorter jes' like everybody, no
better no worse, jes' a good feller. Thar's another feller in that
country who beats him—Dick Yates of Jacksonville. He's a
feller who can beat anybody as a talker. He is thet eloquent
thet he'll make you fergit your own name. Talk about the
American Eagle an' the Star-Spangled Banner! He can jes' lift
you off your feet, an' make you soar an' yell an' hurrah, an'
swing yer hat, an' holler—think ye're Patrick Henry, an' George

Washington, an' Andrew Jackson, an' Henry Clay, an' Bunker Hill an' everything. I've seen him make people hold their breaths, an' wipe their eyes, an' blow their noses, jes' by his talk. He'll be Pres'dent some day!"

But what was the name of the first young man who could make a cat laugh? "Abe Linkern."

And in further sketching "Abe Linkern," Green wanted them to know: "He is the curi'sest feller I ever seed! He could ask more questions than a Philadelphia lawyer could answer. Thar never kem a man inter the neighborhood, but he'd find out jes' the things he knowed. He'd make friends with him by tellin' him stories an' then he'd pump him. I've seen him pump a down-East Yankee 'bout Boston till he knowed more 'bout Boston, an' Plymouth Rock, and Bunker Hill than the Boston feller hisself. When he heerd of a grammar-book he walked six miles to git it, an' when he got through with it he knowed more grammar than the schoolmaster, Mentor Graham."

Arriving in Knox County, young Carr heard Colonel Finch, the leading Whig politician, say: "I've seen Abe Lincoln go into a caucus or convention, and jist git up and talk kind of honest-like, with no fuss, but jist plain sense, windin' up with a story square to the point, and carry the whole outfit, bag and baggage, along with him."

And one day in Galesburg as the boy, Clark E. Carr, was looking away down East Main Street toward the Knoxville Road, he heard a horn blow and saw a big rockaway stagecoach make the turn into Main Street, four horses breaking into a run, the driver half standing, and cracking a whip, while pigs and chickens in the road scattered, and women ran out of the kitchens and waved handkerchiefs and dish-cloths.

As the stage came to a standstill in front of the one-story log post-office on the southeast corner of the public square, a tall stranger was among those who stepped out. Colonel Finch was ready to greet him but another man put himself between Finch, put his hand out to the stranger and blurted, "Abe Lincoln, by God!" "Yes, governor, here I am," said Lincoln, shaking hands with the Honorable William McMurtry, lieutenant governor of the state, a Democrat, and a farmer on Henderson Creek, north of Galesburg. "I'm glad to see you and to be in Knox County. How are you, Colonel Finch? I hear you are keeping those rascally Democrats level here in Knox! How are you, Squire?"

And shaking hands with everybody, even young Clark E. Carr, he swept the gathering with a glance, and said with a wreath of a smile: "That's a good story we had on the governor. You see, an Irishman had a bill before the legislature for some imaginary service he had performed on the canal, which the governor here squelched in the senate. The Irishman's account of it was that his bill had passed the house and he was watching it from the gallery of the senate; that it finally came up, and 'jist as it was about to pass, a big nayger named McMurtry got up and motioned that my bill be laid under the table till the Fourth of July; and that killed it sure.' " After that everybody walked into what was called the "barroom" of the tavern, though no liquor was sold; it was a church and college town; a block from the tavern was to be erected the First Church, of solid walnut.

"Lincoln, how can you keep out of politics?" asked O. H. Browning, a Quincy lawyer with the blood and manners of a Kentucky gentleman. "Nothing going on in politics that I care about. I am trying to become a lawyer," was the reply. And it was suggested that the Missouri Compromise line between slave and free states might be wiped out. "We cannot tell what men will do," said Browning. "Well," was Lincoln's answer, "if anybody should attempt such an outrage while I live, I think I'd want to take a hand in politics again."

When he had gone, Browning remarked that Lincoln was "always a learner," and in that respect was the most notable man he had ever seen. "I have known him for ten years, and every time I meet him I find him much improved. He is now about forty years old. I knew him at thirty, and every time I have seen him I have observed extraordinary improvement. Most young men have finished their education, as they say, at twenty-five; but Lincoln is always a learner. If he keeps out of politics, he will in ten years stand at the head of the profession in this state."

Four miles south of Galesburg, on the Seminary Street road, lived a farmer, Daniel Green Burner, who was born in New Salem, had seen Lincoln go off to the Black Hawk War and had lived there when Lincoln was keeping a grocery store. He told people, when asked, that Lincoln sold whisky in the New Salem store but never drank any himself and never used tobacco. "He would swear under strong provocations, but this was not often. I don't think he made any pretensions to special goodness. The community was raw and green and he was one of us. Lincoln was as full of fun as a dog is of fleas, yet he had no part in the tricks of the Clary's Grove gang. They had queer notions of fun. Once they called up an old man with a wooden leg and made him a prisoner. They then built a fire around the wooden leg, and held the man there till the wooden leg was burnt off."

Burner could run on with recollections. "I have seen Lincoln place a cup of water between his heels, and then folding his arms, bend his tall form backward until he could grip the edge of the cup between his teeth and then straighten himself up, without spilling the water. He would back up against a wall and stretch out his arms; I never saw a man with so great a stretch. He did little things like that to please people.

"Lincoln was the strongest man I ever knew. In the grocery I often saw him pick up a forty-four-gallon barrel of whisky, place it on the counter, and then lower it on the other side. And while Lincoln was full of fun and life, I never saw him dance and he courted no girls. The four years I knew him in New Salem I never saw him with a girl. He did not go to others for his amusement, but if they wanted fun they came to him, and they found him full of it. . . . There was singing school, but Lincoln couldn't sing any more than a crow. So he did not go often."

Thus, in odd corners of Illinois men were telling each other what Abe Lincoln was and wasn't.

Across the state of Illinois, in the towns where Lincoln practiced law for a living, men gained different impressions of him. This and that man had his own little individual portrait of Lincoln. He could, paradoxically, make a cat laugh, and also be the solemnest man in ten states. He was always a learner. It was of a piece with the mental sketch formed by the Quaker, Ira Haworth, who saw Lincoln in Danville and noted, "Lincoln doesn't show at first all that is in him," or the swift characterization in the remark of Leonard Swett, who often tried cases with and against him. "You can never tell what Lincoln is going to do till he does it."

Other lawyers could not say beforehand just when Lincoln would switch the management of his case and be off on a trail not noticed before. He would speak to a jury and give away one point after another. "Yes, we admit this," and "Yes, we admit that." And it would look as though the case were slipping away, when suddenly he would come down with unexpected power on the weakest point of the opposition and bring up his own strongest point. Once, during a criminal trial, a colleague, Amzi McWilliams, whispered to other attorneys, as Lincoln was speaking, "Lincoln will pitch in heavy now, for he has hid."

In silence and in ways covered from the eyes of other men, he struggled, grew, learned, in the years just after he came home from Congress and Washington. The boy who had lain awake nights and wrestled to unravel the big words "in-de-pend-ence" and "pre-des-ti-na-tion" had become a grown man who wrestled to unravel the ways of putting simple words together so that many could understand the ideas and feelings he wanted them to understand. He said, "I am never easy when I am handling a thought, till I have bounded it north, bounded it south, bounded it east, and bounded it west."

He bought a book on logic and studied the science of explanations, how to analyze the absolutely true and the relatively true, the proximate causes and the remote causes, how to untangle fallacies and take them apart piece by piece and show mistakes in reasoning. He heard the word "demonstrate" and said to himself: "What do I do when I demonstrate, more than when I reason or prove? How does demonstration differ from other proof?" He looked in Noah Webster's dictionary and learned that demonstration is "proof beyond the possibility of doubt."

The definition didn't satisfy him; he went to all the dictionaries and books of reference he could find for the meaning of the word "demonstrate" and in the end said to himself that their definitions meant about as much to him as the color blue when explained to a blind man. He said to himself, "Lincoln, you can never make a lawyer of yourself until you understand what 'demonstrate' means."

He bought "The Elements of Euclid," a book twenty-three centuries old. It began with definitions, such as: (1) A point is that which has no parts and which has no magnitude; (2) a line is length without breadth; (15) a circle is a plane figure contained by one line, which is called the circumference, and is such that all straight lines drawn from a certain point within the figure to the circumference are equal to one another; (16) and this point is called the centre of the circle.

Also it began with Axioms or Common Notions: (1) Things which are equal to the same thing are equal to one another; (2) if equals be added to equals the wholes are equal; (3) if equals be taken from equals the remainders are equal; (4) if equals be added to unequals the wholes are unequal; (5) if equals be taken from unequals the remainders are unequal; (6) things which are double of the same thing are equal to one another; (7) things which are halves of the same thing are equal to one another; (8) magnitudes which coincide with one another are equal to one another; (9) the whole is greater than its part; (10) two straight lines cannot enclose a space.

Quietly, by himself, he worked with these definitions and axioms. The book, "The Elements of Euclid," went into his carpetbag as he went out on the circuit. At night, when with other lawyers, two in a bed, eight and ten in a hotel room, he read Euclid by the light of a candle after others had dropped off to sleep.

Herndon and Lincoln had the same bed one night, and Herndon

noticed his partner's legs pushing their feet out beyond the foot-board of the bed, as he held Euclid close to the candlelight and learned to demonstrate such propositions as: "In equal circles, equal angles stand on equal arcs, whether they be at the centres or circumferences," and "Equal parallelograms which have one angle of the one equal to one angle of the other, have their sides about the equal angles reciprocally proportional; and parallelo-grams which have one angle of the one equal to one angle of the other, and their sides about the equal angles reciprocally proportional, are equal to one another."

"In this troublesome world we are never quite satisfied," he remarked once. Dreaminess filtered through him. He planned a speech in Congress; a week passed without his getting a chance to make the speech; and he commented, "Now my in-terest in the subject has passed too."

One night in Danville at the McCormick House, the ladies' parlor was turned into a bedroom for Judge David Davis, who had a bed to himself, and Lincoln and his fellow lawyer, Henry C. Whitney, who slept two in a bed. In the morning a thing hap-pened that Whitney later told in this way:

"I was awakened early, before daylight, by my companion sitting up in bed, his figure dimly visible by the ghostly firelight, and talking the wildest and most incoherent nonsense all to himself. A stranger to Lincoln would have supposed he had sud-denly gone insane. Of course, I knew Lincoln and his idiosyn-crasies, and felt no alarm, so I listened and laughed. After he had gone on in this way for, say, five minutes, while I was awake, and I know not how long *before* I was awake, he sprang out of bed, hurriedly washed, and jumped into his clothes, put some wood on the fire and then sat in front of it, moodily, dejectedly, in a most sombre and gloomy spell, till the breakfast bell rang, when he started as if from sleep, and went with us to breakfast. Neither Davis nor I spoke to him; we knew this trait; it was not remarkable for Lincoln, although this time to which I refer was a radical manifestation of it, a proof that 'true wit to madness, sure, is oft allied.' "

John T. Stuart had remarked to Whitney that Lincoln was a

hopeless victim of melancholy. "Look at him now," said Stuart, in a McLean County courthouse. "I turned a little," said Whitney, "and saw Lincoln sitting alone in a corner of the bar, remote from any one, wrapped in abstraction and gloom. . . . I watched him for some time. He seemed to be pursuing in his mind some specific painful subject, regularly and systematically through various sinuosities, and his sad face would assume, at times, deeper phases of grief. No relief came till he was roused by the adjournment of court, when he emerged from his cave of gloom, like one awakened from sleep."

He was spending more and more time by himself. Books, newspapers, his own thoughts, kept him alone in his room on evenings when the other lawyers on the circuit had all gone to a party and returned to find Lincoln asleep. If he went to a concert, lecture, or negro minstrel show, he would as soon go alone.

The habit stuck to him of reading out loud to himself whatever he wanted particularly to remember, and of reading out loud as he wrote. The proverb about "wits gone a-wool-gathering," he applied to some of his own moods. Whitney noticed him often during a court session "with his mind completely withdrawn from the busy scene before his eyes, as abstracted as if he were in absolute and unbroken solitude." Whitney noticed also: "Lincoln had no method, system, or order in his exterior affairs; no library, clerk, no *index rerum*, no diary. When he wanted to preserve a memorandum, he noted it down on a card and stuck it in a drawer or in his vest pocket or his hat. While outside of his mind all was anarchy and confusion, inside all was symmetry and method. His mind was his workshop; he needed no office, no pen, ink and paper; he could perform his chief labor by self-introspection." For his important business matters he had an envelope marked, "When you can't find it anywhere else, look in this."

The branches and crotches of trees interested him more in the winter-time, stripped of leaves and naked in design, than in the summer, when covered; he searched for basic anatomy of structure.

Finding Herndon reading a new book, "The Annual of Science," he glanced through it and commented that the book was on the right track because it took account of failures as well as successes in its field. "Too often we read only of successful experiments in science and philosophy, whereas if the history of failure and defeat was included there would be a saving of brain-work as well as time. The evidence of defeat, the recital of what was not as well as what cannot be done serves to put the scientist or philosopher on his guard—sets him to thinking on the right line."

These remarks were prophetic, in their way, for Herndon found Lincoln had arrived earlier than usual one morning at the office. Spread before him on his desk were sheets of paper covered with figures and equations, plenty of blank paper, a compass, rule, pencils, bottles of ink of different colors. He hardly turned his head as Herndon came in. He covered sheet after sheet of paper with more figures, signs, symbols. As he left for the courthouse later in the day he told Herndon he was trying to square the circle.

He was gone only a short time, came back and spent the rest of the day trying to square the circle, and the next day again toiled on the famous problem that has immemorially baffled mathematicians. After a two days' struggle, worn down physically and mentally, he gave up trying to square the circle.

He was trying to organize his mind and life so that he could not accuse himself, as he had accused President Polk, of being "a bewildered, confounded, and miserably perplexed man." He wanted to be simple as the alphabet, definite as the numbers used in arithmetic, sure as the axioms or common notions that are the starting-points of Euclid. Had he trusted too much to his feelings, and not reasoned, proved, and demonstrated his propositions clearly enough in his own mind before speaking them during his term in Congress? He wasn't sure. Hadn't he made a sort of fool of himself, and made his friends sorry for him, when he spoke before the Scott Club in Springfield in reply to the Richmond speech of Judge Douglas? He wasn't sure.

He would see if he could be as simple as the alphabet, as

definite as numbers, as sure as a demonstrated proposition in
Euclid. He scribbled notes trying to be as absolute as mathematics.

"If A can prove, however conclusively, that he may, of right,
enslave B, why may not B snatch the same argument, and prove
equally that he may enslave A? . . . You say A is white, and
B is black. It is *color,* then: the lighter, having the right to
enslave the darker? . . . Take care. By this rule, you are to
be slave to the first man you meet with a fairer skin than your
own. . . . You do not mean *color* exactly? You mean the whites
are *intellectually* the superiors of the blacks, and therefore have
the right to enslave them? . . . Take care again. By this rule,
you are to be slave to the first man you meet, with an intellect
superior to your own. . . . But, say you, it is a question of *interest;* and, if you can make it your interest, you have the right to
enslave another? . . . Very well. And if he can make it his
interest, he has the right to enslave you."

Into these notes he put the high human hopes spoken by the
men who made the American Revolution. One note read:

"The ant who has toiled and dragged a crumb to his nest will
furiously defend the fruit of his labor against whatever robber
assails him. So plain that the most dumb and stupid slave
that ever toiled for a master does constantly know that he is
wronged. So plain that no one, high or low, ever does mistake
it, except in a plainly selfish way; for although volume upon
volume is written to prove slavery a very good thing, we never
hear of the man who wishes to take the good of it by being a
slave himself.

"Most governments have been based, practically, on the denial
of the equal rights of men, as I have, in part, stated them; ours
began by affirming those rights. They said, some men are too
ignorant and vicious to share in government. Possibly so, said
we; and, by your system, you would always keep them ignorant
and vicious. We proposed to give all a chance; and we expected
the weak to grow stronger, the ignorant wiser, and all better and
happier together. We made the experiment, and the fruit is before us. Look at it, think of it. Look at it in its aggregate

If A. can prove, however conclusively, that
he may, of right, enslave B.— why may not
B. snatch the same argument, and prove
equally, that he may enslave A?—
You say A. is white, and B. is black.
It is color, then; the lighter, having the right
to enslave the darker? Take care.— By this
rule, you are to be slave to the first
man. you meet, with a fairer skin than
your own.

You do not mean color exactly?— You
mean the whites are intellectually the superi-
or of the blacks, and, therefore have the
right to enslave them? Take care again.— By
this rule, you are to be slave to the first
man you meet, with an intellect superior
to your own—
But, say you, it is a question of interest;
and, if you can make it your interest
you have the right to enslave another.—
Very well.— And if he can make it his
interest, he has the right to enslave you.—

Lincoln writes loose notes trying to reason in politics and human relationships with some of the absolute quality of mathematics. To *prove* a thing isn't enough; he wants to *demonstrate*. By such tests and rehearsals he aims to be trained so that he can meet all comers in debate and overthrow them. He is dropping away from the horseplay and comic sarcasm of his oratorical style of earlier years. The page reproduced above slightly reduces Lincoln's handwriting. The original is in the Barrett Collection.

grandeur, of extent of country, and numbers of population—of ship, and steamboat, and railroad."

Though Lincoln was an entertainer, and when he arrived in Bloomington, Knoxville, or Pekin, men passed around the word that he had come to town and was retailing stories and jokes at a certain store or harness shop, he had his moods. A young man in Bloomington took special notice of these moods. His name was Jonathan Birch and he was licensed to practice law on an examination given him by Lincoln. Birch noticed that an hour or two after Lincoln had been in the court clerk's office, and entertained a crowd, and himself shaken with laughter as he drew his knees up to his chin at the end of a story, he might be seen in the same office or in some law office near by in a changed mood.

Birch noted: "His chair would be leaning back against the wall, his feet drawn up and resting on the front rounds so that his knees and chair were about on a level; his hat tipped slightly forward as if to shield his face; his eyes no longer sparkling with fun or merriment, but sad and downcast, and his hands clasped around his knees. There, drawn up within himself, he would sit for hours at a time. No one ever thought of breaking the spell by speech; he had thrown about him a barrier no one dared break through."

Glimpses of the ways by which history works with the individual—what a little and willing piece of sacrifice a man must be for the sake of his highest purpose—these came to him. "He visited no public places seeking applause; but quietly, as the earth in its orbit, he was always at his post," Lincoln had spoken of Zachary Taylor, murmuring the text, "He that humbleth himself shall be exalted."

To develop an illuminated, mysterious personality, and to be an elusive and dark player on the stage of destiny, is a dream of achievement lightly carried by a man of whom it is said, "He can make a cat laugh." Yet when such a dream does develop in such a man he is hard to follow even when he most explains himself.

The inside changes that began to work in Abraham Lincoln in the four or five years after he came back from Washington had their connection with the changes developing in the heart and mind of the country. He was ready to be the tongue and voice of those changes. As he walked with his long, easy stride, with a head bowed till the chin rested on his collar-bone, with a sober face and eyes of deepening mystery, he was already carrying a load, already in the toils, almost ready to cry, "I shall never be glad again." He was lawyer, politician, a good neighbor and story-teller, a live, companionable man; these belonged to his rôle. He was to be a mind, a spirit, a tongue and voice.

Out of the silent working of his inner life came forces no one outside of himself could know; they were his secret, his personality and purpose, beside which all other facts of his comings and goings were insignificant. He became a seer and sayer; he took responsibility personally; he solved, resolved, and answered terrible questions; or he said, with out-and-out honesty and a desperate toss of his head, that he had no answer, no man could form the answer; only history and the future could bring the answer.

True, he had ambitions; goals beckoned and banners called; but he would wreck and sink the ambition that interfered with his life and personality. "He could make a cat laugh."

In the speeches he was now ready to make, with the American nation for an audience, there would be reason and passion rising so overwhelmingly out of them that some men and women would know they came from other regions than those of personal ambition. He was in the toils of something else than personal ambition. He was beginning to see what a little and willing piece of sacrifice a man must be for the sake of a dark fame.

END OF VOLUME ONE